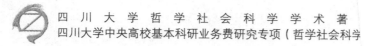

四川大学哲学社会科学学术著
四川大学中央高校基本科研业务费研究专项（哲学社会科学

《公孙龙子》

重释与重译

Reinterpretation and Retranslation of *Gongsun Longzi*

by Dr. Liu Limin

刘利民　著

 四川大学出版社

责任编辑：张　晶
责任校对：夏　宇　敬铃凌
封面设计：墨创文化
责任印制：王　炜

图书在版编目（CIP）数据

《公孙龙子》重释与重译：汉英对照 / 刘利民著.
—成都：四川大学出版社，2015.11
ISBN 978－7－5614－9146－1

Ⅰ.①公…　Ⅱ.①刘…　Ⅲ.①名家－汉、英②《公孙
龙子》－注释－汉、英③《公孙龙子》－译文－汉、英
Ⅳ.①B225.4

中国版本图书馆 CIP 数据核字（2015）第 279864 号

书　名	《公孙龙子》重释与重译	
	Gongsun Longzi Chongshi yu Chongyi	
著　者	刘利民	
出　版	四川大学出版社	
地　址	成都市一环路南一段 24 号（610065）	
发　行	四川大学出版社	
书　号	ISBN 978－7－5614－9146－1	
印　刷	郫县犀浦印刷厂	
成品尺寸	170 mm×250 mm	
印　张	20.25	
字　数	454 千字	
版　次	2015 年 11 月第 1 版	
印　次	2015 年 11 月第 1 次印刷	
定　价	58.00 元	

◆读者邮购本书，请与本社发行科联系。
　电话:(028)85408408/(028)85401670/
　(028)85408023　邮政编码:610065
◆本社图书如有印装质量问题，请
　寄回出版社调换。
◆网址:http://www.scup.cn

献给我的家庭

丛书序

　　四川大学（以下简称川大）是中国近代创办的最早一批高等教育机构中的一个。近十余年来，又经两次"强强合并"，成为学科覆盖面较广、综合实力较强的一所综合性大学。一百多年来，川大的人文社会科学在学校日益壮大的过程中，从国学研究起步，接受现代科学的洗礼，不同的学术流派融合互动、共同成长，形成了今日既立足于中国传统，又积极面向世界的学术特征。

　　作为近代教育机构，四川大学的历史要从1896年设立的四川中西学堂算起。但具体到人文社会科学研究，则可以追溯到清同治十三年（1874年）由张之洞等人创办的四川尊经书院。在短短二十几年的办学历史中，书院先后培养出经学家廖平、思想家吴虞等一大批在近代中国学术思想史上影响巨大的学者，也因此使四川成为国内研究经、史、文章等中国传统之学的重镇。此后，在20世纪相当长的一段时间里，以国学为主要研究对象的近代蜀学成为川大人文社会科学研究的主流，拥有张森楷、龚道耕、林思进、向楚、向宗鲁、庞俊、蒙文通、刘咸炘、李植、李培甫、伍非百等一大批国内知名的学者。

　　近代蜀学在研究内容上以传统学术为主，在观念与方法上则立意求新。廖平的经学思想曾经作为19世纪晚期变法维新的基本理论依据之一，其知识背景上也不乏西学色彩。20世纪20年代成长起来的一批学者如庞俊、刘咸炘等人，更是亲自参与了中国传统学术向现代学术的转变。其中，蒙文通由经向史，同时又广涉四部之学，在晚年更是力图从唯物史观的角度探索中国社会与思想的演进，最能代表这一学术传统的是其包容、开放并具有前瞻性的眼光。

　　自20世纪20年代开始，现代社会科学的深入研究也逐渐在川大开展。1922年至1924年，吴玉章在此教授经济学课程，鼓励学生通过社会科学的研究，思考"中国将来前途怎样走"的问题。1924年，学校设立了10个系，在人文社会科学6个系中，除了延续着蜀学风格的中文系外，教育、英文、历史、政治、经济5个系均着力于新的社会科学研究。这一科系的设置格局一直持续到30年代初的国立四川大学时期。

川大的另一源头是私立华西协合大学（以下简称华大）。作为教会学校，华大文科自始即以"沟通中西文化与发扬中西学术"为宗旨，而尤擅长于西式学问。其中，边疆研究最放异彩。1922年创办的华西边疆研究学会（West China Border Research Society）及其会刊《华西边疆研究学会杂志》（*Journal of the West China Border Research Society*）在国际学术界享有盛誉。华大博物馆以"搜集中国西部出土古物、各种美术品，以及西南边疆民族文物，以供学生课余之参考，并做学术研究之材料"为目标，在美籍学者葛维汉（David Crockett Graham）的主持下，成为国内社会科学研究的另一基地。

华大社会科学研究的特点：一是具有较强的国际色彩，二是提倡跨学科的合作，三是注重实地踏勘；对边疆文化、底层文化和现实问题更为关注，与国立川大校内更注重"大传统"和经典研习的学术风格形成了鲜明对比。双方各有所长，其融合互补也成为20世纪三四十年代两校人文社会科学发展的趋向。从20世纪30年代中期开始，华大一方面延请了庞俊、李植等蜀学传人主持中文系，加强了其国学研究的力量；另一方面致力于学术研究的中国化。一批既有现代社会科学的训练，又熟悉中国古典文化的中国学者如李安宅、郑德坤等成为新的学术领袖。

1935年，任鸿隽就任国立四川大学校长后，积极推动现代科学的发展。1936年5月，川大组建了西南社会科学调查研究处，在文科中首倡实地调研的风气，也代表了川大对西南区域跨学科综合性研究的发端。此后，经济学、社会学、民族学、考古学等领域的学者组织开展了大量的实地考察工作，掌握了西南地区社会文化的第一手资料。在历史学方面，较之传统史学而言更注重问题导向和新材料之扩充的"新史学"也得到了蓬勃发展，并迅速成为国内史学界的重镇。20世纪30年代后期开始，川大校内名师云集。张颐（哲学）、朱光潜（美学）、萧公权（政治学）、赵人儁（经济学）、徐中舒（历史学）、蒙文通（历史学）、赵少咸（语言学）、冯汉骥（考古学、人类学）、闻宥（民族学、语言学）、任乃强（民族学）、胡鉴民（民族学）、彭迪先（经济学）、缪钺（历史学）、叶麟（文艺心理学）、杨明照（古典文学）等一批大师级学者均在此设帐，有的更任教终身，为川大文科赢得了巨大声誉。在不同学术流派的融合中，川大人文社会科学形成了自己的特点：一方面具有传统学术通观明变之长，另一方面又具有鲜明的现代学术意识。1952年，在院系调整中，随着华大文科的并入，更使川大人文社会科学进入了飞速发展的新时期。半个多世纪以来，在继续保持传统优势学科如古典文学、语言学、历史学、考古学、民族学发展的基础上，新的学科如宗教学、理论经济学、敦煌学、比较文学、城市史等也成长起来，涌现出了一大批在国内外学术界受到极高赞誉的学者，为川大文科未来的进一步发展打下了良好的基础。

　　2006年是川大建校110周年，为了继续发扬深厚的学术传统，推动人文社会科学研究的新繁荣，学校决定设立"四川大学哲学社会科学学术著作出版基金"，资助川大学者尤其是中青年学者原创性学术精品的出版。我们希望这套丛书的出版，有助于川大学术大师的不断涌现和学术流派的逐渐形成，为建设具有中国特色、中国风格、中国气派的哲学社会科学做出贡献。

序

——兼论古代哲学的重新双译

一、双译的解释学立场

为了方便，我把刘利民书名中的"重释"与"重译"称为"双译"，好在此书第一章的名字中有"古译今"及"英译文"这样的措辞。

重新双译《公孙龙子》的必要性，他自己已有交代，我赞成，也请读者自辨。他所持的解释学立场，对双译工程有价值，也许具有普遍意义。所以，我想议一议。

第一篇《名实论》的原文：

"天地与其所产者，物也。

"物以物其所物而不过焉，实也。实以实其所实，不旷焉，位也。出其所位，非位；位其所位焉，正也。"

刘的解释：

"大自然以及生长、存在于其中的是实在之物。

"而一个物能被称为那个'物'，其名称的所指则必定并且只能是该物之为该物的概念意义，不能任意过度；这才是我们所议论的'实在性'。这种'实在性'必须充分表征事物的真正本质而无缺失，这应当是意义正确性的基本要求。对这一要求的任何偏离，都会使名称的意义出现偏差。完全满足这一要求则保证了意义正确性。"

根据这样的古译今的解释，于是便有那样的中译英的解释（第一篇）：

Heaven and Earth, with what grow and exist therein, consist of actual objects.

But the reason why an object is said to be that "object" is that its name necessarily and exclusively refers to the conceptual meaning of the object as it is precisely defined, without any shade of undue excessiveness; this should constitute the "actuality" that we talk about. Such an "actuality" is none other than the representation of the true essence of the object so named, without any looseness, which is the very requirement that ensures the correctness of the meaning of the names for objects. Any deviation from such a necessary requirement is bound to result in errors in the use of names. The meaning of a name is correct, only if it satisfies completely this requirement.

刘对自己的解释理念宣称如下："古汉语高度精练，能省的推理和语义部分均予以省略，因而表面上看很不连贯。《公孙龙子》这样的理论性著作因此显得更加难读，非常有必要把句子所隐含的思想表达明确地翻译出来。因此，本书打算在尽可能照顾原文的情况下，多采用意译的方法。"（见本书引言，着重号为钱加）我在《汉语文化语用学》里用了整整一节[1]详细地、明确地反对这种汉译英的翻译方法，即在文学翻译中，反对把句子所隐含的思想表达明确地翻译出来（将隐变明），与刘的解释学立场针锋相对。因为思想表达的隐含性是文学之为文学的基本特点。把文本的思想说得明明白白，就等于取消了文学。翻译把原文本来隐含的东西暴露出来，是帮倒忙，因为你把文学变成了告白于天下的宣称，而文学特别忌讳告白于天下。文学是靠人物形象与人物的命运自己"说话"，不用告白于天下。

哲学，特别是古代哲学又如何呢？哲学追求的是确定性（certainty）。既然如此，哲学的诠释需要的是告白于天下。海德格尔（Heidegger）以来的现代解释学，伽达墨尔（H. G. Gadamer）基于胡塞尔（E. Husserl）人本主义立场，论述了理解的历史性。因为理解者在阅读文本资料时所处的时代，不同于文本所创作的时间、环境、条件和地位，它们都已发生了变化。这些因素必然会影响和制约理解者对文本的理解，因而造成读者与作者在理解上的误差。……伽达墨尔还提出"时间距离"和"视域融合"补充了理解的历史性。……"时间距离"可解放作者，又可解放读者，使得这两者得以对话和融合。……"视域融合"，如果解释者的视界与文本的历史视界相互重叠并融合，可以提升理解的普遍性，获得

1　钱冠连：《汉语文化语用学》（第二版）第六章第三节，北京：清华大学出版社，2002。

一个更高层次的"崭新视域"（参见王寅《语言哲学沉思录》[1]）。以现代解释学的立场看刘的双译，他不过是在处理文本所创作的时间、环境、条件和地位的变化误差；他不过是在面对"时间距离"时，解放作者，又解放读者，使得这两者得以对话和融合；他不过是做了"视域融合"的事，也就是使解释者的视界与文本的历史视界相互重叠并融合；他不过是实验了欧陆人本解释学（哲学）所提倡的"理解的创造性"与"（读者可能会比作者有）更好的理解"〔斯赖尔马赫（Schleiermacher），参见王寅《语言哲学沉思录》〕。做了这些事情之后，获得哲学诠释的确定性，是可以容忍的。

但是我以为，海德格尔以来的现代解释学并不能彻底"解放"哲学翻译，更不消说是古代哲学的今释与接下来的英译。当一个解释者或翻译者将"能省的推理和语义"补足出来，以及将隐变明，能否符合原来文本作者的意图？这是一问。第二问，就算不限于原来文本而采用海德格尔以来的现代解释学立场，容许"理解的创造性"，那么，凭什么你的（译者或解释者的）补足与"创造"，我（读者）就一定要接受？这两问，对于哲学翻译来说，是非问不可的。一方面，与现代哲学一样，古代哲学的解释追求的是确定性；另一方面，哲学就是你思、我思，故你在、我在，或者，你在、我在，故你思、我思。问题是，你思与我思是不同的，即你的解释与我的解释可能是不同的。还有一层，据蒯因（Quine）断言，刺激意义的不确定性使原初翻译（radical translation）也具有了不确定性[2]。让我们把古代哲学原文的每一个判断与命题都当成一个刺激，刺激意义是不确定的，那自然引起不同思者的解释的不确定性。一句话，一路都是不确定性，凭什么我要相信你的这个不确定性解释结论？

但是别忘了，说到底，解释或翻译，最后都是语言性的表述，最终见之于语言形式，故伽达默尔说"所有的理解都具有语言性"。建议考虑卡尔纳普（Carnap）建构理论的"宽容原则"（principle of tolerance）："让我们做出宣称时小心谨慎，考察这些宣称也不妨严格要求，但是让我们以宽容之心放手让这些语言形式通行。"[3]我们是理智性的人，达成共识是人们追求的社会秩序之一。绝大多数人不

1　王寅：《语言哲学沉思录》第十章第十五节"解释学意义观"，北京：北京大学出版社，2014年。

2　V. Quine, *Word and Object*, The M. I. T. Press, Cambridge, Massachusetts, 1960: 31-34.

3　"Let us be cautious in making assertions and critical in examining them, but tolerant in permitting linguistic forms." See Carnap: "Empiricism, Semantics, and Ontology", in *Modern Philosophy of Language* by Maria Baghramian, First American edition, 1999 by Counterpoint, P. O. Box 65793, Washington, D.C., p. 66.

会欣赏对一个对象的认识永远分歧下去，绝大多数人不会对别人接近真实合理的答案死不认账。最终，我们会有一个趋于一致的共识。

二、重新双译：解决重大难题

对早有双译（古译今、中译外）本的一部古代哲学文献（比如说《公孙龙子》），为什么要从头再来？如果只是为了局部的改善，意义不大。如果从头至尾从文献的系统上梳理出新的线索，从这个新的线索里可以看出解决重大难题的契机，那就要从根本理念上推倒原来的定论，那就值得重新双译。作为他的博士论文导师，我了解，刘利民从酝酿他的哲学博士论文开始，就发现先秦名家并非诡辩，从此就致力于摘掉公孙龙"诡辩家"的帽子这一工作。这次重新双译就是对公孙龙子的文献从系统上梳理出新的理论线索，借此机会解决一个重大难题：从理论上正确理解先秦名家并明白地解读他们。这可不仅仅是一个摘掉错误帽子的问题，是事关中国文化在世界上的交流与地位的问题。一方面，这对于他的工作来说，是水到渠成；另一方面，这对于一部早有双译本（古译今、中译外）的古代哲学文献是否还需要重新双译的问题，是一个带根本规律性的回答。回答好了，对古代哲学的双译，有重要的启示。

诡辩是怎么来的？既然是诡辩，就一定是语言性的。在无知的背景下，将白说成黑，不是诡辩。需抬出验证原则纠正的黑白颠倒，那就不是诡辩了。因此，诡辩的表现形式大致上是：一，抬杠，即故意把白说成黑，只需笑一笑就可过去；二，在没有形式逻辑手段帮助语言表达的时代下，提出看似奇怪的命题。

对付语言意义的不确定与歧义，历代的哲学家费尽心思，采取了一些行之有效的办法，一般地说，它们都可以沿用到避免诡辩。比如，借用现代形式逻辑改写日常用语，使一个命题只有一个确定的意义。又比如蒯因使用标准记法（canonical notations）的一整套规整（regimentation）[1]技术，就是用来排除歧义的。除此以外，还可以采用将语言分层（次）、分阶（order）的办法。还可以采用塔斯基（Tarski）提出的"X" is true iff p.[2]全句是工具性语言，括号内是对象语言。这

---

1 Quine, V., 1960, *Word and Object*, The M.I.T. Press, Cambridge, Massachusetts, pp.157-186.

2 参见 "The Semantic Conception of Truth and the Foundations of Semantics" in *Modern Philosophy of Language* by Maria Baghramian, 1999 by Counterpoint, P. O. Box 65793, Washington, D.C., p. 46。

样，就分出了语言的层次。还可以采用区分语言的"使用"与"提及"的办法。提及的语言放进括号、引号之内，或特殊排版、用异体字等。如"Chomsky is a great philosopher of language"中的"Chomsky"是使用，而"'Chomsky'有七个英文字母"内的"Chomsky"是提及，故放置于引号内。提及的"Chomsky"已失去了外延，没有了刚性指称，不能再指称世界上的那个哲学家乔某人了！这里再次验证了公孙龙本人的"指非指"理念：不要以为一提到"reference"，就一定要"to denote"（指到）一个具体的物（或人）！

消解诡辩，可能还有其他一些方法。

公孙龙的一些看似奇怪的命题却不是诡辩。他是在没有形式逻辑手段帮助语言表达的时代下，提出看似奇怪的命题的——尤其当他玩弄"指非指"的理念的时候！正是在这种情况下，我们可以看出公孙龙的伟大之处，他进行了太超前的理性思维，而又缺乏相应的记录与书写规则，他的表述才看上去怪异。明白了这一点，我们再来读刘利民对公孙龙的基本结论，就会会心一笑：

> 如后文所见，我的理解和翻译完全是视以公孙龙为代表的先秦名家为理性主义的语言哲学家这一基本点。这当然是一种有条件的解释。但以笔者之陋见，这尚可称为目前唯一能够全面说明先秦名家所有"诡辩"命题的解释方式。（《引言》）

刘是在说，以"理性主义的语言哲学家"的定位去看公孙龙他们，就能全面说明他们的"辩"一点也不"诡"。

刘利民还指出：

> 如果我们借用现代语言哲学的框架和技术（如"使用"与"提及"的区分等），也许更能融贯一致地表达出公孙龙的语言哲学思想。对此，本书将在正文中阐述。（《引言》）

也就是说，如果公孙龙时代能借用到现代语言哲学的框架和技术（如"使用"与"提及"的区分等），是可以不显出诡辩的。

对刘的这些宣称，我们可以在本书中看到他的解释，我们会发现许多有益的启示。

三、结论

当今的中国，掀起了一股不小的古代中国文献外译的热潮。我的建议是：一，动手双译前，先搞清自己的解释学立场，采取何种解释或者翻译的进路——直译？意译？直译加意译？其他方法（现代解释学派的种种方法）？为何采取这一方法？先把自己的主意打定。二，搞清古代文献原本的基本哲学倾向与实质，并守住它，许多出其不意的精思妙译就会一一冒出。三，最好是为了解决某个重大难题而重新双译一部古代哲学经典（那毕竟是一个大工程啊！），而不是为了一两处改善。以上三点，刘利民的工作都提供了一些有益的启示。

希望以上讨论可为本书读者提供些许帮助，也希望对古代哲学双译的工作有所裨益。

钱冠连

2012年4月12日

于湖北仙桃老家

《〈公孙龙子〉重释与重译》读后感

一、研究《公孙龙子》的困难与价值

《公孙龙子》，由于其文字简奥，以及汉字的多义性，历来解释《公孙龙子》的著作之间有天差地别。但各家的解释却有其共通之处，也就是以各自的合理性来解释《公孙龙子》。这种情况一方面对我们还原公孙龙的原意造成了极大的障碍；但是，另一方面，却提供了各家解读《公孙龙子》的方法、各家所认为的合理性标准，以及解释背后参照系思想、理论等可供探讨的材料。因此，对于《公孙龙子》的研究，除了以《公孙龙子》为研究对象之外，也可以将解读《公孙龙子》的研究成果作为研究对象，并且对后者的观察有助于对前者的了解。从这个意义来看，《公孙龙子》一方面是研究目的，另一方面是研究中介。其中隐含着的是当代研究者所把握的思想，也可以考察出研究者所受中西思想的影响。所以，《公孙龙子》研究的价值是多元的。

对于某一诠释系统的评价，也不可能站在绝对客观的立场予以评析，必须在自觉评价标准的前提下予以审视。

刘教授是我从未谋面的朋友，因为同对《公孙龙子》的解析与其中所涉及的哲学问题感兴趣，而在电邮来往中慢慢彼此了解，建立起既陌生又熟悉的情谊，这是很难得的经历。对于他这本《〈公孙龙子〉重释与重译》的写作，我是由衷佩服他能够用语言哲学的观点将《公孙龙子》做统贯性的解释，一方面开发出新的意义，另一方面也对比出中国哲学思想在表达上的特性，并且还提出许多前瞻性的哲学问题。这本书对我有许多启发与帮助。曾子曰："君子以文会友，以友辅仁。"因此，我将一点读后感想记叙如下，以会吾友。

二、本书研究方法与理论预设

刘教授的研究方法是循着理解、诠释、翻译、重构、比较、评论、提问的步骤进行的。在理解部分，主要是采用王管所撰《新编诸子集成·公孙龙子悬解》之原文，在诠释与翻译部分参考王宏印所著《白话解读公孙龙子》（西安：三秦出版社，1997）和刘玉俊所著《浅论先秦名家》（台北：正谊出版社，2002）。其中刘玉俊并未完成《公孙龙子》全部5篇关键论文的翻译，《通变论》一文没有现代汉语和英语译文，在理论重构方面涉及一些前理解的预设。

基本上这本《〈公孙龙子〉重释与重译》在重释部分颇具系统性。所谓"系统"是指它的诠释已能呈现《公孙龙子》的理论架构与诠释内容的一致性；在他的诠释之下，《公孙龙子》各篇章的理论关联性显示出来，在问题的解决方面，也可以看出《公孙龙子》立场的一致性、观点的互补性，以及视野的连续性。简单地说，在刘教授的诠释下，公孙龙绝不是个诡辩者，而是一个理性主义的哲学家；虽然此一诠释系统对《公孙龙子》的文本仍有笼罩不全的情况，后文再论。

刘教授《〈公孙龙子〉重释与重译》一书的核心问题如其引言所论，"以纯概念思辨的方式追问语义规定性本质是什么，人用语言到底把握了什么样的知识"。刘教授认为这是《公孙龙子》语言哲学的基本精神。此一基本精神的把握有如下几方面的预设：

1. 《公孙龙子》的思想是一种语言哲学。（其参照系是以索绪尔为主的语言哲学思想）

2. 语言之语义有本质性规定，且是人可以把握得到的。（这主要从他对《公孙龙子·名实论》的理解中可见）

3. 由具有语义本质的语言所构成的知识有其特性。（这主要从他对《公孙龙子·指物论》的理解中可见）

4. 有以"非纯概念思辨"为探讨语义或语义本质的方法。（这主要可从他对先秦哲学各家名学思想的理解及与《公孙龙子》思想的比较中可见）

5. 纯概念思辨方式是探究语义本质的方法之一。（这是在对古汉语与英文两种语言特性的比较之下，指出《公孙龙子》如何摆脱古汉语语法限制的探究方法）

6. 公孙龙是以纯概念思辨方式探究语义本质的。（这是在前述比较之后，对《公孙龙子》探讨方式与表达方式特性的肯定）

7. 公孙龙以纯概念思辨方式探究的知识特性是可以把握的。（这是作者对

《公孙龙子》诠释、研究后所做之肯定）

事实上，以上所分析的七点是相互支持、彼此印证的整体。将《公孙龙子》理解成怎样的理论形态，就选取怎样的诠释参照系；选用了怎样的参照系，也就将《公孙龙子》解释成怎样的理论形态。此种研究过程上的循环，并无损于此一诠释系统的价值，因为其诠释结果只要能取得根据文本而来的最大一致性，就是好的诠释系统。所谓一致性的程度乃是相对的，相对于其他诠释系统而论。如果我们从预设中的每一项来检视这本书，可以看到作者是基于什么理由认为《公孙龙子》思想的基本精神是语言哲学。

在比较、评论方面，刘教授介绍了西方语言学的发展，将西方语言的特性与基本元素与中国语言做比较。他指出："古汉语虽然缺乏语形或将逻辑符号化、形式化，但不能因此断定中国古代哲学中没有语言精确性研究。古汉语不具有西方语言中的性、数、格、时等，而是在一个'字'中包含诸多意义，此一特性对于催生形而上学理性思辨有着独特的价值。"除了中西语言学的比较之外，刘教授也在第四章[1]对先秦名家思想的专题研究中，将索绪尔与《公孙龙子》比较，与解读《公孙龙子》的伍非百思想比较。通过诸多比较、理解，刘教授指出解读名家文本的重要方法在于运用现代语言哲学的分析工具之一，即蒯因（Willard Van Orman Quine）的《语词和对象》（*Word and Object*）一书中"使用"（use）与"提及"（mention）的区分，通过此一区分可以解开许多名家、辩者看似诡辩的命题。

最后在提问方面，刘教授关心的是，由于古汉语的结构形式并不突出，公孙龙走不出形式分析的路，只能走语义研究的路。那么，这条路我们今天能否接着走下去？公孙龙关于语义确定性原则的论述可以给现代语义学的启发是什么？又由于体验的个体差异性、环境差异性、文化差异性等，语义的人际交流如何可能，如何才能达到主体间的共识？公孙龙提出的"唯乎其彼此"原则是否值得我们高度重视？若依照公孙龙的思想推论，抽象的概念不一定是隐喻性的，因为抽象概念必须有自己的"此性、彼性"，且必然不同于具体概念的"此性、彼性"。那么，语义本质不相同的概念之间又如何能够映像？若是将两者分别视为完全独立的本质意义规定性，那么抽象概念又是如何从具身体验中形成的呢？……刘教授的提问虽然没有给出明确的答案，但他试图解决问题的观点隐藏在本书的许多角落，这需要读者们细细体会，自己去发掘。

1　李先生在此提到的几篇文章及第四章专题研究，是我在初稿中收录的本人近年来发表的论文。在此书定稿过程中，其中的观点已经融入了第三部分中，因而决定删去。这里为了保持李先生的原文而未做改动。——刘利民注

三、本书结构

　　刘教授这本著作的结构非常有逻辑性，是以意义的转换作为思路开展的脉络。第一章呈现《公孙龙子》的原典、今译、英译。由于从原典到今译需要理解，从中文到英译也需要理解，于是第二章说明第一章理解的根据、公孙龙思想所涉及的哲学问题，以及公孙龙对这些问题解答的观点。然而，我们又如何确证作者对《公孙龙子》的解读是正确的呢？于是作者在第三章中指出古代、现代中西学者对《公孙龙子》的误读、理解与评价，进而指出正确理解、解读《公孙龙子》的方法，并定位《公孙龙子》为语言哲学，且先秦名家是理性主义哲学家。

　　基于前面各部分的论证，作者的理解在一定程度上取得了内在一致性的诠释，刘教授在第四章对先秦名家的某些部分做了更深入的专题研究，其中《语言切分出的意义世界》主要是针对《公孙龙子》中《名实论》《指物论》的思想与西方语言学的比较。《先秦名家在形容词语义中的哲学盘旋》一文通过对"白狗黑"等先秦名家"诡辩"命题的研究，指出这些命题是先秦名家的理性主义哲学思想命题。他们所反映的正是与西方哲学不同的，具有古汉语语言特色的理性主义哲学思辨路径。《语言元范畴化与公孙龙语言哲学》一文指出，公孙龙对于元范畴化语义概念的思辨是自觉的，他的语义反思中既有本体论也有认识论的明确意识。公孙龙基于汉语言后设范畴化认知而对"名"的意义本质进行了语言哲学反思。《先秦语言哲学流派问题再探》一文则指出，鉴于先秦不同哲学思想流派对于"名""实"等概念的理解、思想的取向与层面并不相同，所反思的对象、方法也大相径庭，先秦儒、道、墨、法、名等各派的共同特征，是很难成立的，也因此凸显出公孙龙是以纯概念思辨方式探究语义本质的。

　　此外，在本书的附录部分还有先秦名家"诡辩"命题古译今、英译及解说，与前面各章的相关诠释意义相连，相映成趣。

四、从内容上看的一些问题

　　（一）《公孙龙子》一书的文本确立问题

　　关于《公孙龙子》的版本，明清两代以来有陶宗仪《说郛》本、《道藏》本、《十二子》本、周子义《子汇》本、《绵眇阁》本、王缧堂《廿二子全书》本、张海鹏《墨海金壶》本、钱熙祚《守山阁》本等，一般认为以《道藏》本为最早，为各本所从出，并较各本为善。但据南京大学哲学系杨俊光先生考证，认为《说郛》本更早于《道藏》本，文字亦互有长短，它之所本，可能还属于《道藏》以外的另一个系统。

现以含芳楼影印的明正统《道藏》和万历《续道藏》本为据，考察本书的文本[1]。

1. 在《名实论》中"天地与其所产者"据《道藏》为"天地与其所产焉"。

2. 在《白马论》中"有白马，为有白马之非马，何也？"据《道藏》为"有白马为有马，白之，非马，何也？"。

3. 另"天下非有无色之马"据《道藏》为"天下非有无色之马也"。

4. 再者"使马无色，如有马已耳，安取白马？"据《道藏》为"使马无色，有马如已耳，安取白马？"。

5. "以有白马不可谓无马者，离白之谓也。是离者，有白马不可谓有马也。"据《道藏》为"有白马不可谓无马者，离白之谓也。不离者，有白马不可谓有马也"。

6. 在《坚白论》中"得其白，得其坚，见与不见离。不见离"，据《道藏》为"得其白，得其坚，见与不见与不见离"。

7. 在《通变论》中"而牛之非羊也、羊之非牛也"据《道藏》为"而羊牛之非羊也、之非牛也"。但依前后文意看，前者之改变较正确，《道藏》原文反而有误。

8. 在《通变论》中"羊牛足五"据《道藏》为"牛羊足五"。

9. 在《指物论》中"使天下无物，谁径谓非指？"据《道藏》为"使天下无物指，谁径谓非指？"。

（二）《公孙龙子》诠释方面的问题

在《名实论》中"谓此而行不唯乎此"据王启湘应改为"谓此而此不唯乎此"。

在《名实论》中"知此之非也，知此之不在此也，明不谓也"。据俞樾及王启湘应改为"知此之非此也，知此之不在此也，则不谓也"。如此才能与后文"则不谓也"相应。

1. 在《名实论》中："故彼彼止于彼，此此止于此，可。彼此而彼且此，此

---

1 关于李贤中教授以下提出的版本问题，我已采用脚注的方式，在正文中做了一定回应，提出了自己的看法。参见《公孙龙子》译文部分。——刘利民注

彼而此且彼，不可。"陈澧本、辛从益本、守山阁本皆作"故彼彼……"，周昌忠、陈宪猷、徐复观等绝大多数当代学者的处理皆将"彼彼"连读，本书则断为"故彼，彼止于彼；此，此止于此，可。彼此而彼且此，此彼而此且彼，不可"。姑且不论谁是谁非，在本书第55页[1]引《墨经·经说上》"正名者彼此。彼此可：彼彼止于彼，此此止于此。彼此不可：彼且此也。彼此亦可：彼此止于彼此。若是而彼此也，则彼彼此此也"就有不一致的断句。

2. 在《坚白论》中"而坚必坚其不坚。石物而坚"原释"坚硬就是使不坚硬的东西坚硬起来的性质"，宜断句为"而坚必坚，其不坚石、物而坚"，解释为"坚性本身就是坚性，它不需要使石头或某物坚硬，才具有坚性，其本身就是坚性"。

3. 《通变论》："青白不相与而相与，反对也。不相邻而相邻，不害其方也。"要引入五行方位思想才解释得通顺。

4. 在《指物论》中依《道藏》"使天下无物指，谁径谓非指？"其中"物指"有重要意义，不能解释为"并非指称的物"。

5. 在《指物论》中将把握三种不同含义：（1）"指认"，即以手指指物；（2）"指称"，即以名指物意义上的指；（3）"指"的名称本身，而推论公孙龙主要是在谈论用名称指称事物的问题。依个人来看这样的理解是有不足的。

6. 《指物论》"使天下无物指，谁径谓非指？""天下有指，无物指，谁径谓非指？"其中的"物指"是解开"非指"或"而指非指"的关键，此一"物指"的意义是认识主体与认识对象经由"指涉作用"所构成的双向关系；由于认知主体所把握到的认知结果是主客合作的结果，或主体经由客体性质的把握而成。因此，才可以讨论或说明"而指非指"的意义。这种主客二元的认知架构贯通着《坚白论》与《名实论》相关原文的诠释[2]。

从"物指"意义的厘清中可发现《公孙龙子》并不仅仅是语言哲学，正如刘教授在《语言元范畴化与公孙龙语言哲学》一文中所主张的，其中也涉及认识论与形而上学的相关问题。就其探讨议题的分布来看，《坚白论》《指物论》与《名实论》是探讨认知方法、认知可能性、认知之结果到正确表达原则的确立。而《名实

1　这是本书初稿中收录的论文所引。在本书定稿中，由于删除了论文收录部分，此引文亦不存在。——刘利民注

2　李教授在此提出了批评意见。我认为有的有道理，如第一条，我用脚注方式在译文章节中做了说明；第四条李教授的解释与我的翻译没有出入；其余几条则属于学术研究争议。关于这类争议问题，我在有关《公孙龙子》的翻译说明章节与重释公孙龙思想的章节中有论述，供学者参考。——刘利民注

论》《通变论》与《白马论》则是探讨正确表达原则与产生概念的思维过程以及正确表达的范例说明。因此，整部《公孙龙子》处理了认知、思维与表达三个层面的哲学问题，而不仅限于语言哲学。如此的理解将可取得与《庄子·齐物论》中对于《公孙龙子》《指物论》批评的更多对话可能性，并彰显先秦名学相关文献的丰富意义。

至于刘教授所提出的问题：公孙龙提出的"唯乎其彼此"的原则是否值得我们高度重视呢？根据周云之教授在其《名辩学论》的立场，正名的对象必须是语词之名，同时也必须是概念之名。公孙龙的《名实论》包含哲学正名与逻辑正名，所谓哲学正名是指名实一致，特别是实先名后的存在次序。而唯乎其彼此的正名原则，则是指在思想界中——概念的独立性，其彼、此各有分别，不得混乱。至于约定俗成的语词正名原则，则是从《荀子·正名》思想引申而出，在表达界，同名异谓与异名同谓是被允许的，只要在人们相互沟通的场域中，大家达成共识即可。例如："机车"可以指交通工具，但在台湾年轻人的日常表达中也可指一个很不上道的人。在表达界中"机车"是一个语词，但是在思想界中交通工具的"机车"与很不上道者的"机车"却分别指两个不同的概念。公孙龙提出的"唯乎其彼此"原则其价值正是凸显了每个概念的独立性，这是思想界中的逻辑正名原则，值得我们高度重视，并加以研究。

五、结语

我秉持诠释经典时的符合性、把握创造性的要求来撰写这篇读后感，因为对古籍诠释的评价应涉及以下几个方面：

1. 诠释的文献是否与古代文本相符。

2. 对作品语言的诠释是否符合古代语言的用法。在解释古籍时，必须注意关键词之字源意义、作者生活年代，或成书年代的时代意义，以及作品本身的脉络意义。例如："指"在卜辞、金文、大篆中的字源及演变意义，在孟子、庄子、荀子、墨辩中的时代意义，以及在《公孙龙子》一书中的脉络意义，都是必须考察的。

3. 解释本身是否符合逻辑。解释本身必须前后一致，不能自相矛盾，这是人们对解释的最基本要求。

4. 对作品思想的诠释是否与当时社会的思想文化背景相契合。任何思想都是在一定的社会历史环境中，在一定的思想文化背景下产生的。在某一特定的社会历史环境中存在的思想虽然各不相同，相互冲突，但它们共同构成了一个大的思想文化背景。这个大背景把每一位作者的思想对象、理论的性质，甚至思考问题的方式都限定在一定的范围之内。因此，在解释《公孙龙子》时，必须考虑时代背景的相关因素。

5. 哲学家之所以为哲学家定然有其创见，既然有其创造性的部分，在考虑以上几方面的符合性要素之外，当然也必须容许新的解读观点与相应参照系的运用。历来《公孙龙子》之所以难以解读，正是由于诠释方法上的不对应造成的。

刘教授《〈公孙龙子〉重释与重译》这本书重点在于上述第三点与第五点，第四点也做了一些先秦名学发展的历史考察，以及古汉语的限制性说明。他对《公孙龙子》的解释确实具有前后一致性。把握《公孙龙子》创见的部分则是这本书的特点所在：他在对古汉语与英文两种语言特性进行比较之后来审视解读名家的思想，提供了一个新的解读观点，是很有贡献的。他运用自己的语言学及语言哲学的学术背景，将公孙龙思想以语义问题的分析、离析来解释《公孙龙子·坚白论》中的"离"，也有独到的见解，呈现了公孙龙思想的分析性格，是我很欣赏的部分。正如他自己很有信心地说："那么本书的解释和翻译是否成功了？这个还是留给读者，留给历史去评价吧。但我作为译者非常自信，我的解释比现有的解释更能合理地、内在一致地说明名家的全部命题。这至少说明，本书的解释框架比现有的任何理论框架都更接近名家的思想倾向。"的确，本书是在我所读到《公孙龙子》相关著作中相当有内在一致性的著作，对于我在先秦名辩学及中国哲学方法论的研究也有相当的帮助。我相信在有心的同道彼此讨论、相互激荡下，先秦名家的智慧将逐步得到解读、展开，进而运用于现代认知、思维、表达的各个层面。

李贤中
台湾大学哲学系教授
2012年9月25日

C目录
ONTENTS

引　言

翻译旨在沟通，实现跨语言的思想、感情交流与理解。翻译的理想目标当然是严复提出的信、达、雅。这话说起来容易，做起来难。且不谈"雅"的至善要求，就连最基本的"忠实于原文"标准，也不是轻而易举就能达到的。原因就在于翻译的对象是语言意义，而语言意义极其复杂，难以完全充分把握。按语言哲学家蒯因的观点（Quine，1960：185-212），不仅跨语言之间的翻译具有不确定性，即使是一种语言内，以一个陈述句对另一个陈述句进行释义也具有不确定性。这是由于单个语句的意义无法确定，要理解说话人使用的语句的意义，就必须把它放到说话人的信念系统中，参照他相信什么、具有什么知识结构而进行。看来，翻译充其量只能是近似地沟通。既然只能近似地沟通，我们所能做也应该做的，就是不断地探讨、反思、改进翻译，使之一步步接近准确。于是，重译旨在更好地沟通，更好地实现交流与理解；这也就是重译之所以必要的理由。

《公孙龙子》需要重译，主要出于以下四个理由。

第一，公孙龙的文章在历史上背负着"诡辩"的错误标签，没有得到严肃认真的解读；即使是在今天，虽然他已经得到"正名"，被承认为中国先秦的哲学家，或逻辑学家，或理论科学家，或语言学家等，但这么多的"家"也至少说明，《公孙龙子》古文今译各种版本对他的思想众说纷纭，理解很不一致，甚至相互冲突。本书将在"重新理解《公孙龙子》"这一部分中专门讨论这个问题。至于国外学者的理解，更是错得离谱，让人不知所云。如，A. C. 葛瑞汉把公孙龙的"物莫非指，而指非指"解释成这样："万事万物都是指认出的，而指认并不是将它指认出来。"（Graham，1990：213）如此现状说明我们还有必要重新研读公孙龙的文章，做出更准确的解释和翻译。

第二，对于公孙龙思想的再探讨，很可能有助于我们重新认识中国古代哲学的理性主义思想，从一个角度为"中国哲学"正名，促进中西方思想文化交流。在中外不少学者看来，说中国古代有自己的哲学，是可疑的；德里达（2001：10）就曾明确说过，中国古代只有思想，没有哲学，因为哲学是欧洲形态的东西，是与欧洲语言相联系的，是古希腊的发明。不少中国学者认为，一个重要原因就是古汉语的结构特征不利于中国思想家产生古希腊式的思辨性形而上学。然而，公孙龙的思想分明表明，这种认识恐怕并不正确。不过，这方面的论证还有待通过研究公孙龙的原著来梳理。对于孔子、孟子、老子、庄子、墨子等一系列先秦哲学家，人们已经认识得相对深入了，理解也没有太大的差异，所需要的是进一步挖掘其中细微精妙的思想。而对于先秦名家，如前所述，人们的意见花样百出。这明显不利于中外哲学思想传统的交流。

第三，译者陋闻，所见的《公孙龙子》完整译文（汉、英译文）仅有王宏印所著的《白话解读公孙龙子》（西安：三秦出版社，1997）和刘玉俊所著的《浅论先秦名家》（台北：正谊出版社，2002）。其中刘玉俊并未完成《公孙龙子》全部五篇关键论文的翻译，没有拿出《通变论》的现代汉语和英语译文。从英文表达看，这两部译著水平是很高的，且都从中国先秦时期哲学家这个视角来翻译《公孙龙子》，王宏印还给出了详尽的说明，解释公孙龙的哲学和逻辑思想。但是，我认为，他们的译文还未能充分展示出公孙龙理性主义语言哲学的基本精神：以纯概念思辨的方式追问语义规定性本质是什么，人用语言到底把握了什么样的知识。因而他们的译文中还有不少值得商榷之处。以公孙龙最著名的"白马非马"论文为例。刘玉俊认为这篇文章的中心是辩证地揭示个别与一般之间的对立统一关系，而王宏印则认为公孙龙在"同中求异"，以证明逻辑和辩证逻辑相结合的方式揭示实在与概念、内涵与外延的关系等。我非常不赞成将公孙龙的思想视为某种辩证思维。事实上，我们将会看到，公孙龙对概念意义的确定性本身给予了高度的关注与思辨，其中涉及严格的实在层面和语言概念层面的意义区分。这里没有任何辩证思维的影子。如果按照现有这两个译文的理解来翻译，那么我们就很难把握公孙龙文章所表达的思想的严格逻辑性，结果仔细读之，感觉公孙龙的思想虽有一定逻辑性，但漏洞不少，译文的篇章之间，甚至一篇文章的前后论述都存在内在不一致性，甚至自相矛盾，还需要加以澄清。如果我们借用现代语言哲学的框架和技术（如"使用"与"提及"的区分等），也许更能够融贯一致地表达出公孙龙的语言哲学思想。对此，本书将在正文中阐述。

第四，由于公孙龙等名家思想家"专决于名"，即一门心思专注于语言问题的反思，他们的思想在语言学理论中也独树一帜。这对于我国语言学理论形成自己的学术流派具有重要的启发意义。中国语言学现有的学派，无论是唯理主义还是经验主义，都是从国外引进的。这在外语界尤甚，而在汉语界，学术思想活跃得多，他们基于汉语的特征而形成了研究取向的分野。但是，即使在汉语界也还没有诞生在世界上独具特色的语言学理论学派，而其中重要的原因就是我们对自己的语言哲学传统挖掘不深，没能从中汲取足够养分。对《公孙龙子》的研究极有可能给予我们以思想的启发。

鉴于以上原因，我力图在本书中对《公孙龙子》的五篇文章以及惠施的"历物十事"和"辩者二十一事"等三十一个命题做出新的翻译。如后文所见，我的理解和翻译完全是基于视以公孙龙为代表的先秦名家为理性主义的语言哲学家这一基本点。这当然是一种有条件的解释。但以笔者之陋见，这尚可称为目前唯一能够全面说明先秦名家所有"诡辩"命题的解释方式。这是不是一种终极解释？我不敢妄言，只是说现有的种种解释框架均不能够完全解释所有命题，因而与此相比，本书的框架更具解释力。这应当是符合科学研究精神的。如果将来学术界提出了更有说服力的解释，我当然应当接受。

鉴于此，我并不宣称本书的译文和讨论忠实地再现了公孙龙及他所代表的先秦名家的思想，因为历史毕竟是不可复制的。但我也不认同尤金·奈达（1993）的翻译"功能对等"说，因为毕竟还是存在着正确、错误的可能判断。模仿阐释学的话说，虽然一千个阐释者尽可以阐释出一千个公孙龙，但所阐释出的却只能是公孙龙。由于我们不大可能建立一种判定《公孙龙子》译文是正确还是错误的标准，我姑且接受关于真理的融贯论（coherence theory of truth），而把译文所表达的思想内容是否具有内在融贯性作为检查翻译可靠性的原则。

这里，我所谓的"融贯"（coherence）指的是，对于一个语句的理解，译者应当努力使之与全文，乃至全书的其他语句所表达的命题意义具有思想理解的一致性。正如杜世洪提出的那样，融贯恐怕并不是语句、语篇本身的问题，而是涉及基于理性、知识、意向而在交往中涌现出来的（杜世洪，2012）。按照这个原则，我认为一个语句的翻译不应拘泥于表层的遣词造句，而应当使得所理解、译出的意义能够在由其他语句共同构建起来的思想理解框架中得到合乎逻辑的说明。至于这个理解框架的正确与否，我将在第二部分《〈公孙龙子〉翻译说明》和第三部分《重新理解〈公孙龙子〉》中做出说明，为自己辩护。

这就涉及直译和意译的选择。如果我们囿于原文而选择完全直译，很可能掉入陷阱。古汉语高度精练，能省的推理和语义部分均予以省略，因而表面上看可以很不连贯。《公孙龙子》这样的理论性著作由于这个原因而显得更加难读，因而非常有必要把句子所隐含的思想明确地翻译出来。本书打算在尽可能照顾原文的情况下，多采用意译的方法。

随着近几年对先秦名家"诡辩"问题研究的深入，我的确有些新的认识，深感我们现有的认识公孙龙的框架值得反思，因为它们之下所产生的《公孙龙子》

思想解释不具有良好的融贯性。因而本书打算梳理近几年来我对公孙龙及先秦名家的思想实质的研究，并在此基础上对《公孙龙子》进行现代汉语和英语重译，旨在以本人绵薄之力引起讨论，促进对公孙龙等先秦名家的语言哲学思想的认识，并由此反思中国古代哲学、语言学思想，推动中外思想文化的相互理解与交流。

本书的结构安排如下：

第一部分为《公孙龙子》一书六篇文章的古译今译文。其中，原文采用王琯所撰《新编诸子集成·公孙龙子悬解》版本。

第二部分为翻译注解，表达译者对原文的理解和对一些难题的解释。

第三部分讨论为何要重新翻译《公孙龙子》以及对公孙龙子的理解框架问题。我将先讨论关于先秦名家的传统误解以及现代的种种相互并不一致的解释，然后从汉语特征及其对哲学思想产生的价值出发，讨论为什么说先秦名家是理性主义语言哲学家。

附录将庄子《天下篇》中记录的先秦名家代表人物惠施的十个命题（"历物十事"）和其他辩者的二十一个命题（"辩者二十一事"）也进行了翻译；同时附上译者对这些命题的认识和解说。目的在于以同一哲学框架对先秦名家的命题进行具有融贯性的解说，并强化对《公孙龙子》五篇文章的思想理解。

最后需要说明的是，本书中的翻译肯定得基于译者本人近几年关于公孙龙子和名家的研究；其中一些观点已经发表于《哲学研究》、《四川大学学报·哲学社会科学版》、《外语学刊》、《外国语文》、《语言哲学研究》、*ProtoSociology*等刊物，以及由四川大学出版社2007年出版的本人的专著《在语言中盘旋》。之所以这里不揣谫陋，再次发表其中一些内容，是为了支撑本书中关于先秦名家文献的翻译，同时也为了将自己的新近研究之所得集中呈现在读者面前，引起讨论和批判。若仅仅是翻译加翻译说明，这一点是做不到的。既是发表过的论点或研究结论，本书内容不免有交叉重复；在请读者海涵的同时，注意文章的侧重点，或许可引发研究兴趣。此外，本书还引用了其他研究者的观点，这些观点均在文中注明出处；在对他们表示感谢的同时，我必须声明，如有失误都是本人造成的，与他人无关。

第一部分
《公孙龙子》古译今

第一篇 名实论

【原 文】

天地与其所产者，物也。

物以物其所物而不过焉，实也。实以实其所实，不旷焉，位也。出其所位，非位；位其所位焉，正也。

以其所正，正其所不正；疑其所正。

其"正"者，正其所实也；正其所实者，正其名也。其"名"正，则唯乎其彼此焉。谓彼而彼不唯乎彼，则彼谓不行。谓此而行不唯乎此，则此谓不行。

其以当不当也，不当而乱也。

故彼，彼当乎彼，则唯乎彼，其谓行彼。此，此当乎此，则唯乎此，其谓行此。其以当而当也，以当而当，正也。

故彼彼止于彼；此此止于此，可。彼此而彼且此，此彼而此且彼，不可。

夫名实，谓也。知此之非也，知此之不在此也，明不谓也。知彼之非彼也，知彼之不在彼也，则不谓也。

至矣哉，古之明王！审其名实，慎其所谓。至矣哉，古之明王！

【古译今】

大自然以及生长、存在于其中的皆是实在之物。

而作为物之名的"物"，其所指则是物之所以是且只能是该物的概念性意义，不能泛化过度；这就是我们所议论的"实（实在）"。此一"实在"必须充分符合物的真正本质而无缺失，这即是我们说的"位"，即语义正确性的基本要求。对"位"的任何偏离，都会使名的意义出现不恰当或偏差。完全满足"位"的要求则名的意义也就正确了。

这一意义正确性要求理当是用来矫正名的意义偏差的标准，也是质疑〔现有的］正名是否合理的标准。

由此观之，正名应当是确定"实在"的本质。只有"实在"的本质得到了确定，名称的正确意义才得到了确立。而正名的原则就是"名称本质意义的唯一性"。说出"彼"的名称，却不唯一地指称彼事物，那么"彼"就不应当用于言说那个事物。说出"此"的名称，却不唯一地指称此事物，那么"此"就不应当用于言说该事物。

如果非要这么做，那就是把正确的名称用于不正确的对象；正是这种做法导致了名称使用的混乱。

因此，言说"彼"时，"彼"的意义必须是一切彼必然具有，并且只有彼才具有的"彼性"；这时才可以用"彼"来言说彼事物。言说"此"时，"此"必须是一切此必然具有，并且只有此才具有的"此性"。这时才可以用"此"来言说此事物。这样，事物的名称与其本质意义就相符合了；只有当名称表达了事物的本质，名称的正确性才得到了确定。

因此，用"彼"来言说彼，则"彼"必须而且只能指称彼之彼性；用"此"来言说此，则"此"必须而且只能指称此之此性；这才是正确的。若以"彼"来言说此，使得"彼"既指称彼性又指称此性；或者用"此"来言说彼，使得"此"既指称此性又指称彼性，这些都是不正确的。

所谓"名"与"实"的关系，本质上说，就是正确地使用语言进行指称的问题。如果确定"此"并不指称此性，即知道语词"此"所指的此性并不存在于所言说的此对象之中，那就很清楚，不能使用"此"来言说此对象。如果知道"彼"所指的彼性并不存在于所言说的彼对象之中，那么很显然，不能用"彼"来言说彼对象。

英明的古代先王是多么了不起啊！他们认真审视名称的意义与其所指之实在本质的关系，从而在说话中谨慎地使用名称。这也正是他们的英明之处！

第二篇　白马论

【原　文】

"白马非马"，可乎？

曰：可。

曰：何哉？

曰：马者所以命形也，白者所以命色也；命色者非名形也，故曰："白马非马"。

曰：有白马不可谓无马也。不可谓无马者，非马也？有白马，为有白马之非马，何也？

曰：求马，黄、黑马皆可致。求白马，黄、黑马不可致。使白马乃马也，是所求一也；所求一者，白者不异马也。所求不异，如黄、黑马有可有不可，何也？可与不可，其相非明。故黄、黑马一也，而可以应有马，而不可以应有白马；是白马之非马，审矣！

曰：以马之有色为非马，天下非有无色之马。天下无马，可乎？

曰：马固有色，故有白马。使马无色，如有马已耳，安取白马？故白者非马也。白马者，马与白也。马与白，马也？故曰："白马非马也"。

曰：马未与白为马，白未与马为白。合马与白，复名白马。是相与以不相与为名，未可。故曰："白马非马未可"。

曰：以有白马为有马，谓有白马为有黄马，可乎？

曰：未可。

曰：以有马为异有黄马，是异黄马与马也；异黄马与马，是以黄马为非马。以黄马为非马，而以白马为有马——此飞者入池而棺椁异处——此天下之悖言乱辞也。

曰：以有白马不可谓无马者，离白之谓也。是离者，有白马不可谓有马也。故所以为有马者，独以马为有马耳，非以白马为有马。故其为有马也，不可以谓"马马"也。

曰：白者不定所白，忘之而可也。白马者，言白定所白也。定所白者，非白也。马者，无去取于色，故黄、黑皆所以应。白马者，有去取于色，黄、黑马皆所以色去，故唯白马独可以应耳。无去者非有去也，故曰"白马非马"。

【古译今】

［客问：］说"白马不是马"是正确的吗？

主答：当然正确。

问：为什么？

答："马"是用来命名形状的名称，"白"则是用来命名颜色的名称。命名颜色的名称不能用来命名形状。这是我说"'白马'不是'马'"的依据。

问：有白马，就不能说没有马。既然不可以说没有马，它不就是马吗？你说有白马就是有白马而不等于有马，这是什么道理？

答：若要追问"马"所命名的概念意义，则黄马、黑马都符合其意。而要追问"白马"所命名的概念意义，则黄马、黑马不符合其意。假定"白马"等于"马"，那么这两个概念的意义必须同一。既然意义必须同一，那么"白"与"马"就不能有意义差别。既然意义不能相异，那么［刚才所论的］黄马、黑马却存在符合其意与不符合其意的矛盾情况，这又是何故？这是因为符合还是不符合原本是两码事，却被混为一谈因而不明确了。因此，即使把"黄、黑马"视为同一性概念，它可以用来确定"有马"的意义，却不能用来确定"有白马"的意义。这说明，"白马"不等于"马"。难道还不够清楚吗？

问：你这是以马有颜色来论证"不是马"的问题，但世界上并没有无色的马。那么是不是可以说世界上不存在马呢？

答：实存的马当然有颜色，所以才有白马。但我们说"马"时，"马"的概念并无颜色；有"马"只意味着有"马"本身，怎么会等于"白马"呢？因此，关键在于"白"本身并不是"马"的本质。"白马"是"马"与"白"构成的复合名称。难道说其中的"马"与"白"都指"马"的意义吗？因此我说，"白马"不是"马"。

问：马不必是白的，它也是马，白不必是马，也是白。"马"与"白"相组合，构成了复合名称"白马"。你把复名中的意义组合说成因性质不同而不可组合，这种做法是错误的。所以，说"白马不是马"并不正确。

答：那么用"有白马就是有马"的句子来说"有白马就等于有黄马"，这样行吗？

问：不行。

答：这就是说有"马"与有"黄马"是两回事，于是"黄马"与"马"区分开来了。既然"黄马"与"马"可以区分开，这说明"黄马"所指的概念意义不等于"马"所指的概念意义。既然确定"黄马"并不是"马"，却偏要说有"白马"就是有"马"，这就像说鸟在池塘中生活、棺材和椁不在一处一样，无异于天下最自相矛盾、混乱不堪的语言命题！

答：所谓"有白马就不能说没有马"，关键在于应当把"白"本身抽离出来单独讨论。这一分析使得"有白马"不等于"有马"。说"有马"所凭借的依据，只能是以马的概念意义为"马"这一名称的所指，而不能以"白马"的所指为有"马"的概念；因为照此推下去，"白"也就等同于"马"，就等于说有"马马"［，这至少十分别扭吧］！

12

答：白并不限于具体物体而为白；将具体物体的白色忘掉，而抽离出白本身，这才是正确的认识。［日常语言中，］"白马"中的"白"被限于具体的物体的白颜色了；一旦被限定，则所说的"白"并不是白本身。"马"的概念意义并不包含任何颜色定义，因而黄、黑马都可以作为"马"的具体实例；而"白马"的概念则包含白的性质，黄、黑马就不是其具体实例了；只有白马才是"白马"的具体实例。显然，包含特定本质意义的概念必然不等于不包含该特定本质意义的概念；所以我断言"'白马'不是'马'"。

第三篇　坚白论

【原　文】

坚白石三，可乎？

曰：不可。

曰：二，可乎？

曰：可。

曰：何哉？

曰：无坚得白，其举也二；无白得坚，其举也二。

曰：得其所白，不可谓无白；得其所坚，不可谓无坚；而之石也之于然也，非三也？

曰：视不得其所坚而得其所白者，无坚也。拊不得其所白而得其所坚，得其坚也，无白也。

曰：天下无白，不可以视石；天下无坚，不可以谓石。坚白石不相外，藏三可乎？

曰：有自藏也，非藏而藏也。

曰：其白也，其坚也，而石必得以相盛盈。其自藏奈何？

曰：得其白，得其坚，见与不见离。不见离，一一不相盈，故离。离也者，藏也。

曰：石之白，石之坚，见与不见，二与三，若广修而相盈也。其非举乎？

曰：物白焉，不定其所白；物坚焉，不定其所坚。不定者兼，恶乎其石也？

曰：循石，非彼无石。非石，无所取乎白石。不相离者，固乎然其无已。

曰：于石一也，坚白二也，而在于石，故有知焉，有不知焉；有见焉，有不见焉。故知与不知相与离，见与不见相与藏。藏故，孰谓之不离？

曰：目不能坚，手不能白。不可谓无坚，不可谓无白。其异任也，其无以代也。坚白域于石，恶乎离？

曰：坚未与石为坚，而物兼未与为坚。而坚必坚其不坚。石物而坚，天下未有若坚；而坚藏。白固不能自白，恶能白石物乎？若白者必白，则不白物而白焉。黄黑与之然。石其无有，恶取坚白石乎？故离也。离也者因是。力与知果，不若因是。且犹白——以目、以火见。而火不见；则火与目不见，而神见。神不见，而见离。坚——以手，而手以捶；是捶与手知而不知，而神与不知。神乎，是之谓"离"焉。离也者天下，故独而正。

【古译今】

[客问：]说坚硬、白色、石头是三个东西，这正确吗？

主答：不正确。

问：那么说它们是两个东西，正确吗？

答：正确。

问：这是为什么？

答：未感知坚硬时，完全可以感知白色，这说的是感知为二；未感知白色时，完全可以感知坚硬，这也说的是感知为二。

问：感知到了白色，当然不能说没有白色；感知到了坚硬，也不能说没有坚硬。然而对于石头也应该同样推论啊，难道这不说明"坚""白""石"是三个东西吗？

答：用眼睛看，不能看到坚硬，而看到了白色，眼睛感觉不到坚硬的存在；同样，用手摸，不能摸到白色，而摸到了坚硬，手摸感觉不到白色的存在。

问：如果自然界中不存在白色，那么我们无法看到石头；如果自然界不存在坚硬，则又无法说石头是硬的。坚硬、白色、石头理应不可分离，那么说这三个对象存在于一体，可以吗？

答：有必要弄清楚独立存在性，它与未被感知到还不同。

问：石头必须同时是白色并且是坚硬的才能成为完整意义上的石头。你所谓的"独立存在性"该怎么理解呢？

答：看到石头的白色，却摸到石头的坚硬，这说明被显现于感知者与不被显现于感知者是相互独立的。不被显现者被分离开来，它并不取决于被显现者的存在而存在；因此它自身存在着。这种自身的存在就是我所说的独立存在性。

问：〔就算按照你的显现或未显现于感知的观点来看，〕石头的白色、石头的坚硬也是被感知到的两个东西，都是第三个对象即石头的属性；正如长和宽构成了面积不可分割的属性一样。这不说明坚、白与石头是不可分离的吗？

答：具体对象可以是白的，但白并非限定于某个对象才能为白；具体对象是坚硬的，但坚硬并非限定于某个对象才能是坚硬。既然不限定，那么这些属性可为万物所兼有。那么，为何偏要说坚硬、白色只能存在于石头中呢？

问：观察任何一块石头，它都必须具有坚、白的属性，否则不能叫作石头。若没有石头，则无从谈论白色石头。坚、白都不可能从石头中抽离，它们是石头固有的属性，永远如此！

答：具体到石头，其属性当然与之一体。坚硬与白色作为两个属性同时存在于石头中，所以才会出现有的被感知到、有的未被感知到，有的显现、有的不显现的现象。但是显而易见，可感知的对象与不可感知的对象不可能同时是同一的，所显现者也不可能同时又是所未显现者。其原因就在于各自的独立存在性；既然独立存在，为何不能分而析之？

问：眼睛看不到坚硬，手摸不到白色，但确实不能说没有坚硬，也不能说没有白色。这只不过表明不同感官的知觉功能不同，不能相互替代而已。坚硬与白色仍然存在于石头中，怎么又是独立于石头的呢？

答：坚硬并非因为它存在于石头中，才是坚硬，也不因为它存在于世上任何物体之中才是坚硬；坚硬就是使不坚硬的东西坚硬起来的性质。若说是石头使得不硬的物体坚硬，则世上找不到这种坚硬。坚硬就是坚硬这种性质本身。〔同理，〕白自身若不是必然为白，怎么能够使石头或者其他物体具有白色？如果白自身必然为白，那么白不必存在于物体中也是白。黄、黑色也是这个道理。如果石头中没有坚硬与白本身，那么坚硬、白色石头的观念是从哪儿来的？这些对象来自于分而析之、单独考察。分析的方法适用于各种对象之为其本身的不同性质。基于实在的接触及感官体验而得到的初步知识，远不如通过适应其本质存在方式而获得的理性知识更具真理性。以白为例——白颜色只能是用眼睛看，且只有在有光时才能看到。但事情的真相是，光本身并不保证见到白，光加眼睛本身也并不能把握白，是心灵（思维）把握住了白本身。心灵不是直接看到了白，而是通过抽离而把握了白之为白本身。坚硬通过手来感知，而手又以捶打为感知方式；表面上看似乎是手通过捶打动作而把握了坚硬性，实际上并非如此。心灵不是直接获得坚硬的体验的。所谓心灵，即把对象分而析之，加以认识和把握。分析是认识万事万物的方法，只有用此方法所获得的知识才是为真的。

第四篇　通变论

【原　文】

曰：二有一乎？

曰：二无一。

曰：二有右乎？

曰：二无右。

曰：二有左乎？

曰：二无左。

曰：右可谓二乎？

曰：不可。

曰：左可谓二乎？

曰：不可。

曰：左与右可谓二乎。

曰：可。

曰：谓变非不变，可乎？

曰：可。

曰：右有与，可谓变乎？

曰：可。

曰：变只。

曰：右。

曰：右苟变，安可谓右？苟不变，安可谓变？

曰：二苟无左，又无右，二者左与右奈何？羊合牛非马，牛合羊非鸡。

曰：何哉？

曰：羊与牛唯异，羊有齿，牛无齿；而牛之非羊也、羊之非牛也，未可。是不俱有，而或类焉。羊有角，牛有角；牛之而羊也，羊之而牛也，未可。是俱有而类之不同也。羊牛有角，马无角；马有尾，羊牛无尾。故曰："羊合牛非马也。"

非马者，无马也。无马者，羊不二，牛不二，而羊牛二。是而羊而牛，非马可也。若举而以是，犹类之不同。若左右，犹是举。

牛羊有毛，鸡有羽。谓鸡足一，数足二；二而一，故三。谓牛羊足一，数足四；四而一，故五。羊牛足五，鸡足三，故曰："牛合羊非鸡。""非"，有以非鸡也。与马以鸡，宁马。材不材，其无以类，审矣。举是谓乱名，是狂举。

曰：他辩。

曰：青以白非黄，白以青非碧。

曰：何哉？

曰：青白不相与而相与，反对也。不相邻而相邻，不害其方也。不害其方者反而对，各当其所，若左右不骊。

故一于青不可，一于白不可，恶乎其有黄矣哉？黄其正矣，是正举也，其有君臣之于国焉，故强寿矣。

而且青骊乎白，而白不胜也。白足之胜矣而不胜，是木贼金也。木贼金者碧，碧则非正举矣。

青白不相与，而相与；不相胜，则两明也。争而明，其色碧也。

与其碧，宁黄。黄，其马也，其与类乎！碧，其鸡也，其与暴乎！

暴则君臣争而两明也。两明者昏不明，非正举也。

非正举者，名实无当，骊色章焉，故曰"两明"也。两明而道丧，其无有以正焉。

【古译今】

问：二中存在一吗？

答："二"中不存在"一"。

问：二意味着有右边吗？

答："二"没有"右边"。

问：二有左边吗？

答："二"没有"左边"。

问：右可以被称作"二"吗？

答：不能。

问：左可以被称作"二"吗？

答：不能。

问：左和右合起来可以说是"二"吗？

答：可以。

问：说变化等于并非不变化，可以吗？

答：可以。

问：右如果与另一物相结合，可以说有变化发生吗？

答：可以。

问：变成了几？

答："右"。

问：右若已经变了，怎么还称之为"右"？如果它没变，又怎么能说变了？

答："二"自身并无"左"，也无"右"，那它的"左"与"右"又从何谈起？如果说"羊"与"牛"合起来不是"马"的话，那么"牛"与"羊"合起来更不是"鸡"。

问：此话怎讲？

答：羊与牛有区别，因为羊有上齿，而牛没有上齿。然而单凭此就说是牛就绝无羊的属性，是羊就绝无牛的属性，这并不恰当。两者并不共有全部属性，但我们确实有可能将它们归入一类的理由。羊有角，牛也有角。但因此说牛就等于说羊、或者说羊就等于说牛，这也不行。两者共有"有角"的属性，却的确又不同类。"羊牛"指称有角类，而马没有角；"马"指称长尾类，而羊、牛没有长尾。鉴于此，可以说："'羊'与'牛'合起来不是'马'。"

所谓"非马"，指"羊牛"概念中不包括马的本质。在包含两个元素的这一"非马"的概念中，"羊"不是"二"，"牛"也不是"二"，但"羊牛"却是"二"。这个"二"指称"羊牛"概念的共同性质，而不指称马的性质；这肯定是正确的。以这个例子来说明问题，强调的是概念本质的不同。前述的"左""右"问题，也应当这样来理解。

牛、羊有皮毛，而鸡有羽毛。若谈论"鸡足"，则此"鸡足"构成了概念之"一"，而数数鸡的足，则肯定为二只。这样，二合一，则得到"三"只鸡足。同样，谈论"牛羊足"，则它构成了概念之"一"，而数数牛、羊的足，则肯定为四只。于是，"四"与"一"相合，则得到"五"只足。"羊牛"类有五只足，而鸡只有三只足，因此我说"'牛羊'更不意味'鸡'"。"不意味"所说的是"羊牛"的概念意义绝不可能包括"鸡"的任何性质。如果给定"马"和"鸡"两个选择［来说"羊牛"意味哪一个］，那我宁可选择"马"。这是因为"鸡"的特征与"羊牛"更无相近之处，根本没有任何理由将其纳入此概念之中。这道理显而易见。我举这些例子是为了说明名实混乱的原因，即名的意义因指称了错误的实质而不正确。

问：还有其他例证吗？

答：[有的。比如：]"绿"与"白"混合不是"黄"，"白"与"绿"混合也不是"淡绿"。

问：这又怎么理解？

答："绿"与"白"是两种原色，并非由相互的特征混合而成；即使混合，两者本质上也还是形成反差的独立两色。它们各有其清楚而确定的范围且不相近，即使把两者混合在一起，也无损于两者各自的原色性质。既然性质无损，那么作为两者本质的反差理当依然存在，各有各的确定性。就如同前述的"左"和"右"一样，不能混为一体。

因此，把两者混合而成的一体称为"绿"是不行的，称之为"白"也是不行的。既如此，怎么可能称之为"黄"呢？"黄"指称另一种独立原色，是有其正确指称对象的。就如同一个国家中的国王与大臣一样，只有各自符合自己的规定性，才有可能长久摆正相互关系。

绿色如果混合于白色，白色不再以纯正白色而胜出。白完全可以不断冲淡绿而侵蚀绿，却最终无法战胜之，因为绿虽然被白所侵蚀，但两者混合成了淡绿。淡绿是色调不同的杂色，而不是定义明确的原色。"淡绿"并无确定的色调本质，因而不是意义明确的名称。

"绿"与"白"并不能混合一体；如果非要混合，两者都无法胜出，因为它们会争相显示自身性质。结果便是既非"绿"又非"白"，成为意义范围无法确定的不同色调的"淡绿"。

因此，[要组合成一个类的话]与其选择"淡绿"，我宁可选择"黄"。"黄"，如同我先前说的"马"一样，至少还可以因具有单色性质而被归入[原色]类！"淡绿"，则相似于先前说的"鸡"的例子，其色调千差万别，因而性质不能确定，不能归入性质确定的类中！

性质不确定，正如国王与臣子混乱争斗，都力图以自己为标准。这种争斗的结果，则是本质更加不明确，于是两者的名称也就没有了正确的所指。

没有了正确的所指，则名称与意义实在就脱节了，就像杂色一样，没有了颜色的确定性。我称之为"性质自我显示之争"。在这种争斗之中，根本的本质规定性已经失去了，也就无法用来确定一个名称的意义是否正确。

第五篇　指物论

【原　文】

物莫非指，而指非指。天下无指，物无可以谓物。非指者天下，而物可谓指乎？

指也者，天下之所无也；物也者，天下之所有也。以天下之所有为天下之所无，未可。

天下无指，而物不可谓指也；不可谓指者，非指也；非指者，物莫非指也。

天下无指而物不可谓指者，非有非指也。非有非指者，物莫非指也。物莫非指者，而指非指也。

天下无指者，生于物之各有名，不为指也。不为指而谓之指，是兼不为指。以"有不为指"之"无不为指"，未可。且指者天下之所兼。天下无指者，物不可谓无指也。不可谓无指者，非有非指也。非有非指者，物莫非指，指非非指也，指与物非指也。

使天下无物，谁径谓非指？天下无物，谁径谓指？天下有指无物指，谁径谓非指，径谓无物非指？

且夫指固自为非指，奚待于物而乃与为指？

【古译今】

物之为"物"无一不是由名称指称而成，然而指称并不等于指认具体物[1]。如果世上万物没有名称来做指称，则物就无法被称为"物"〔从而被认识〕。〔可是，既然〕指称并非在世界上天然地存在，那么能说物就是物自身的指称吗？

指称并不是天然存在着的，而物却是实在存在于自然界中的。把存在的东西理解为不存在的东西，这是不正确的。

如果没有名称来进行指称，那么物就不能用"物"来言说。物不能说等同于"物"，因为物本身与"物"的指称意义不是一回事。既然两者不是一回事，则

1　李贤中教授不赞成把原文此句中的"指"区分为"指称"与"指认"（见李先生的读后感）。对此，我保留自己的认识。这其实也不完全是我个人的看法。具体的讨论参见第二部分关于这个问题的讨论。——刘利民注

"物"就是由名称指称而成的东西了。

如果没有指称，那么物就无法用"物"来言说，这并非是说名称不能指认具体物。名称并非不能指认具体物，是因为物之为"物"无一不是由名称指称而成。然而，"物"都由指称而确定，但指称［所指意义］却不等于对物的指认。

说指称并无实际存在，指的是万物虽然各有各的名称，但具体物本身并非名称的真正所指。具体物不是名称的所指，却把它说成是名称的所指［概念性意义］，这不是对指称的正确理解。把"存在着的不等于指称的实在之物"当作"不实际存在的指称意义"是不正确的。理由在于，指称的对象是世界上同类事物兼有的共性。世界上实际不存在指称，然而却不能说物不能由"物"来指称。"物"并非不能用来指认具体物，并不是因为"物"作为名称其作用是标记具体物。指称不是指认具体物的标记，"物"的指称是物之为该物的本质意义。因而指称并不等于指认；换言之，指称与具体物的关系不是指认的关系。

假如世界上无物存在，谁又会去讨论"并非指称的物"？没有物的存在，谈论"指称"又有何意义？自然界若存在指称，而却没有概念作为指称对象，那还谈什么"并非指认"？又如何能够说没有任何"物"不是由指称而成为"物"？

那么，指称既然不等于指认具体物，为何一定要认为指称固定于具体物而只充作其指认标签呢？

第六篇　迹府

【原　文】

公孙龙，六国时辩士也。疾名实之散乱，因资材之所长，为"守白"之论。假物取譬，以"守白"辩，谓白马为非马也。白马为非马者，言白所以名色，言马所以名形也；色非形，形非色也。夫言色则形不当与，言形则色不宜从，今合以为物，非也。如求白马于厩中，无有，而有骊色之马，然不可以应有白马也。不可以应有白马，则所求之马亡矣；亡则白马竟非马。欲推是辩，以正名实而化天下焉。

龙与孔穿会赵平原君家。穿曰："素闻先生高谊，愿为弟子久，但不取先生以白马为非马耳！请去此术，则穿请为弟子。"

龙曰："先生之言悖。龙之所以为名者，乃以白马之论尔！今使龙去之，则无以教焉。且欲师之者，以智与学不如也。今使龙去之，此先教而后师也；先教而后师之者，悖。"

"且白马非马，乃仲尼之所取。龙闻楚王张繁弱之弓，载忘归之矢，以射蛟兕于云梦之圃，而丧其弓。左右请求之，王曰：'止。楚人遗弓，楚人得之，又何求乎？'仲尼闻之曰：'楚王仁义而未遂也。亦曰人亡弓，人得之而已。何必楚？'若此，仲尼异'楚人'与所谓'人'。夫是仲尼异'楚人'与所谓'人'，而非龙'白马'于所谓'马'，悖。"

"先生修儒术而非仲尼之所取，欲学而使龙去所教，则虽百龙，固不能当前矣。"孔穿无以应焉。

公孙龙，赵平原君之客也；孔穿，孔子之叶也。穿与龙会。穿谓龙曰："臣居鲁，侧闻下风，高先生之智，说先生之行，愿受业之日久矣，乃今得见。然所不取先生者，独不取先生之以白马为非马耳。请去白马非马之学，穿请为弟子。"

公孙龙曰："先生之言悖。龙之学，以白马为非马者也。使龙去之，则龙无以教；无以教而乃学于龙也者，悖。且夫欲学于龙者，以智与学焉为不逮也。今教龙去白马非马，是先教而后师之也；先教而后师之，不可。"

"先生之所以教龙者，似齐王之谓尹文也。齐王之谓尹文曰：'寡人甚好士，以齐国无士，何也？'尹文曰：'愿闻大王之所谓士者。'齐王无以应。尹文曰：'今有人于此，事君则忠，事亲则孝，交友则信，处乡则顺，有此四行，可谓士乎？'齐王曰：'善！此真吾所谓士也。'尹文曰：'王得此人，肯以为臣乎？'王曰：'所愿而不可得也。'"

"是时齐王好勇。于是尹文曰：'使此人广庭大众之中，见侵侮而终不敢斗，王将以为臣乎？'王曰：'钜士也？见侮而不斗，辱也！辱则寡人不以为臣矣。'尹文曰：'唯见侮而不斗，未失其四行也。是人未失其四行。其所以为士也然。而王一以为臣，一不以为臣，则向之所谓士者，乃非士乎？'齐王无以应。"

"尹文曰：'今有人君，将理其国；人有非则非之，无非则亦非之；有功则赏之，无功则亦赏之，而怨人之不理也，可乎？'齐王曰：'不可。'尹文曰：'臣窃观下吏之理齐，齐方若此矣。'王曰：'寡人理国，信若先生之言，人虽不理，寡人不敢怨也。意未至然与？'

"尹文曰：'言之敢无说乎？王之令曰：'杀人者死，伤人者刑。'人有畏王之令者，见侮而终不敢斗，是全王之令也。而王曰：'见侮而不斗者，辱也。'谓之辱，非之也。无非而王非之，故因除其籍，不以为臣。不以为臣者，罚之也。此无而王罚之也。且王辱不敢斗者，必荣敢斗者也；荣敢斗者是，而王是之，必以为臣矣。必以为臣者，赏之也。彼无功而王赏之。王之所赏，吏之所诛也；上之所是，而法之所罪也。赏罚是非，相与四谬，虽十黄帝，不能理也。'齐王无以应焉。"

"故龙以子之言有似齐王。子知难白马之非马，不知所以难之说，以此，犹好士之名，而不知察士之类。"

【古译今】

公孙龙是战国时代〔（公元前475—前221年）著名〕的辩者。他对于当时名实不副、语言交流混乱的状况深感痛心，为此他凭着自己的天赋，提出了"'白'本身存在"的理论。他利用事物现象做比喻，与人展开"'白'本身存在"的辩论，其中著名的论断为"白马非马"。〔他认为，〕说白马非马，是说"白"是命名颜色的名称，而"马"是命名形状的名称。既然颜色不是形状，形状也不是颜色，那么谈论颜色，就不应当涉及形状，而谈论形状也不应当涉及颜色。然而人们事实上将两者混淆在一起，这是不正确的。就像在马厩中找白马，但厩中没有，只有其他颜色的马，于是这些颜色的马不能被当做白马找出来。之所以不能作为白马，是因为所要寻找的马在那儿并不存在。〔按他的论点，〕既然白马不在，那么白马竟然就不是马了。他试图以这样的论辩来矫正名称与实在之间的关系，由此教化世人。

公孙龙与孔穿在赵国的平原君家中遇见了。孔穿提出："我久闻先生品德高尚，早就想做您的学生了。但是我拒绝接受您的'白马非马'论！如果您放弃这一理论，则我请求做您的学生。"

公孙龙回答说："先生的话自相矛盾。我之所以有名气，恰恰是由于我提出的'白马'论！如今您要求我放弃这一理论，那我就没有什么东西可以教你了。一个人要拜师学艺，总是在思想和学识上不如所拜的老师。而您让我放弃自己的思想和学识，这等于先教育别人，然后再拜别人为老师。这不是自相矛盾吗！"

"而且，'白马非马'的命题，孔子本人也接受。我听说楚王曾打算在云梦狩猎场张开繁弱大弓，将忘归飞箭上弦，用它射杀水中怪兽。然而弓却丢失了。侍从们要求去把弓找回来。楚王说：'别去了。楚人丢了弓，而楚人捡到了弓，又何必去找呢？'孔子听说此事后说：'楚王的话表现出了仁义，却并不完善。完全可以说"有人丢了弓，有人捡到了弓"，何必一定要说"楚人"呢？'这么看来，孔子也认为'楚人'跟他说的'人'不是一回事。肯定孔子把'楚人'区别于'人'，却又否定我把'白马'区别于'马'，这是矛盾的。"

"先生既然修习儒家思想，却又否定孔子所接受的理论；想要跟我做学生，却又否定我能教给您的思想。这么一来，我公孙龙再强一百倍，也无法在您面前充当老师啊！"对此，孔穿无以应对。

公孙龙是赵国平原君家的门客；孔穿是孔子后裔。孔穿与公孙龙会面时，对他说："鄙人住在鲁国，在下面听到了关于您的传闻，十分仰慕先生的智慧，赞赏先生的品行，早就想拜在先生门下学习，直到今日才终于见到先生。然而我不选取先生的地方只有先生的'白马非马'论。请您放弃'白马非马'理论，则我孔穿恳求当您的弟子。"

公孙龙说："先生这话说得可矛盾了。我公孙龙的理论精髓恰恰就是'白马非马'论。您要我放弃这一理论，则我没什么可教你了；找一个没什么可教的人当老师，这是矛盾的。况且要跟我学习，总是在思想和学识上不如我。现在却让我放弃'白马非马'主张，这等于先教育然后再拜为老师；先教而拜师，这说不通。"

"您刚才用来开导我的意思，很像齐王与尹文说的话。齐王对尹文说：'大王我非常看重德才皆备的人，但齐国却没有德才皆备的人，这是为什么？'尹文说：'我想听听大王说的德才兼备的人是什么样的人。'齐王答不上来。尹文说：'假如现在有这么个人，他侍奉国王非常尽忠，对父母非常孝顺，交朋友非常诚信，跟乡亲们关系和睦。有这四种德行的人，可以称为德才皆备者吗？'齐王回答说：'当然好啦！这正是我所说的德才皆备之人。'尹文问：'大王得到这样的人，愿意委任他为大臣吗？'齐王答道：'我当然愿意，但我却还未得到这样的人。'"

"当时齐王好勇。于是尹文问他：'若这个人在大庭广众之中，受到欺负、侮辱而不敢还击，大王还会让他做大臣吗？'齐王答道：'难道这种人也叫作德才皆备？受到侮辱而不还击，这是耻辱！这种耻辱之人大王我不会任用为大臣的。'尹文则提出：'他只不过是受了侮辱而不斗争而已，其他四种德行并未失去。既然这个人并未失去关键的四种德行，那么他被称为德才皆备应该是对的。然而，大王要任用他为大臣，同时又不任用他为大臣，这是否意味着您所说的德才皆备之人同时又并非德才皆备之人？'对此，齐王无言以答。"

"尹文说：'如今有的国王以这样的方法来治理国家：人一犯错就给他以惩罚，不犯错也给他以惩罚；人有功就给他以奖赏，无功也给他以奖赏；但国王却反过来认为他手下的人不治理，这样可以吗？'齐王回答说：'不行。'尹文说：'大王我私下曾观察过大王手下官员治理齐国的情况，他们的做法就跟我刚才说的差不多。'齐王回应说：'大王我治理国家若真的像先生所说的那样，那么治下的人们不治理，我也不会怪他们。不过，［情况］还不至于到那地步吧？'"

"尹文说：'没有根据，我敢这么说话吗？大王曾下令说"凡杀人者一律处决，凡伤害他人者，一律惩治。"［于是］有人害怕大王的律令，受到了屈辱也不敢反击，这是大王的律令导致的后果。然而大王却说："受到侮辱不敢反击，这是耻辱。"说那是耻辱，也就否定了他的行为。其行为本身合法，而大王却否定了，并因此取消他的官员资格，不让他做大臣。不让他做大臣就是对他的惩罚。这样，他没有违法，大王也惩罚了他。况且，大王认为不敢打斗是耻辱，那么就必定认为敢打斗就是光荣。把敢打斗视为光荣，也就肯定了打斗的行为，会任用敢打斗者为大臣。任他为大臣就是对他的奖赏。他没有功劳却得到大王的奖赏。大王所奖赏的行为，正是手下官员们要铲除的行为。君主奖励的行为，正是法律所要惩处的行为。这样一来，奖赏、惩罚、正确、错误四者之间相互背离、混乱了；那么就算国王有十倍于黄帝的才能，也无法把国家治理好。'听了此话，齐王无以应对。"

"因此，我认为你刚才劝我的话与齐王的话类似。先生只知道要拒斥'白马非马'的理论，却不知道以什么为依据来拒斥它。这就和［齐王］只知道要求德才皆备之人，却不知道什么是德才皆备之人类似。"

第二部分
《公孙龙子》翻译说明

　　《公孙龙子》一书一共有六篇文章，其中《迹府》记录了公孙龙的言论和事迹，显然不是公孙龙的作品；其余五篇具有论述内容的一贯性，且明显独树一帜，迥异于儒、道、墨诸家学派思想。李贤中（2011：3）说，这五篇文章"每篇都直接涉及'认识'问题，并且有其完整的理论体系"。从语言概念意义入手，反思人的认识问题，这十分符合先秦名家"专决于名"的语言理性思辨特征，因而这五篇应该是公孙龙所作。但目前出版的专著中，对于书中六篇文章的排序并不统一。如，周山（1997：199–200）列举了伍非百、冯友兰、谭戒甫等学者的排序，一共13种之多，且并未涵盖所有排序方式。每一种排序都有学者自己的看法做支撑。

　　我认为，我们可以这样来排序，即《名实论》《白马论》《坚白论》《通变论》《指物论》，而《迹府》不是公孙龙所作，放在最后就可以了。之所以这样排序，是因为这是公孙龙思想的一个较为完整的呈现。

　　《名实论》作为纲领性文件，公孙龙在文中说明了写这一系列文章的理由，并且提出了正名的基本依据和原则，理当排列第一。接下来的《白马论》《坚白论》《通变论》三篇文章则是对其基本依据和原则的进一步阐述，且这三篇文章一步比一步深入：《白马论》指出了概念与实在是不在一个层面且具有不同性质的问题；《坚白论》进一步指出了概念意义的独立性本质，并提出概念产生于分析的方法这一重要命题；而《通变论》继续澄清概念意义的确定性本质问题。我们可以注意到：在这几篇文章中，"指称"的问题，尤其是论辩当中出现的关于指称是什么的形而上学反思，从而正确把握指称之本质的问题一步步凸显出来。若不解决这个问题，公孙龙在其纲领性文件《名实论》中提出的思想、原则就得不到有力的支持，也就得不到正确的理解。因而，他必须写作《指物论》，专门针对指称的本质及人们对指称意义本质的误解做理论的澄清。

　　我认为这样安排这几篇文章的顺序可以对公孙龙的思想发展有一个较合理的展示。

1. 关于《名实论》

《名实论》应该是公孙龙正名思想的纲领性文件。文中，公孙龙提出了正名的基本依据和原则，并进行了论述。所以，本书把这篇文章列为第一篇。从总体布局来看，这篇文章首先肯定了事物是客观存在的这一前提，但文章并不以讨论事物的存在为目的，而是马上转向了名称意义正确性的基本保证问题的讨论。文章的中心思想应当是关于"唯乎其彼此"这一理性主义正名原则的阐述，可以说是公孙龙的语言哲学的基本立场。这篇文章的构成如下：（1）先确定什么是名称的正确意义，即如果要正名，应当以什么为依据；（2）提出并阐述理性主义的正名原则；（3）强调只有应用这样的原则才能保证语言交流的准确性。

首先，为了确定名称的意义正确性依据，公孙龙提出了"物""实""位"三个基本概念，而这正是本文最大的难点。现有的解释一般把"物"理解为质料，"实"则是质料必定占有空间这一性质，而"位"则是位置、方位等（如：冯友兰，1962：339-340；周昌忠，2005：260-261；等）。此外，人们一般也把"正"作为与上述三个基本概念并列的第四个基本概念或曰范畴。但这种理解有一个问题：如果公孙龙是以讨论事物的客观存在为出发点，并接下来论证语言意义的正确性，那么中间应该有一个过渡，即说明客观事物的存在是怎么成为意义的依据的。而这一点，在现有的译文中没有。公孙龙似乎从事物的客观存在一下子就跳到了正名的原则，于是文章的构成脱节了。

我认为，要解决这个问题，我们应当重新审视我们对上述几个基本概念的解释。文章不是在讨论事物的客观存在性质，而是从一开始就在讨论语言意义的正确性依据。因而这几个概念不是经验层面的概念，而是语言逻辑层面的概念。公孙龙在第一句中肯定了事物是客观存在的，但随即转向了语言问题：当我们说"物"的时候，"物"的意义就不再等于客观事物，而是指称物之为物的概念。作为概念的"物"不需要占据空间，所以"实"不应是指事物必须占据空间的实体，而指"物"的本质性意义。这才应当是"物以物其所物，实也"这个命题的真正含义。公孙龙想说明的是："'实'乃'所指'，并不等于'名'或'原本之物'。"（李贤中，2011：27）所谓"原本之物"当指康德意义上的"物自体"（thing-in-itself）。

这样的解释应当是有依据的。"名实之辩"不是关于"名"与"实"的关系吗？公孙龙想追问，我们所说的"实"到底是什么？他认为这个"实"已经不是客观实在本身。虽然"实"作为本质有赖于实在事物，但一旦我们要求澄清"名实关

30

系"以正名，那么这个"实"不是指事物的实体性实在，而是指人关于事物本质的概念性把握。这种概念之"实"只能是事物本质的表征，不多不少，也不能有任何偏离，这就是"实"应当具有的"位"，即更抽象的意义正确性的基本要求。只要满足了这个基本要求，那么名称的意义就正确了。而任何偏离都导致"不在位"而出错。由此看来，文中的"正"并不是一个与上述三概念相同位的概念，它就是"正名"的"正"，即如何正确使用语言的保证问题。因此，我同意李贤中（2011：28，43）所说："'位'就是'所指'（'实'）与'名'相符合的正确关系。"

这也表明公孙龙的思想与墨家思想不是一回事。墨家的"实"是客观实在，他们的意义理论其实是一种符合论，即所说的与实在的相符，那么意义就正确了。但公孙龙的思想则是语言逻辑层面的意义理论，他想提出的是，只有当名称的确指称了事物的本质时，名称的意义才是正确的。由此看来，先秦名家并非有学者认为的那样是"别墨"（胡适，2000：133-134），他们是与墨家思想倾向不同的哲学家。

这里需要说说对"疑其所正"一句的理解和翻译。句中的"疑"字被理解为"定"（王宏印，1997：94；李贤中，2012：113），这恐怕不一定是正确的。从上文看，公孙龙已经提出要以正确的内涵本质来正名，那么接下来他应当提出对现有的正名方法的质疑，并由此提出自己的正名思想原则。毕竟，他作为名家思想的代表，一个基本倾向就是澄清"名"与"实"的基本概念，以保证正名本身的正确性。所以，这里的"疑"不应理解为"定"，而应理解为"质疑"。同时我也认为此句不应当如刘玉俊（2002：55）所译"去怀疑对物固有本质的正确认识"。公孙龙是在对当时正名的基本理论和方法进行质疑，力图提出自己的理性主义思想方法。

这样的理解就能够把第一段之后的下文接起来，因为第二段一开始，公孙龙就提出，他所讨论的"名""实"本质意义标准应当用来矫正不正确的名称意义，并质疑、反思当下所进行的所谓"正名"是否恰当，即"疑其所正"。有了这个过渡，公孙龙接下来提出正名的基本原则，即"唯乎其彼此"就是顺理成章的了。这个原则是对什么是在"位"什么是不在"位"的进一步展开。

在阐述"唯乎其彼此"的原则时，公孙龙反复用了"此""彼"这两个字。由于古汉语抽象名称与普通名称没有形态区别（如像英语那样的this，thisness），且汉语不是字母文字，没法用"性质X、性质Y""事物x、事物y""X存在于x中"之类的表达方式来说明问题，因而理解起来颇为困难，导致传统解释中"此应当由此物充当"（冯友兰，1962：339）之类的不清晰翻译。

我认为，这些被反复使用的字应当有抽象程度的区分。当然，从一个方面讲，它们已经是一种抽象了，因为它们并不具体指"这个东西"或"那个东西"，而是如同西方语言的字母（A，B，X，Y等）一样，被用来作为抽象的符号标记。但是公孙龙所用的"此""彼"本身还有进一步的抽象程度区分，其中一些被用来表示"此性，此的性质""彼性，彼的性质"。这么一看，公孙龙文中所谓的难句，如："故彼，彼当乎彼，则唯乎彼，其谓行彼"，其原意其实是非常清楚的："言说'彼'时，'彼'必须是一切彼必然具有，并且只有彼才具有的'彼性'；言说'此'时，'此'必须是一切此必然具有，并且只有此才具有的'此性'。"他认为只有这样，人们使用语言表达的概念才是正确的。公孙龙事实上从语言逻辑的层面上提出了与亚里士多德的逻辑基本定律（排中律、不矛盾律）非常接近的语言逻辑定律；或者更大胆言之，他提出的就是逻辑基本定律的古汉语版本！

顺便提及，多数学者把句中的"在"理解为"时空位置上的变化"（如李贤中，2011：32）。这种理解可能没有揭示出公孙龙真正想表达的思想内涵，翻译出来的内容很可能不具有思想的融贯性。如王宏印（1997：339）将此句翻译为"...when one calls 'this', but this does not correspond to it..."等等。且不谈其中的代词指代不明问题，按照这种"时空位置"观翻译，那么词与物相对应的理解也就把公孙龙的思想呈现为亚里士多德式的"符合论"了，而以此来看待公孙龙的其他文章，就不容易理解他关于"白马非马""二无一"等命题到底要说什么，也更难以解释他的《指物论》一文中的重要思想了。所以我认为，这里的"在"应当作"存在于"解。

出于上述考虑，我为了翻译出原文中"在"此中的那个"此性"的含义而采用了"thisness""thatness"两词。这一想法受到了亚里士多德的《范畴篇》《形而上学》英译文的启发，其中他使用的希腊语"*tode ti*"一语被译成了"a this"或"thisness"[1]。虽然哲学界关于亚里士多德的概念到底是"殊相"还是"共相"仍存在分歧，但这并不妨碍本译文采用此译法。在英语中，后缀"-ness"的作用就是把形容词转换为相应的名词，指称的即是该形容词所描述的那种性质。例如："redness"表示"红色性质"。这种性质应该能够被视为"共性"的，因为"红的性质"为所有红色物体所共有。哲学家阿尔斯顿（1988：2）也曾采用诸如"sharpness""treeness"之类的形式来讨论柏拉图的"理念"，认为其理念无非

1　参见：尼古拉斯·布宁、余纪元编，《西方哲学英汉对照辞典》，江怡等译，北京：人民出版社，2001，第3页。

就是实在化了的语言意义分析，如从所有的树中概括出"树性"本质。显然，这种"树性"是普遍的，是一切树所共有，且仅树所有的本质属性。这就是我采用这两个译法的理由，在本译文中这两个语词指称的就是"此"与"彼"的本质。我认为这样翻译将使得译文从精神实质上十分接近真正的关于Being的形而上学思辨，可在一定程度上展示公孙龙的思想风貌。

所以，"thisness"之类的表达不是本人的生造。虽然这样的译文读起来有些别扭，但是公孙龙的文章表述，如"知此之在此"在汉语中也属于"不合常规"。由于我通过在翻译文本中界定其中一些"此"指的是"此性"（the essence of this），从而为"thisness""thatness"做好了语义铺垫，所以我认为这样的译文既能使读者了解公孙龙要表达的意义，又在一定程度上保持了原文的某种风味。

我正是在这个基本想法的引导下对这篇文章进行翻译的，并且认为这样的翻译能够使得文章成为一个整体，清晰地突出其语言哲学的核心思想。顺便提及一下，这里使用的"语言哲学"一语，不是西方20世纪分析哲学意义上的概念，而是广义的指通过对语言问题，尤其是语义问题的形而上学反思，试图确定人到底把握了什么样的知识，这种知识如何具有正确性的哲学思考。中国古代哲学虽然没有西方哲学意义上的本体论和认识论，但这并不妨碍中国哲学家从一开始就从语言的哲学反思入手，反思世界与人生的根本道理。如我们在下面几篇文章中将看到的，公孙龙事实上是在做这样的反思。本书中的"语言哲学"一语，除专门说明者外，都是在这个意义上使用的。

此外，我还想提及的是，在《名实论》结尾，公孙龙用了"先王是多么贤明"之类的语句，但他这么做并不是像有的学者所说的那样表明了公孙龙的政治态度。公孙龙只是用这个来说明正确的正名有多么重要。如伍非百（1983：516）所言，"两赞明王而言'审其名实，慎其所谓'，其重视'唯谓'之义深矣"。在那个时代，利用君王之名分来提高自己理论的重要地位，这是完全可能的，也是我们可以理解的。

最后，关于古文原文版本，我参考李贤中教授的读后感做几点说明。

（1）按《道藏》本，文章第一句中的"者"为"焉"。不过，无论哪个版本的用词均不影响整句的句意。

（2）李教授指出，按王启湘的修改，"谓此而行不唯乎此"一句的"行"字应为"此"。他认为这一改动应当是正确的。若是，则更印证了本书译者对公孙龙原文命题的理解和阐释是正确的。

（3）原文中"故彼彼止于彼"一句的断句，李教授指出其他许多版本均为

"故彼，彼"等，即在两个"彼"之间加一个逗号。这一改动的确会使原文理解更加明确，不过并不影响本书的解释和翻译。

（4）"知此之非也，知此之不在此也，明不谓也"一句中的"明不谓"，李教授认为应改为"则不谓也"。这一改动使得语句更加符合上下文，也说明本书的理解和翻译是准确的。

2. 关于《白马论》

《白马论》是论辩体，该文事实上构成了对公孙龙"唯乎其彼此"正名原则的具体论证之一。我们在《名实论》中看到，这个正名原则说的就是"这一个"，必须而且只能是这一个；要将一个正确的名称应用于一个事物对象，那么这个名称所指的本质必须存在于那个事物当中，而且这个事物不能既具有这个本质，又具有另一个本质。

这对于单名，当然不成问题。"人"应用于具有人的本质的对象，"马"应用于具有马的本质的对象，而"白"则应用于具有白色本质的对象。但是，"白马"之类的复合名称却给公孙龙造成了麻烦，因为"白马"所命名的对象既具有马的本质属性，又具有白的本质属性。那么"唯乎其彼此"的原则在此还能坚守吗？为了保卫"唯乎其彼此"原则，公孙龙必须对这个问题做个解释，他必须说明"白马"不是"白"和"马"两个单名意义的简单叠加，而是单独具有自己的意义唯一性。这应当是理解和翻译这篇文章的关键所在。把握了这一点，这篇文章的论述理当是十分清楚了。

需说明的是，公孙龙并不否认客观世界中的白马是马，跟其他颜色的马一样，但是他的重点在于论证"马"和"白"两个名称所指称的是概念性实在。公孙龙的论辩起点是："马"是命名特定形状的名称，而"白"是命名特定颜色的名称，两者不能混用。但他的目的在于说明：之所以两种名称不能混用，是因为它们各自表征的实体具有不同的性质，即"马"的概念本身并不包含任何颜色的属性，而"白"也不是必然跟马相联系才是白，白就是白本身。

从整篇文章来看，公孙龙反复在语句逻辑的层面回答对手的问题，也说明他注重的不是经验层面而是语言层面。该文的层次其实并不难把握，主要有二：一是论证"白""马""白马"是三个不同的独立的概念，因而"白马"不是"马"；二是抓住对手的语言概念逻辑漏洞，进一步区分经验和语言逻辑两个层面，从而说明公孙龙自己观点的合理性。

在第一部分中，公孙龙的对手总是从经验层面进行论证，说世上的马都有颜色，而白马只是其中一种颜色的马，因而白马只能是马。而公孙龙则说，世上的马的确有颜色，所以才会有白马；但是他马上指出，在语言概念层面，"马"是无色的，而"白"是与"马"性质不同的概念。这里需要指出，传统的解释在此并未突出公孙龙的这一意图。

例如，关于"求马，黄、黑马皆可致；求白马，黄、黑马不可致"一句，人们认为这是从经验的层面提出论据。若是，那么这个论据无疑非常无力，漏洞明显，因为对手应当马上就可以反问公孙龙："既然求马，黄黑马可以来，那么白马也可以来，这不就证明白马是马了吗？"然而，我们在文中却没有发现对手以这样明显的逻辑漏洞来反驳公孙龙！这显然说明，我们传统的理解是错误的。我认为，传统的理解没有将接下来的一句很好地结合起来，即"使马无色，如有马已耳，安取白马？"，而这一句非常重要。传统解释将"使"一词理解为"假使"，结果后面一句也成了一个经验命题，即"如果马无色，怎么会有白马"。这样，公孙龙的命题被转换成了经验命题，而被误解了，也与后面的论述脱节了，怎么解释都很勉强。事实上，这里的"使"应当是"使得"的含义，公孙龙的意思是说，我们应当把"马"作为概念意义，而概念性的"马"并不需要颜色作为其定义性本质；既然"马"仅仅指称"马"的本质，怎么会在其中找到"白马"呢？这样的解释才能使整篇文章的思想具有连贯性。

紧接着，公孙龙开始论述"白马"是一个复名，其意义并非"白"加"马"，而是一个与后两者同位的概念，即"白马"之为"白马"本身。他不是讨论"马"与"白马"之间的种属关系，而是将"马自身"（horse-in-itself）、"白自身"（whiteness-in-itself）、"白马自身"（white-horseness-in-itself）并列起来，把复名与单名的地位等同起来，由此将复名与单名表达的本质意义同等看待，力图从本体论的层面上说明"马"之为"马"、"白"之为"白"、"白马"之为"白马"各自的"此性"或"彼性"本质，以维护他的"唯乎其彼此"的正名原则。这就与《名实论》的思想吻合起来了。我们今天当然可以指责他的论证在逻辑上不成功，但毫无疑问的是，这是一种在语言概念层面的盘旋，即从语言意义的层面对名称与其所指的实在的关系，进而对人用语言把握了什么样的知识这一根本性问题所进行的哲学思辨。这当然应该算是语言哲学。

顺便提及，我认为，由于古汉语的特殊结构，公孙龙无意之中提出了与现代认知语言学的"构式"相似的概念。如果我们把"白马"视为一个独立于"白"和"马"的构式，那么依据公孙龙的看法，不是进入"白马"短语构式的语词决定了其构式义，而是构式义与其中的词各自具有了特定的语义角色和功能。这一点，对我们今天也颇有启发意义。

在第二部分，公孙龙抓住对手的逻辑漏洞对自己的观点做了进一步的阐述。公孙龙先是设下一个语言逻辑圈套，即问："以'有白马为有马'，谓有白马为有黄马，可乎？"对手果然上当，因为无论是从经验层面还是从语言逻辑层面上看，都肯定不能用"有白马就是有马"一句来表达"有白马就是黄马"的含义。公孙龙立刻抓住对手的漏洞，进一步证明，"马"的概念是无色的，"白"就是白色的本质，人们日常理解中并未分清概念的内在逻辑定义，因而认真追问就可能出现逻辑问题。如果"白"在"白马"中具有"马"的定义性质，那么说"白马"就等于说"马马"，而这是无意义的；而如果"白"因此又不具有"马"的性质，那么"白"就是独立于"马"的，因而从语言概念的层面上讲，"白马"必定具有"白马"的性质，而不再等于"马"的性质。

这里需要指出，若不加引号来理解公孙龙这里的推论，则很可能出现学者所批评的逻辑推理错误，因为从"白马为马"和"黄马为马"并不能推出"白马为黄马"（李贤中，2011：77）。的确如此。但是，如我上一段所言，如果加上引号，那么公孙龙就是在语言层面分析。他没有做"白马为黄马"的推论，而是从力图反思人们的语言表达的角度来进一步说明"白之为白"和"马之为马"本身的概念意义问题。

所以我仍然认为，公孙龙借此成功地证明"具有某一本质之物必然不是不唯一地具有此本质之物"，从而维护他"唯乎其彼此"的正名原则。这似乎很类似于巴门尼德式的命题，即"那所是者必然是，并且不可能不是"。公孙龙的"白马非马"论证可以说是一种汉语版本的巴门尼德式命题。

最后，李贤中教授读后感中的几点意见需要说明。

（1）按《道藏》本，"有白马，为有白马之非马，何也？"一句断句为"有白马为有马，白之，非马，何也？"。仔细考察之，语句的断句和表述形式虽然有异，但事实上句子表达的命题意义并无不同，均为客方对公孙龙的质疑，即"有白马就是有马，怎么能说马是白的就不叫做有马？"。

（2）"天下非有无色之马"这句话之后，《道藏》本在句末加上了语气词"也"。不过，语气词的加与不加对句意理解均无影响。

（3）"使马无色，如有马已耳，安取白马？"句在《道藏》本中为"使马无色，有马如已耳，安取白马？"。其实，只有中间一个分句词序不同。应当说，《道藏》本的词序更为合理，也与本书的理解更一致，即表达"有马之为马本

36

身"。这也从一个侧面说明本文的理解是正确的。

（4）"是离者"在《道藏》本中为"不离者"。但若从上下文及本句句意看，公孙龙表达的是："按照这样的概念分析以观之。"（关于"离"的语义，后文将有阐述。）《道藏》本改为"不"字，反而导致语义矛盾：既然"不离"，那么白马必定就是马了，而这与公孙龙接着表述的语句命题完全相左。故本书采用王琯原文。

3. 关于《坚白论》

《坚白论》是《白马论》的进一步展开。在《白马论》中，公孙龙提出了"白"本身与"马"本身应当分而析之的思想，而在本文中，他则进一步以论辩的方式阐述分析的方法和理由。

从语言角度看，这篇文章应当是比较好理解的，所以在很多地方，本书的解释与传统解释也并没有太大差别。但传统解释没能凸显公孙龙的写作意图，虽然看到了他类似于柏拉图式的"理念"的思想倾向性，但现有的译文还不能充分体现其实质。文章中关键的几个词就是"藏""自藏"和"离"。传统翻译各有所不同，但一般都把"藏"解释为"把什么东西隐藏起来"，"自藏"因此也就是"自我藏匿"，"离"就是"分离"。这其实也无不可，然而问题在于现有的译文基本上都是在经验逻辑的层面上解释这些关键词，结果没有充分体现出公孙龙的思想倾向。

例如，从公孙龙文中的表述"离也者，藏也"来看，"藏"应当不仅仅是"藏起来"，而是一种独立于人的感官知觉的存在性，这种存在性由"分离"来把握。如果进一步追问：到底什么被"分离"出来了？这种分离是不是简单的经验层面的客观事物与其属性的分离？答案显然是：事物与其属性客观上不可分离，我们不可能把红花的红色属性和花本体经验地分离，亦不能把石头本体与其坚硬属性经验地分离。既然如此，那么公孙龙所说的能够被分离出来的只能是概念，是人对事物及其属性的分别认识！由此我们非常清楚地看到，公孙龙所说的正是"分析"的认识方式！分离出来之后的概念被"藏"起来，实际上说的就是它具有独立于客观事物本身的存在性。如果按以往的英译，译成"Separation, as I understand it, is concealment"，则完全没有表达出公孙龙的思想。结合下文关于"离"的思考，本文将此句翻译成"Such a state of independent existence is what I mean by 'being in and of itself'"。按此，"藏"表达的是"存在"。

为了充分理解公孙龙的思想倾向，我认为应当从理性主义哲学的高度再进行一番说明。首先，中国古代没有西方哲学意义上的形而上学本体论和认识论，古汉语中也没有相应的"存在""分析"之类的语词，但这并不妨碍中国古代哲学家思考这类问题。公孙龙所做的正是这样的思考，只不过他只能依赖汉语给他提供的表达方式而已。

他这篇文章的论证思路是这样的：坚硬和白都是石头的属性，但是人的各种感知方式（眼睛看和手摸）只能分别感知到石头的硬度或者白色，这证明坚硬和白色是相互独立的，也是独立于石头的；当一种知觉起作用的时候，它只能获得其中一个属性，不能同时感知另一个属性，这证明这两种属性各自具有不同的本质；同时，坚硬并不只是石头的属性，世上还有其他坚硬的东西，白也是这样，这证明坚硬和白都是独立于石头的不同性质的东西；那么如果说石头存在，我们就没有理由说坚硬和白本身不存在。

这样来看，公孙龙的思想其实很有柏拉图式的客观唯心主义之嫌，但需要注意，公孙龙并未像柏拉图那样论证唯一的实在是"理念"（或曰"相形"）。同时，公孙龙也并非以"主观的认识结果来说明客观的事物，亦即客观的事物必须符合主观的认识"（李贤中，2011：67）。公孙龙真正反思的是：人用语言到底把握了什么样的关于实在世界的知识？

从这个角度视之，我认为"藏"在此文中既有传统理解的"藏起来"，更有如"自藏"所表达的那样更为抽象的"存在性"。这是使得藏起来之所以可能的原因。公孙龙文中的"有自藏也，非藏而藏也"一句非常清楚地说明了他的这一观点，"自藏"这种"藏"与一般的"藏"不是一回事。我们看看这句话他是怎么说的。当对手从经验的层面提出，如果没有白，那么我们看不见石头，如果没有坚硬，我们也无法说"石头是硬的"，那么由此推出"坚、白、石其实是一体的"这一命题的时候，公孙龙回复，这就需要提出"自藏"的问题，而且这种"藏"不是一般说的知觉不到的"藏起来"。一个存在着的东西不一定能被知觉到，而它能够被"藏"起来，原因就是它有"自藏"的性质。即使"藏起来"了，那个属性还是那个属性本身。"藏起来"可以从经验层面上说，亦即我们的感知一次只能知觉到一种属性，其他的属性我们知觉不到。然而公孙龙认为，问题在于一个属性之所以能被藏起来，正是因为它有自身的独立的存在性，即属性本身"自藏"。这种存在性并不依赖于任何感、知觉，也不附属于任何具体事物；它本身存在，并且就是事物之所以如此的必要前提。"自藏"是对象能够被"藏起来"的根本原因。

那么这个"自藏"怎么把握呢？公孙龙提出了"离"的方法论概念。我认为，这个"离"并非日常语言意义上的"分离"，而是一种语言概念的抽象，即以理性的思考，把属性从具体事物中提取出来，单独加以考察以确定其意义本质。这当然是一种分析的方法。公孙龙在论证的后面部分反复说明，"离"并不仅仅是"手摸不能感知白色"或者"眼睛看不能看到坚硬性"，"白"和"硬"是"神见"的，即是心灵或曰思维所把握的概念对象。换言之，"离"不是感知经验层面的分离，而是思维层面的分而析之。因为感觉器官的感受不是知识，而是心灵加工、理解的结果，即与具体事物分离了的关于属性的概念本身才构成真正的知识。且公孙龙强调只有这种"离"的方法，即分析的方法，才是确定概念意义的唯一正确方法（即"离也者天下，故独而正"）。公孙龙关于只有心灵才能把握真知识的认识非常接近柏拉图的心灵把握理念的思想。

如果仅仅把"离"字理解为"分离"，那么翻译出来的句子很可能让读者不能准确把握公孙龙的思想。如王宏印（1997：331-333）的译文："Separation is concealment... only mind can see... Even mind is incapable of... without separating it." 我认为此句译文并未清晰地传达出公孙龙的思想，甚至可能导致不理解或误解。而如果将"离"理解为"关系的断离"，则不免生出"倘若万物皆独立互离，认识主体就只能于自身认识自身，那么主、客对立的指向性可认识如何可能"（李贤中，2011：78）之类的疑问。

鉴于此，我认为，关键词"离"可以大胆地翻译成"analysis"。虽然中国古代并无"分析"的概念，但是从公孙龙的文章来看，他的观点就是"分离出来进行单独考察"，即要求将这些概念从具体事物中分离出来进行单独考察以把握其本质。这实质上就是"分析"。因而使用"analysis"来翻译公孙龙提出的获得知识的最根本方式，跟以前的译文"separation""'apart' phenomenon"等相比，更能映衬出公孙龙的分析理性思想，使整篇文章的意图更加明确。

人们也许会反对说，先秦时代的"离"字并无"分析"的含义。这确实是个问题，但我认为这是就当时的常规惯用语义而言，并不一定必须以此来解释哲学的特别含义。如果公孙龙的思想已经具备"分析"的成分，那么理当能够容忍这个语义出现在这篇文章中。此外，语义是变化的，极有可能由于某个个体的特定使用而后传播开来作为社会接受的语义。这是社会语言学研究已经证实了的现象。现代语言如此，古代语言仍然会如此。于是，假如公孙龙真的是想表达"分析"的概念，那么他为何不能成为中国第一个使用"离"来表达这一概念的哲学先驱呢？

我认为，公孙龙在这篇文章中，不仅提出了名称意义的概念性实在这个真正的哲学观念，而且提出了语义的概念性实在产生于人的思维的理性分析这一重要命题。这一点是以前关于公孙龙的哲学研究没有提及的。而我认为这恰恰是十分关键的：谁说汉语语言特征不利于形成关于"理念"的形而上学？显然，这篇文章完全不是诡辩，而是货真价实的语言哲学论文。

最后需说明的是，上文说公孙龙的"自藏"概念非常接近柏拉图的"相（理念）"，但两者还不是一回事。后者的"相"是唯一真实的存在，而实在的万事万物不过是"相"的摹本；而前者的"自藏"虽也有实存性，但可以被感知，由心灵分析（即"离"）来把握对象。公孙龙把属性作为实存的对象，却并未明确提出这是唯一的实在。在这点上，他的思想与惠施的"天与地卑，山与泽平"等命题（参见本书附录1.3节）所表达的倾向是一致的，都是基于汉语"词无定类"的特征，从反思形容词语义的本体论依据而提出的理性主义哲学观点。

最后，关于原文，李贤中教授指出了两点，这里我做如下说明：

（1）原文中"见与不见离。不见离"一句在《道藏》本中为"见与不见与不见离"。但我认为，《道藏》本的断句不仅不符合汉语语法，还导致语义歧义："'见'与'不见'都与'不见'离"，还是"'见'与'不见与不见'离"？若是后者，则属于无意义语词重复；若是前者，则无法解释"不见"如何与"不见"离。而王琯的断句却是很清楚的："见"与"不见"相离，然后接着说明什么叫作"不见相离"。

（2）最后一段中，"而坚必坚其不坚。石物而坚，天下未有若坚"一句，李贤中教授建议重新记标点为"而坚必坚，其不坚石、物而坚"。但我认为，这样改动的话，紧接着的一句"天下未有若坚"反而被孤立起来，解释会很生硬。此外，即使按李教授的建议修改，也并不与本书的解释和翻译相矛盾。故本书还是采用王琯的断句。

4. 关于《通变论》

《通变论》也是论辩体，公孙龙通过辩论进一步论证名称指称特定唯一本质的意义规定性，以维护"唯乎其彼此"的正名原则。公孙龙从"二"的概念就是二本身，不是两个"一"入手，通过几个语言概念的思辨，力图说明一个语词只能指称一个具有本质唯一性的对象。

本文翻译的难点如下：

（1）关于"二无一"一节。论辩双方谈及的"左""右"可能让读者困惑。笔者同意王琯的解释，即"左""右"都是"一"的含义。为了帮助读者理解清楚，本文将之译成"有一左（右）边"。在日常生活等经验场合，一个物在左边，一个在右边，两者加起来等于二，这是常识。但公孙龙要说明的是，当我们使用"二"这一名称的时候，其意义应当并且只能是二本身，而不能指两个一，因为"一"只具有一的本质。如果用"二"指称两个一，那么就违反了"唯乎其彼此"的原则，因为这时的"二"既指称二，又指称了一（参见第二部分《名实论》翻译说明）。公孙龙的正名原则是，"此"名称的应用是正确的，当且仅当此具有此性，并且此中不具有任何彼性。这正是公孙龙在文中的中心思想。

另外，关于文章中的这段对话，我认为现有的翻译理解可能有问题：

> 曰：右有与，可谓变乎？
> 曰：可。
> 曰：变只。
> 曰：右。
> 曰：右苟变，安可谓右？苟不变，安可谓变？
> 曰：二苟无左，又无右，二者左与右奈何？羊合牛非马，牛合羊非鸡。
> 曰：何哉？

客问：右如果加上了另一物，那么是否可以说是变化？公孙龙答：是的。接下来，客问的"变只"，目前有人解释为"变成了什么"。如果这样解释，那么下文公孙龙的回答其实答非所问，显得不合逻辑，甚至"右苟变，安可谓右"到"牛合羊非鸡"这几句中，到底哪几句是客问哪几句是公孙龙的回答也就在对话段落划分上出现混乱，不易理解了。

因此，我决定采用王琯的解释和对话段落划分，即"变只"的意思就是"变成了几"。客问显然打算将公孙龙诱导入一个陷阱，因为从经验的层面看，右边的一个物再加上一个物，一定等于二。这样，客问就成功地说明"二中有一"了。但公孙龙并未上当，仍然回答"右"。于是客问只好再追问：右如果已经变了，怎么还叫作右？如果没变，怎么又能说是变化？这才是符合逻辑的追问。对此，公孙龙指出，"二"本来就没有左、右，它的左、右又从何谈起，这本来就是个假问题嘛！接着，他提出了"羊合牛"的命题进行进一步说明。

我的这个解释与现有的翻译不一致，但是明显更符合文章对话的逻辑性。

（2）"羊合牛非马、牛合羊非鸡"的命题，不是如不少人理解的那样，是关于类别范畴的讨论，而是关于概念意义本质规定性的讨论。公孙龙的论证是这样的：羊和牛当然是两种不同的动物，因而不能说"羊"就是"牛"或者反之

（参见本书附录2.3、2.9等）。但是跟马相比，牛和羊都具有共同的属性（如"有角"），而两者都不具有马的属性（如"有长尾"），因此牛和羊的特性都与马形成了更大的反差，因而相对于马而言更有可能合起来成为一个复合概念"羊牛"。这一概念作为一个独立的"一"，其中不包括马的性质。然而，假如又增加一个选项"鸡"，并且如果非要选择"马"或者"鸡"跟"羊牛"相合而成为一个复合概念，那么公孙龙说他宁愿选择"马"，而不选择"鸡"。道理很简单：鸡跟马相比，与羊牛的相似性更少，因而与"马"相比，更不可能与之合成一个独立的概念。这当然是对的，即便按照现代生物学的分类，马与牛、羊的类属虽然差别也很大，但这三者至少都是胎生动物，而鸡与它们的差异则更大，因为鸡是卵生动物。

需要说明的是，公孙龙并不是在讨论动物的分类，而是从语义逻辑的层面论证一个名称所指对象只能是具有本质唯一性的"一"。他夸大"鸡"与"羊牛"的本质性差别，目的在于论证这两个"一"不可能在任何意义上构成一个纯真的"二"。我们不妨推想，若以"有生命"为类，那么公孙龙很可能提出"合石与鸡羊牛非动物"（笔者杜撰）之类的命题来。这是因为，他所关注的是"二"的语义本质规定性。公孙龙从正、反两个方面证明：一个纯真的"二"不能由任意两个"一"叠加而成，纯真的"二"必须是具有共同本质特征、相同的理性规定性的语义概念。人要使用语言来准确地交流思想、把握世界事物的本质，就必须对"二"进行分析，认识语言所指的那个"二"的根本性意义；否则，就可能导致"乱名"，即语言与意义脱节，而无法把握、表达真的知识。因此，我认为公孙龙的命题是语言哲学的命题，而不是生物学的命题，因为他是在通过思辨名称意义的本质来反思人们用语言获得的关于世界的真知识应当是什么。

（3）接下来的关于颜色的讨论，更进一步证实了笔者的理解。这一节的解释难点包括公孙龙涉及传统"五行""方位"的论述，以及他关于国王与丞相之间的政治伦理的论述语句。传统解释五花八门，甚至认为公孙龙是以道家的阴阳思想在论证颜色问题，或者他的着眼点是政治伦理等。其实这些理解是错误的，至少与该文前面讨论的思想倾向以及公孙龙的其他论文的讨论内容很不融贯。笔者认为，公孙龙的这些语句并非说明他真的在使用五行方位的思想来对颜色、属性定位，说明颜色之间互不相克，如"金克木"之类（参见：王宏印，1997：47；李贤中，2011：43）。毕竟公孙龙生活在两千多年前，那个时代流行的用语、说法他当然可以用之。但如果以五行方位来解释公孙龙的理论，则我们至少可以问这样一个问题：为什么他在其他文章及本文其他地方的思想讨论从不涉及阴阳五行，而这里他却兀然提出五行来支撑自己的观点？有这个必要吗？不仅没有这个必要，而且这样的解释与公孙龙文章的整体内容和论证方式并不吻合。因此我认为，公孙龙只不过是借用这种表达法做比方而已，从他的其他几篇文章的论述内容与方式，以及《迹府》中关于公孙龙的记述看，我们找不到任何迹象表明他信奉五行方位论。至于他关于国王与大臣关系的语句，则只是为了借之以强化他的观点。那么他讨论的到底是什么呢？

我认为，他讨论的核心与前文是一样的，都是论证语义的本质唯一性，不过所使用的例证是颜色而已。例如，从经验层面看，绿色混合进白色，那么所得到的就是淡绿。但是这不是公孙龙思考、讨论的东西。他力图从语义逻辑的层面说明，绿与白指称完全不同性质的两种颜色，各是各，不容混淆；即便将两者混合起来，"绿"仍然指称绿这种正色，而"白"仍然指称白这种正色；两个名称的指称对象（两种正色）是确定的，不容改变的；所谓的淡绿既不是绿也不是白，而是一种无法确定准确意义的杂色。语义逻辑和事实均是如此。从逻辑上讲，"绿"只能指称绿，不能指称不是绿的颜色，"白"亦如是。从经验上讲，绿和白的含义是我们能够准确把握的，而什么是淡绿，多淡算淡却实在不好定义。既然如此，那么淡绿就不是一个具有确定定义的概念，因而该名称无法正确地指称一个对象。

这就是为什么公孙龙接下来要再次明确提出，如果要在淡绿和黄两者中选择一个来跟绿和白合成一个独立的"一"，那么他宁可选择黄，因为黄色至少是可以准确定义的一种正色，而不是淡绿那样无法定义的杂色。这一论证方式与"羊合牛非马、牛合羊非鸡"如出一辙。更确切地说，公孙龙就是以这两个例证来最后说明"二"作为一个概念，只能指称二，而不能同时指称两个"一"。

我们当然可以指责公孙龙的论证太过简单、牵强，但我认为，从语言概念层面看，他的论证从其视角看，是能自圆其说的。他这种论证的方式对于两千五百多年前的中国哲学还是有思想启发意义的，也维护了他的"唯乎其彼此"的正名原则。也正是出于这一认识，我的《通变论》译文与现有其他学者的译文差异很大，而我自认为这样翻译能够更加融贯且清晰地传达出公孙龙的思想。

最后，关于李贤中教授的读后感提到的有关本文的三点，我说明如下：

（1）按《道藏》本，文中的"而牛之非羊也、羊之非牛也，未可"为"而羊牛之非羊也、之非牛也，未可"。但我认为，王琯的语句是正确的，因为不仅依据上下文从推理上更连贯，而且关于"羊牛"不等于"羊"也不等于"牛"的问题，公孙龙已经做了解释，这里没必要重复。

（2）李教授提到，《道藏》本中，"羊牛"顺序是"牛羊"。不过，这个调整对于原句意义的理解和翻译毫无影响。

（3）关于"不害其方也"的理解，按李贤中教授的意见，应该结合"五行方位"思想进行解释。但我对此持有不同意见，认为公孙龙的观点与阴阳五行没有关系。我已经在上文中做了说明，此不赘述。

5. 关于《指物论》

《指物论》被公认是先秦文献中最难理解的一篇。全文总共只有268字，其中"指"字就有48个，占全文总字数的17.91%。对"指"字的含义的理解，的确是理解《指物论》全文思想的关键。对"指"的不同解释，导致了对公孙龙这篇文章主要思想的不同，甚至是对立的、令人困惑的认识。但是，各种解释虽然纷繁复杂，却始终离不开"语词""指云"这个大方向。因此，说该文就是关于指称问题的讨论，应该是不离谱的。

我倾向于同意林铭均和曾祥云（2000：180-181）的解释，即"指"在《指物论》全文中有三种不同含义：（1）"指认"，即以手指指物；（2）"指称"，即以名指物意义上的指；（3）"指"的名称本身，公孙龙主要是在谈论用名称指称事物的问题。他们认为，"物"的问题，公孙龙已在《名实论》中做了界说，在《指物论》中无须再重复说明。我基本上也持此观点。

然而，我进一步认为，这篇文章的理解可以结合先秦名家辩者的"指不至，至不绝"命题（参见本书附录2.13）。名家思想家非常清楚地认识到，世上万物当然有其客观存在，但是人们说"物"的时候，实际上说的是"物"的"指"，而不是物本身。也就是说，物的存在是一回事，而人用语言所把握的"物"不再是物本身，而是关于物的本质意义的概念性知识。语词指称"物"的概念意义，而不等于把具体的物指认出来。也就是说，语义并不在于具体的、个体的物本身。

文章开篇第一句："物莫非指，而指非指。"本句中的三个"指"全是名词；其中，"物"是"物"之名，而第一个"指"的意思是"指称"，第三个"指"的意思则应为"指认"。这样，这个句子的命题意义就十分清楚了：万物都是由于语言的指称作用而成为"物"的，但是指称并不等于指认具体的物。这正是"指不至，至不绝"力图表达的命题。"总之，'物莫非指，而指非指'意义，即凡是对象物皆必须透过指涉作用而呈现。但这被指出而呈现之物，已不同于对象物。"（李贤中，2011：18）公孙龙"一方面肯定了认知过程无法不透过指涉作用，另一方面也看到了认知的结果并不同于原先的认知对象"（李贤中，2012：149）。这一解说是非常正确的。

也有人把这篇文章视为一个论辩体，这或许无不可。但事实是，原文并无由"曰"字构成的对话结构，所以没有必要一定要划分出对话。自问自答的风格是完全允许的。该文中的问题极有可能是公孙龙自己的提问，就像我们今天写文章一样，可以假想对手提出问题，然后我们自己给予回答。

公孙龙在提出了"物莫非指，而指非指"这一中心命题之后，接着论证说："天下无指，物无可以谓物。"他明确指出：如果没有语言，则物就没有办法被称为"物"。那么，既然在自然之中，物就是物而并没有名称，那么语词的指称是否等于直接把具体物指认出来呢？公孙龙认为不是。物本身是自然界中的存在，但它们本身并没有"名"。名称是人用来谈论事物的方式，因此名称的所指对象并非具体的物，而是关于物的概念。语词指称的概念并不等于物本身。

那么人如何把握事物的意义呢？公孙龙说，"非指"说的是物本身并没有名称。自然界之物没有名称，因而不可能每个物都用一个具体的名一个一个指认出来，但这并非是说世界上存在着不能用名去指称的事物。关键在于，"物"作为名词，其所指不是具体物，而是物之为物的概念意义。公孙龙的意思非常清楚：万事万物的名称是人使用语言对之进行认识的结果。因此，人的语言词汇的意义不是物本身，而是物之为物的本质性意义抽象。

接下来，公孙龙做了重要论述，要求严格区分经验层面的"指认"和语言概念层面的"指称"。他提出，具体的物可以由其名称来指认，但指认只是挑选出具体物表达而不是其本质，因而不是"指称"。不是指称而称其为"指称"，这是混淆了"指认"与"指称"。把关于"物"的概念的指称理解为具体物的指认，正是导致名实关系失序的原因。事物"无指"是说事物本身没有自然的指称。但说事物本身没有指称，不是说它们不能被指认，而是说"物"的本质意义只能通过语言名称来表征并把握，否则人就无法认识世界。"指称"并非不能用来指认物，但"指认"与物本身却都远远不是"指称"的意义。两者是不同性质的问题。

公孙龙明确指出："具体物不是名称的所指，却把它说成是名称的所指（概念意义），这不是对指称的正确理解。把'存在着的不等于指称的实在之物'当作'不实际存在的指称意义'是不正确的。"他的论述并不涉及老子式的"无"概念，而是一种地地道道的逻辑反思，没有任何玄得不可捉摸的东西。在这点上，我不同意这种解读："就存有层次而言，所指之物与所谓之物皆属同一个层次——'无'。"（李贤中，2011：20）不知这个判断从何谈起。

鉴于此，我没有像以前的英译（如：王宏印，1997：337）那样，把《指物论》中的"指"译为"signifier"，"非指"译为"that which is signified"，因为那样做的话，必然会遇到无法解释的语句。例如下文中的"非有非指者"之类的翻译就会遇到难题（此句若译为"there is no that which is signified"的话，其句意是不清楚的）。李贤中则认为"非指"与"物指"一样，是关键概念（参见李先生给本书所做的《读后感》）。他认为，"物指"即是"认识主体与认识对象经由'指涉作用'所构成的双向关系"，而"非指"则当与之对应，是主体经由客体性质的把握而成。我认为，李先生这里事实上区分了直接的"指涉"与间接的概念意义"指称"两个层面。对此，我是同意的，若不做这样的区分，很难解读这篇文章。但是，我不赞同把"非指"视为独立的概念。"非指"在全文中应当解读为"不是""指"，因为若不分开的话，会出现句法不通问题。以第一句的后半句"而指非指"为例，"指"和"非指"这两个名词并列，不符合汉语语法，也无从推断两个成分的关系；但若将之理解为"此'指'并非'彼指'"，则不仅符合古汉语语法，也与公孙龙的"唯乎其彼此"正名原则高度一致。再说，若"非指"是独立概念的话，公孙龙理当认真地说明其含义，就像他论证其他"指"一样。而这我们并未在文章中发现。

故此，本文参考了以前的译文，采纳了它们的合理之处，但是我自认为我的译文的新意就在于用"reference""denotation"这两个词来翻译不同的"指"。我认为，这两个词的运用使得公孙龙《指物论》这篇公认的先秦文献中"最难啃的骨头"的论述具有思想的融贯性。开篇第一句"物莫非指，而指非指"，我将之译成："Things are known as 'things' by virtue of reference, but reference does not mean merely the denotation of specific things."这使得全文的中心思想一下子非常明白：公孙龙不是在讨论指称与事物的关系，而是在讨论指称的性质本身；他的逻辑是非常清楚的——名称可以用来实指具体对象，但实指并不等于指称；他认为在名实之辩中，人们把这两个概念混为一谈了，所以要求澄清之，以便从理性的高度把握语词的指称意义的本质。

这篇文章中，公孙龙提出的重要思想是：正名的关键不在于考察名称与实在是否相符，而在于考察语义是否符合其本质规定性。这就使得我们能够更好地理解他在其他几篇文章中反复讨论"白马非马""二无一""离坚白"之类的"怪命题"的原因。我们确信，这些不是诡辩，而是与客观实在之物没有直接关联的、对于名称所指意义的本质本身的严格的形而上思辨。李贤中（2011：46-47）指出："实""变化的起点在于肯定'物'的存在，其变化的终点在于'名'，亦即概念内涵之确定……其所依据者即'位'之贞定。"我基本同意这一断言，不过我认为公孙龙的文章不是在谈"实"的变与不变，而是关注语言词汇所指称的概念具有什么本质意义这个根本性的认识问题。

即便是如前述的《通变论》一文中多次使用了"变"这个词，公孙龙的理论反思兴趣也在于：变化中那不变的、能够被人用语言词汇来固定下来的东西是什么？简言之，这一思想倾向很接近于古希腊哲学家之从"多"中追求"一"。对公孙龙而言，这个"一"就是"指称"的本质意义。他深切感到人们在语言使用中并没有弄清楚用一个名称去标签一个实在对象与用名称表征事物的本质这两者之间的区别，因而认为如果要正名，这两个概念必须得到梳理和澄清。这恐怕是他写这篇文章的动因。

严格区分经验层面的"实指"和概念层面的"指称"，这正是"正名"必须要解决的问题。《指物论》一文始终围绕什么是指称这个问题展开。从这个意义上讲，这篇文章应当是前几篇文章思想的提炼和升华。这也是我将这篇文章放到最后的理由。

认识到"正名"问题的关键在什么地方，才能够回答如何才能以理性主义的原则真正地正名，从而保证人对世界的认识是真的。这正是公孙龙写这篇文章的根本意图。但由于这个问题的复杂性和抽象性，同时由于古汉语无形态变化，句法松散灵活，以及先秦时代哲学本体论和认识论的不在场，公孙龙的这篇文章给后来的解释者造成了很大的困难。我的这种翻译理解或许也只能算一家之言，但我认为，这样的解释不仅使得整篇文章具有内在的思想逻辑性，也使得这篇文章与公孙龙的其他文章具有思想融贯性。因此我认为，我的解释和译文虽然与现有的解释和译文差异颇大，但应当是站得住脚的。

两千多年前的中国先秦哲学家公孙龙子竟然进入了关于指称与意义问题的理性主义思辨这一20世纪西方语言哲学反思的核心问题，不能不说是中国思想史的一个奇迹。

最后，关于李贤中教授提出的关于"非指"的意见，我再次回复如下：

按《道藏》本，此句为"使天下无物指，谁径谓非指？"。这多出来的"指"字的确非常影响原句意义。李贤中教授指出，如此变之，"物指"将成为一个独立概念。这也是历来理解的一个难点。本书对此暂时搁置而采用王琯版本，是因为"物指"若是一个独立概念，为何公孙龙不像他讨论"指""非指"一样，开篇即提出来，而是反复讨论"指非指"，最后才出现"物指"的提法？即便是按《道藏》版本，"物指"也只在文末的设问句中出现了两次，很难由此断定这是公孙龙提出的与"物""指"相提并论的重要概念。我认为不把"物指"作为独立概念，反而有助于我们理解《指物论》全文的中心议题：语词的"指称"是概念，而不是具体物；语词虽然可以用来指认具体物，但从本质上讲，其语义内涵是关于物之为物的本质意义。李教授认为"物指"是理解"非指"的关键，但如此一来，就不好解释公孙龙为何没有在一开始就把"物指"的概念与"非指"概念一起提出来，而是在已经讨论完中心思想之后，在以设问方式强调论题重要性的时候才提出"物指"概念了。李教授的意见是建立在他不同意"指"字的"指称"与"指认"区分的认识上的。而我认为，正是这一区分使得《指物论》全文的思想融贯起来了。关于这个区分，我在上文中已有说明，此不赘述。

6. 关于《迹府》

《迹府》不是公孙龙所写的，而是关于他的一些故事。文中的文字并不难懂，也没有特别需要解释的。但有一点，正由于该文并非公孙龙所作，所以其中的一些表述其实与公孙龙的思想不是一回事。

该文第一段说公孙龙一生坚持自己的"白马非马"观点，与人论争，"欲推是辩，以正名实而化天下焉"。这是符合公孙龙论辩的目的的，本书的翻译也是基于这一点来审视公孙龙作品的。但该文说公孙龙"假物取譬"，即以具体物来做比喻，恐怕不准确。这表明该文作者的理解不是在语言哲学层面的，而是基于常规经验来看待公孙龙的理论。理解的关键就在于对"物"的认识。前文已经谈到，公孙龙所说的"物"既可能是具体实在之物，也可能是"物"之为"物"的概念意义本身，即在抽象的语言哲学层面上，对"物"的意义本质规定性进行的形而上学思考。

《迹府》的作者只注意到了前者而没有上升至后者，所以他把公孙龙"白马非马"的论证解释为在马厩中找白马找不到，因而白马不是马。这是完全错误的。但译文不能擅自纠正这个错误，只能照实翻译。这里说明这一点，是为了提醒读者注意，一般人的思考模式与哲学家的思考模式不同，两者不在一个层面上。这也是公孙龙之所以被误解的原因。

另外，在《迹府》的最后一段中，我们可以看出，公孙龙对孔穿的真正不满在于他认为孔穿根本没有理解他的理论的实质。"子知难白马之非马，不知所以难之说"这句话说的就是：你知道要拒斥我的"白马非马"理论，但根本不知道以什么为基础来拒斥它。在说此话之前，公孙龙已经以很严密的语言逻辑推理说明了齐王使用某个语词（"士"），但不知道该语词的准确意义，因为他对语词所指称的那个本质定义缺乏认识和把握。

须注意的是，公孙龙对孔穿的要求进行的反驳是从逻辑思想的角度进行的，明显具有理性主义色彩。同时，他在文章的最后非常明确地指出，孔穿并没有理解他的语言哲学思想却要急于反对这种思想。这种无的放矢的批判其实说明公孙龙与孔穿的思想并不在一个层面上。

如果这里引用的公孙龙的话确实是一个真实的记录，那么这句话正好从另一个角度验证了本书翻译思路的正确，即公孙龙所谈的理论问题，并不是实践层面的问题，而是有关指称、意义本质等抽象的语言哲学问题。公孙龙是货真价实的理性主义语言哲学家。

译后记

严复说，译事三难，信、达、雅。不仅英汉翻译如此，古汉语翻译成现代汉语仍然如此。《公孙龙子》的文章被公认为先秦文献中最难读懂的，其中以《指物论》尤甚，该文被称为"最难啃的骨头"。既如此，译文恐怕实难做到"雅"。于是，译者降低标准，以准确为基本要求。但这也难以办到。由于公孙龙只有这几篇文章，历史上又被抨击、拒斥，现代的解释也多种多样，很难说本书真的能够恢复其思想的原貌。

那么，译者能做的，就只能是基于自己的解读，尽可能在公孙龙的文章之间寻找某种内在的能说明问题的联系，尽量使译文具有意义的融贯性。至于他人的译文和注释，译者在着手翻译之前曾经阅读过，但感觉都还没有能够取得这种融贯性。这也正是译者重译的原因。因此，这里谈的翻译说明极有可能已经融入了已读过的译本，但肯定地说，基本思路与他人有差别。为了尽量保证译文思想表达的融贯性，译者只按照自己的思路进行解释，以贡献一家之言。

第三部分
重新理解《公孙龙子》

1. 对《公孙龙子》思想的种种解读

之所以要重新理解并重译《公孙龙子》，就是因为这本书虽然是先秦名家思想的集大成之作，也是其纲领性文件，但有史以来一直得到不同的，甚至相互对立的解读。既然如此，说这些解读是误读亦无不可。

公孙龙的生平散见于古文献记录。他生活于战国时代，赵国人，曾在平原君赵胜家做门客。作为先秦名家学派的代表人物，在长达百年的先秦思想大辩论，即"名实之辩"中非常活跃，影响颇大。提起公孙龙，人们首先想到的就是他的"白马非马"论。相传公孙龙牵着白马欲过一关口，把守关口的官兵按规定不准他的马通过。公孙龙则当场论证说他牵的是白马，而白马不是马，使得官兵无言以对，只好放他与马通过关口[1]。据史书关于公孙龙的记载，我们大致得知他好与人争辩，毕生坚持辩护他的"白马非马""坚白石二"等主张。然而，公孙龙以及他所代表的先秦名家的命题与常识相悖、苛察缴绕，他们的思想及方法不为当时的人们所理解，因而被斥为"诡辩"，被排斥、打击，终于衰落了，以至于后来的学术精英竟然因为读不懂公孙龙的书而恨不得把书烧掉！（杜国庠，1963：6）

也许正是这个原因，先秦名家的作品基本上流失殆尽。惠施等著名人物的言论仅有极少量残片传今。所幸还有公孙龙的文章保存了下来，使我们有一窥先秦名家思想风采的机会。公孙龙虽然著述颇丰，据说多达好几万字，但是流传至今相对完整的作品却只有《公孙龙子》中收录的五篇文章，即《名实论》《白马论》《坚白论》《通变论》和《指物论》。另有一篇《迹府》记录的是公孙龙的一些言行。其中一些思想跟其他五篇一致，但其阐述和解释则有不一致之处。况且该文中有部分完全重复，这表明该文不是公孙龙所作。尽管如此，本书还是将《迹府》作为《公孙龙子》的一部分加以翻译，供读者参考。

那么，先秦名家被斥为"诡辩"的命题有哪些？人们又是怎么批判他们的？这些批判合理吗？我们先来看看公孙龙的"白马非马"命题、"二无一"命题和"离坚白"命题。其中，关于"离坚白"的解释基本一致，即公孙龙试图把

---

1 公孙龙生平事迹记录详见：王琯撰，《公孙龙子悬解》，北京：中华书局，1992年，第2-8页。

"坚""白"抽取出来，说它们是实实在在存在的。于是，凭这一命题，公孙龙即被判为"唯心主义"哲学家。但是，再唯心的哲学家也不会说"白马不是马"，也不会说"二"当中不包含两个"一"吧？那么公孙龙为什么要提出这样的命题？这类命题与他的"离坚白"思想是什么关系？这倒没怎么追究了，"诡辩"的标签一贴，万事大吉：唯心主义者不诡辩，谁还诡辩？或许正是这种理解，使我们错失了认识公孙龙及他所代表的先秦名家思想实质的机会。至于公孙龙的另一篇论文《指物论》，历来被认为是先秦文献中最难解读的文章，一块"最难啃的骨头"（周山，1997：234）。结果，说公孙龙是唯心主义者的人指责这篇文章为唯心主义的文献，而说他是"诡辩"家的人也把这篇文章视为"苛察缴绕"，让人思想困惑的诡辩之作。

除了公孙龙在他的文章中提出并论证的种种"诡辩"外，惠施和其他先秦名家辩者的命题则只是记录在《庄子·天下篇》中的"诡辩"语句。这些"诡辩"似乎更加离谱。

一、惠施的"历物十事"

（1）"至大无外，谓之大一；至小无内，谓之小一"；

（2）"无厚，不可积也，其大千里"；

（3）"天与地卑，山与泽平"；

（4）"日方中方睨，物方生方死"；

（5）"大同而与小同异，此之谓小同异；万物毕同毕异，此之谓大同异"；

（6）"南方无穷而有穷"；

（7）"今日适越而昔来"；

（8）"连环可解也"；

（9）"我知天下之中央，燕之北越之南是也"；

（10）"泛爱万物，天地一体也"。

二、辩者的"二十一事"

（1）"卵有毛"；

（2）"郢有天下"；

（3）"犬可以为羊"；

（4）"马有卵"；

（5）"丁子有尾"；

（6）"山出口"；

（7）"龟长于蛇"；

（8）"白狗黑"；

（9）"鸡三足"；

（10）"火不热"；

（11）"轮不碾地"；

（12）"目不见"；

（13）"指不至，至不绝"；

（14）"矩不方，规不可以为圆"；

（15）"凿不围枘"；

（16）"飞鸟之景未尝动也"；

（17）"镞矢之疾，而有不行不止之时"；

（18）"狗非犬"；

（19）"黄马骊牛三"；

（20）"孤驹未尝有母"；

（21）"一尺之棰，日取其半，万世不竭。"

在没有上下文的情况下，我们恐怕只能理解其中几个命题。如：辩者提出的"一尺之棰，日取其半，万世不竭"命题与现代数学、物理学的极限理论，或物质无限可分的理论假设高度一致。又如：惠施的"至大无外，谓之大一；至小无内，谓之小一"命题极有可能是关于"最大"之为最大、"最小"之为最小的概念意义的哲学反思（大到不再有外部空间，即为"最大"，小到不再有内部空间，即为"最小"；这就是"最大"之为最大和"最小"之为最小的本质意义）。

除此以外，从常识看，其他命题足够怪异，多数纯属无稽之谈。"白狗"怎么会同时又是"黑狗"？"鸡"怎么会有"三足"？"天"如何可能跟"地"一样"卑（低）"，"山"又如何可能跟"泽（湖）"一样"平"？说"我知天之中央（宇宙的中心）"同时位于"燕之北"（北方的燕国以北）和"越之南"（南方的越国以南），这不是胡话吗？

也许正因为此，先秦名家从一开始就遭到了各家各派的抨击。其中少数批判属于学理性批判，是讲道理的。但是多数是不讲道理的攻击。令人遗憾的是，无论是讲道理的，还是不讲道理的，批判者大都没能弄清楚先秦名家在说什么，为什么要那么说。那么，人们是如何批判公孙龙、惠施等名家的呢？我们选择一些有代表性的言论来看看吧。

《公孙龙子》重释与重译

1.1 先秦时代对名家的批判

先看与名家同时代的墨、儒、道几家是怎么批判名家的。

1.1.1 后期墨家

墨家不同意公孙龙的命题，《墨经》针锋相对地提出："白马，马也；乘白马，乘马也。骊马，马也；乘骊马，乘马也"（《小取》）；"［火］必热，说在顿"（《经下》），又说"见不见不离，一二相盈，广修，坚白……抚坚得白，必相盈也"（《经说下》）等。这是因为他们认为语言名称应当是对实在的描述："声出口，俱有名……言也者，诸口能之，出名者也。名若画虎也……所以谓，名也。所谓，实也。名实耦，合也。"（《经说上》）既然如此，语言意义应当以是否符合实在来确定："以名举实，以辞抒意，以说出故……效者，为之法也；所效者，所以为之法也。故中效，则是也；不中效，则非也，此效也。"（《小取》）

点评：

墨家的视角显然是经验论的，与名家不一样。名家论证"'火'不热"，而墨家却论证说火就是热的；公孙龙力证"'白马'非'马'"，而墨家针锋相对，说白马就是马，因为乘白马就是乘马。这样的对立是很自然的，因为从公孙龙的文章中，我们明显看出，他是在概念层面上进行语义逻辑反思，而墨家是在经验层面批判名家思想。墨家明确提出，名称是用来刻画、描述客观事物的，因而名称的意义是否正确，应该看意义是否与客观实践的效果相吻合；吻合就是正确的，而不吻合则是错误的。按照这样的思想倾向，墨家当然会反对"白马非马"之类的论点，因为我们骑着白马难道就不是骑着马吗？这样说也太荒谬了吧！不过，显然墨家没有站在名家的理性主义语言哲学的立场说话，他们对名家的批评只能说从经验主义的角度看是合理的，却并未对名家思想构成真正的否定。关于语言意义，一方在经验实在层面说话，另一方则从形而上学层面谈问题；层面不同，当然也就不会相互构成否定了。可以推知的是，墨家可能理解了名家的思想，只是不同意后者的唯理主义语言哲学立场；然而两者都是具有追求知识的确定性基础的中国古代哲学家。如果他们的思想没有湮灭，相互之间的争论继续下去，那么中国传统思想将呈现出另一幅画面。

1.1.2 儒家

与后期墨家完全不同的是，儒家对名家的批判近乎谩骂。儒家代表人物荀子这样说："不法先王，不是礼义，而好治怪说，玩琦辞，甚察而不惠，辩而无用，多事而寡功，不可以为治纲纪；然而其持之有故，其言之成理，足以欺惑愚众；是惠施、邓析也。"（《荀子·非十二子篇》）"奸事、奸道，治世之所弃，而乱世之所从服也。若夫充虚之相施易也。'坚白''同异'之分隔也，是聪耳之所不能听也，明目之所不能见也，辩士之所不能言也，虽有圣人之知，未能偻指也。不知无害为君子，知之无损为小人。工匠不知，无害为巧；君子不知，无害为治。王公好之则乱法，百姓好之则乱事。而狂惑戆陋之人，乃始率其群徒，辩其谈说，明其辟称，老身长子，不知恶也。夫是之谓上愚，曾不如相鸡狗之可以为名也。"（《儒效篇》）"凡邪说辟言之离正道而擅作者……明君临之以势，道之以道，申之以命，章之以论，禁之以刑。"（《正名篇》）

点评：

荀子的批判可谓是气急败坏。虽然他自己确实也有自己的语言观，提出过"名无固实，约之以命实，约定俗成，谓之实名"（《正名篇》）之类正确的理论，且跟孔子"法先王"先验主义正名思想相比，他还具有现实主义思想，提出过语言的意义来自于感知并由思维进行加工（即所谓"心征"）的思想，但毫无疑问，他完全没有弄懂名家到底在说什么，因而只有骂人家妖言惑众、扰乱纲纪而已。他的咒骂几近泼妇骂街。不仅如此，他还要求用尽行政、学术、刑法等一切手段消灭名家的言论。这也太霸道了！即使是持有某种经验主义立场，也应当学学墨家，以哲理观点批判对方的命题，但他没有这么做，而是从实用的治国秩序、政治伦理的角度攻击对手。这种无的放矢的攻击其实只能说明一点：荀子的经验主义思想并不是自觉的，有哲学基础的，只不过沿袭了孔子"经世致用"的思想特质而已。荀子的思想并未上升到哲学理性反思的层面，无法理解名家思想的哲学实质，他以实用政治的角度对名家语言哲学的批判完全是出于无知的无的放矢。不过，后来儒家思想在中国封建社会中占统治地位，他的抨击对名家的理性思辨性思维模式带来了毁灭性的打击。

1.1.3　道家

道家代表人物庄子："桓团、公孙龙，辩者之徒，饰人之心，易人之意，能胜人之口，不能服人之心，辩者之囿也。"（《庄子·天下》）"合同异，离坚白；然不然，可不可；困百家之知，穷众口之辩。自以为至达。"（《秋水》）"知诈渐毒、颉滑坚白、解垢同异之变多，则俗惑于辩矣。故天下每每大乱，罪在于好知。"（《胠箧》）"惠施多方，其书五车，其道舛驳，其言也不中。""惠施不辞而应，不虑而对，遍为万物说。说而不休，多而无已，犹以为寡，益之以怪，以反人为实，而欲以胜人为名，是以与众不适也。弱于德，强于物，其涂隩矣。由天地之道观惠施之能，其犹一蚊一虻之劳者也。其于物也何庸！……惜乎！惠施之才，骀荡而不得，逐万物而不反，是穷响以声，形与影竞走也，悲夫。"（《庄子·天下》）

点评：

庄子跟惠施关系不错，所以对惠施是很客气的了，说可惜了他的才能。但他对公孙龙和名家辩者则没有那么温和，指责他们以辩论来堵住别人的口，使得人们的思想无所适从，何其奸诈歹毒啊！可见，庄子也没有理解名家思想的实质。既然他承认名家辩者们能"胜人之口"，甚而至于以此"困百家之知"，为何他自己不去探究、论证他们不能"服人之心"的道理呢？其实在我看来，庄子恐怕不是不想，而是不能罢了。他在自己的文中断章取义地记载了惠施、公孙龙及其他名家辩者的言论，而且自鸣得意，以自己那种相对主义、不可知论的"高明"来贬低名家思想，殊不知这恰恰给我们留下了证据，不仅说明了名家的理性主义哲学思想本质，而且反证了庄子逻辑思想基础缺乏的特征。庄子堪称文豪，但在逻辑分析性思辨上他却十分低能。这也正好说明，为何庄子的思想倾向跟荀子不是一回事，双方的立场甚至是对立的，但是在对名家的抨击上，两者却异口同声，同样不得要领，并没有把握别人在说什么，却蛮横地批判一气。

中国古代思想以"经世致用"为要，名家的理性的形而上学思辨特质显然不见容于当时的社会及学术思想的主流，甚至相互对立的学派也批判名家。除了墨家能够基于自己的经验主义认识论立场对名家展开有意义也有思想价值的争论外，其余的也就只有挖苦、谩骂的本事，无力提出有思想价值的批判。名家与墨家之争在他们与其他各派之间缺乏一种话语理解的"共晓性"（杜世洪，2012：200）。

先秦之后，随着儒家思想一统天下，中国哲学的理性主义思辨传统事实上中断了。名家的思想一直到两千多年后的清末，西学东渐时才再次引起学者们的注意。不过，这时候名家的著述除了公孙龙相对完整的五篇文章外，几乎全部失传，只留下少数没有上下文的只言片语。这也使得现代学者对公孙龙的思想做出了各种各样的甚至是互相冲突的解释。

1.2 现代人的种种阐释

我们现在又是怎么看待公孙龙以及他所代表的先秦名家的呢？以下是一些有代

表性的意见。

1.2.1　意识形态批判及"诡辩"说

直到现代，还是有人把公孙龙的思想看作是诡辩，甚至仍然以意识形态作为批判公孙龙的视角。郭沫若（1945：280–283）认为，公孙龙的"诡辞差不多都是观念游戏"，这些诡辞不是毫无政治意义的逻辑思想，而是为没落阶级的"反动言论"作掩饰的东西，不仅没有进步意义，反而"把先秦的初期学者的革命意义完全否认了"。然而郭沫若却并未证明公孙龙的思想是如何为反动统治者服务的。有讽刺意味的是，在"文化大革命"期间某学报一篇署名为"外语系大批判组"（1974）的题为《"白马非马"是对孔丘"正名"的挑战》的文章却说："公孙龙大约是会懂得'哈巴狗是狗'这样的常识的。但他为什么硬要坚持'白马非马'这样看来有些违反常识的论题呢？道理很简单，这是战国末期阶级斗争的需要，批判孔丘'正名'的需要。"这下，公孙龙又被赞为"革命英雄"！

另一些人虽然不以意识形态来解说公孙龙，但也指责公孙龙的东西不过是诡辩。章太炎（1906：386，395）认为，"若惠施、公孙龙辈，专以名家著闻；而苟为钘析者多，其术反同诡辩""若鸡三足狗非犬之类，诡辩繁辞，今姑勿论"。杨钘（2003：77）说："惠施与公孙龙的观点虽有不同，但却都不从实际感受出发，所以他们所做的论断，都是反常识反事实，也和现实的经验相反，结果都成为诡辩。"韩东晖（2001）说，以公孙龙为代表的形名派"因为辩而辩，自相矛盾，终流于诡辩"，只不过他们的诡辩"在哲学上却有相当的意义"。即使是对名家思想观点持正面肯定意见的学者中也有人认为至少诸如"孤驹未尝有母"之类的命题属于诡辩（张新，1996：211–212），或者认为其中有些命题"不过是谬误以及毫无意义的语词游戏"（Liu，2003：300）。

点评：

把名家命题说成诡辩，然后不去理会，这很容易；但就像历史上那些读不懂公孙龙的书就要求把它们烧掉的人一样，也太过轻率了。万一那不是诡辩，我们不就错失认识中华文化瑰宝的机会了吗？即使是诡辩，也需要解释解释为什么名家非要诡辩。既然我们承认名家那些明显反常识的诡辩竟然在哲学上有意义，那么应当追问的是这种意义是什么。最起码，我们也需要解释为什么名家的命题有的是哲学，有的又是诡辩或者无意义的语言游戏。如果名家真的是哲学家，那么我们说他们在诡辩，是否说明我们看待他们思想的视角、框架不正确或者不恰当？至于以阶级和阶级斗争的视角来看待名家的命题，则可能是风马牛不相及的。至少，公孙龙为什么要用"诡辩"的方式来满足当时"阶级斗争"的需要，这是难以得到说明的。更何况，荀子强调社会政治秩序，要求名与实的辩论为"治国"做出贡献，而名家却与荀子针锋相对，这是不是说明名家就反对当时的统治阶级呢？恐怕我们无法得出这样的结论。用意识形态框架批判名家大约只与荀子的情绪化指责在一个档次，没有思想启发价值。

1.2.2　唯物论或者唯心论说

冯友兰对先秦名家的评价是很高的，他曾说过："除一起即灭之所谓名家者外，少有人有意识地将思想辩论之程序及方法之自身，提出研究。故知识论之第二部，逻辑，在中国亦不发达……中国哲学史中之只有纯理论的兴趣之学说极少，若此（名家学说——刘利民注）再不讲，则中国哲学史更觉畸形。"（2000：8，147）但他也曾将公孙龙的哲学视为"客观唯心主义"（1962：325），主要理由是公孙龙虽然对主语（对象）和谓语（属性）之间的不同做了详细的分析，但是他把两者割裂开来，加以抽象化、绝对化。侯外庐等（1957：419）则认为："中国的古代社会，在逻辑史上也有唯物主义和唯心主义的斗争，因而产生了名辩思潮两条战线的分裂。一方面是向上的发展，发端于墨子，而完成于墨经作者及荀子、韩非。另一方面是向下的堕落，滥觞于曾子，放大于思、孟，溃决于庄、惠，而枯竭于公孙龙、邹衍。前者之所以称为'发展'，是因其将名辩的方法净化而成了形式逻辑的科学。后者之所以称为'堕落'，则因其丧失了名辩思潮的积极内容，而蜕变成概念游戏的'诡辩'。"他们把惠施的"诡辩"称为"相对主义唯心思想"，而公孙龙的"诡辩"则为"绝对主义唯心思想"。这些论述是很有代表性的。

与此同时，另一些学者则反对他们的看法。如屈志清（1981：50-51）提出，公孙龙的名实论坚持了朴素的唯物论；他的坚白论也并没有把人的神智作用视为万能，因而也就基本上同唯心论的先验论划清了界限，是属于唯物论反映论的见解。刘玉俊（1995）提出：惠施与公孙龙"这批学者坚持的是同一哲学理论和观点，他们的主要哲学倾向是唯物主义的自然观，朴素的对立统一规律之辩证法思想和朴素的辩证唯物主义的认识论"。曾祥云（2004）更是高调指出："不无讽刺意味的是，被指控为彻头彻尾的唯心论者的公孙龙，竟然会说出这样再'唯物'不过的话来：'天地与其所产焉，物也。……''夫名，实谓也。'在这里，如果我们套用列宁评价黑格尔《逻辑学》的话来评价公孙龙哲学，那是再也合适不过的了：'这是纯粹的唯物主义！'在《公孙龙子》'这部最唯心的著作中，唯心主义最少，唯物主义最多'，矛盾？然而'这是事实'！"

　　杜国庠则认为公孙龙的哲学既不是唯物主义的，也不是像黑格尔"绝对精神"那样的唯心主义，因为公孙龙的理论"是由感觉的分析出发的，是由感觉性的'物''物指'达到非感觉性的抽象的'指'的。……（而这表现了公孙龙）出于要从事物的现象进一步去找寻更本质的东西的企图。这是值得注意的"（1955：23）。但杜国庠把公孙龙的哲学称为"多元的客观唯心主义"（1955：61）。

　　点评：

　　由此观之，说公孙龙是唯物主义或是唯心主义都能在他的言论中找到依据，也都能言之凿凿。公孙龙确实像柏拉图那样，割裂了事物及其属性，并对它们的抽象加以某种意义上的实体化，认为它们独立存在，这明显是唯心主义的。但是，公孙龙又再明白不过地承认世界是物组成的。这就有问题了。唯物与唯心两个主义是截然对立的，如果承认世界是物的世界，就不能同时又承认世界不是物的世界，反之亦然。那么公孙龙怎么能认为世界同时是物的世界而又不是物的世界呢？这是不是说明，唯物论或唯心论的哲学本体论视角或者框架并不适用来审视公孙龙与名家的思想？至少，这个框架的确不能完全说明公孙龙以及其他名家人物提出的命题。比如，公孙龙的"离坚白"确实接近柏拉图式的客观唯心主义，但他的思想却是以承认世界是由具体实在之物所构成为前提的。这又该如何解释？

　　当然，有一点我们得承认，无论如何，唯物与唯心的认识框架做出了一个重要贡献：否定了公孙龙的思想是诡辩。这使得我们有理由继续看看他们到底在说些什么，且不一定非要把公孙龙及先秦名家人士要么归入唯物主义阵营，要么归入唯心主义阵营。

1.2.3　逻辑学理论说

　　胡适在1917年所写的《先秦名学史》（1983：111）中最早提出，名家学派"继承了墨翟伦理和逻辑传统，并在整个中国思想史上，为中国贡献了逻辑方法的最系统的发达学说"。陈荣捷（Chan，1973：232）曾这样说："几乎所有中国古代哲学主要流派都极其关注名与实的关系问题，或者关注其社会、道德意义（如儒家），或者关注其形而上重要性（如道家），或者是为了政治控制（如法家）。但他们中没有任何一家对于这个问题的逻辑方面感兴趣。……唯一主要关注逻辑问题的只有逻辑学派。……它们是唯一致力于探索诸如存在、相对性、空间、时间、特性、实在，以及因果等问题的一个学派。虽然它们的中文名称叫作'名家'或'名辩'，但它们并不局限于名与实的符合。它们的形而上学和认识论还是初级的，但它们真正地、首要地追求着纯粹的知识。……这在中国历史上是独一无二的。"周云之（1994：106-107）指出："在先秦逻辑史上，第一个比较自觉地把名实问题从逻辑理论的高度做出研究和概括的，就是公孙龙。……研究《公孙龙子》，如果不能从逻辑上发展其中的正名学说，甚至简单地用他的哲学唯心主义来批判，否认他的重要逻辑正名学说，将是一个莫大的失误。"

然而，孙中原（1987：172）曾经对公孙龙文章的逻辑进行了详细的分析，结论却是：公孙龙虽然的确是一个"相当不错的兼职逻辑学家"，但他又的确是"著名的诡辩家"。庞朴（1979：73，75）指出："形式地看来，公孙龙倒是恪遵形式逻辑〔A是A〕的规则的。问题在于，他根本违反了辩证逻辑，违反了思维的辩证法。"违反了辩证法，当然只能是诡辩了。龚家准（1989）提出，"白马非马"命题违反了同一律、矛盾律、充足理由律等一系列逻辑规律，偷换概念，改变概念之间关系，或者干脆不讲道理；认为公孙龙的《白马论》论的是个"假命题，讲的是些歪道理，但由于其文结构严密、简练、环环相扣，因而不愧为一篇出色的诡辩文章"。

点评：

用形式逻辑来分析公孙龙的文章，我们确实发现他的推理有问题。但是，公孙龙是在用"白马非马"命题来研究逻辑规律吗？违反了一系列逻辑规律的文章竟然还可以结构严密、环环相扣，这不是很可疑的吗？至少，我们得再仔细看看，这到底怎么可能？可不可以换个角度看，假如公孙龙不是在研究形式逻辑推理，而是在谈别的，那么用逻辑学的眼光去衡量他的文章恐怕不那么合适。尤其是辩证法，极有可能根本不适合用来审视公孙龙的文章。我们从公孙龙的文章中压根儿找不到关于辩证思维的线索。鉴于公孙龙的文章千百年来一直被误读、误解这一事实，我们在没有真正读懂公孙龙到底在说什么之前，就把形式逻辑等应用于他的文章的解释，这恐怕是完全错误的。顺便说明，这里说的"辩证"不是古希腊苏格拉底式的通过论辩、思辨而达到真理的证明那个意义上的"dialectics"，而是诸如"个体与一般的对立统一""否定之否定"之类的理解。这本身是个大题目，本书不打算展开。但现有的理解多是在后面这种意义上使用"辩证"一词的。公孙龙的文章中没有这类论述。非要这样去理解他的文章，则真的可能与他真正要表达的思想相去甚远。

1.2.4 理论科学说

于是，一些学者把公孙龙和先秦名家辩者们视为理论科学家。例如，董英哲等（1995）提出，《庄子·天下》中所记载的名家命题除了"鸡三足"和"孤驹未尝有母"两条属于诡辩之外，其余的都不仅不是诡辩，而是蕴藏着丰富的科学思想之说。董英哲等（2001）还撰文详细讨论了名家在数学、物理、天文、地理、力学、声学、热学、生物学、医学等领域的成就与思想。李耽（1998：228-229）则干脆说，"惠施是个理论数学家和理论物理学家，而不是应用数学家和实验物理学家"，因为"惠施《历物十事》，全部是用逻辑（包括形式逻辑和辩证逻辑，主要是辩证逻辑）推理得到的，与《墨经》不同，《墨经》既重逻辑推理，又重试验，并重视古人经验"。此外，我们还可以检索到关于先秦名家具体命题的专文研究，如关于"飞鸟之景，未尝动也""一日之棰，日取其半，万世不竭"等命题的研究。这些论述的确展示出了先秦名家这类命题与现代科学的理论认识，例如极限理论等，具有高度的一致性。

点评：

说墨家是科学家，这说得过去。阅读《墨经》，可以发现其中关于声光力物理学、数学、逻辑的命题十分丰富，不禁令人赞叹中国古代竟有如此优秀的科学思想、科学定义和科学结论。但先秦名家则不然，我们没有证据证明他们是跟墨家一样的科学家。他们似乎对实践经验与经验科学并不感兴趣，而是一门心思"专决于名"，与人就名称的意义问题进行争辩。最难解释的是，"白狗黑""火不热""白马非马""我知天之中央燕之北越之南是也"等命题，无论如何也不可能得到科学的解释。于是，理论科学论者不得不留下尾巴：除了一些有科学性的命题外，其余的还是诡辩。这就是我们面对的困惑，具有科学精神的一群学者为什么要同时提出诡辩命题？公孙龙还写文章专门详细论述"白马非马""二无一"等诡辩命题，这不会是为了闹着玩吧？既然名家是科学家、数学家，那么公孙龙作为名家思想集大成的代表人物，为什么偏要去论证"二不是两个一"？这些说不通的问题表明，我们把公孙龙们视为理论科学家这一想法恐怕是值得商榷的。

1.3　国外学者的误解

国外的中国古代哲学研究者也做过汉语言与公孙龙思想的研究，但他们的研究也很有问题，值得质疑。例如，陈汉生（Hansen，1983：31-32）认为，古汉语缺乏名词的单复数屈折变化，因而其名词是类似于西方语言的不可数名词的"物质名词"。这一特点使古代中国思维不能产生出西方哲学那样的概念抽象来作为认识的中介。汉语名词的命名中，名与实的一对一关系使得汉语的本体抽象是一种"部分论的"（mereological）抽象，即"对于任何一个抽象的物体集（abstract set of objects），都可以通过将该集合中的所有元素都视为非连续的质（discontinuous stuff）来构建出一个具体的分体物（concrete mereological object）。鉴别该集合中的不同元素就等于在时空中鉴别同一质的不同部分。对名进行认知也就等于学会将实在区分为其名所命名的分体的质"。换言之，汉语名词的命名不是像西方语言那样基于某种抽象概念、属性、本质或者理念形态的观念，而是基于识别事物的界限，这个特点使得中国思想倾向于产生一种"行为唯名主义"。结果，中国古代思想由于语言的原因无法形成概念的抽象，因而"共相论"的问题无法提出。

陈汉生（Hansen，1983：151-170）认为，公孙龙的确是在有意识地就语言问题进行思辨，不过公孙龙的"白马非马"悖论（paradox）事实上就是关于名的本质的严格解释：一个名必须总是"挑选出"（pick out）同一种物体。公孙龙并不否定"白马是马"，但"白马"这一兼名中的"马"与"马"字所指的绝对不是同一种东西，因为两个"马"指的不是同一类物质。从这个意义上看，陈汉生认为公孙龙的观点就是，兼名中的名与单独使用的名不具有同一性，因而公孙龙的"白马非马"只不过是在坚持"一名一物"（one-name-one-thing）的正名规则。陈汉生说，公孙龙正确地察觉到后期墨家关于"兼名"的理论中的问题，但是他比墨家更加坚持错误的见解，即把所有的语词都视为"名"。公孙龙的"离白马"事实上提出，"白马"作为兼名与"白"和"马"分别使用之间没有语义关系而出错，因为这样的话，这些"名"实际上什么也不能命。于是，公孙龙的辩解漏洞百出，陷于荒谬。

另一位研究者葛瑞汉（Graham，1990：200-209）的观点似乎自身就不一致。一方面，葛瑞汉提出，公孙龙的"白马非马"所要表达的思想是，白（作为颜色）与马（作为形状）相兼的整体不是马（形）的一部分。公孙龙不是将"马"的名应用于"白马"整体，而是用于其中一个部分，即"马"形，而"白"色则处于形之外。于是，既然整体并不是其部分，当然"白马"就不是"马"。而他认为公孙龙的命题因此是非常合逻辑的，而公孙龙的论敌却将"整体与部分"的逻辑分析误解成了种属关系的混淆。那么，以"马"命形的时候，"白"（色）何以能够处于形之外呢？葛瑞汉（Graham，1990：208-209）认为，这是中国古代哲学对事物的思考方式导致的：中国哲学没有思考事物"是"某种相形，而是思考它们"有"某种形状或颜色（things are conceived, not as being their shapes, but as "having shape and color"）。由于缺乏表示共相抽象的词汇（如whiteness，hardness等），古汉语的"坚"（is hard）、"白"（is white）可作为动词来描述事物（如石头），但不是作为"being"而是"having"那种颜色或硬度。在这方面，葛瑞汉的观点与陈汉生是很接近的。

另一方面，古汉语词性不分、转换自由的语法特点使得中国哲学家倾向于从内部认识事物，而不是像西方哲学那样从外部认识事物，因而后者那种把知识客观化的努力在前者就不能实现。葛瑞汉认为，公孙龙正是利用古汉语的特点，将论辩推至有利于自己的观点，将本来仅仅是下位概念的词作为同位概念来使用。这样，公孙龙的论敌就进入了语言的迷宫，无法认清"白"与"马"事实上根本不是同位语词，"白"是"马"的下位成分，因此也无法肯定地说，"马并非白与马，而是一只白色的马"。因此，葛瑞汉认为，公孙龙的悖论本来是站不住脚的，是很容易驳斥的，之所以没有被驳倒，是因为古汉语不能区分上下位词，导致认识上种属关系与整体/部分关系纠缠在一起。

但是，我认为葛瑞汉在分析中过于想当然地在原文上进行加减词语或变动词语位置。这种做法很难说是可靠的。这很可能是由于葛瑞汉对汉语理解不透彻造成的。比如他对公孙龙《指物论》的分析非常有问题。如同陈汉生将"指"字理解为"挑选出"（pick out）一样，葛瑞汉将这个字解释为"pointing things out"（把物体指出来，指涉），而完全没有顾及"指"字在汉语中的多义性。他把"物莫非指，而指非指"解释为"When no thing is not the pointed-out (what the name points out), to point out is not to point it out"（当无物是由名所指涉出的时候，指涉并不是指涉出此物）（Graham，1990：213），"指非非指也，指与物非指也"解释为"It is not that to point out is not to point it out, it is pointing out combined with things which is not pointing it out（并非指涉不是指涉此物，指涉与事物之结合才不是指涉此物）"（Graham，1990：215），如此等等。这类解释只能让读者云里雾里，不知所云，于是只好断言公孙龙是诡辩家。

点评：

陈汉生认为公孙龙的思想着重于对"名"的语义问题进行思辨，这是对的；他从"离坚白"的角度来认识"白马非马"命题也是有道理的（下文将说明这一点）。从"物质名词"假设及其"行为唯名论"观点来看，陈汉生的解释对于了解公孙龙与墨家思想的差别或许有一定帮助，但是他这种不顾及公孙龙整体哲学思想的分析法，无疑大大降低了公孙龙思想的哲学价值。他的解释并没能驳倒冯友兰的"共相论"观点。恰恰相反，如果我们进一步追问公孙龙所"离"出来的东西是什么，那么我们完全可以发现，公孙龙所提出的可以离物而自藏，因而自在的不变者正是"共相"。虽然古汉语没有"共相"一词，但是，公孙龙的"白者必白"中的"白者"、"马无色"中的"马"等，除了指"共相"之外，还可做何解释？而这又进一步说明，古汉语完全能够使人产生出概念的抽象。于是，陈汉生的"行为唯名论"理论也就站不住脚了。

葛瑞汉从古汉语特征和整体与部分的角度分析公孙龙的思想，有一定的思想启发价值。如我稍后将要谈到的，正是语言对先秦思想家构成了困惑才会产生公孙龙等名家，力图澄清语言尤其是语言意义的本质问题。但若公孙龙真的只是在利用古汉语语法松散的结构来达到诡辩的目的，则其思想其实也就没什么价值了。或许这也正是葛瑞汉理论中出现一方面"逻辑完全正确"，另一方面又的确"容易驳倒的悖论"这样不一致的认识的原因吧。

国外学者对汉语言的把握，以及他们对中国传统思想的把握可能有问题，他们是站在自己的角度来考察汉语和汉语文化思想的。借用杜世洪（2012：201）的说法，他们即使在"语脉"层面也与中国人的理解没有足够的"连贯因子触点"。但不可否认的是，他们的语言框架的确体现了他们各自的语言分析智慧。这些框架本身因此也是有研究价值的。

这里我把国外学者的误解陈述出来，不是为了抱怨他们，而是旨在说明本书的目的之一就是为名家"正名"，说明他们是货真价实的理性主义哲学家。从更大的意义上讲，本书也想为整个中国传统哲学"正名"，即便是在西方形而上学思辨这一严格意义上说，哲学也是普遍的，而不是语言特有的，汉语土壤完全能够培养出真正意义上的哲学。

1.4 语言哲学解读

如果说上述理解多多少少是误解，那么接下来我们看到的语言哲学理解却为我们反思并重新解释公孙龙及先秦名家的思想实质提供了钥匙。进入90年代之后，或许在语言哲学以及中西比较哲学研究的影响下，国内学者有意识地从语言哲学的角度对公孙龙思想进行研究。他们的研究更具启发意义。

周昌忠在1991年就出版了《公孙龙子新论——和西方哲学的比较研究》一书，首次明确提出公孙龙的哲学是思辨的哲学、知性的哲学、语言分析哲学（1991：10-14）。他说（1991：113）："《公孙龙子》哲学的主体是分析的语言哲学和逻辑学。可以说它独步先秦哲学，致力于从语言分析来突破常识，……进而构造了一个相当丰富的关于语言本身的哲学理论。"2005年周昌忠又出版了《先秦名辩学及其科学思想》一书，把公孙龙思想与西方哲学，特别是西方语言哲学思想进行比较，进一步凸显了公孙龙思想的分析性和理性主义倾向。总体来看，周昌忠认为，公孙龙主张实在论的本体论，一方面肯定客体的实在性，同时又肯定共相的实在性；在认识论上，公孙龙主张知性旨在认识共相，因而其思想中富含逻辑性，论述也涉及同一律、矛盾律等形式逻辑问题；而在语言哲学上，公孙龙提出了含义与指云（弗雷格意义上的意义与指称——刘利民注）的划分，客体词和概念词的划分，指云的客观性、决定、辨识、变化等一系列思想。

崔清田（1997：26-32）不同意将名学、辩学视为逻辑学，但他指出了一个要点：公孙龙的名实关系讨论与众不同的是，他把语言与思维严格而清楚地区分开来，"他在讨论语言和语言的对象时所使用的词是'名'和'实'，而在讨论思维和存在的关系时所使用的词是'指'与'物'"（1997：145）。崔清田（1997：169）进一步指出："公孙龙的名学理论是关于语言的理论。《公孙龙子》中关于名、实、指、物的论述及'白马非马''坚白相离'等讨论都是为了说明一个问题，语词的意义是什么。公孙龙认为，名的意义是它所指的实，但由于名和实必须由指来联结，所以在他的理论中，名的直接意义是指。公孙龙的名学理论与西方语言哲学的观念论相似。"17世纪英国哲学家洛克（Locke，2001：510）曾说过："语词的作用就是把观念可感地标示出来，语词所代表的观念就是它们固有的直接的意义。……语词以其主要或曰直接意义仅仅代表的是使用语词的人心中的观念而已。"崔清田认为公孙龙的见解与洛克的这种观念论思想是一致的。

重要的是，崔清田（1997：169-170）还指出：在西方，语言哲学是在经历了本体论、认识论转向之后才出现的，而在公元前3世纪的中国居然出现公孙龙专门以语言意义作为研究对象的理论，这似乎有些不可思议。他指出，公孙龙思想的出现虽然有名辩思潮发展的必然性，但公孙龙的语言哲学没有像西方语言哲学那样对认识论进行充分研究的哲学土壤，因而虽然名噪一时，却很快就消亡了。

林铭均和曾祥云（2000：19）也认为，中国名学的定位应该是以"名"为研究对象的思想理论；名学的"名"不是以具体的单个的名作为研究的对象，而是只研究名的一般。他们不同意将先秦名辩学与古希腊的逻辑学相比较，因为名学的"名"并不等于西方传统逻辑的"概念"，辩学的"辩"也不与"逻辑"相当。他们认为，应该从"名"的实质本身来看待先秦名学。那么"名"的实质是什么呢？第一，"名"的本义就是对事物命名；第二，命名，与人们认识文化交流活动密切相关；第三，"名"具有表征对象的指谓功能和用以交流思想的交际功能（林铭均、曾祥云，2000：39）。由此观之，公孙龙不是诡辩家，而是"对中国名学做出卓越贡献的名学家、符号学家"，"《公孙龙子》可以说是我国古代唯一的一本专门探讨名学问题即符号学问题的名学理论专著"（林铭均、曾祥云，2000：161，164）。

《公孙龙子》重释与重译

点评：

研究公孙龙以及其他先秦名家思想家的学者们终于进入了语言哲学视域。上述学者提出的观点中有三点特别值得重视：一，公孙龙的哲学是语言哲学，而且是分析的语言哲学；二，中国古代的语言哲学表现为以汉语言以"名"为中心的形而上学反思；三，公孙龙的语言哲学是先秦思想辩论的必然发展，这种发展已经产生了本体论和认识论的哲学思想元素。

我觉得这种发展不是偶然的。相反，我认为西方语言哲学是从西方哲学的本体论、认识论发展而来的，而中国哲学则可能走的是一条相反的道路，即从语言的反思中诞生本体论和认识论哲学。从语言意义本质的思辨来力图认识、把握世界与存在，这不是西方哲学的专利，中国古代哲学家也有着同样的思考。再者，维特根斯坦说，"语言休假了，哲学问题就产生了"（*PI.* §38）。哲学当然有其研究的对象，如概念、本质、存在、认识等，但是如果没有语言，这些问题不可能出现。维特根斯坦是对的，西方哲学起源于语词和语句意义的追问，即脱离语言使用的语境与说话人而孤立地追问语言所表达的概念、命题意义的本质是什么，又如何才能为真。正是这种求"是"与求"真"的冲动让西方哲学家走上了哲学的道路。中国哲学的起源也应是同样的道理。

不过，就目前的语言哲学解读本身来看，也还有一些问题，如公孙龙的陈述的确显得与西方哲学家的思想吻合；但在一些地方，我们发现他的思想与洛克思想吻合，另一些地方又发现他提出了逼近柏拉图的"理念"的思想；那么如此各不相同，甚至冲突的思想何以使公孙龙的思想具有融贯性？此其一。

其二，公孙龙真的提出了类似于弗雷格的"含义"与"指称"的区分吗？这是个很令人疑惑的问题。对于弗雷格，指称是客观的、实在的对象，而含义是引导我们对这个对象进行思考的方式。但在公孙龙的论述中，我们实在看不出这样的思想倾向。其他的区分亦复如是。此外，如前所述，公孙龙的思想到底是不是逻辑，争议很大。但若不承认他的论述的逻辑性，我们也可能不好解释他的思想。那么，能否区分纯语言层面的语义逻辑与经验感知层面的逻辑从而考察公孙龙的思想呢？假如说古希腊的亚里士多德提出逻辑学思想的起点就是语言的分析，特别是关于句法结构的意识和思辨，那么依据汉语言特征进行分析、思辨是不是也可能构成公孙龙逻辑学思想的起点？这个问题尚未见讨论。

其三，如果我们同意公孙龙的思想是理性主义的语言哲学思辨，那么我们也就应该重新对《公孙龙子》一书进行翻译，尤其需要翻译成外文，以向世界哲学界进行介绍。这一翻译还应当包括对"历物十事""辩者二十一事"的融贯性阐释，因为即便是对惠施和先秦名家辩者的思想倾向持正面肯定看法的学者，也是从万物整体论、认识相对论的角度对他们进行解释的（参见：李贤中，2012：第3章），而这样的解释对于理解先秦名家基本思想的实质恐怕并无助益。先秦名家思想需要重新理解。这个工作目前尚未见到有人做过。这也正是本书撰写的意义。

我认为，就现有的语言哲学解释框架看，由于解释者在他们的分析中没有充分注意汉语语言特性的问题，而采用西方语言哲学的现成概念或理论来考察先秦名家，就不免提出说服力不那么强，或者不能得到证据支持的理论解释。这么看来，语言哲学的理论框架并没有问题，但我们还必须考虑汉语语言本身的特性。先秦名家思想家们如果真是在进行关于语言问题，尤其是语言意义问题的形而上学哲学思辨，那么他们的思辨只能基于汉语语言提供给他们的条件，因而必然具有汉语语言的特色。这是理解先秦名家思想的关键。

2. 中西语言与中西哲学的关系问题

说一种思想是语言哲学，那么其主要特点应当是从语言问题，尤其是语言意义问题的反思入手，试图说明人类到底把握了什么样的关于世界的知识，人的知识如何才是正确的。但是这个问题为什么会出现呢？这是因为世界是无穷的、变化的，而语言的手段却是有限的、受规则约束的。既然人只能以语言的手段来把握世界，表达关于世界的知识，那么世界与语言之间就出现了巨大的不对称：人只能用有限的方式认识无限的世界，只能以不变的规则去理解变化多端的对象。于是，这种认识、理解怎么才具有真理性就成了一个值得反思的问题。如果人"不得不活在语言中"（钱冠连，2005），那么对于这个人赖以生存的理性"家园"做一番考察实在是必要的。此其一。

其二，人们用语言所描述的对象，有些是可以直观把握的，而有些则无法把握。比如，"如果天下雨，地上必然湿"描述了天下雨导致地上湿这样的事实。这种描述是否为真，只需要看看描述与事实是否相符就行了。但是"如果仁慈，就不可能残忍"这句话所描述的内容就不那么容易确定为真了。道理很简单：我们可以观察到下雨、湿润等现象，但是我们无法观察到一种叫作"仁慈"的对象。可以实在把握的，当然没有什么问题，但是不能实在把握的，就需要追问那是什么，它到底具有什么性质。

这也意味着，人用语言所谈论的对象是有不同的层次的。这就是我在《在语言中盘旋——先秦名家"诡辩"命题的纯语言思辨理性研究》（刘利民，2007）一书

第二章中，为了解释先秦名家的思想而提出的"语言性认知操作三模式论"所要谈论的问题。语言性"认知操作三模式论"要点是：人类的思维本质上说是语言性的认知操作，语言使用者在日常、科学、哲学三个不同模式中的思维操作所使用的语言都是同一种语言，只不过他们用语言所操作的对象性质不同而已。哲学话语不等于日常话语，哲学语法也不等于日常语言语法。然而，哲学的语言却没有超越的特权。哲学家用来谈论思想、语言本身的语言与日常生活中用来谈论事物和事件的语言是同样的自然语言。即使是逻辑语言，也源自自然语言。在日常层面，人们的认知操作是用语言来对实在的事物与事件进行言说，那么科学层面的认知操作则是以语言结构化的方式对抽象的对象（关于客观事物的属性、规律等的概念、命题）进行间接操作，而哲学层面的认知操作就是用语言来对语言本身进行操作。显然，日常层面的操作对象和验证方式都是直接经验的，因而具有完全的经验确定性；科学层面则只有间接确定性，因为科学研究所构建的概念、命题本身不是客观实在对象，不具有直接经验确定性；而在哲学层面，其概念、命题等对象及对这些对象的把握完全不具有经验确定性，它们只能依赖分析性思辨。

后来我在《语言元范畴化与公孙龙语言哲学》（《外语学刊》，2011年第1期）一文中进一步阐释了这一观点：无论是西方哲学还是中国哲学，虽切入点完全不同，但最终都源于语义的"元范畴化"（meta-categorization）反思。所谓"元范畴化"，是我对认知语言学的概念"范畴化"的理论延伸。所谓"范畴化"指的是人对于世界万物给人的体验的切分与归类，以赋予种种体验以秩序和结构加以命名，从而形成概念并进行认识和把握这样一种认知方式。在日常语言中，人们所切分的是具体的事物、事件给人的感知经验。此层面的范畴化所形成的概念性语义本质上是对直接体验的概括（如"日、月、山、水、冷、热"等）。但范畴化并不止于对实在事物与事件，而是将以相同的机制对知觉经验层面的语义进行再范畴化（re-categorization）。如对上句中的具体概念再范畴化而形成"天体、物体、类别、属性、关系"等上位概念。

再范畴化基于对感知经验的第一步范畴化，就与感知经验没有直接联系，即不是对客观事件给人的感知而是对概念性意义的范畴化。于是再范畴化形成的概念更加抽象，不能直接由经验来判定意义，因而至少从经验的角度讲，更有可能导致意义的不确切，甚至误解。因此人们不得不对再范畴化形成的语义概念进行进一步反思，力图保证自己关于世界的理解具有确定性、普遍性和必然性。这时候，元范畴化就是必需的了。"必然性""偶然性""现象""本质"等就是对再范畴化的概念、命题进行的更高层次的范畴化。这是形而上学的范畴化，因为它已经远离经验，本质上是用语言对语言意义本身的分析与考察。需指出的是，元范畴化的语言认知性质与范畴化和再范畴化不同。范畴化与再范畴化层面的切分、归类、抽象等都是对意义内容的操作，即实义性的概念化（substantive conceptualization）。但元范畴化则不是单纯的对语言的切分和概念化，即不是在再范畴化之上重复的再范畴化，而是出于对语义本身可靠性的疑惑，对于语言范畴化和再范畴化本身的正确性的反省和思辨，是对于范畴化认知的评价性概念化（evaluative conceptualization）。这应当是"元"的含义。在我看来，这便是哲学概念的本质。

　　我的理论的关键观点是哲学产生于对语言意义的元范畴化反思。任何一个民族都用语言来言说世界，并由此对世界进行理解和把握。那么只要他们对语义本身发出疑问并进行思辨性分析，都能够产生出理性主义的思维方式。各种语言之间肯定存在巨大的差异（例如，英语与汉语），但是语言作为人认识世界的方式却具有共性。任何民族都能走上理性主义的道路，而他们所使用的具体语言的形态性差异即所谓语言个性特征，仅仅决定了他们通向理性主义的路径有所不同而已。

2.1　西方哲学与西方语言特征

　　张志林曾这样说过："人类的一切文明都是在造句。"[1]他当然不是指小学生式的造句练习，而是指人类总是用语言构建、深化、发展思想。思想，正是人类文明的核心，整个人类文明就是在语言中的盘旋。即便是物质文明，也首先是人不断用语言表达出来，即提出新的理论，然后才通过实践性操作而物化所形成的。而对于语词概念、语句命题以及这些概念和命题指导之下的行为实践的正确性保证进行分析、反思，就是哲学逻辑反思的起点。

　　西方哲学起源之初，其先贤对语言的反思是自觉的。柏拉图明确提出："语言这个论题，可能正是一切论题中最重要的论题。"[2]（*Cratylus*，427e）亚里士多德也曾明确指出，他以求真为目的的逻辑思辨就是力图在语言中盘旋出必然的结论："我所谓完美的三段论，是说除了所陈述的语句之外，不再需要任何别的东西就能够得出必然的结论。"[3]（*Analytica Priora*，24b）

1　这是中山大学张志林教授2007年4月在四川大学进行学术交流期间与包括笔者在内的语言学专业师生所做的一次谈话中所说的。此论点虽未正式发表，但笔者非常赞同这一说法，故此引用。

2　所引柏拉图的话出自：*The Collected Dialogues of Plato* (16th edition), edited by Edith Hamilton and Huntington Cairns, New Jersey: Princeton University Press, 1996.

3　所引亚里士多德的话出自：*The Basic Works of Aristotle*, edited by Richard McKeon, New York: Random House, Inc., 1941.

从他们的理论来看，他们也确实是在语言中对所"是"以及所"是"之为真进行着语义反思的认知操作。关于柏拉图的"理念"，阿尔斯顿说："柏拉图使我们注意到语言的一种普遍特征，这就是，一个给定的通名（例如'tree'）或形容词（例如'sharp'）可以在同样的含义上被真实地应用于大量的不同个体。他的见解是，仅当存在有某一个由（每个个体所分担的）那种所论及的普遍词项所命名的实体，如树性（treeness）、锐利性（sharpness），普遍词项才可能在同样的含义上被应用于许多不同的个体；否则，这便是不可能的。"（1988：2）由此观之，柏拉图的"理念"论"实际上是一种语言分析"（赵敦华，2001：46）。

而关于亚里士多德及其逻辑与语言反思，崔清田（2004：131）指出："亚里士多德结合希腊语言的实际，获得了直言命题的主谓结构（系词与实词同属谓词）。以主谓结构为基础，又有了命题的分类、名词的周延性、命题的对当关系、命题的换位、三段论的构造、三段论的格与式、三段论的划归等三段论理论的内容。所以，离开希腊的语言，离开命题的主谓结构，就不可能建立三段论，不可能有亚里士多德逻辑。亚里士多德逻辑和他的三段论是对应着西方语言的结构而建立的。"

既然哲学起源于语言的反思，那么西方哲学经由本体论，到认识论，再到语言论的发展就是很自然的了。整个20世纪，西方哲学家自觉地从语言分析的角度来对待形而上学，使西方哲学出现了17世纪认识论转向（epistemological turn）之后的又一次转向，即语言论转向（linguistic turn），力图通过分析语言来探索人把握世界的方式，从语言的角度重塑西方哲学的问题（Baghramian，1999：Introduction）。无论怎么转向，无论问题形态怎么变化，西方哲学传统的根本性追问（"是"与"真"）始终未变。人所认识的那个对象到底是什么，如何才能保证人的所知为真，这始终是西方哲学的关注中心。

一个重要问题是，西方语言的结构虽然复杂而精细，但是语言毕竟不是逻辑，语言有其自身的模糊性和歧义性。这种模糊性和歧义性与复杂而精细的结构相结合，很容易导致要求澄清形式意义的冲动。在促使西方人的思想自然地进入理性思辨的方面，西方语言的三个句法特征是关键性的：（1）系词"to be"；（2）名词的具体与抽象词义的形式化区分；（3）主谓分明的陈述句结构。这些关键性特征极有利于西方思想家从句法和语义两个角度进入元范畴化的反思，即形而上学的思辨。

首先，西方哲学的核心范畴"Being"本身就是系词"to be"[1]的动名词形式。按卡恩的研究（Kahn，1986），由于"to be"集系词、断真和存在用法于一身，这个词具备作为形而上学范畴概念的条件。作为系词，"to be"从语言学角度看，联系主语和谓语而构成陈述句；从认知角度讲，它联系主体和关于主体的述谓而构成命题。在形式为"x is y"的陈述句结构中，"x"和"y"都是变项，唯一不变的是"is"，那么由"is"所联系的两个变项在什么条件下构成正确的命题？这样的疑问使得"to be"的重要性凸现出来了。在西方语言中，"to be"正好又可以表示存在，比如说，"God is"。如果一个物"is"，那么这个物就具有了存在的规定性；如果一个物"is not"，则没有存在的规定性。西方语言中的系词"to be"所具有的这两个意义结合到一起，恰好与西方哲学家对于存在、本质是什么的追问相匹配。"'是者'的哲学意义是'实体'，而'实体'的每一种意义都可以通过对系词'是'的逻辑功能的分析而得到。"（赵敦华，2001：68）

第二，名词的形态变化与名词所指称对象密切关联。以英语为例，泛指个体的单数可数名词前一定要加上不定冠词"a""an"，泛指的复数名词前则不加不定冠词，但必须在词尾加上"-s"或者其变体；而特指名词前面需要加上定冠词"the"。若是由普通名词衍生出的抽象名词，则以词缀加以标示，如"bird + -ness = birdness"或者"active + -ity = activity"。普通名词可以实指个体的事物，也可以指称关于普通事物的类的概念，而抽象名称只能指称抽象出来的概念。

这些都不外乎西方语言的常识，但是这些常识对于西方哲学家们自然、顺利地进入关于概念、命题的形而上学思辨却意义重大：因为这些名词从句法形式上明确划分出了"一"与"多"、"具体"与"一般"、"现象"与"本质"等西方哲学一开始就注意思辨的二元语义。在"多"中求"一"，经由"具体"而追问"一般"，从"现象"中发掘"本质"，这种哲学理性的思辨与其所基于的语言抽象过程非常自然和谐地统一了起来。这也正是陈汉生（Hansen，1983：34-36）所强调的"概念形成机制"，即使得"物的共性（thing-in-common）能够在形而上的、语义的和认识论的意义上，作为本质、理念，或特性等而出现"的语言机制。一言以蔽之，西方语言所特有的名词的形式有利于导致语言使用者关于普遍者的自觉。

最后，主谓分明的句法结构也是一个重要的环节，因为关于什么意义的词可以占据主语的位置、什么结构可以作为对主词的正确陈述等的反思，极可能导致关于本体性和命题逻辑的抽象认识。

1　"to be"及其形变是欧洲语言的特征，如在古希腊语中为"einai"，德语中为"sein"，法语中为"étre"等。这里以英语为例。

《公孙龙子》重释与重译

张东荪（1985：338-339）曾这样说："哲学上的本体是由名学（指亚里士多德的逻辑学——刘利民注）上的主体而来。"他论证说：

> 无主体便不能成为言语。譬如说"花红"，即是说"花是红的"，同时亦就含有"此是花"。所以这个"此"字是不能少的。因为"花"在"此是花"一句中是云谓而不是主体。虽则在"花是红的"一句中是主体而不是云谓。可见无论如何推到最后总不能不有一个赤裸裸的"此"。这便是说，一切云谓都是加于主体上的。虽可累积起来，但却离不开主体。所以亚里士多德以为主体是云谓所加于其上的，而其自身却不能变为云谓加于他物之上。否则，思想上的三个法则，（即同一律、矛盾律与排中律）皆不能成立。……总之，他是把主体与云谓分作截然不同的两种。……只有主体而无云谓，则不成为"言"。只有云谓而无主体则不明"所言"。所以一个成为言语的句子必须有主体和云谓。亚里士多德的这个主张实在是根据西方人（狭义之言，即希腊）的文法。然而这样的文法却代表了西方人的"心思"（mentality）。亚里士多德把这样的西方人思想习惯加以整理做成系统的说明，遂成"亚里士多德的名学"（Aristotelian logic）。这样的名学支配了西方人（广义的）数千年。

在张东荪（1995：334-349）看来，汉语缺乏产生西方哲学意义上的形而上学思辨所必需的结构特征。具体来说，汉语没有词尾变化，主语和谓语不能清楚地分别开，而这对于中国思想的影响表现在四个方面：第一，主语不分明导致中国人没有"主体"（subject）的观念；第二，主语不分明导致谓语亦不成立；第三，由于没有词尾变化，以至于没有时态与语态等语格；第四，没有逻辑上的"辞句"（proposition）。

那么既然西方哲学的思辨性取向非常自然地与语言形式化特征密切联系在了一起，而汉语没有这样的特征，我们能否判断说西方形而上学意义上的理性思辨不可能在汉语土壤中诞生呢？

2.2 汉语言与中国哲学的思辨之路

关于汉语和西方语言的根本差别，王力先生在谈到汉语主语省略现象时曾这样说："就句子的结构而论，西洋语言是法治的，中国语言是人治的。法治的不管主语用得着用不着，总要呆板地要求句子形式的一律；人治的用得着就用，用不着就不用，只要能使对话人听懂说话人的意思，就算了。"（王力，1984：53）这意思很清楚，汉语不是以句法为中心的语言，而是以语义为中心的语言。上一节所论及的对于西方形而上学思辨理性的产生与发展起了关键作用的语言特征，恰恰是中国传统哲学发端之时的先秦古汉语所缺乏的。

其一，先秦古汉语没有作为系词使用的"是"，更遑论集系词、存在语义、断真功能于一体的"是"。语言学家王力（2000：378）指出："在先秦的史料中，肯定的句子，主格与表明语之间没有系词。"不仅那时候的汉语没有系词"是"，即便是在现代汉语中，作为系词的"是"也不表示存在。中国传统哲学没有经由"是"而进入形而上学思辨的语言条件。

其二，古汉语没有词素，因而也谈不上词素变化。古汉语的名词、动词、形容词在形式上没有任何区别。此外，单复数、抽象名词与具体名词、可数与不可数等词汇的句法特征完全缺乏。"道听途说"与"道不可言"两句中的"道"，一形而下，指具体事物，一形而上，指十分抽象的玄学概念，却无一丝一毫语言形式的区分。故有人说这种语言特征不利于中国哲学家像西方哲学家那样自然地知觉到语言形式所呈现的"一"与"多"的概念性问题，因而不具有从语言形式中抽象出"共相"并加以形而上学反思的动机（Hansen，1983：32-42）。

其三，古汉语的主语在形式上并不完整、明晰。张东荪（1995：334-349）指出，古汉语由于没有词尾变化，因而主语和谓语不能清楚地分别开，而这对于中国思想有根本的影响：因为主语不分明，中国人没有"主体"的观念，因此没有产生明确的逻辑上的命题。

可见，导致西方哲学本体论形而上思辨的重要语言形态因素，在古汉语中都不存在或者形式上不完整。古汉语缺乏产生出西方哲学那样的元范畴化概念、命题的语言条件。西方哲学的核心学科本体论（Ontology），在"being as being"的意义上，的确无法诞生于古汉语语言土壤之中。

但是，逻辑语言不也是从日常语言中抽象脱胎出来的吗？语言学家霍凯特（Hockett，2002：286）说："我们称之为逻辑和数学的这些准语言系统来源于语言的语法核心。……逻辑和数学的主要特征在很大程度上就是许多语言或大多数语言的语法核心所共同具有的特征：从亚里士多德到现在，逻辑学的历史只不过是不断舍弃一种具体语言的过分专门的特征而已。"

这意味着，即使我们只从形式入手研究逻辑语言问题，结果还是发现，逻辑语言的源头是自然语言。我们今天所讨论的数理逻辑等与古人所讨论的语言逻辑在思想实质上是一样的，只不过我们讨论的纯粹逻辑经过历史发展，已经舍弃了与具体语言联系的特征而已。因此，我们恐怕不能因为古汉语缺乏语形，或者古代哲人没有像亚里士多德那样把逻辑符号化、形式化，就断定中国古代哲学中没有对语言意义之精确性的追究。

表面上看，这种无形式区分的语言特性的确不利于分析性思维的出现。然而，我却认为，这一特性对于催生形而上学理性思辨有着独特的价值。

汉语不重句法形式，却有独一无二的"名"的意合特征。汉语的"名"不仅限于名词，而且涵盖了动词、形容词等一切语言之"名"。世上万事万物皆以"名"的语言方式出场于我们的思想；而物与物的关系、物的特性等亦复如是。这一情形直接导致两个问题：

第一，既然人只能通过语言来把握世界与人生，那么语言之"名"与客观之"实"之间到底有何种关系，"名"到底能否使人准确地认识、理解"实"？

第二，"名"既可指云实在之物，也可指云非实在之义（如形容词用来指云特性），那么显然有的意义是"实"而有的则是"虚"，即同一个"名"，其意义可以有也可以没有本体地位，那么"名"的意义的依据到底是什么？

不难看出，如果中国古代哲学家以"名"的意义作为元范畴化认知的核心，即以汉语"名"为中心的特征，追问"名"的意义到底该如何确定，这一追问最终必将导致"名"的意义的本体论依据的反思，同样产生关于"是"之为"是"的思辨。如前所述，公孙龙的作品非常明显地提出了汉语语言特色的"是"与"真"的问题。汉语的结构特征完全不是中国传统思想中诞生出形而上学哲学思辨的障碍。

中国哲学史上第一场大辩论就是著名的"名实之辩"，辩论的中心就是"名"与"实"、"言"与"行"的关系。导致这场大辩论的，便是中国第一位哲学家孔子的"正名"论。奈依（Nye）曾编辑了一本《语言哲学：宏大的问题》的西方语言哲学文集。但是，在这本书的"总论"一开始，奈依（Nye，1998：ix-x）却首先引用了孔子的《论语·子路》中关于"正名"的那一段著名的论述，并指出：孔子的言论提出了一个根本性问题，即语言对于人的重要性问题；因为什么是"意义"、什么是"理性"、什么是"真理"是西方哲学从古希腊开始就一直不懈追问的问题。西方哲学思想，特别是形式逻辑产生的东西，才在对人说话必须要有意义、有理性、符合其真的追问中产生出来。中国古代思想家从一开始就对语言问题给予自觉的、高度的关注，并从语义的角度提出了带根本性的问题，这一事实由此可见一斑。

中国传统哲学关注的对象主要是人伦纲常、道德秩序、社会实践等，虽然也有求知（例如墨家的经验主义科学思想），但与以古希腊哲学为源头的西方哲学求知识之为真的取向相比，所提出的问题是以入世为指向的，旨趣迥异。但是，中国传统哲学一开始没有提出知识之为真的问题，并不等于后来也不会出现对此问题的追问。如果哲学确实发源于语言意义的割裂式反思，那么从逻辑上说，中国思想家同样可以通过对语言意义的割裂式反思催生自己的形而上哲学。虽然汉语缺乏西方语言那样的形式化句法特征，中国思想家没有条件从句法的视角进入哲学思辨，但是汉语的特征也给他们提供了概念元范畴化认知的另一独特路径：从对"名"的意义的反思来考察人的思想。中国古代思想史上第一场大辩论就是关于语言与实在关系的"名实之辩"，这绝非偶然。

后面我们将会看到，正是因为各家各派在名与实问题上各自使用不同的概念，因而辩论无法分出胜负或者取得一致。要进行有意义的辩论，必须首先反思什么是"名"，什么又是"实"。这就是先秦名家以"专决于名"的态势登上辩论舞台的理据。

无论是以客观世界为思考对象，还是以道德伦理等价值问题为思考对象，人的思考都必须以语言概念以及由语言概念构成的命题来进行。离开了承载概念意义的语词，离开了表达命题判断的语句，人的思想断无可能。既然如此，人总会或迟或早开始对语言问题本身进行反思。中国传统哲学发展中，也一定会有人努力对自己所使用的语言、语言表达的意义本身进行思考，在语言中盘旋出理性的思想。道理非常简单：只有弄清楚了我们所用的词、所说的话到底有什么意义，这些意义的本质到底是什么，我们才能够在牢靠的基础上进一步追问世界与人生到底意味着什么，我们才能保证自己对世界与人生的认识和把握是正确的。

2.3 "使用"与"提及"——语言哲学分析技术的启发

2.3.1 古汉语标点符号的缺失与"使用"和"提及"的区分

最早促使我思考名家解释方式的，是现代语言哲学的分析工具之一——"使用"（use）与"提及"（mention）的区分。先秦古汉语的特征之一就是其书面语没有标点符号。这为名家的语言哲学分析造成了一定障碍。为了克服语言的这一不便之处，先秦名家必须也只能利用汉语的特点来限定自己论辩的范围，并表明自己的思想。若此为真，那么首先，把名家命题理解为"诡辩"事实上是没有弄清楚名家论辩的语言哲学层面；其次，名家的命题很可能就是在"使用"与"提及"无法区分的语言条件下，从汉语语言特点出发所进行的语言哲学思辨；第三，一些目前被认为"无解"的命题很有可能就是他们关于自己的论辩范围的解释性划定或是他们的语言分析方式。于是，本书打算从"使用"与"提及"入手来考察他们的命题，但本书不限于西方语言哲学对"使用"与"提及"的现有区分，而是力图给出一个自己的新解释。

"使用"与"提及"的区分在语言哲学中有非常重要的本体论区别意义。简言之，我们"使用"一个语词来指称一个对象，但"提及"一个语词则与对象无关，而是指称语词本身。（详细论述可参见蒯因的《语词和对象》一书。）这很好理解。当我们说"蟑螂是虫"时，句中的"蟑螂"指的就是蟑螂这种昆虫。这个句子表达的命题意义可以用任何一种语言来表达，且同样为真（如：英文"A cockroach is an insect"等）。但是，如果我们不是使用而是提及"蟑螂"这一语词，那么同样的意思能否进行跨语言的翻译并且保持其真值就很难说了。当我们说"'蟑螂'是个双声叠韵词"这句话的时候，其中的"蟑螂"不是指一种害虫，而指该语词本身，因为我们旨在考察"蟑螂"这个词本身的结构和语音特征。这时我们该如何将之翻译成英文，并且使之为真？从字面层面看，肯定不可译，即使硬译出来也无法让人理解（"'Cockroach' is a two-character vowel-rhyming word"是什么含义啊），此英文句也不可能为真。我们充其量可以通过汉语拼音和英文近似词语混合的方式进行某种"翻译"；或许再加上注脚解释，我们才可以让英语人士弄懂汉语结构，并理解这个语句，但这实际上也完全是在谈论语言，而与蟑螂是否存在、是否昆虫等毫无关系了。

可见，使用与提及的确是很要紧的区分。一个名词出现在句中，加了引号即是被提及，不加引号则是被使用；前者指称的是该语词本身，而后者则指称一个对象。这个区分对于我们解读先秦名家的文本有重要的思想启发意义：引号的加与不加或许还可以用来区分出语句命题意义的经验事实层面和语言反思层面！

西方语言哲学的这一分析技术，只可用于谈论一个对象与提及一个语词的区分。但如果我们把这个区分加以发挥，即一个名称加上引号之后不一定仅仅限于提及这个名称，而是更进一步从语言意义的层面对名称所代表的概念进行反思，那么我们极有可能将之应用于先秦名家思想的理解，而且这种理解极有可能是合情合理的。

在这一启发之下，我的思考是这样的。先秦名家很可能已经明确提出了关于经验与语义两个不同反思层面的命题意义的区分。他们之所以提出那些十分怪异的命题，目的正是在于告诉人们他们所做的不是关于客观实在，而是关于语言概念意义问题的反思。他们只能以这种"诡辩"命题的方式来突出他们在语言中反思、盘旋的语言哲学思想特征，其根本原因在于古汉语不仅仅如前所述没有任何形式化句法特征，甚至连标点符号都没有。当时的人们无法像现代汉语使用者那样凭借引号来判定一个名称到底是在指称一个对象，还是在指称名称自身。例如："基因是决定生物性状的密码"和"'基因'是个近乎完美的音译词"。当我们看到前面一句时，我们判断其真假主要的方法就是寻找事实依据；而当我们看到后面一句话时，肯定知道这句话没有任何事实能够用来判定其真假，因为它说的是这个语词本身，而不是关于世界上任何对象的任何事实。古汉语没有标点符号，给先秦时代的人们带来了很大的困难。

于是我们完全可以设想：假如先秦名家需要在论辩中着重说明他们自己的思想是在语言中的盘旋，是关于语言概念意义本身的反思，而不是关于经验事实的陈述，那么在古汉语缺乏标点符号的条件下，他们该怎么办？又能怎么办？举个例说吧。先秦名家若要表达这样的命题："山存在，但山的意义并不实际存在，我们所谈论的'山'并不是实实在在的山，而是作为语词意义的'山'"，那么他们可能采用的手段是什么？

如果我们把现代语言哲学的"使用"与"提及"的区分加以发挥，即先秦名家"使用"语词是为了指称一个实在对象，而"提及"一个语词则是为了反思该语词本身的概念意义，那么我们可以获得关于名家命题解释的启发：先秦名家以语句表达的方式，把自己的论辩范围规定在语言意义之内。也就是说，他们在论辩中，需要用语句来说明，相互辩论的对象不是客观实在之物，而是在语言意义当中进行追问：意义是哪儿来的？有什么依据？如何才能正确地把握语词的意义？一旦这样理解，先秦名家的语言哲学思想昭然若揭，他们的理性主义精神一下子就呈现在我们面前。

2.3.2 反思"x出口"命题

那么，名家有没有留下线索使本书的设想得以立足呢？我认为是有的。一个典型例子就是先秦名家辩者的"山出口"命题，这是当代哲学家认为"无解"的命题（如：胡适，2000：171；任继愈，1983：495；陈鼓应，1983：899，等）。于是，有人认为这是混淆语言概念的"悖论"（沈有鼎，1992：210），或者认为这是"说异为同"（即把不同的东西说成相同的东西）（张岱年，2005：163），如此等等。这说明，关于这个命题的意思，我们还需要考察。说这是科学命题，那么名家可能是在讨论山是由火山口喷发而形成的吗？如果是，那么火山不也是山吗？

为何必须"出口"？若说是"悖论"，那么这个命题与什么逻辑定理矛盾，是怎么构成悖论的？而要说这是"说异为同"，那么名家把山与什么说成是相同的？这显然说不通。

其实，学者们早已注意到，唐代的僧人成玄英已经将这个命题的含义解释为"山名出自人口"。沈有鼎在说这是个悖论之前，也曾这样说："我说'山'时，不是在发出没有意义的声音，它是有意义的声音（在本例意指实在的山），而出自我口。"但即使这样说了，他还是认为这是个悖论；至于为什么是悖论，他则没有说。叶锦明（2003：195）在评论沈有鼎的观点时提出"如果'山出口'一条的意思就是'山'这个字的发音由口而出，那么此条就是混淆了语言层次，属于范畴错误。照现代的学术习惯，此条当写成"'山'出口"。这就是我想说的话了，但是叶锦明却没有说明该不该这样加引号改写，为什么要加引号改写。我认为，必须这样改写，只有这样改写我们才能真正由此切入，完整地说明先秦名家的语言哲学思想。

假如先秦时代的古汉语有标点符号，那么我想名家人士将会直接利用，从而避免人们将他们的语言意义反思命题混同于经验事实命题。而由于标点符号的缺乏，名家没有引号这一关键的语言技术资源可资利用，他们只能用语句表达的方式，告诉自己的论辩对手，论辩的层面是出自人口的名称本身的概念意义，而不是实在的对象！

这一视角可以从荀子对名家的攻击中得到一定佐证。

荀子说"'山渊平'，'天地比'，'齐秦袭'，'入乎耳，出乎口'，'钩有须'，'卵有毛'，是说之难持者也，而惠施、邓析能之"（《荀子·不苟》），又说"君子之学也，入乎耳，着乎心，……小人之学也，入乎耳，出乎口"（《荀子·劝学》）。

显然"出乎口"的确是名家反复强调的命题。不过荀子认为，正人君子获得的知识命题是必须牢记于心、成为思想的一部分的，而名家之流的"知识"命题只不过是为了过过口瘾，是无聊的有害的语言游戏而已。

这当然是荀子的误解，他根本没有弄懂语言概念与经验事实两个完全不同层面意义反思的价值，但是他把名家辩者们的"入乎耳，出乎口"命题与其他命题并列，说明"出乎口"是先秦名家在辩论中常见的、让人时时注意到的命题。这不难解释，因为他们总是力图把自己的论辩范围限制在语言概念意义的层面上，要求自己的对手注意，辩论所涉及的是"出乎口"的名称的概念性意义，而不是实在存在着的具体对象，不能将语言意义与经验事实层面混淆起来！什么东西只是在论辩中

"入乎耳，出乎口"？当然不是实实在在的物体，只能是关于物体的语言言说。

这就可以理解"山出口"命题了。我认为成玄英的解释是对的，也赞同叶锦明提出的"'山'出口"之改写。这是名家在论辩中明确声明自己的命题属于语义分析并且命题句中的语词是"提及"性使用的一个技术手段。庄子碰巧记录下了"山出口"命题，自鸣得意地向人们证明名家命题属于无稽之谈：山就是山，是实实在在存在着的，怎么可能从人口中蹦出来？由于"入乎耳，出乎口"是名家常见的提醒，他们极有可能还说过"火出口、马出口、白出口、坚出口、色出口"等命题来讨论某一名称，他们可能以此方式来界定过论域范围。而这恰恰是庄子、荀子们没有弄清楚的。

因此，我认为"山出口"这个命题对于理解先秦名家的"诡辩"命题非常关键，这是一个十分难得的历史记录，是认识和解释名家命题的宝贵线索。本书对公孙龙以及其他名家辩者的"诡辩"命题的解释和翻译皆基于这一关键线索。名家向人们展示的思想是，山固然是客观存在，但如果没有语言，则山不可能被命名为"山"；人们对一个对象的意义的把握并不等于那个对象本身，因为一个名称的概念意义可以脱离其所指的客观对象。客观对象本然地存在着，它们自身并不存在真与假、正确与错误的问题，但作为人的认知理解的概念意义却肯定存在着真与假、对与错的问题，而这正是"正名"问题之所以被提出的根本原因！于是，"正名"并不一定等于名称与实在的符合，名称的意义具有自身的认知逻辑规定性，因此正名理当以确定这种认知逻辑规定性为核心要点。

可不要忽视这些"'x'出口"！把这些"'x'出口"中的"x"替换为"火、马、白、坚、色"等名称，我们似乎就可以窥见先秦名家到底要说什么。

公孙龙最著名的诡辩命题不就是"白马非马""离坚白"吗？那么如果他不是在说客观世界中实在存在的白马不是马，而是强调说"'白'出口""'马'出口""'坚'出口""'白'出口"，因而它们不等于客观世界的白色、马、坚硬性，我们不是能很明显地看出他的思想是真正理性主义的语言意义的思辨吗？道理再明显不过了：既然"马"是人用语言表达的概念，而"马"这个名称又能够指称实际存在的马，也就是说"马"的意义具有客观实在之物作为其本体论依据，那么"白"和"坚"之类的名称理当也能够指称某种存在的对象，以使得它们的意义有确实的本体论依据。马作为具体的个体事物，那么"白"之类的形容词作为名称是不是也应该以实际存在的白色本身作为其意义本体呢？然而，我们又无法找到不是任何事物属性的白自体（whiteness-in-itself），那么"白"的意义依据如何确定？亚里士多德说具体的个体才是真实的存在，而它们的属性（颜色、坚硬性等）则没有独立的存在，只是"依附性存在"。但如果它们只有依附性存在，人们又如何确定其本质定义呢？公孙龙等思想家反思的正是这样性质的问题，即货真价实的本体论形而上学问题！

以此视角来认识名家命题，我们恍然大悟：他们真的是在语言中盘旋着思想，力图从语义确定性、正确性依据的反思中认识人关于世界到底把握了什么样的知识。由此来看待惠施的"天与地卑、山与泽平"命题，我们可以发现，这是他在形容词语义中的哲学盘旋，所追问的是名称意义的可靠性本体论依据。汉语没有词尾变化，因而形容词与名词一样，都是以无差别的形式作为名而使用的。那么一个很自然的追问就是："天、地、山、泽"等名称的意义有具体实在之物作为其来源和依据，那么"卑、平"之类的名称，其意义的来源和依据又在哪儿？是否真的存在着"卑自体、平自体"之类的东西？所以，我认为，以前关于这个命题的解释（即这是惠施的"合同异"相对主义思想的体现，他说的是高、低、平与不平是相对的）是不正确的，最起码这种解释与前述惠施与庄子辩论中体现出的强烈的理性主义思想倾向严重地不吻合。

同理，当先秦名家辩者提出"白狗黑"命题的时候，他们所说的并非世界上白色的狗都是黑色的。这样说没有意义，不是有价值的思想。他们实际上说的是"'白'出口"中的"白"是命名颜色的词，而"'黑'也出口"中的"黑"也是命名颜色的词。于是由于颜色等于颜色，那么我们是否能说"白"的意义与"黑"的意义等同，具有同样一个本体作为依据呢？这事实上问及"颜色存在吗""颜色本身是什么颜色"这样的形而上学问题。我们完全有理由相信先秦名家曾经说过"色出口"命题！遗憾的是，记录他们命题的书被毁掉了，而碰巧记录下名家命题的庄子、荀子等人却没有能够理解名家的思想实质。

3. 名家的理性主义思想出现的缘由

先秦名家对语言意义本身的反思是先秦"名实之辩"的深入发展。这个话题必定要涉及最主要的先秦思想流派，即儒、道、墨（此外还有法家、阴阳家等，但他们的主要思想中对语言与实在的问题并无更独特的见解，故略去）。需要马上说明，这几个流派均有自己的体系，且每一个都可以写出专著论之，绝非本书寥寥数语可以说明白的。好在本书的任务不是阐释各家各派，不用全面、深入论述他们的思想。我仅仅想通过他们在语言问题上所持的基本立场和观点，看看先秦名家为什么要提出"名本身"的问题来，由此反衬先秦名家的语言哲学特质。

关于名家的思想倾向，李贤中（2011，2012）认为他们具有相当的理性自觉，其理性的反思聚焦于"认识"和"表达"的问题。李贤中指出，先秦名家"有独树一帜的思考形态，于当时既有的学说中发掘新的问题，发展不同的探讨方式，建构思辨性的名实思想，如此应变创新的求知态度，拓展了该时代的思想领域，不可不谓当时思想上的突破与进步"（李贤中，2012：130）。我认为这一评论是很到位的，因为它指出了名家独树一帜的思想创新，而这一思想创新又是以思辨性为根本特征的。

3.1 孔子的"正名"论

长达百年的中国历史上首次思想大辩论，即先秦"名实之辩"由孔子发起。孔子首先提出了"正名"的主张："名不正，则言不顺；言不顺，则事不成；事不成，则礼乐不兴；礼乐不兴，则刑罚不中；刑罚不中，则民无所措手足。"（《论语·子路》）简言之，孔子把当时的社会动荡归因于语言交流的障碍以及由此导致的思想混乱。名称与实际脱节了，语言交流混乱了，思想无法相互理解了，还怎么谈得上社会秩序、伦理道德？这里，孔子给予了语言以极重要的地位，把"名"看作是一切社会秩序赖以确立的基础。这引发了先秦哲学的"名实之辩"，先秦哲学各家各派全都被卷入了这场哲学思想大辩论。

但孔子虽然提出"正名"，却并非以反思语言意义而追问认识的真理为取向。

首先，孔子的"正名"主要是正名分，即所谓"君君、臣臣、父父、子子"（《颜渊》）。"正名"主要是个社会秩序问题，是道德关怀而不是语言分析。虽然他也要求人们重视语言、丰富语言（如：他提出要"多识于鸟兽草木之名"），且极其关注名称的正确指称（如：他认为当时的酒具"觚"已经不具备先王时代的外形特征，不能再被称为"觚"，因为名不副实了），但是从孔子的整个思想倾向看，其关注中心是"克己复礼"之"仁"。他把恢复过去的社会制度、伦理道德视为己任，并无通过语言分析以求意义之为真的冲动。

其次，孔子的"正名"是要求"实"符合"名"的规范，即语词意义的正确性应当以先王时代的"实"为标准，因为那个标准表达了名称所指对象的实质。而孔子所处的时代，人们虽然沿用过去先王制定的名称，但其所指已经不是先王规定的"实"，而是背离了"实"的本质，因而变得混乱不堪，使得人们交流出现障碍，直至手足无措，无所适从，整个社会失范，纲常崩溃。所以孔子才要求"名"的意义以先王规定的"实"为依据：先王时代的"实"作为一种意义标准，是不可改变的。如果要说孔子的"正名"要求算是一种语言哲学的话，那么显然他的倾向是先验论的。他的这种名实观有点儿像柏拉图借苏格拉底之口所提出的"语言立法者"观点，即古代某先贤拥有洞悉一切事物本质的本事，因而对用哪个名称来标签哪个事物做出了正确的规定，让后人能够正确地用语言对世界进行表达。

但两者的思想观点也仅仅是有点儿像而已。柏拉图的取向是求真的理性思辨，所提出的是关于语义理论是哲学"本质论"（或语言学"命名论"）。孔子的取向则是恢复理想的社会秩序的身体力行式实践，他关于名实关系的思想是以伦理道德、政治秩序的结构建立为指向的。就连作为其核心思想范畴的"仁"，孔子也没有明确提出其定义，而是以种种描述性陈述来强调行为实践，如"刚毅木讷近乎仁""仁者乐山……仁者静……仁者寿""仁远乎哉？我欲仁，斯仁至矣"（《论语》），等等。可以确定的是，孔子既没有从逻辑上也没有从经验上说明"仁"的内涵。不仅如此，即便是我们承认这些语句就是关于如何成"仁"的"限定性描述语"，我们也不知道到底如何才能"乐山"，怎样做才算是"刚毅木讷"，什么才是"近乎""仁"，"近乎"毕竟不等于"是"！这样的陈述甚至连对行为的指导价值都是模糊的、可疑的。孔子思想并非旨在求知识之为真，其取向与古希腊哲学家在思想气质上相去甚远。

3.2 荀子的"正名"论

儒家的另一代表人物荀子则提出了语言"约定俗成"论："名无固宜，约之以命，约定俗成谓之宜，异于约则谓之不宜。名无固实，约之以命实，约定俗成，谓之实名。"（《荀子·正名》）不仅如此，荀子指出，人靠感官所获得的对外部事物的感受是有可能不准确的，因此这些感受需要经过"心征"（人脑的思维加工）来进行分析和辨别，然后才能使人真正掌握事物的异同。荀子超越了孔子，他力图为"正名"寻找认识论依据。

荀子虽然也抱怨"今圣王没，名守慢，奇辞起，名实乱，是非之形不明"，要求"正名"，但他提出的观点是"制名以指实"（《荀子·正名》）。他说得很明白：要制定不同的名称来指云不同的事物。他不是要求矫正"实"，使"实"符合于"名"，而是要制定"名"来描述"实"。这与孔子的"正名"的方向完全不同。从他对"共名"和"别名"的讨论中可看出这一点。他说：

> 故万物虽众，有时而欲无举之，故谓之物；物也者，大共名也。推而共之，共则有共，至于无共然后止。有时而欲偏举之，故谓之鸟兽。鸟兽也者，大别名也。推而别之，别则有别，至于无别然后至。……物有同状

而异所者，有异状而同所者，可别也。状同而为异所者，虽可合，谓之二实。状变而实无别而为异者，谓之化。有化而无别，谓之一实。此事之所以稽实定数也。此制名之枢要也。（《荀子·正名》）

显然，荀子不仅注意到了名称概念的层级性，而且提出要依据事物的实际状况和特征来定名；有时候同一个名可能指不同的实，而有时候不同的名却都指同一个实。因此，必须考察具体事物的实际状况，才能够确定名称是否恰当。这是很重要的思想，它说明在荀子的"正名"思想中，"实"已不仅仅是先王规定的意义标准，而且包括客观实在。这在认识论意义上占有很重要的地位，可能是因为荀子受到了墨家经验主义哲学思想的影响。

荀子在"正名"的目的上，跟孔子是一样的。他在《正名篇》中说"王者之制名，名定而实辨，道行而志通，则慎率民而一焉"，又说"制名以指实，上以明贵贱，下以辨同异"。这就是说，君主制定名称来确定各人的名分；名分确定之后，人的地位、等级就分明了，社会道德规范就可以施行，君主也就可以使人民服从于自己的意志而一统天下了。可见，在目的上，荀子同孔子一样，所关注的仍然是社会秩序和伦理道德，本质上仍然是道德行为实用主义，然而在方法及范围上，荀子与孔子却并不完全相同。

很遗憾，荀子并没有再进一步发挥他的"心征"说，对作为语言认知理据的"实"作为知识的普遍性、必然性进行分析性追问。荀子之所以就此止步，是因为其语言哲学思想的基本取向与孔子是一致的："正名"的目的主要在于定名分、明高低尊卑之分，以恢复社会秩序，确立君主的一统天下。因此，他虽然在制名的机制、原则等问题上提出了科学的观点，具有一定的经验实证精神，但却强调制名的终极权力应该交给君主。其思想中这种混合了经验论与先验论而产生的矛盾性说明他那些科学的认识论观点缺乏理性反思基础，因而无法深入下去。

3.3 老子的"无名"论

儒家要"正名"，道家却提出"无名"。老子《道德经》开篇第一句话就是"道可道非常道；名可名非常名"（第一章）。

与孔子让"实"来符合"名"相反，老子认为"物"是可以"名"的，但是"名"的意义应该顺应物之"道"，也就是事物赖以存在、变化的某种本质性或规律性的东西。人靠"名"来对"物"进行认识、言说。然而，"名"却不是万事万物本来就有的，是人在用"名"来言说世界，而这个"名"的意义却只能是"道"

的体现。既然如此，"正名"是行不通的；人为的"正名"所正的只能是具体事物的"名"，而体现在这些"名"中的"道"的意义，即统摄这些"名"所指之物的存在和变化的终极意义却是语言所无法"正"的。人们说话与做事一样，只能顺应"道"，并在顺应中领悟"道"的本然意义。

按我的理解，老子的"道"是一个高度抽象的形而上学概念，但却无法定义，因为我们无论如何不能说"道"是什么。一旦使用"道是……"的句型来言说"道"，那我们等于将"道"贬低成一个语言所"名"的普通一物，而作为普通一物，它又必须由"道"而生，顺"道"而变。这将使我们陷入逻辑矛盾：作为万物生长变化依据的"道"不是万物生长依据的"道"。所以，为了避免这一逻辑矛盾，老子说"道可道，非常道"。在对"道"进行分析性探究方面，语言是无能为力的，这是道家语言哲学思想消极的一面。

按照老子的观点，"正名"是不可能的。这并不是说老子提出了理论来否定孔子的正名要求和理论。毕竟老子所谈的"实"与孔子所谈的"实"不是同一个层面的东西；前者是形而上的，而后者则是形而下的。不过，在客观上，老子的思想对孔子正名的理论构成了否定。老子认为，意义的终极依据不在于物，而在于道。名称当然可以用来言说具体事物，比如把杯子叫作"杯子"，狗叫作"狗"或"犬"等，但是杯子之所以是杯子因而被叫作"杯子"，狗之所以是狗因而被叫作"狗"，其意义却由"道"所规定。而"道"由于是世界的终极道理、终极依据，本身却不可言说，即所谓"名可名非常名"。真正的意义在"无名"；既然"无名"，那又有何"名"可正？客观地看，老子的"无名"思想由此而解构了孔子的"正名"。

老子的"道"是一切事物形而上的本源和依据，万物由此而生，顺此而变，"道"即是世界的终极道理。这在精神上与本章前面所提到的赫拉克利特提出的"Logos"很相似："道"与"Logos"都是万事万物的形而上本原，也都涉及人的语言这个根本性问题。这是老子和赫拉克利特各自对中西方哲学的伟大贡献。两者之间不同的是，赫拉克利特的"Logos"是可言说的，它引起了西方哲学以语言反思切入，对世界的道理、人的认识进行分析性追问；而老子的"道"则不可言说，割裂了"言"与"意"，阻塞了人通过语言分析反思把握世界、认识道理的道路。这是很自然的发展。赫拉克利特的"Logos"所代表的客观世界之道理就在语言之中，它需要人们通过思想去理解、把握，从而获得对世界的理性认识。"Logos"本身意味着言语与思想的根本同一性，人可以并且只能凭借语言来思考，来把握真知。而老子的"道"却只能领悟，无法用语言表达出来，更不用说清晰地表达出来了。这或许能够解释著名的李约瑟难题：中国古代科学技术成就辉煌，为何现代科学无一诞生于中国？科学需要的是分析性思维，科学的定义、疑问、假设、结论等需要清晰的语言来表达，而"道"的思维重领悟、整体，不利于分析性思辨模式的产生。

3.4　庄子的"言不尽意"论

庄子的语言哲学思想与老子一脉相承。在"言"与"意"之间，庄子更着重意义，而不是语言本身。庄子说："言者所以在意，得意而妄言。"（《外物》）在庄子那里，语言与意义是可分离的。说话总是要表达意义的，一旦获得了意义，语言本身便不重要了。在他看来，"得意"虽必须通过语言，但意义却不在语言中，"可以言论者，物之粗也；可以意致者，物之精也；言之所不能论，意之所不能察致者，不期精粗焉"（《庄子·秋水》）。可以用语言直接表达的，仅仅是事物现象而已，但事物的本质却只能去意会。

但是，庄子并未像韩东晖（2001）所说的那样，把语言视为"糟粕"。事实上，庄子对语言有深刻的认识。庄子认为语言是用来指实的符号："名者，实之宾也"（《庄子·逍遥游》）；意即是主，而名称是宾，宾随其主，名称用来描述意义。他指出，名称与事物没有必然联系，"道行之而成，物谓之而然"（《庄子·齐物论》）；"昔者子呼我牛也而谓之牛；呼我马也而谓之马"（《庄子·天道》）。这不仅说明庄子已经有了语言约定论思想，而且说明他反对像孔子那样把名称的作用理想化。事物本身并没有名称，事物的名称完全是人用语言所说而成的。这意味着，语言是人命名、把握事物的工具。其思想即使按照当代语言学或符号学的观点来看，也是正确的。

不过，由于庄子在知识问题上持有相对主义或不可知论，其正确的语言观点并不成体系，没有深入下去。这一点从庄子的另一个论述，即著名的"轮扁斫轮"的故事中可看得更清楚。轮扁告诉桓公说古圣贤的书其实是糟粕，因为圣贤已死，他们所写的书的真正意义已经无法弄清楚了。轮扁以他自己斫轮的经历说："斫轮，徐则甘而不固，疾则苦而不入，不徐不疾，得之于手而应于心，口不能言，有数存乎其间。臣不能以喻臣之子，臣之子亦不能受之于臣，是以行年七十而老斫轮。古之人与其不可传也死矣，然则君之所读者，古人之糟粕已夫！"这意思是说，轮扁自己制造轮子的时候，斫轮的动作慢了就会松懈而不牢靠，而动作快了却又难以斫进木头；但这种技术体会他自己能够得心应手，把握住分寸，却不能用言语来传授给儿子，儿子也无法从自己这里学到这个技巧，所以他自己年至七十了还得亲自制作轮子。由此观之，古人写书的时候所体验到的那种意义，怎么能够通过语言传递呢？既然语言传递不了原意，古书就是糟粕了！这里，语言似乎只具有描述现象的功能，但是现象背后所必须依赖的那个让某个现象不得不如此的本质性的东西（也就是其"道"），却是语言无法描述的，只有通过用心领悟言外之意才能得到。

因此，庄子不赞成辩论。他说："夫道未始有封，言未始有常，为是而有畛也。"（《庄子·齐物论》）他认为真意只能整体领悟，因为"道"是一个整合的总体，不可进一步分析，无法通过辩论来说透彻。庄子接下来说："请言其畛：有左有右，有伦有义，有分有辩，有竞有争，此之谓八德。六合之外，圣人存而不论；六合之内，圣人论而不议。"（《庄子·齐物论》）谁是谁非的争议，必然有左右、伦理、等级、区别、辩论、异议、争执等，这些是"德"，即形而下的东西，而不是在言说"道"，即形而上的意义依据。"大道不称，大辩不言。"最深奥的真理是不可以命名来言说的，最有力的论辩是无需用言语的。名是虚的，实是玄的，正名是不可能的。

从庄子的言论中，我们发现他比老子更明确地指出了人类语言表达意义的局限性，同时也发现了庄子的相对主义和不可知论思想："道"并不在语言中，也不是任何东西，因而它不能被明确地分析和认识，每个人只能通过自己的体验来领悟。

3.5 墨家的经验主义"正名"立场

与儒家和道家语言哲学思想根本不同的是墨家的经验主义思想。

墨家肯定"名"的形而下功能："所以谓，名也。所谓，实也。"（《墨经·经说·上》）"有之实也，而后谓之；无之实也，则无谓也。"（《墨经·大取》）墨家认为，名的指称就是实在之物，而"实"是第一性的，"名"是第二性的，从属于实的。墨家的经验主义名实观与孔子的先验论名实观形成对立，也与道家的思想格格不入，因为墨家认为"名"是可以正的，名的意义就是其所指之实，而"实"不是像道家所说的那样在于玄之又玄、不可把握的"道"，也不是儒家所说的先验标准，而是客观实在之物。

墨家认为语言意义应当由客观实践来验证："效者，为之法也；所效者，所以为之法也。故中效，则是也；不中效，则非也，此效也。"（《墨经·小取》）这显示出墨家在"名"与"实"、"言"与"意"关系问题上的实证主义思想倾向。不过，墨家虽然着重科学实证，但他们没有对严格、精密、普遍适用的证明方法提出强烈要求（崔清田，2004：158）。这个指责当然有道理，墨家毕竟还不能像近代科学家那样提出一整套研究的程序。他们的着眼点在于人的知识来源于实践，其最大特点还是在于以实践检验来追求"实"之真实性。

有意思的是墨家和名家的论辩。谭戒甫（1983：63-75）曾列出表格，把包括"辩者二十一事"部分命题在内的名家言论与公孙龙的思想归入"形名家之学"类，而把主要由后期墨家命题构成的言论归入"名家之学"类，两相对照，旨在说明名家不等于形名家，两者的思想和命题完全不同，甚至矛盾。谭戒甫的"形名家"，在本书中，也就是名家，而他的名家在本书的框架中则应当是后期墨家。从谭戒甫所列出的大量矛盾命题来看，名、墨两家的思想的确是对立的：名家说"白马非马"（《公孙龙·白马论》），墨家则论证"白马，马也"（《墨经·小取》）等。但有一点十分重要：墨家关注的是经验之真，而名家关注的是理性之真。例如，名家说"'火'不热"（《庄子·天下》），其中"火"是作为语词表达的概念而不是现实中的现象；也就是说，"火"在这里是作为语词概念而讨论的，名家追问那个"不热"的"火"的概念意义；而墨家反驳说"火热，说在顿"（《墨经·经说·下》），又说"火，谓火热也，非以火之热我有，若视日"（《墨经·经说·下》）。墨家说的是客观实在中的火这个现象。名墨两家的"实"显然具有巨大差别。墨家的"实"就是指实在之物，是经验层面的概念；而名家的"实"，是语言概念，是理性层面的东西。

3.6　名家思想产生之必然

可见，先秦"名实之辩"中，各家各派对"名""实"问题都提出了自己的关于语言及其意义的理论，各执一词，争论激烈。那么"名"到底为何能够表达"实"？各家在"名"上并无多大差异，但是关于"实"则似乎说的不是同样的对象。如果"实"就是实实在在的具体事物，为什么不能直接用名称作为标签，为何有人认为名称作为标签，其意义却在另一个更一般的名称，并且最终只能在于不可言说的"道"那里？有人认为事物应当符合意义的先验标准（实），否则就不能用正确的名称来言说；而另一些人则认为事物就是事物，人只不过用语言词汇来模拟、刻画事物，因而语言的意义（"实"）就是事物。于是，问题出现了：我们所说、所辩论的"实"到底是什么？语言所表达的"实"是什么？如何才能正确地表达实在？这类问题必定有人注意到并且提出来，促使人们对人用语言把握的是什么，如何才是关于世界的真正知识这类根本性问题进行理性反思。这正是先秦名家所做的工作。

由这一点看，我不完全同意李贤中（2012：130）所说的"名家秉承正名思想的渊源，接受无名思想的转化，与立名思想相互詟应"的说法。名家的确是在力图正名，但是显然他们的思想与道家的无名思想旨趣南辕北辙，而与墨家思想虽相互訾议，却共有对真的追求。我认为正是由于孔子正名思想引发了众多的争议与辩论，语言、意义与认识问题凸显了出来，而要回答这类问题，非常有必要澄清"名实之辩"所涉及的基本概念，即"名"是什么，"实"又是什么。这是名家思想之所以产生的历史、思想理据。

"只有认识到语言是符号，语词有歧义，歧义有不同作用，必须分析所指的是什么，然后才有可能想得确切。"（金克木，2006：76）名家之所以开始对语言意义问题本身进行反思，是因为先秦哲学围绕"正名"的争论一定会导致哲学家对"名"之为名、"实"之为实的本质进行澄清。儒家"循名责实"，盯住名而追问实，强调先验的理想标准；道家提出"名可名，非常名"，盯住实而追问"道"，强调"道"不可言而须领悟的倾向最终却导致了求知意义上的消极性和相对主义；墨家"按实定名"，盯住实而追问名，力图以经验主义的立场来确定语言意义的正确性。由于他们各自的"名""实"意义并不完全同一，那么要达成一致或者争论出个结果是不可能的。辩论涉及的关键概念如此不一致，只可能导致无谓的争论，更糟糕的是导致思想的进一步混乱。于是在这种局面中，名家才会出现，提出"专决于名"，盯住名而追问名的意义本身，走上了理性主义思辨的语言哲学之路，尽管他们在中国历史上是昙花一现。

那么，先秦名家的思想为何昙花一现、一起即逝呢？

这与名家的思想与常识无涉，是一种关于语言意义本身的元语言反思（即一种高度抽象的哲学思辨）不被当时的广大受众所理解和接受有关，也与他们受到了儒家、道家等先秦哲学主流学派的歪曲和抨击有关。如前所述，荀子对名家大加抨击、谩骂。既然名家思想他看不惯也弄不懂，他干脆要求凭借政治权力，动用意识形态、学术、行政、法律等一切手段对名家的"邪说辟言"予以打击。荀子的思想专制主义倾向在此暴露无遗。但这也造成了名家名声不良，其思想后人无法解读的后果。杜国庠（1955：7-8）曾指出，《公孙龙子》一书不可能是后人的伪作，因为其内容一般人无法理解。杜国庠引用了宋濂的《诸子辨》对《公孙龙子》的评论："予尝取而读之，白马非马之喻，坚白异同之言，终不可解。……苟欲名实之正，亟火之。"对此，杜国庠说："自己读了不懂，恨不得赶快把人家的书烧掉，这是什么话！"荀子就是如此，他不懂名家的命题及其意义，却蛮横地要求"禁之以刑"。

荀子的学生韩非子继承了荀子的思想，的确制定了法律来禁名家思想。崔清田（1997：73）指出：对韩非子而言，"法既是立国之本，也是一切思想言行的最高准则，而抽象地讨论诸如'坚白'之类的问题，会使人们产生对法的无端猜测，从而动摇封建专制的政治统治"。如果分析性思维真的在人们的思想中生根，那么他们对封建专制肯定会提出质疑，因为分析性思维的本质特征就是追问。站在封建专制立场上的韩非子似乎对此有种本能的意识。然而这样一来，名家思想就难逃被消音的命运了。

4. 先秦名家是理性主义语言哲学家的依据

本书说名家是"理性主义语言哲学家"，就有必要先阐明一下这个词的含义。严格意义上讲，"理性主义"一词指称笛卡儿等人以降的认识论哲学思想传统，即真正的知识只应当是运用人的理性而获得，知识的基础不能建立在不可靠的感觉资料之上。我不是在这个严格意义上使用这个词的，因为这种传统在中国历史上不存在。关于名家，我这里用"理性主义"来讨论，其含义是名家那种力图通过诉诸理性而不是通过实践经验或某种神秘感悟来确定语言意义的思想倾向。中国哲学一开始确实不是以求真知为取向的，通过分析获得"真理"的问题也从未被提上中国传统哲学的议事日程，但如我们前面的讨论所见，先秦名家等哲学家最终还是走上了以分析思辨为特征的理性主义思想之路。正是在先秦的"名实之辩"中，名家登上了舞台，先是为了澄清辩论的基本概念，然后在此过程中形成了他们自己关于语言意义的理性主义思想。

如前所述，"语言哲学"在严格意义上讲，指的是20世纪西方哲学的研究潮流，即"语言哲学力图理解语言的本质以及语言与说话人，他们的思想以及世界之间的关系。……这不仅仅包括哲学家们对语言问题的兴趣大幅度提高，而且是以语言分析的方式来重塑千百年来的哲学问题"（Baghramian，1999：Introduction）。这里使用"语言哲学家"一词来言说公孙龙和先秦名家显然不可能是在这个严格意义上进行的。不过，从广义来讲，一个思想家如果是从语言和语言的意义方面进行反思，进而涉及人与世界的关系、人的认识，他所提出的问题是语言意义是哪儿来的、依据是什么、意义的本质是什么、如何保证语义的正确性、人用语言所把握的知识到底具有什么性质等根本性问题，那么这个思想家应当算作语言哲学家。我是在这样一个广义范围内使用"语言哲学家"一词的。

除前述的理据之外，我把名家视为"理性主义语言哲学家"还有如下三个文本依据。

4.1 依据一

首先从所谓"别墨"谈起。也许在不少命题上，名家与墨家有相近、相似的陈述，也都关注名称、实在等，于是谭戒甫等学者视名家为"别墨"，即跟正统墨家有些差别的一个墨家派别。

然而，我们从名、墨两家的论述来看，两者的基本哲学立场完全不同，不应视为一个学派。名、墨两家只有少数命题相同（如，名家说"飞鸟之景，未尝动也"，而墨家也说"景不徙，说在改为"，两者都认为"影子本身是不动的"），而多数命题则不同（如，名家认为物质无限可分，而墨家则认为分到一定的程度，如到了端点，则无法再分了）。重要的是，两者的讨论层面是不一样的，一个说的是语言概念层面的问题，另一个则说的是经验实在层面的问题。如张岱年（2005：159）所说，名、墨两家"实际上是一言指，一言物，是就不同的观点立论的"。这个判断说到点子上了。"言指"，即不涉及实在存在的事物，而专注于指称本身的思辨，这在公孙龙的论辩体文章《白马论》《坚白论》和《通变论》中表现得十分明显，而他的《指物论》一文正是专门讨论什么是指称、指称与具体事物到底是何关系、应当如何区分这个很抽象的语言哲学问题的。

我认为，公孙龙几篇文章中的辩论对手其实就是墨家人物。理由有二：

第一，儒家、道家等学派的思想关注政治伦理、道德秩序、人生修养等问题，不关注知识以及知识如何得到正确性保证的问题。孔子、老子、荀子、庄子等思想家当然都谈到过语言的问题，但是他们对于追问什么是真知识似乎并无理论兴趣和完整表述。而老、庄等道家人物则明显有相对主义倾向。他们关注的话题或思想倾向在公孙龙的论辩体文章中并无任何体现。公孙龙和对手的辩论涉及的问题是，当一个人说到某个概念的时候其概念意义的性质到底是什么，如何确定其为真。孔、老、荀、庄都不是公孙龙的论辩对手。

第二，公孙龙与他的论辩对手之间的几场辩论明显地展示了两者在概念意义如何确定问题上的基本立场的对立，而这个对立显示了他们各自具有经验主义和理性主义的特征。公孙龙的论辩对手总是从经验层面，以符合论对公孙龙的命题进行攻击，即力图以名称的意义是否符合实际来确定名称使用的正确性；而公孙龙则针锋相对，从语言本身的层面，以概念的形而上学理性思辨的方式回复，即力图把语义正确性基础建立在人的理性对意义本质的把握之上。公孙龙的论辩对手提出的观点，与《墨经》中记载的后期墨家的经验主义哲学立场完全吻合，而公孙龙恰恰认为这种立场只具有实在正确性，不构成对语言意义本身的正确性论证，所以他总是试图说服对手，实在层面之外还有一个需要理性反思以确定意义正确性的语言概念层面，两者不能混淆。

这几篇文章完全可能是名家与墨家之间辩论的记录。我可以大胆地说，先秦名家当时辩论的真正对手很可能只有墨家，因为只有这两家对纯粹知识的问题，即对于所"是"如何为"真"有理论兴趣。庄子自以为是，记录下惠施及辩者们的只言片语，用来进行挖苦、抨击，很可能是因为庄子并未听懂名墨之争而断章取义。

其实，《公孙龙子》一书中的《迹府》就向我们展示了公孙龙的理性主义逻辑思想倾向。如前面第二部分翻译说明中所述，他面对孔穿要他放弃"白马非马"论然后拜他为师的要求，以逻辑的推论指出了其自相矛盾之处，并且非常清楚地陈述，他自己与孔穿的思想不在同一个层面，孔穿并未理解他的理论实质就错误地认为他的理论是错误的。我们可以自信地说，一个习惯于用逻辑思考的理性主义者，在他的日常生活言论中也会表现出逻辑思考的特征。

4.2　依据二

名家的另一代表人物惠施也是这样的理性主义者。这一点我们可以通过庄子与惠施之间著名的"濠梁之辩"看清楚。《庄子·秋水》记录了这场辩论。

庄子与惠子游于濠梁之上。庄子曰："鯈鱼出游从容，是鱼之乐也。"

惠子曰："子非鱼，安知鱼之乐？"

庄子曰："子非我，安知我不知鱼之乐？"

惠子曰："我非子，固不知子矣；子固非鱼也，子之不知鱼之乐，全矣！"

庄子曰："请循其本。子曰'汝安知鱼乐'云者，既已知吾知之而问我。我知之濠上也。"

非常清楚，惠施所追问的是，庄子说出"鱼是快乐的"这个判断句有何确切的逻辑依据。他关心的不是鱼到底是否快乐，也不关心庄子是否知道鱼是快乐的，而是追问庄子的"鱼之乐"这个认知判断是从哪儿来的，如何才是可靠的、不可怀疑的。惠施完全不打算从经验的角度，根据鱼的客观样态来归纳出某个结论。他不关注知识本身，而是关注获得知识的前提条件，即知识必定为真的逻辑必然性。惠施要求的是对判断性命题的正确性、可靠性的理性证明。

要说"诡辩"的话，庄子毫无疑问是诡辩家，因为他面对惠施有力的逻辑追问，无力应对，只好偷梁换柱，把"如何"换成"何处"，以此来躲避惠施的思想锋芒。庄子自鸣得意，认为自己比惠施更具智慧，其实这只是表明了庄子在求真知问题上的浅薄，说明庄子并无逻辑分析的大智慧。或许有人会说，庄子获得知识的方式是"情感移入"（empathy），是经验的类比推论。这当然无不可，我们可以从鱼的行为样态得出"鱼之乐"的推论。但是，显然这样的推论并不一定可靠，因为这种推论具有很强的主体性色彩，其所得"知识"并不一定具有必然性。惠施所追问的正是为了获得必然正确的知识所需要的前提条件是什么。

类似的例子还有《德充符》中的记载：

惠子谓庄子曰："人故无情乎？"

庄子曰："然。"

惠子曰："人而无情，何以谓之人？"

庄子曰："道与之貌，天与之形，恶得不谓之人？"

惠子曰："既谓之人，恶得无情？"

庄子曰："是非吾所谓情也。吾所谓无情者，言人之不以好恶内伤其身，常因自然而不益生也。"

惠子曰："不益生，何以有其身？"

庄子曰："道与之貌，天与之形，无以好恶内伤其身。今子外乎子之神，劳乎子之精，倚树而吟，据槁梧而瞑。天选子之形，子以坚白鸣。"

这段对话也清楚地显示了惠施对语义确定性的追求："情"是"人"的定义性意义之一，"人"之为"人"必然有"情"，否则便不能以"人"谓之。庄子则反复说人之所以叫作"人"是因为上天给了他们形体。这显然是错误的，因为有某种事物的外形并不等于就是那种事物；石头雕刻的人显然不是人。即使我们把庄子的"形"理解为"形体"，那也不是对"人"的根本性定义；人之为人关键是理性。按现代心理学的认识，人的情感是环境刺激与主体对自身与环境刺激的认知相互作用而产生的心理现象；有的情感（喜、怒、哀、乐等）人与动物共有，而有的情感（道德、意志、爱情、爱国主义等）则是人类特有的。故此，"情感"理当是人之为人的确定性特征之一。由此观之，惠施是正确的，而庄子是错误的。整个对话中，庄子并未正面回答惠施的问题，而是反复求助于"天道自然"之类的无法确定的概念，最后干脆对对手进行人身攻击。庄子的言论反映出他思想中并无任何澄清概念意义的分析性成分，因而也无法进行逻辑思维，这也正好反衬了惠施的理性主义倾向。

由此可见，惠施的思想追求完全不满足于关涉现实中实在之物的经验式推论，更不接受任何主观性臆测和玄想。只有货真价实的理性主义者才会采取这样的态度来对待概念的准确意义问题，才有这样的分析性追问方式。很多人以为这类对话体现出庄子的"哲理智慧"，认为庄子是赢家。在我看来完全不是那么回事。真正的输家是庄子，他的思想并无严格意义上的哲学意味；面对惠施的理性追问，庄子并无招架之力，只好求助于诡辩。不过，得感谢庄子的自以为是，因为这给了我们一个管窥先秦名家理性主义思想风采的机会。

4.3　依据三

更直接的依据来自幸存下来的公孙龙的五篇文章。其中的《名实论》和《指物论》两篇正是公孙龙的理论纲领性文件，宣示了公孙龙的语言哲学立场、原则和方法。

《名实论》开篇即说："天地与其所产焉，物也。"这句话明白无误地宣布，公孙龙绝不否认世界事物的客观存在。他把这个判断放在全文的第一句，足以说明他认为客观存在的事物正是人认知的源头。这种以客观事物为认识基础的思想与惠施"遍为万物之说"的思想指向在实质上是完全一致的。

对于公孙龙而言，物是第一性的，实在的物是存在的本体，也是人的认识的来源和基础，离开了物也就谈不上什么物之为物。然而，客观事物的存在是一回事，人对客观事物存在的本质的认识则又是另一回事。人对事物的真正认识只能通过思想概念的分析性认知操作才能进行，而这离开了语言是不可能的。毕竟，人是凭借语言而拥有世界的（李洪儒，2006）。因此，公孙龙在承认事物的客观存在的基础上，力求审查人怎样通过严格的语言抽象思维来认识和把握客观实在，即物作为实存之物本来就存在，问题是人以"名"把握了什么"实"，如何把握"实"。

对此问题，公孙龙提出了他的语言哲学原则——"唯乎其彼此"：

> 其名正，则唯乎其"彼"、"此"焉。谓"彼"而彼不唯乎彼，则"彼"谓不行。谓"此"而行不唯乎此，则"此"谓不行。……故"彼"，"彼"当乎彼，则唯乎彼，其谓行彼。"此"，"此"当乎此，则唯乎此，其谓行此。[1]

公孙龙指出，一个语词的意义必然有严格的规定性，要正确地使用语词来称谓事物、交流思想，就必须严格考察其语词意义的本质，澄清并规定指称"这一个"和"那一个"的语词意义。他认为，言说"彼"时，"彼"必须表达一切彼必然具有，并且只有彼才具有的"彼性"；言说"此"时，"此"必须表达一切此必然具

1　引文中"彼""此"二字的引号为笔者所加。

有，并且只有此才具有的"此性"；只有这样，语言的使用才是正确的，人们的思想认识因此才具有确定的普遍性和确定性。这事实上就是亚里士多德的经典逻辑基本定理（不矛盾律和排中律）的古汉语版本，因为公孙龙所要表达的就是：一个对象必定是那个对象，它不可能既是"这个"对象，同时又是"那个"对象；也就是说，一个对象就是其自身，不能同时又不是自身。

先秦古汉语没有系动词"是"，因而公孙龙无法就"是"进行句法形式意义的追问，但是他的"此""此"、"彼""彼"的反复盘旋，其中心与古希腊哲学家在精神气质上完全一致。公孙龙是在先秦古汉语的条件下，对"是什么"以及这个"是什么"如何为真的问题进行思考。他的表达看上去很拗口，因为汉文字不是字母的，而是象形的。西方人可以用字母来作为一般性概念的抽象符号，汉语则没有给公孙龙提供同样的手段，因而他只能利用汉语的特点来进行抽象意义的表达。如果我们用"P""Q"之类的字母符号来替换公孙龙文中的"此""彼"等，那么我们会看到，公孙龙讨论的正是P必定是P，而不能同时又不是P；一个对象不能同时既是P，又是Q。这难道不是非常接近亚里士多德的逻辑定理"$P \vee \neg P$"与"$\neg (P \wedge \neg P)$"吗？

同样如前文所述，公孙龙的《指物论》力图通过反思指称的本质来阐释人把握了什么样的关于世界的知识这样一个哲学问题。凭借语言，人对世界事物的认识不局限于具体的物，而能够通过语言的范畴化作用来对世界进行抽象概括性认识，即人用语词来对世界进行切分，从而对万事万物进行范畴化认识、把握。现代语言学理论自发端始就持这个看法（索绪尔，1949：157）。而这一认识在公孙龙那里早已有了萌芽。在他看来，语词可以命名具体对象，但作为指称，其所指意义并不一定与客观具体之物直接、必然地联系着。客观事物原本无名，"物"由概念表征、语言表达而成为"物"，是人用来范畴化事物，形成对事物本质的认识的方式；语词指称的是概念性意义，而不是个体之物本身，因而"指称"并非等于对具体的物的"指认"。

这也就是名家著名命题"指不至，至不绝"的基本含义：语词并不直接达于具体事物，而是指称由人脑从事物中抽象出来的意义。语言使思想成为可能，而思想又使人得以超越具体的经验性感知，能够对客观事物进行理性的抽象性认识。名家的这个基本理论，即便是今天，人们也普遍赞同。既然如此，对语言意义的反思就非常必要，因为语言表达了思想，那么探索如何正确地说，事实上也就是在探索人如何才能确切地想。

尽管有一些表达问题、逻辑问题，公孙龙的五篇论文的思想体系仍称得上

完整:

（1）在《名实论》中，他提出事物是客观存在的，而事物之名称却不是事物的标签，而是其本质意义的指称符号；事物与事物之间具有本质差异，所以一种事物只能具有其固有本质而不能同时具有其他事物的本质，因此正名的原则就只能是"唯乎其彼此"。由此，公孙龙提出了非常接近于亚里士多德逻辑基本原理（不矛盾律和排中律）的古汉语版本原则。

（2）在《坚白论》《白马论》《通变论》中，公孙龙以"白马"与"马"、"二"与"一"、"坚"与"白"等概念作为分析对象，详细阐述了他在《名实论》中提出的"唯乎其彼此"原则。其中尤以《坚白论》极为重要，他在文中提出了"自藏"的概念，"坚、白"正是基于这个概念而具有了观念实在性，非常类似于柏拉图式的"理念"。公孙龙还十分明确地指出，这类"理念"是由心灵（思维）通过"离"（分析）的方法所把握的。类似于柏拉图，他认为真正的知识是心灵凭着理性分析而把握的。他的思想无疑是一种理性主义哲学思想。

（3）在《指物论》中，公孙龙进一步明确要求严格区分"实指"（denotation）和"指称"（reference），认为这是两个不同层面的逻辑概念，即前者是经验层面概念，而后者则是语言概念层面概念。他明确指出，指称是人对世界万物意义的真正认识和把握，人也只有凭借语言的这种指称功能才能够得到关于世界的真理性知识。前面四篇文章事实上讨论语言、指称、概念性质问题，因而我认为这篇文章应当是总括与提升。

4.4　结论

这些思想，只有货真价实的理性主义者才会提出，才能提出，因为只有他们才具有这样的思想高度与角度。公孙龙等先秦名家的确是在通过语言和语言意义问题的形而上学反思而思考人把握世界的内涵及方式等哲学问题，因此他们是中国古代思想史上罕见的、独树一帜的理性主义语言哲学家。

我曾经在《语言元范畴化与公孙龙语言哲学》[1]一文中提出："公孙龙对于元范畴化语义概念的思辨是自觉的，他的语义反思中既有本体论，也有认识论的明确意识。若按他的路径走下去，中国古代哲学极有可能出现'此性''彼性'到底是实存还是非实存这样的类似于西方中世纪唯名论与唯实论之争。坚持"此""彼"具有独立存在性的一方（如公孙龙）极有可能成为柏拉图式的理念论者，而反对公

1　刘利民，《语言元范畴化与公孙龙语言哲学》，《外语学刊》，2011(11)，第16页。

孙龙实在论的一方则会坚持意义不过是"名"的属性，其验证应该经验地进行（如后期墨家），从而走向唯名论。中国古代哲学完全可能由此诞生西方哲学意义上的形而上学和逻辑学，不过其路径将是由语言哲学而进入本体论、认识论，这有异于西方哲学。"

5. 结束语

本书以此为框架对公孙龙子和名家命题做了新的解释，即以语言哲学反思的"意脉"来构建名家话语的"连贯性"（coherence）。这当然可以说是一种有条件的解释，但这不是机会主义的，而是在特定语言框架下的融贯性理解。也许有人会说这不过是一种历史建构主义意义上的解释。对此，我不否认。两千多年前活生生的生活场景、思想交锋确实再也无法复制。然而，我不同意这一说法，即一切解释都是当代解释。如前所述，纵然一千个译者可以译出一千个哈姆雷特，但他们所译出的只能是哈姆雷特，而不能是爱因斯坦。换言之，我们对名家思想的解释应当与名家的思想气质相吻合，即我们所解释的名家至少应当是历史文献中记录的生平、佚事所反映出的名家，而不能与之矛盾。前面提出了几个证据，说明名家是理性主义的思想家，而且当代学术界也多承认他们的确是先秦罕见的理性主义思想代表，那么为什么我们不应该重新审视名家的作品和命题，从而更具融贯性地展现他们的理性主义哲学思想呢？我以为本书所做的正是这样一件工作。

那么本书的解释和翻译是否成功，这个还是留给读者，留给历史去评价吧。但我作为译者非常自信，我的解释比现有的解释更能合理地、内在一致地说明名家的全部命题。这至少说明，本书的解释框架比现有的任何理论框架都更接近名家的思想倾向。

在我的初稿出来之时，我曾经给一些朋友看过。西南大学的杜世洪博士给我发出了这样一个疑问：千百年来的难题难道就这么解决啦？他认为即使是一种"终极解释"，也是有条件或者有前提的解释。对此，我并无异议。假如未来的研究中，人们提出更有说服力的框架，从而更合理地解释了名家的文章与命题，我当毫无保留地乐见其成并接受之！

附　录
先秦名家"诡辩"命题古译今及解说

1. 惠施"历物十事"

1.1〔原　文〕

至大无外，谓之大一；至小无内，谓之小一。

〔古译今〕

"极大"以至于本身之外没有了更多的空间，这就是"极大"之为"极大"的本质；"极小"以至于本身之内没有了更多的空间，这就是"极小"之为"极小"的本质。

〔解　说〕

这一命题是惠施关于"极大"与"极小"的本质的定义性思辨。其中的"一"应当解释为"极大"之为"极大"或"极小"之为"极小"的本质本身。由于汉语没有类似于英文的"Oneness"之类的语汇，惠施以"一"作为概念意义的本质并进行纯理性的反思。之所以是纯理性的，是因为这个命题显然无法经验地验证，只能是逻辑的思辨。

1.2〔原　文〕

无厚，不可积也，其大千里。

〔古译今〕

面积本身无厚度，不可累积，却可以大至千里。

〔解　说〕

这是惠施关于"面积"的本质意义的思辨，这是学术界基本同意的。需注意的是，惠施不是在研究如何丈量面积，而是在追问"面积"本身的本质。

1.3〔原 文〕

天与地卑，山与泽平。

〔古译今〕

"天"与"地"一样的"低"，"山"与"湖"一样的"平"。

〔解 说〕

如果不加引号，惠施的这个命题无疑没有意义或者是相对主义的错误，因为经验告诉人们，天不可能与地一样低，山和湖也不可能一样平。但是加上引号之后，我们可以窥见，惠施所反思的是名称意义的本体论依据问题。"天、地、山、湖"作为名称，可以靠实在的存在作为其意义依据，那么"卑、平"之类的形容词之名，其意义依据如何客观确定？汉语词类无语素形式的特征促使惠施对"名称"意义的确定性问题产生了形而上学的追问。因此，此命题绝不是所谓"相对性"问题的思考，也不涉及伦理道德判断。

有人认为，这个命题说的是"是天反衬出地的低，是山反衬出湖很平"，即"与"的意思是"使成为"，没有天的"高"我们也就无法认识地的"低"，而没有山的"不平"我们也就无法认识湖的"平"。由于惠施的言论只是孤零零的一句话，这不失为一种解释。但我认为，这种解释不符合惠施其他命题以及名家其他言论的思想气质。有属性A才相对有属性B（如：有高才有低，大是相对于小而言，等等），这其实是老子和庄子的论说方式。而就我们所知，庄子与惠施的思想倾向是截然不同的；庄子把这个语句作为与其他"诡辩"相同性质的命题记录下来，也反证了他并不同意惠施的思想。因此，我认为不宜用庄子来解释惠施。如果说庄子的思想是相对主义的，那么惠施应当不满相对主义，而寻求意义、知识的确定性。所以，我认为这个命题是惠施关于名称意义，特别是形容词意义的本体论依据的追问。

在此，我还得再议论一下对"卑"的翻译。有人提出，"卑"应当译成"卑下、卑微"，理由是中国古代的"天"为"乾"、为"阳"，代表"男性、父亲"等，而"地"为"坤"、为"阴"，代表"女性、母亲"等；前者在那个时代具有支配地位，而后者只有从属地位；跟前者相比，后者的社会地位是卑下的。这种说法或许有一定道理。但是，从惠施的其他命题所关注的对象、他自己的"泛爱万物"的宣言以及庄子关于惠施"遂万物而不返"的评论等线索来看，惠施用本命题的前半部分关注伦理道德问题，而后半部分关注客观事物的可能性非常小。惠施关注的应当是哲学形而上问题。因此，我坚持将"卑"译成"低"。当然，即便可以将之译成"卑微"，这也并不能改变本书的解释立场，即惠施仍然可能在追问："卑微"之为"卑微"本身，其语义的本体论依据是什么？

1.4〔原　文〕

日方中方睨，物方生方死。

〔古译今〕

太阳升至顶点的"瞬间"也就是它西斜的"瞬间"，万物出生的"时刻"也就是它们死亡的"时刻"。

〔解　说〕

如果不加引号，那么表面上看，这仿佛是个相对主义的命题，即一个对象是难以把握的，它既是此，又是彼。这也是通常的解释。但这一解释与许多其他命题的精神格格不入，而一个思想家一般不可能同时持有理性主义和相对主义的立场。这个命题极有可能是关于"方"（瞬间）的本质的思考。如果把时间视为一条长河，那么这条长河将由无数个"方"组成；没有一个个"方"，则没有时间的概念。既然有时间的概念，则"方"理应存在。然而正如以太阳正、斜或事物的生、死为例所表明的那样，"方"本身是无法经验地把握住的：一旦说出"方"字，则所指之"方"必已流逝。人所处的此"方"总是异于彼"方"。那么"方"到底是什么？"方"以何种方式存在？人能否把握"方之为方"的本质？惠施借语义分析所追问的应当是关于时间的本质如何把握的问题。这样的解释才符合惠施其他命题的思想倾向。（可参见1.3条的解说。）

1.5〔原　文〕

大同而与小同异，此之谓小同异；万物毕同毕异，此之谓大同异。

〔古译今〕

"大同"（共相）与"小同"（相同性）不是一回事，相同性是指具体事物的相似或者差别，而万事万物所具有的本质性相同或者差异，才是我们所谓的"大同异"（共相）。

〔解　说〕

　　这一命题传统上被解释为惠施的"合同异"立场，即一种相对主义的立场，试图消弭事物之间的差异，因而认为任何事物之间既同又不同。然而，这可能不是一种正确的理解。其实，从命题本身来看，这应当是很清楚的：惠施认为"大同"与"小同"不是一个形而上学层面的概念；前者指的是万事万物之间所具有的本质规定性的相同或者差异，这显然应当是一种柏拉图意义上的"共相"之同异；而除此以外，日常语言所说的"相同"和"不同"则只不过是事物表面的相似性或者差别。惠施认为日常语言概念表达的"同异"并不一定代表事物的本质，因而要求从理性的高度确定事物的本质的"同"与"异"。本书的这一解释与其他学者的解释有不同，但却与惠施思想的理性主义倾向相吻合。

1.6〔原　文〕

　　南方无穷而有穷。

〔古译今〕

　　南方的延伸既无极限又有极限。

〔解　说〕

　　现有解释认为，这个命题是在反思"极限"的问题。这应当是有道理的。但如果将这一命题解释为相对主义的"无边而有限"则可能是不对的，因为有限与无限本身就是一对矛盾。而如果解释为"有穷"包含在"无穷"当中，则那属于辩证思维，并不一定符合惠施的思想。惠施的确可能在反思极限的问题，但其进路应当是理性主义关于空间性质本身的形而上学反思。同前述1.4小节对时间的反思一样，惠施追问的问题可能是：时间中的各个瞬间，人们似乎无法经验地把握住，但可以通过语言对时间以及瞬间的切分来认识和理解；而空间问题也是一个同性质的问题，无限性是人无法经验地把握的，但却可以用语言从有限空间中推击出无限空间的观念。人能够体验到此空间、彼空间等有限空间，但是对有限空间的体验并不等于空间的本质。空间的本质不能单纯地由人的经验来证明。于是关于空间的言说的确定性、真理性也十分有必要进行理性的分析。这一解释更加符合惠施的思想倾向。

1.7〔原　文〕

今日适越而昔来。

〔**古译今**〕

"今天"启程去越国，而"昨天"就到达了。

〔**解　说**〕

对这个命题的传统解说恐怕有误，因为人们认为此句表达了惠施的怀疑主义和时间相对主义思想，即庄子式的认知怀疑主义。我之所以说传统解说完全错了，是因为庄子在自己的著作里反复说他跟惠施的思想旨趣不是一回事，从庄子的记述来看，他跟惠施的辩论构成了他的相对主义与惠施的逻辑理性之间的巨大反差。因此，以庄释惠理当确定为不正确。不过，单从字面意义来看，这个命题确实不好解释。按照惠施思想的精神取向，本书试做如下解释。

惠施很有可能试图经由"今"与"昔"的时态性意义反思存在本质问题。这个问题的引发可能与先秦古汉语缺乏系词"是"有关。假如汉语有像西方语言那样的集述谓、断真、存在于一体的系词，那么惠施很可能直接就如西方哲学那样从"to be"入手，思考存在的同一性。但先秦时代的古汉语既没有动词"to be"，且其动词也没有任何时态的形式变化，因而惠施借着从名词"今""昔"的语义入手进行具有古汉语特色的关于存在的同一性问题的思辨。

这个命题中的"今"和"昔"两个词应该加上引号。我们不妨假设惠施的思辨针对的是事件。事件的发生总有时间顺序。某人"现在动身去越国"是个事件，但该事件发生之后，如果要用语言来叙述这个事件，那么语言所表达的"这个事件"肯定不可能指称"当下"发生的事件，而一定是指"过去"（尽管是刚刚过去的"过去"）已经发生的"那个事件"了。从逻辑上讲，"那个事件"当然不等于"这个事件"。语言使得我们可以区分一个事件历时性存在和共时性存在的状态。于是，关键的问题就是："过去"状态的"这一个"是否与"现在"状态的"这一个"具有存在同一性？如果一个事物会从一种状态变化成另一种状态，那么它的存在还具有同一性吗？我们能说一个已经变化了的对象还是那个对象吗？"今适"与"昔来"两个词语同在一句、共述一事，很可能是为了放大"过去"与"现在"存在的时态性，以便突出人的思想如何从状态的变化中把握住存在的同一性本质这一重大问题。本书这一解释是否得当可以商榷，但它的确符合公孙龙的"唯乎其彼此"的正名原则，因而也符合先秦名家思想的一般特征。

1.8〔原　文〕

连环可解也。

〔古译今〕

相互死扣着的连环是可以"解开"的。

〔解　说〕

从经验的层面看，死扣的连环当然无法解开。但是从语言的层面看，问题总有解决方案。既然连环连得上，那么其逆过程就是"解开"，这至少存在一种概念性的可能。甚至"无解"本身也是一种"解"。这样解释或许很勉强，但与惠施力图从语言意义层面反思问题的视角是一致的。

从这个角度视之，这个命题更深层的含义可能是：客观事物的存在及其存在方式是一回事，而人凭借语言所获得的思想则可能是另一回事。人的思想，或者说人的语言意义世界，与客观世界不必然具有一对一的匹配关系。在客观世界中不可能的事物及其现象，在语言意义世界中是完全有可能的。有的事情在实际经验中是不可能的，而在语言创造的意义世界中，一切都有可能。

1.9〔原　文〕

我知天下之中央，燕之北越之南是也。

〔古译今〕

我知道宇宙的中心就在北方的燕国以北和南方的越国之南。

〔解　说〕

从字面意义看，这个命题无疑是胡说。几乎所有人都接受这一解释：惠施以这个命题说明地球是圆的。然而，这个解释却不正确，因为地球是圆的这一认识在先秦还没有。当时的天文学认为地是平的、静止的。本书认为，这个命题的解释关键在于"我知"。这也是这一命题与其他命题的不同之处，因而也是非常宝贵的关于理解名家思想的提示。

惠施极有可能在反思这样的问题：一个命题前面加上了"我知道"之后，它的真值如何判定？或者如我们现在所认识的那样，"我知道"是一个断定行为，而本身并无真值？对于一个陈述句P，我们总可以从经验或者逻辑上判断其为真还是为假（例如："金属遇热膨胀""若甲高于乙，且乙高于丙，则甲必然高于丙"）。但是，当我们说"我知道P"时，其真值应该如何判定？如果P为真，那没问题，整个语句仍然为真；但若P为假，则问题就复杂了。"知道P"表示"有了P的知识"；而如果P为假，则不能成为知识，所"知道"的是错的。困难在于，是说话人在说"我知道"，所以即使P为假，这个说话人也陈述了他"知道P"这件事。也难怪有人干脆说"我知道P"是一个断定行为，不涉及真假。可是，这也有问题：若他不是说"我知道"而是说"我相信"，这两者有没有差别？显然差别是存在的。"我知道"陈述的是一个为真的事实性内容，可以加上"我知道"而不改变其为真的性质。但是"相信"则不然，无论相信的内容P为真还是为假，都只是那个说话人相信的内容，不一定是事实，别人无法否定这一点。这样来解释应该很符合惠施的理性主义思辨特征。

总之，这个问题牵涉很多关于知识之为真的逻辑问题，而惠施很有可能早就在思考这类问题了。他的理性主义思想被湮灭实在是中国思想传统的巨大损失。

1.10〔原　文〕

泛爱万物，天地一体也。

〔古译今〕

认识一切事物，宇宙万物必有统一的规则。

〔解　说〕

许多人把这个命题看作对惠施前面九个命题的总结，认为他提纲挈领地指出万物都不是绝对的，对事物的认识和把握又都具有相对性。但如同前文所说，这样的解释是以庄释惠，并不正确，也无法解释为何庄子作为一个相对主义者要把惠施的命题当作他自己反对的思想而记录下来的原因。

就此前解释的命题来看，其中没有证据证明那些命题与实在之物有什么联系，也没有发现关于人的经验或体验的论证线索。惠施对于伦理道德、人生政治没有多少兴趣，但他喜欢研究"物"，且在追求知识上面兴趣广泛。但惠施的思想也不像后期墨家那样具有浓郁的经验主义色彩，而是对于知识本身的逻辑必然性保证，对语言意义之为真的理性分析有特殊的兴趣。惠施的爱好是对万事万物都要求毕显其真，他的思想类似于古希腊哲学家的思想，即试图从杂多中追问一，从现象中追问本质。这样的理解才能使这个命题在哲学实质上与惠施的其他命题一致。

本书完稿之前，我读到了李贤中教授所著之《名家哲学研究》（2012），其中作者释此句含义为："若想认识这个世界，先爱这个世界吧！"李教授把惠施当作以认识为对象的哲学家，这我是赞同的，我其实也可以按李教授的理解做翻译。但是在李教授看来，惠施的"爱"意味着"联系人与人的疏离，打消人与物的隔阂……唯有同情的了解诸事万物……方能有包容各种不同之物论，了然各论有限之观点，及其相对观点下所论之物"。这我不敢苟同。作为名家代表人物，惠施应当以犀利的语言逻辑眼光"专决于名"，以反思事物之名的意义本质为其职责，何况惠施与庄子的辩论也的确清楚地表明了惠施的逻辑分析性思辨特质。如果说这是一个极易导致相对主义认识论思想的命题，那么我认为这与名家的思想立场是格格不入的。

2. 辩者"二十一事"

2.1〔原　文〕

卵有毛。

〔古译今〕

蛋里面"有"毛。

〔解　说〕

按照名家的理性主义语言哲学思想倾向，这个命题应当是关于"有"的意义的反思。以下还有三个命题（2.2，2.4，2.5）都具有同一句法形式，即"x有y"。这些语句中的"有"如果仅意为"拥有"则没有意义，名家辩者应当是在"存在于"的意义上使用"有"，由此反思"存在"的意义。

汉语"x有y"判断句的一个意思就是"y存在于x中"（另一个意思是"x拥有y"，但这与哲学的存在关注不是一回事）。如果x中确实存在y，那么人能够感知、认识y在x中的存在，用"有"来表达这一事实。但是说"x无y"（例如"卵无毛"）时，"无"表达了一个什么事实？"无"的意思就是"没有、不存在"。那么不存在的事实能是事实吗？"有"可以实在、正确地理解和把握，但是"无"能否可以同样实在、正确地理解和把握？对于不存在者的认识和言说将具有什么样的真理性？若真是这样，那么名家辩者所反思的对象就是类似于西方哲学的"to be""being"之类的非经验的、纯理性存在的性质问题。

2.2〔原　文〕

郢有天下。

〔古译今〕

宇宙就"在"郢国。

〔解　说〕

此命题的理解可参阅2.1命题的解说。宇宙当然不在郢国，但是当我们说出这个句子的时候，由于这是一个不存在的事实，那么我们如何能够保证它道出了一个真理？

2.3〔原　文〕

犬可以为羊。

〔古译今〕

"狗"也可以是"羊"。

〔解　说〕

传统解说在此是正确的，因为这个命题显然不是从经验的层面说狗这种动物可以是羊这种动物。因而，这很明显是关于名称的讨论。先秦名家想要指出的是，事物的名称不是天生就有的，而是约定俗成的指称。名称与事物的本质之间并无必然的、可论证的联系。这也与公孙龙的《指物论》一文的思想吻合。同时，也可参见本书第二部分翻译说明中关于《通变论》译文的解释。

2.4〔原　文〕

马有卵。

〔古译今〕

马"是"有卵的。

〔解　说〕

此命题的理解可参阅2.1命题的解说。

2.5〔原　文〕

丁子有尾。

〔古译今〕

青蛙"是"有尾巴的。

〔解　说〕

此命题的理解可参阅2.1命题的解说。

2.6〔原　文〕

山出口。

〔古译今〕

"山"是口中说出的名称。

〔解　说〕

　　许多人认为此命题无解，也有人认为它说的是山有口，如火山口。但这是错误的，因为这是以经验层面来看待语言哲学的命题。唐代的成玄英曾解释此命题为"山出自口中"，我认为这是正确的。其中的"山"应当加上引号，因为名家辩者在此强调，此句中的"山"不是指实际存在的山，而是"山"这个音所表征的概念。由于古汉语没有标点符号，辩者们没有其他方式来表达类似于西方语言哲学的"使用"与"提及"的概念，而只能采取语句表述的方式，强调他们的论辩层面不是经验，而是语言概念本身。他们以这种方式把自己的论辩限制在语言哲学的范围之中。如果此一理解正确，那么这个命题将是名家语言哲学思想层面的直接证据。

2.7〔原 文〕

龟长于蛇。

〔古译今〕

乌龟比蛇更"长"。

〔解 说〕

从经验知识看，蛇肯定比龟长，所以这个命题被庄子作为谬论记录了下来。关于庄子记录的传统注释认为，蛇的身比龟长，但是命没有龟长。但这是事实性判断，根本不是诡辩。这个句子的理解关键确实在于"长"这个形容词。蛇身的"长"是空间性概念，而龟寿的"长"却是时间性概念。正是在这里，名家辩者发现了问题：两种性质不同的长度却只有一个"长"字来指称，那么长之为长自身到底是什么？不要说古人，就是现代人也没有拿出一个圆满的回答：时间与空间特性的描述使用的是同一个形容词，那么这个形容词作为名称所指称的是一种什么本质意义或共相？人如何能够用同一语词把握性质不同的对象？这些无疑是哲学的问题，既涉及本体论，又涉及认识论。这样的理解符合先秦名家的理性主义思辨特质。

2.8〔原 文〕

白狗黑。

〔古译今〕

"白"狗是"黑"的。

〔解 说〕

白色的狗当然不可能同时是黑色的，否则便违反了逻辑基本定理。所以这个命题不应当理解为对经验事实的描述，而是名称意义的概念层面反思。我认为，其真意应当与公孙龙的"白马非马"命题一致[1]。其基本点是：命名颜色的名称不能命名形状，而必然且只能命名颜色。那么名家的问题就是："白"这一名称命名颜色，"黑"也是；那么既然颜色等于颜色，可以说"白"等于"黑"吗？其更深层

1　参见本书第二部分关于《白马论》的翻译说明。

次的追问在于：颜色本身有颜色吗？这显然不是一个经验命题，而是一个形而上的本体论问题。从名家辩者的其他命题所表现的思想倾向看，他们的确可能在思考、追问这样的问题。庄子的记录只是在他不理解名家思想实质的情况下的断章取义。

2.9〔原 文〕

鸡三足。

〔古译今〕

鸡应有三只"足"。

〔解 说〕

传统解释也比较一致，即按照公孙龙在他的《通变论》中表达的思想，将此命题解释为语词概念意义的"鸡足"和具体实在的鸡足共同构成了三只"鸡足"。这一解释比较合理。

但需要特别注意的是，名家辩者以这类形式的命题巧妙地告诉人们，名称的意义不是实在对象。语言为人们创造了概念的世界，其中各种各样的"物"不再是实物而是概念本身。概念本身才是"真"的知识。具体的鸡足作为实在物，在每一只鸡都不一样（如：颜色、肥瘦、长短等），并且迟早都会消失的（鸡总是要死的），甚至可以是残缺的。但是，如果一物被称为"鸡足"，那么它必定指称一切鸡足所共有的，并且只有鸡足才具有的本质；离开了这一本质，则该物不能被称为"鸡足"。这种一切鸡足必须具有并且只有鸡足才具有的本质，作为语义，是永恒的、完善的、不变的，因而是"鸡足"的本质性意义，而这才是人用语言所把握住的关于鸡足的真正的知识。这才是真正的理性主义的认识论立场。

以下一些命题，如2.10，2.11，2.12，2.14，2.15和2.19，亦应当作这样的理解，否则从经验事实的层面，这些命题只可能是无意义的诡辩。

2.10〔原 文〕

火不热。

〔古译今〕

"火"是不热的。

〔**解　说**〕

此命题的理解参阅2.9命题的解说。从经验层面看，火毫无疑问具有热的属性；但是从语言概念的层面看，"火"的意义并不具有热的属性。

2.11〔**原　文**〕

轮不碾地。

〔**古译今**〕

"轮子"是不碾地的。

〔**解　说**〕

此命题的理解参阅2.9命题的解说。从经验层面看，轮子当然要碾地；但是从语言概念的层面看，"轮子"的意义并不碾地。

2.12〔**原　文**〕

目不见。

〔**古译今**〕

"眼睛"是看不见东西的。

〔**解　说**〕

此命题的理解可参阅2.9命题的解说。公孙龙在他的《坚白论》中明确地论述过，人能看到物体及其颜色，是因为有光线、有眼睛，但是光线和眼睛本身并不能看，而是心灵把握了这些对象。他的解释与名家辩者的解释在形而上学思想倾向上是相同的。只不过本命题着重的是，作为名称的概念意义，"眼睛"并不是用来看东西的。

2.13〔**原　文**〕

指不至，至不绝。

〔**古译今**〕

指称并不达于具体事物，具体事物是无穷无尽的。

〔**解　说**〕

有人（如冯友兰）解释说"指"意思为"共相"，所以这个命题说的是事物的共相可知而不可见；也有人把"指"说成是用手指把事物指认出来。前者有道理，但后者则是错误的。

我认为，这很可能是名家辩者们的纲领性命题，是理解他们思想层面的依据之一。该命题的意义与公孙龙的《指物论》中提出的思想是完全一致的。公孙龙在文中指出"物莫非指，而指非指"，意即"物之为'物'无一不是由名称指称而成，然而'指称'并不等于指认具体物"。本命题中的"指"也就是公孙龙所提出的"指"，即指称。在辩者看来，人只能用语言名称来认识和把握世界，但是名称的意义是概念，并不是具体事物，即名称的指称并不直接涉及客观实在之物，因为客观的实在之物是无法逐一枚举并命名的。名称的意义是人的认识概括的结果，是从事物中抽象出来的共有特征。这是名家语言哲学的一个非常了不起的思想。这分明证明，名家已经发现，在客观世界之外还有一个语言所构建的纯理性的语义世界。意义世界的概念性存在才是真的，也就是普遍的、确定的知识，使人能够对无穷尽的、千变万化的客观世界进行理性把握。因此，我同意冯友兰的意见，即后半句的"至"应当为"物"。

2.14〔原　文〕

矩不方，规不可以为圆。

〔**古译今**〕

方尺画不出方本身，圆规也画不出圆本身。

〔**解　说**〕

此命题的理解可参阅2.9命题的解说。用尺子和圆规当然能分别画出一个个方形或圆形，这是经验事实。但是方形之为方形必须具有方的本质，圆形也是如此。而这个本质已经是概念，而不是方形或者圆形的东西。那么尺子当然无法画出方的概念，圆规也画不出圆的本质。于是，我们可以理解名家辩者为何要以这种"诡辩"的方式提出自己的思想：因为先秦古汉语中没有类似于西方语言（如英语的"round"和"roundness"等）的表达手段。

2.15〔原　文〕

凿不围枘。

〔古译今〕

"卯眼"并不围住"榫头"。

〔解　说〕

此命题的理解可参阅2.9命题的解说。在经验事实层面，卯眼当然围住榫头；但是从语言概念的层面看，"卯眼"的意义并不是围住榫头。

2.16〔原　文〕

飞鸟之景未尝动也。

〔古译今〕

飞鸟的影子从来不动。

〔解　说〕

此命题被解释为飞鸟动，而飞鸟的影子不动。这是可接受的。后期墨家也有同样的命题，即"景不徙，说在改为"。即使用今天的科学眼光来看，这也是正确的理论。不过，鉴于名家思想的思辨特性，我认为名家辩者可能借此更加深入地反思"运动"的本质是什么。鸟飞行的运动是鸟这个物体自身的位移，但是鸟的影子显然不能运动，只能是鸟的位移的投影。这样看起来是运动的现象，有的其实可能并不是运动。因此，名家很可能要求确定运动之为运动本身的本质意义，而不是简单地停留在经验观察的层面上。

2.17〔原　文〕

镞矢之疾，而有不行不止之时。

〔**古译今**〕

　　快速飞行的箭在每一时刻既动又不动。

〔**解　说**〕

　　关于这个命题的解释没有什么异议，即它说的就是飞着的箭既动又不动。但是学者们以运动的辩证法来看待此命题，则与名家的理性主义思想不相吻合。我认为，这个命题与古希腊芝诺悖论，即"飞矢不动"命题是很相似的。如果说芝诺悖论的价值在于指出感性的认识必须由逻辑分析来把握才能上升为理性的真知的话，先秦名家的命题也应当做此解释。在名家辩者看来，"飞行"显然是一个过程，但这个过程可以分析为任意多个极小的瞬间；那么在这些极小的瞬间中，箭头到底应该被定义为是在运动（"行"）状态，还是在静止（"止"）状态呢？说它处于两个状态中的任何一个，并以此来定义"疾"，都不无问题：若是在"行"，那么箭头在任意一个瞬间却只能"在"一处，不可能同时又"在"另一处，而"在"即意味着"止"；但若是在"止"，则一连串的静止又如何能够构成运动？"止"与"疾"的语义定义是相矛盾的。于是，从理性的角度看，"疾"的本质到底是什么？这就是辩者们追问的问题。

2.18 〔**原　文**〕

　　狗非犬。

〔**古译今**〕

　　狗不是犬。

〔**解　说**〕

　　此命题包含一个深刻的哲学含义：狗幼小的时候被称为"狗"，而成年后则称为"犬"。但是存在的同一性却不允许"成为"。一个对象要么是那个对象，要么不是那个对象。存在本质上应当是超验的。这一反思极可能很像古希腊巴门尼德关于"是"与"成为"的思辨。下面的命题2.20也应做此理解。

2.19 〔**原　文**〕

　　黄马骊牛三。

〔古译今〕

"黄"马、"有色"牛加起来等于三。

〔解　说〕

此命题的理解可参阅2.8和2.9命题的解说。"黄"命名一种颜色，而"骊"也命名颜色。"马"命名一种动物，"牛"也命名一种动物。因而，它们是三个概念。

2.20〔原　文〕

孤驹未尝有母。

〔古译今〕

孤驹从未有过母亲。

〔解　说〕

可参阅2.18命题的解说。由于汉语动词没有时态的变位，所以名家辩者使用"未尝有"来突出时间的问题，而这一点传统的解释并未强调。名家真正做的很可能是透过"孤驹"的语义分析来思辨存在的同一性问题。孤驹曾经有母，但"曾经有"无论在经验上还是在形式上都绝不等于"当前有"。说"孤驹有母"是语义矛盾，但是说"孤驹无母"则是大白话，无法凸显名家的命题意图。而这个命题使用"未尝有"，一下子就把存在同一性问题摆了在人们面前。"曾经有母"的驹和"当前无母"的驹是不是指同一驹？过去和现在两种存在状态之中的"驹"哪一个更真实，更应当是"有无"一语所把握的存在？这无疑是涉及"是"与"成为"的一个深刻的存在本质问题。这与惠施的命题（参见命题1.7）具有同样的性质。

2.21〔原　文〕

一尺之棰，日取其半，万世不竭。

〔古译今〕

一尺长的木棍，取其一半，然后每天取其一半的一半，那么永远也不可能将它切分完。

〔解 说〕

关于这个命题，学术界的理解没多少争议，都认为这是一个符合现代数学的极限论的思想。我也同意这个解释，但想指出一点，先秦名家辩者的这一思想是从纯粹语言概念的思辨中提出的，而不是先有实践经验而后从中概括、推论得出的。他们反思的问题是物质是不是无限可分。这与他们的一般性思想倾向是一致的。值得注意的是，先秦后期墨家也谈论过"可分性"问题，但他们出于经验主义立场，认为物质不是无限可分的，分到一定的点，即"端"，就无法再分下去了。在实在世界，这也是一个经验事实。后期墨家的经验主义因此也反衬出了名家辩者们在无限可分观点上的理性主义。

译后说明

除了这里译出的记载于庄子著作中的三十一个命题外，先秦名家辩者的一些命题还散见于其他文献，如荀子的文章等。但那些命题也都没有离开"历物十事"和"辩者二十一事"的范围，故不必再收入。

上述命题按照庄子文中记载的顺序列出。但很明显，这些命题其实都可以按照它们的内容进行重新分组。这里列出译者在另一本著作《在语言中盘旋——先秦名家"诡辩"命题的纯语言思辨理性研究》（四川大学出版社，2007年）中所做的分类，供读者参考。分组的理由参见上述翻译解说。

（1）惠施"历物十事"

第一组：1.1，1.2，1.5，1.10

第二组：1.3

第三组：1.4，1.6，1.7，1.8

第四组：1.9

（2）辩者"二十一事"

第一组：2.6

第二组：2.13

第三组：2.16，2.17，2.21

第四组：2.7，2.8

第五组：2.3，2.18

第六组：2.1，2.2，2.4，2.5，2.20

第七组：2.9，2.10，2.11，2.12，2.14，2.15，2.19

关于"历物十事"和辩者"二十一事"的现代汉语解读，我曾在《四川大学学报·哲学社会科学版》（2007年第2期）和《哲学研究》（2009年第9期）上分别发文研究。这里附上的现代汉语和英语译文，在原有的研究上增加了新的心得。

英文部分

目 录

ONTENTS

Foreword

1. On the Interpretative Standpoint of Liu's Twofold Translation of *Gongsun Longzi*

For convenience, I refer to Liu Limin's "reinterpretation" and "retranslation" as "twofold translation". This causes no misunderstanding, since in the first part of his book there are phrases denoting "modern Chinese version" and "English version".

Liu has already elaborated on the necessity of the twofold translation of *Gongsun Longzi*, which I agree and the readers can find it in the book. What I want to discuss here is the interpretative standpoint he holds, which I think is not only valuable for the twofold translation itself, but also of general academic significance.

The original text of "On Name and Actuality" is:

"天地与其所产者，物也。

"物以物其所物而不过焉，实也。实以实其所实，不旷焉，位也。出其所位，非位；位其所位焉，正也。"

Liu has translated it into English in this way:

> *Heaven and Earth, with what grow and exist therein, consist of actual objects.*
>
> *But the reason why an object is said to be that "object" is that its name necessarily and exclusively refers to the conceptual meaning of the object as it is precisely defined, without any shade of undue excessiveness; this should constitute the "actuality" that we talk about. Such an "actuality" is none other than the representation of the true essence of the object so named, without any looseness, which is the very requirement that ensures the correctness of the meaning of the names for objects. Any deviation from such a necessary requirement is bound to result in errors in the use of names. The meaning of a name is correct, only if it satisfies completely this requirement.*

As to the reason for this translation, Liu has claimed in this way: "... the classical style of the Chinese language is highly condensed and concise, omitting in some cases the process of reasoning or any semantic components that can be omitted, leaving the readers to infer on what connections between statements and even between sentential elements should be. This makes theoretical works such as *Gongsun Longzi* extremely difficult to read; and for this reason, it is quite necessary to <u>express in clear terms what has originally been cached</u>, left out or assumed. Therefore, I decide to use frequently the method of indirect translation while trying to stick to the original diction." (See his "Introduction", the underline is my addition.) In one of my books, entitled *Pragmatics in Chinese Culture*,[1] I have used an entire chapter to oppose clearly and definitely such an approach to Chinese-English translation, especially the expression of what is implied in the sentences in the translation of the works of Chinese literature (to make the implicit explicit). This idea of mine stands in tit-for-tat conflict with that of Liu's. To me, the implicitness of ideas is one of the basic characteristics of literature, and if every single idea is expressed directly and clearly, it is tantamount to the elimination of literature itself. It would be more of a hindrance than a help if a translator reveals in clear wording what is implied, because in that case he would be making a public notice of literature, from which literature is anxious to shy away. Literature "speaks" by means of its figures, the image created and the development of its plot, and is not a public notice.

What about philosophy, then, especially ancient philosophy? Philosophy seeks after certainty. For this, the interpretation of philosophy requires clear and unmistakable language. In modern hermeneutical tradition since Heidegger, H. G. Gadamer has expounded the historicity of interpretation, based on Husserl's humanistic viewpoint. The era in which an interpreter reads a textual material is necessarily different from that in which the text was originally written, with changes in the time, environment, condition and position. These factors are bound to influence or to exercise constraints on the readers in their interpretation of the text, resulting in a discrepancy between the readers and the original author. ... To supplement the

---

1   Qian Guanlian, *Pragmatics in Chinese Culture*, Beijing: Tsinghua University Press, 2002: Section 3, Chapter 6.

historicity of comprehension, Gadamer has proposed the ideas of "time distance" and "fusion of horizons".... "Time distance" emancipates both the author and the readers, bringing the two parties to fusion through dialogs. ... "Fusion of horizons", that is, if interpreters' field of vision overlaps with that of the text in history, then an upgraded level of "new range of vision" can be achieved, thus improving comprehension in general. (cf. Wang Yin[1]) In the light of the modern hermeneutical viewpoint, we find that Liu's twofold translation is no less an effort to deal with the discrepancy of time, environment, condition and position between the era of the original and our present times. He just faces the "time distance", attempting to emancipate both the readers and the author in order to bring them together through dialogs. He is engaged in nothing but "fusion of horizons", i.e. to achieve certain overlapping and fusion of the horizon of the interpreters today and that of the original text in history. He has only experimented what European humanistic hermeneutics (philosophy) has proposed, namely the "creativity of comprehension" and "better comprehension (the readers may have than the author)" (Schleiermacher, ibid.). Having done these, he has achieved the certainty of philosophical interpretation, and this endeavor is tolerable.

However, I do not think modern hermeneutics since Heidegger is truly able to "emancipate" philosophical interpretation, still less than the reinterpretation of ancient Chinese philosophy and the retranslation into English that follows suit. When an interpreter or translator expresses in clear terms the "reasoning and language meaning that is cached" and makes the implicit explicit, can it be an expression of the intention of the original author? This is the first question. And there is the second question: even if we free ourselves from the constraints of the original texts and adopt the standpoint of modern hermeneutics since Heidegger, allowing the "creativity of comprehension", how can you (translator or interpreter) convince me (reader) that I must accept your supplement and "creation"? For a translation of philosophical literature, these two questions cannot be shrugged off. On the one hand, the interpretation of ancient philosophy as well as modern philosophy must seek after certainty; and on the other, philosophy is essentially that you think therefore you are and I think therefore I am. Or, you are and I am, and therefore you think and I think. The problem is, there is

---

1　Section 15, Chapter 10 of Wang Yin's *Meditations on Philosophy of Language*, Beijing: Beijing University Press, 2014.

a difference between you think and I think; that is, the interpretation of yours and of mine may not be the same. What is more, according to Quine, the indeterminacy of the stimulus meaning makes the radical translation indeterminate.[1] Suppose we regard every judgment and proposition in the texts of ancient Chinese philosophy as a stimulus, which is indeterminate, then we have to conclude that this will lead to the indeterminacy of interpretation in different ones who think. In a word, there does not seem to be anything determinate and why then must I believe this indeterminate interpretation of yours?

But, please don't forget that an interpretation or a translation is after all an expression in language, or realized in linguistic forms. This is why Gadamer believes that all comprehension is linguistic. I would suggest Carnap's "principle of tolerance": "Let us be cautious in making assertions and critical in examining them, but tolerant in permitting linguistic forms."[2] We are all rational beings and to arrive at certain agreement is one of the social orders that we pursue. Most of us would not appreciate an endless disagreement in the understanding of an object. Nor would most of us deny desperately any close-to-truth answer provided by another thinker. In the end, we shall come to an agreement.

2. The New Twofold Translation: Solution to a Major Point of Difficulty

Why should one start anew in retranslating any classical philosophy literature (such as *Gongsun Longzi*), when we have already had translated versions in modern Chinese and English? It is certainly trivial, if it is nothing but a minor improvement. But a retranslation is inevitably necessary, if new clues are found through an in-depth analytical reading of the literature system, which throw a new light on the important points of difficulty, indicating the possibility of shaking the ideological foundation of the established conclusions. As his PhD dissertation advisor, I know that Liu Limin

---

1   V. Quine, *Word and Object*, The M.I.T. Press, Cambridge, Massachusetts, 1960: 31-34.

2   See Carnap: "Empiricism, Semantics, and Ontology", in *Modern Philosophy of Language* by Maria Baghramian, first American edition, 1999 by Counterpoint, P. O. Box 65793, Washington, D.C., p. 66.

has been engaged in ridding Gongsun Long of the label of "paradoxical sophist", ever since he found that the pre-*Qin* Ming Jia (or School of Names) thinkers were not talking sophistic paradoxes at the start of his doctorate project research. This twofold translation of his has indeed come up with new theoretical clues through his critical reading of Gongsun Long's literature system. On the basis of this, a major point of difficulty is tackled: a reasonable reinterpretation of the theory of the pre-*Qin* Ming Jia. This is not just a matter of redressing the wrong imposed on them, but of far greater significance concerning the position of Chinese culture in international exchanges. The course of his research naturally leads to this success on the one hand. And on the other, he has offered a radical answer to the question whether such a twofold translation of the classical literature is indeed necessary or not, since there have already been versions by foregoing scholarship. Such a radical answer, if tenable, is of important head-starting value for the translation of ancient philosophy in general.

Why should there be sophistic paradoxes? Paradoxes are necessary of language. To say the white is the black out of ignorance is not a sophistic paradox. Nor is a proposition paradoxical, if it can be rectified in the principle of verification. Roughly speaking, to be a sophistic paradox, it could be 1) to argue for the sake of arguing, or deliberately referring to the white as the black, which needs only to be laughed off; or 2) to put forward deceptively grotesque propositions in the era when there was no device of formal logic to clarify the meaning of language expressions.

Generations of philosophers have been racking their brains in dealing with the indeterminacy and ambiguity of language meaning and turned up with some practical methods for it. Generally speaking, these can be employed to avoid sophistic paradoxes. For instance, one can use modern formal logic to rewrite natural language expressions to ensure that a proposition has only one definite meaning. Another example is Quine's canonical notations in a whole set of regimentation techniques,[1] which aim at ruling out ambiguities. There are also other methods, such as the stratification and ordering of language. According to Tarski's proposal of "X" is

---

1   V. Quine, *Word and Object*, The M.I.T. Press, Cambridge, Massachusetts, 1960: 157-186.

true iff p,[1] the entire sentence is the instrumental language and the one in brackets is the object language. In this way, language is stratified. In so doing, one adopts the distinction between "use" and "mention". What is mentioned is put into brackets, quotation marks or in special fonts or variant forms, etc. For example, in "Chomsky is a great philosopher of language", the word "Chomsky" is used, while in "'Chomsky' has seven letters", the word "Chomsky" is mentioned and quotation-marked. The "Chomsky" so mentioned does not have any extension, meaning that it does have a reference. It no longer refers to the philosopher named Chomsky who exists in the world! Here, we find another verification of Gongsun Long's idea of "to refer is not the same as to denote": it is wrong to say that a reference means necessarily the denotation of a specific object (or a human being)!

To clear up sophism, there may be other ways.

The seemingly strange propositions of Gongsun Long's are in fact not sophistic paradoxes. They are the propositions that he put forward at the time when he could not resort to formal logic to clarify the meaning of language expressions, which is why they looked strange: especially when he juggled with his idea of "reference is not the same as denotation"! It is exactly here that we perceive the greatness of Gongsun Long, who was proposing ideas far ahead of his time under the condition that there were no formal rules proper for recording his speech and for writing down his ideas, which explains why his statements appear to be grotesque. With this point in mind, we can give our understanding smile, when we read Liu Limin's conclusions on *Gongsun Longzi*:

> *My comprehension and translation are based on the standpoint that the pre-Qin Ming Jia thinkers, represented by Gongsun Long, were a group of rationalist philosophers of language. Mine is, of course, a conditional explanation, but as far as I know, this is the only explanation that covers in a self-consistent manner all and every "paradoxical" proposition of Ming Jia's. I do not claim that this is the ultimate explanation, but do believe that it is much more reasonable and*

---

1   See "The Semantic Conception of Truth and the Foundations of Semantics" in *Modern Philosophy of Language* by Maria Baghramian, 1999 by Counterpoint, P. O. Box 65793, Washington, D.C., p. 46.

coherent than any interpretations available. ("Introduction")

Liu is saying that Gongsun Long and his fellow Ming Jia thinkers are not talking sophistic nonsense at all and their propositions do make sense, if Ming Jia people are looked upon as "rationalistic philosophers of language".

Liu Limin has also pointed out:

I believe that if the analytical techniques of modern western philosophy of language (such as the distinction of "use" and "mention") are applied, we may present more coherently, hence more convincingly, the ideas of philosophy of language Gongsun Long has expressed in his discourses. About this point, more will be said in my later discussion. ("Introduction")

In other words, if Gongsun Long had had the availability of frameworks and techniques of modern philosophy of language (such as the distinction of "use" and "mention") for his work, his propositions would not have appeared to be sophistic paradoxes.

We can find in this book Liu's explanations of his claims like these, from which we can benefit a lot.

3. Concluding Remarks

China today is witnessing an enthusiasm to translate ancient Chinese literature into foreign languages. My suggestions concerning this tide are 1) that the translator had better make clear his/her own hermeneutical standpoint before setting out doing translation and accordingly decide the translation approach to be adopted, whether it be direct translation, indirect translation or both, or some others (as those of modern hermeneutics), on the basis of an understanding as to why such an approach is proper; 2) that the translator should have a mastery of the essential philosophical tendency of the ancient writings and stick to it consistently, in order to come up with exquisite versions full of insightful ideas; and 3) that it is more advisable to retranslate certain ancient philosophy literature for the purpose of resolving a major theoretical conundrum than just to make a few minor improvements. Liu Limin's twofold translation does have provided readers with beneficial illuminations in all these three aspects.

I hope the above discussion is of some help to the readers of this book and of some reference value to the enterprise of the translation of ancient philosophy literature.

(English version by Liu Limin)

Professor Qian Guanlian

Guangdong University of Foreign Studies

April 12, 2012

Review on *Reinterpretation and Retranslation of* Gongsun Longzi

1. Research on *Gongsun Longzi*: A Difficult But Worthy Job

The research on *Gongsun Longzi* is difficult, because the original was written in a style at once terse and profound and in the Chinese language characterized by polysemy of its expressions, which is why the interpretations of *Gongsun Longzi* have hitherto turned out to be enormously different from each other. The only thing in common is that various interpretations have their own self-consistent rationale. Such a situation makes it extremely hard for us to re-apprehend the ideas of Gongsun Long's as they should truly be; but on the other hand, it offers us different viewpoints of various interpretations that are worthy of further investigation, in terms of their approaches to the interpretation of *Gongsun Longzi*, their criteria considered to be reasonable and their ideologies and theories underlying the different interpretations. Therefore, researchers of *Gongsun Longzi* are justified to take the present researches on and interpretations of *Gongsun Longzi* as their objects for study, in addition to *Gongsun Longzi*, the book itself. And the observation on the former may well be of help to the understanding of the latter. In this sense, the book *Gongsun Longzi* is both the purpose and the medium of our study. It enables us to perceive what the modern researchers implicitly apprehend and to examine the influences of Chinese and western ideas on them. For this reason, the value of the research on *Gongsun Longzi* is indeed multi-dimensional.

Of course, there is no such a thing as absolutely objective standpoint by which one can evaluate an interpretation system and what one can do is to inspect it on the basis of a self-complete criterion.

Professor Liu has been my friend whom I have never met. It is for interpreting

Gongsun Longzi and uncovering the philosophical issues therein that we come to know each other via emails, which gives us an appreciable experience of a friendship at once distant and close. On this book of his, entitled *Reinterpretation and Retranslation of* Gongsun Longzi, I do have a high comment, not only because he is able to give a coherent interpretation of *Gongsun Longzi* in the light of philosophy of language, imbuing it with a new understanding, but also because he has raised quite a few prospective philosophical questions as the result from a comparative inquiry into the peculiar way of expressing ideas in traditional Chinese philosophy. His book is of head-starting value for me. Master Zeng Shen, a famous Confucian disciple, once said, "A gentleman's present to the friends is his essay with an eye to achieving benevolence." Following Zeng's advice, I'd like to note down herein what I think about after reading his book, as a present to my friend.

2. The Approach and Theoretical Postulate of the Book

Professor Liu approaches the research in this procedural sequence: comprehension, interpretation, translation, reconstruction, comparison, comment and question-raising. For reference in comprehension, he has adopted the original of Wang Guan's, entitled *New Collection of Masters' Writings:* Gongsun Longzi *and Its Unsettled Issues*, which is in standardized traditional Chinese characters, and for reference in interpreting and translating, he has used the two available works, *Vernacular Style Interpretation of* Gongsun Longzi by Wang Hongyin (Xi'an: San Qin Press, 1997) and *A Preliminary Study of Pre-*Qin *Ming Jia* by Liu Yujun (Taipei: Zheng Yi Press, 2002). In the latter, Liu Yujun has completed the translation of four essays of Gongsun Long's into modern Chinese and English, the essay "Tong Bian Lun" (literally, "On Change") not having been translated. In the theoretical reconstruction, there are certain postulates for comprehension involved.

On the whole, the book *Reinterpretation and Retranslation of* Gongsun Longzi is quite systematic in reinterpretation. By "systematic", I mean it has the coherence of the presentation of the theoretical framework of *Gongsun Longzi* and the content of interpretation. His reinterpretation has established the relevance of the theories formulated in all the essays in *Gongsun Longzi* by protruding the consistency of the viewpoints in the classic, the mutual compatibility of the arguments and the sequential development of the ideas. To put it in simple terms, Professor Liu has interpreted Gongsun Long as a rationalist philosopher and not at all a sophist as he was traditionally labeled. As to the cases of incomplete coverage of Liu's reinterpretation system, I shall have more comments later on.

As he claims in the "Introduction", Professor Liu has the core question in mind when writing *Reinterpretation and Retranslation of* Gongsun Longzi, namely "a purely theoretical inquiry, by means of speculation on concepts, into what is essential to semantic necessity and what is the nature of knowledge that man acquires and expresses in language". Liu believes this is the fundamental spirit of Gongsun Long's philosophy of language. This understanding of his appears to be based on the following theoretical assumptions:

1) Gongsun Long's thought is a philosophy of language (Liu's framework appears to be primarily Saussurean philosophy of language);

2) The meaning of language has its essential stipulation, which can be mastered by man (this can be seen from Liu's comprehension of "On Name and Actuality" in *Gongsun Longzi*);

3) Language with its essentially determined meanings constitutes knowledge that has its own properties (this is perceivable from Liu's understanding of "On the Nature of Reference" in *Gongsun Longzi*);

4) There is a "purely conceptual speculative" approach to the inquiry into language meaning and its essence (obvious in Liu's comparative study on the various theories about the name issues in *Gongsun Longzi* and those of the other different schools in pre-*Qin* philosophy);

5) Purely conceptual speculation is one approach to the exploration of the nature of language meaning (by a comparative study on the linguistic features of classical Chinese and English, Liu has illustrated how *Gongsun Longzi* was able to get rid of the restriction imposed on philosophical inquiry by the lack of syntactic devices in the Classical Chinese language);

6) Gongsun Long was inquiring into the nature of language meaning by purely conceptual speculation (this is a positive affirmation on the ideas and expressions in *Gongsun Longzi*, based on the foregoing comparisons);

7) The properties of knowledge as understood by Gongsun Long in the mode of purely conceptual speculation can be apprehended and appreciated (this is Liu's definite confirmation of *Gongsun Longzi,* resulted from his reinterpretations).

These seven viewpoints are mutually supportive and corroborative and form a complete system. Certainly, what theoretical pattern *Gongsun Longzi* is understood to have depends on the choice of the framework for interpretation. In other words, it is the framework of interpretation that determines one's comprehension of the ideas in *Gongsun Longzi.* Such a circular procedure of research does not dwarf the value of the interpretation system, because it would be the best system, so long as it achieves maximum coherence of text decoding. Of course, how great the so-called coherence can be is an evaluation relative to the other interpretation systems. But if we can examine this book in accordance to all and every of its theoretical assumptions, we see for what reasons the author has explained *Gongsun Longzi* as being essentially a philosophy of language.

In comparison and comment, Professor Liu introduced briefly relevant theories of western linguistics and compared the features of key philosophical significance of the western languages and those of the Chinese language. As he points out, "The Classical Chinese language did lack syntactic devices and means to symbolize or formalize logic, but one cannot say just for this reason that there existed no mode of thought in classical Chinese philosophy over the exact meaning of language. The grammatical forms of the western languages, such as gender, number, case, tense, etc., were absent in the Classical Chinese language, but it was characterized by characters which have multiple semantic senses in each of them. This feature is of unique value in giving rise to metaphysical speculative thought in China". Apart from comparison of the language features, Professor Liu has also presented his special topic research in the Appendix, including comparative studies on Saussure and *Gongsun Longzi* interpretation, such as the work of Wu Feibai's. Through these comparative studies, Liu comes to point out that an important approach to the reinterpretation of Ming Jia texts lies with the application of one of the analysis techniques of modern philosophy of language, namely, the "use" and "mention" distinction, as used by Willard Van Orman Quine in his *Word and Object*. This distinction is the key to the re-comprehension of quite a lot of Ming Jia debaters' seemingly paradoxical propositions.

Finally, in raising questions, Professor Liu is concerned with this issue: since the syntactic structure of the Classical Chinese language was not formally clear, Gongsun Long could not set onto the path of formal analysis and the only way for him to follow was semantic analysis. Should we today continue the way Gongsun Long opened? What illumination for modern semantics can we have from Gongsun Long's arguments on the principle of meaning certainty? How is interpersonal language exchange possible and how can the inter-subjectivity be achieved, since there are individual experiential differences, environmental differences and cultural differences? Does it worth the while to give our great attention to Gongsun Long's principle of "the exclusive essence of 'this' and of 'that'"? According to Gongsun Long's reasoning, abstract concepts are not necessarily metaphorical, because they should have their own "thisness" or "thatness", which are different from the thisness and thatness of concrete concepts. If so, how can mapping be possible between concepts of different semantic nature? If both are regarded as having the essential stipulations independent of each other, how then can abstract concepts be formed from the so-called embodied experiences? ...Professor Liu has not given a definite answer to these questions, but his viewpoint concerning the answer is concealed in all the parts of this book, which requires the readers to perceive.

3. The Structure of the Book

The book by Professor Liu is logically structured, centering on the clue of meaning transformation. Part I is patterned by the original of Gongsun Long's essay-modern Chinese version-English version. Certainly, comprehension is needed both in translating from the classical original into modern Chinese and in translating from modern Chinese into English, and therefore Part II offers the grounds for comprehension in Part I, the philosophical issues involved in Gongsun Long's speculative thinking and his viewpoints with which he tackled the issues. And then, how can we be sure that the author's interpretation of *Gongsun Longzi* is correct? To this, the author has given in Part III a discussion on the misunderstandings and problematic interpretations and evaluations of *Gongsun Longzi* on the part of ancient thinkers and of scholars at home and abroad in modern times, on the basis of which the author has further illustrated the correct approach to the reinterpretation of *Gongsun Longzi*. The book has established *Gongsun Longzi* as a document of philosophy of language, and the pre-*Qin* Ming Jia as rationalistic philosophers of the time.

To some extent, the author does have achieved a coherence of reinterpretation based on his arguments in the previous chapters, and in the Appendix,[1] Professor Liu presents his specialized research on different aspects of pre-*Qin* Ming Jia's thought. Of the papers included in the part, his "The World of Meaning Constructed by Language Parsing" is a comparative study of the ideas in "On Name and Actuality" and "On the Nature of Reference" in *Gongsun Longzi* with the relevant western linguistics ideas. His "Philosophical Speculations of Pre-*Qin* School of Names on the Meaning of Adjectives of the Classical Chinese Language" discusses the so-called "paradoxical sophisms" of pre-*Qin* Ming Jia's, showing that these are essentially philosophical propositions rationalistically oriented. These propositions are the evidence that the Ming Jia thinkers were following the path towards rationalist philosophy determined by the unique characteristics of the Chinese language that differs from that followed by western philosophy. In "Meta-categorization of Language and Gongsun Long's Philosophy of Language", he points out that Gongsun Long was self-conscious in his speculation on the meta-categorization of semantic concepts, demonstrating his clear awareness of the philosophical questions of ontology and epistemology. Liu highlights Gongsun Long's philosophical reflection on the nature of "name" meanings on the basis of the Chinese language in the mode of meta-categorized cognition. Finally, the article, "Re-examining the Issue of Pre-*Qin* Schools of Thought in Philosophy of Language", points out that it is quite incorrect to attribute some common feature to the pre-*Qin* Confucianism, Daoism, Mohism, Legalism, and Ming Jia, because each of them differs greatly from the rest in their comprehension of "name" and "actuality" on the basis of their own different ideological orientations, levels of thoughts and approaches to inquiry. In this discussion, the author highlights Gongsun Long's

---

1 The three essays mentioned by Professor Lee were originally included as a part of this book in its draft version, which have been left out because the ideas presented in them have been incorporated in Part III of this version. The former Chapter IV in the first draft is not included here. —Liu's note

approach of purely conceptual speculation on the essence of language meaning.

In addition, the Appendix presents the translation of pre-*Qin* Ming Jia debaters' propositions, traditionally labeled "paradoxical non-sense" from the classical Chinese into modern Chinese as well as into English, with a translator's interpretative note attached to each item. These translations and interpretations are highly relevant with the ideas in previous parts, forming a further support in another dimension.

4. Some Problems with the Content

A) Some issues concerning the versions of *Gongsun Longzi*

There have been different versions of *Gongsun Longzi* since the *Ming* and the *Qing* Dynasties, such as the ones in Tao Zongyi's *Shuo Fu*, in *Tao Zang*, in *The Twelve Scholars*, in Zhou Ziyi's *Scholarly Collections*, in *Mian Miao Ge Collection*, in Wang Xiangtang's *Collections of the Twenty Two Scholars*, in Zhang Haipeng's *Mo Hai Jin Hu Collection*, and in Qian Xizuo's *Shou Shan Ge Collection*, etc. It is generally acknowledged that the version in *Taoist Scriptures* is the earliest, from which the other versions are derived, and more likely to be true to the original. But according to the study of Mr. Yang Junguang of Philosophy Department of Nanjing University, the *Shuo Fu* version might be even earlier than the *Taoist Scriptures* version and with some different dictions, its source is considered to be in a system other than that of *Tao Zang*.

Now, let's make a comparison of the two textual versions, one from the orthodox *Tao Zang* (referred to as *TZ* below) of *Ming* Dynasty and the other from the *Extended Tao Zang* (referred to as *ETZ* below) of Wanli Period of the same dynasty, for an inspection of the texts adopted in this book of Liu's. [1]

a1. In "On Name and Actuality", the name of "者" in "天地与其所产者" (*ETZ*) is "焉" (*TZ*).

a2. In "On White Horse", the sentence "有白马，为有白马之非马，何也"

---

1   To the questions Professor Hsien Chung Lee poses here about the versions of the classic, I have given my answers by means of footnotes to the original texts of *Gongsun Longzi*. These version differences do not change the meaning of the original, except a9. For this reason, there is no change of my English version. As to a9, I have given an explanation in a footnote to the English version. —Liu's note

(*ETZ*) is punctuated into "有白马为有马，白之，非马，何也" (*TZ*).

a3. In the same text, the sentence of "天下非有无色之马" (*ETZ*) is followed by a function term "也"："天下非有无色之马也" (*TZ*).

a4. In addition, "使马无色，如有马已耳，安取白马" in *ETZ* is phrased as "使马无色，有马如已耳，安取白马" in *TZ*.

a5. Finally, in the sentence "以有白马不可谓无马者，离白之谓也。是离者，有白马不可谓有马也", the wording of the phrase "是离者" in *ETZ* is changed into "不离者" in *TZ*.

a6. In "On Hardness and Whiteness", the sentence "得其白，得其坚，见与不见离。不见离" in *ETZ* is different from the *TZ* expression of "得其白，得其坚，见与不见与不见离".

a7. In "On Change", the *ETZ* sentence of "而牛之非羊也、羊之非牛也" differs from that in *TZ*, "而羊牛之非羊也、之非牛也". From the context, the former appears to be more correct, while the latter more problematic.

a8. In the same essay, the phrase of "羊牛足五" in *ETZ* has an inverted order of "牛羊足五" in *TZ*.

a9. In "On the Nature of Reference", the sentence of "使天下无物，谁径谓非指" in *ETZ* has another character added in: "使天下无物指，谁径谓非指" in *TZ*.

B) Some problems with the interpretations of *Gongsun Longzi*

b1. In "On Name and Actuality", the character of "行" in the sentence "谓此而行不唯乎此" should be changed into "此", according to Wang Qixiang's study.

b2. In "On Name and Actuality", two characters should be changed in the sentence "知此之非也，知此之不在此也，明不谓也", making the sentence to be "知此之非此也，知此之不在此也，则不谓也", according to both Yu Yue's and Wang Qixiang's studies. In this way, the sentence appears to correspond more with the following sentence in structure.

b3. Again in "On Name and Actuality", a statement goes: "故彼，彼止于彼；此，此止于此，可。彼此而彼且此，此彼而此且彼，不可"; In the versions of Chen Li's, Xin Congyi's and *Shou Shan Ge Collection*, there is no comma between the second and the third characters and the sentence appears to begin with "故彼彼", which is also adopted by most of the modern scholars, such as Zhou Changzhong, Chen Xianyou and Xu Fuguan. In this book of Liu's, the prevalent punctuation pattern is not followed. It is another story who is right or wrong, but this book also quotes some statements from the *Mohist Scripture*, which goes: "正名者彼此。彼此可：彼彼止于彼，此此止于此。彼此不可：彼且此也。彼此亦可：彼此止于彼此。若是而彼此也，则彼彼此此也". There is an inconsistency in terms of punctuation.

b4. In "On Hardness and Whiteness", the sentence "而坚必坚其不坚。石物而坚" is translated to be "Hardness is just that which hardens the non-hard objects". I suggest a punctuation of the original as "而坚必坚，其不坚石、物而坚" and a translation of it into "Hardness is just hardness in itself. It is hardness without making stones or anything hard."

b5. In "On Change", the thought expressed in "青白不相与而相与，反对也。不相邻而相邻，不害其方也" should be more suitably explained by introducing in the ideas of the Operation and Location of the Five Elements.

b6. In "On the Nature of Reference", the phrase of "物指" in the sentence "使天下无物指，谁径谓非指" is an important concept, which cannot be explained by "things that are not references".

b7. In "On the Nature of Reference", there are three different senses proposed: first, "ostensive denoting", meaning the labeling of a thing with a name; second, "reference", meaning the denotation of the essence of things; and third, "signifier", the name itself. This is the basis on which Liu infers that Gongsun Long was discussing the issue of using name to refer to things. Personally, I do not think this understanding is sufficient.

b8. To understand the statements of "使天下无物指，谁径谓非指" and "天下有指，无物指，谁径谓非指" in "On the Nature of Reference", the key term to the interpretation of "非指" or "而指非指" is the phrase of "物指". This phrase means a two-way relationship between the cognizing subject and the object for cognition via a "referring function". The result of cognition that the subject has obtained is a result of the cooperation between the subject and the object; it is what the subject has had via mastering the properties of the object. This should be the true meaning of the phrase "而指非指". Such a framework of subject-object dualism coheres with the interpretation of the original texts of "On Hardness and Whiteness" and "On Name and Actuality".[1]

If we clarify the idea of "非指", we find that *Gongsun Longzi* is not just a works on philosophy of language. Just as Professor Liu himself has stated, Gongsun Long's ideas involve epistemological and metaphysical issues. In terms of the distribution of topics, the three essays of "On Hardness and Whiteness", "On the Nature of Reference and "On Name and Actuality" are an exploration of the way to and the possibility of cognition, with an establishment of the principles for a correct expression of the result of cognition. And "On Name and Actuality", "On Change", and "On White-horse Not-horse" are exemplary illustration of the principles for correct expressions and the thinking processes that lead to the formation of concepts. Thus, the whole book of *Gongsun Longzi* has dealt with the three philosophical questions of cognition, thinking and expression, beyond the scope of philosophy of language. Thus understood, there appears to be a greater possibility of dialogs with the criticisms against Gongsun Long's "On the Nature of Reference" by Zhuangzi in his essay "On Knowing Things", hence highlighting the rich thoughts in relevant literature concerning the study of name in pre-*Qin* period.

Professor Liu has raised the question that we should attach a great attention to Gongsun Long's principle of "the exclusive essence of the *thisness* in this or the *thatness* in that". Is it really worth the while? In my opinion, also as Professor Zhou Yunzhi has proposed, in his *On the Study of Name and Debate*, the target for the rectification of names must be the names at once at the linguistic and the conceptual levels. Gongsun Long's "On Name and Actuality" does contain philosophical and logical rectification of names and his philosophical rectification requires the correspondence between the name and the actuality, especially in the existential order of actuality first and name second. And his principle of the exclusive essence, however, refers to the independence of concepts in the world of thought, where the this and the that are distinctive in themselves and cannot be confused with one

---

1　I appreciate Professor Lee's criticisms listed above. Because his criticism of b1 does seem quite reasonable, I have adopted it by adding a footnote to the original version of *Gongsun Longzi*. And b4 is not different from my understanding. As to the rest of the items, Professor Lee has expressed some different opinions from those of mine, about which I have given my reasons for understanding in Parts II and III, respectively of translator's notes and of the framework for reinterpreting *Gongsun Longzi*. —Liu's note

another. As to the rectification principle for conventionalized words, the idea finds its source in Xunzi's essay "Rectification of Name", where the use of the same name to denote different things or vice versa are allowed, so long as people can reach an agreement in their verbal communication. For instance, the term "机车" (motor vehicle) can refer to means of transportation, but among the young people in Taiwan, this phrase is also used to refer, in their everyday speech, to a person who is slow to get into the right track. In language expression, "机车" is just one phrase, but in the world of thought, it refers to two totally different concepts. The value of Gongsun Long's principle of "the exclusive essence of the *thisness* in this or the *thatness* in that" lies exactly in that it protrudes the independence of every concept from one another. Such a logical principle for the rectification of names is of great importance and we should give it our great attention of study.

5. Concluding Remarks

This review of mine on the book is based on the requirements of both compatibility and originality in the interpretation of historical classics, which include the following points.

1) The texts used for interpretation should match the classic original.

2) The interpretation of the textual expressions must conform to the language usage in ancient times, which involves the points of the etymology of the key terms, the period in which the original author lived and the book was written, and the coherence of ideas in the classic works. To give an example, the term of "指" must be examined in terms of its etymological source and semantic evolution in ancient times: how it was originated in writings such as *Buci* (oracles carved on bones, before 11th century BC), *Jinwen* (inscriptions carved on bronze, before 7th century BC), *Dazhuan* (ancient seal-style writing, before 7th century BC), etc.; what its semantic meaning was during the times of Mencius, Zhuangzi, Xunzi and Mohism and what it might mean in *Gongsun Longzi* itself.

3) The interpretation itself should be logically sound and the ideas interpreted consistent without any self-contradiction, which is the most basic requirement for interpreting the classics.

4) There is also the question of the compatibility of the explanation of a classic works with the social and cultural background at the time it was written. Any thought is a product of the social-historical environment and of the ideological culture. There might be differences and conflicts between the then prevalent ideas, but they constituted together a more general background of ideology and culture. Such a general background had a constraint on the contents of thought, the nature of theory and even the approach to thought over questions on the part of every single writer of the time. Therefore, one should take the relevant factors of the time into consideration in explaining *Gongsun Longzi*.

5) The essence of being a philosopher is the originality of thought. Since originality is essential, new dimensions and frameworks for reinterpretation must be permitted, in addition to the above-mentioned points. The reason why *Gongsun Longzi* has proved to be very difficult to understand is exactly that there is no standardized approach to its interpretation.

Professor Liu's *Reinterpretation and Retranslation of* Gongsun Longzi has given an emphasis to the third and the fifth points above and also to the fourth point, with his efforts on the historical perspective of the development of the study of names in pre-*Qin* period as well as examinations of the limitations of the Classical Chinese language. His interpretation of *Gongsun Longzi* is indeed consistent from the beginning to the end. This book of Liu's is characterized by his unique apprehension of the original thought in *Gongsun Longzi*: he has made a considerable academic contribution in this field by opening a completely new way to the study of the ideas of Ming Jia's via his comparative examination of the peculiar morphological features of the classic Chinese language and of the English language. Making use of his scholarly background in linguistics and philosophy of language and interpreting Gongsun Long's ideas in the framework of language meaning analysis, he has achieved an insight in explaining the character of "离" (pronounced "lí", literally "to separate"), a central concept in *"On Hardness and Whiteness"* in *Gongsun Longzi*, and his explanation has highlighted the analytical spirit of Gongsun Long's thought. This is the point I appreciate particularly of his book. Just like Liu has said confidently in the book: "Is my reinterpretation and retranslation successful? I leave this question to the readers and to history. But as the translator, I am quite confident that my translation is more reasonable and more coherent than all the other versions available at present in explaining all and every proposition of Ming Jia thinkers'. This shows at least that the framework of my book approximates more closely to the thought tendency of Ming Jia thinkers, compared with any existing frameworks for interpretation". Indeed, of the books related to *Gongsun Longzi* study that I have read so far, this book is highly consistent internally and is of significant value of reference for my own researches on the methodology of Classical Chinese philosophy as well as on the pre-*Qin* debates on name and logic. I believe that with the active and insightful exchanges of ideas among the like-minded scholars, we can push forward and deepen our understanding of the philosophical wisdom of the pre-*Qin* Ming Jia and apply what we understand thereof to the various issues of cognition, thought and expression in modern times that we face.

(*English version by Liu Limin*)

Professor Hsien Chung Lee
Department of Philosophy, Taiwan University
September 25, 2012

Introduction

Translation aims at the exchange of ideas between peoples who speak different languages. Ideally, a translation is encouraged to satisfy what criteria Yan Fu has proposed, namely "*faithfulness, expressiveness and elegance*". This is easier said than done, however. Even the primary criterion of faithfulness proves quite difficult to satisfy, still less than the high level requirement of elegance, or keeping the stylistic flavor in a perfect manner. The fundamental difficulty lies with the fact that translation works on meaning, which is extremely complex and even too erratic to apprehend. According to W. V. O. Quine (1960:185-212), there is a radical indeterminacy not only of the translation between two languages, but also of the paraphrase between two sentences within the same language, the fundamental reason being the indeterminacy of the references, hence the uncertainty of the meaning. In his view, there is no way to determine the meaning of a single sentence just by itself; to understand what a sentence means, one should put it against the entire belief system that the speaker has, to see what he holds to be true and how his knowledge is structured. It seems then that translation can, at the very best, achieve an approximate communication, and a perfect and complete translation remains an ideal only. This leaves ample room for retranslation and a translator should not stop reflecting on and criticizing the translated versions, so as to turn up with what might be a better version that approximates more closely what the original writer truly intends to convey.

In this spirit, I believe that four reasons make the retranslation of *Gongsun Longzi* necessary.

Firstly, the essays written by Gongsun Long have traditionally been mislabeled "sophistic paradoxes" and not correctly understood. Even at present, when he has been given his due justice and regarded respectively as pre-*Qin* philosopher, logician, theoretical scientist or linguistic thinker, what he actually is is still a perplexing problem. Available interpretations of his essays are not only widely different from but frequently in conflict with each other. About this situation, I shall give a more detailed study in the later part on *Gongsun Longzi*. As to the experts abroad, the erroneous interpretation of *Gongsun Longzi* even borders on being nonsensical, landing the readers in such a perplexity that they would consider Gongsun Long nothing but a nonsense-talker. Let's look at an example here. A. C. Graham interpreted the beginning sentence of Gongsun Long's essay "On the Nature of Reference", "物莫非指，而指非指", in this way: "When no thing is not the pointed-out (what the name points out), to point out is not to point it out." (Graham, 1990: 213) How much sense could a reader make of this interpretation? Such a status quo invites us to re-read *Gongsun Longzi* with renewed insights, in order to come up with a more satisfactory reinterpretation and retranslation of his essays.

Secondly, a coherent explanation of *Gongsun Longzi* is conducive to a better understanding and appreciation of the rationalistic ideas of philosophy in ancient China, hence justifying a traditional Chinese philosophy and promoting philosophical idea exchanges between China and the external world. This effort is necessary because quite a few scholars in the world as well as in China are doubtful that there was a philosophy in ancient China. J. Derrida (2001: 10), for example, declared in Shanghai early in 1990's, where he lectured to a group of Chinese philosophers, that there are thoughts but no philosophy in Chinese tradition, because philosophy is something European, closely associated with European languages, and invented by the ancient Greeks. Many, including quite some Chinese philosophers themselves, believe that one reason why philosophy could not have come into being in China is the barrier laid out by the Chinese language, as its loose syntactic structure is not favorable for the occurrence of the speculative metaphysics of "being qua being". Yet, as I shall show with my study on Gongsun Long's sayings later on in this book, such an opinion is seriously mistaken. But this point awaits further clarification by a careful and coherent investigation into *Gongsun Longzi*. Of all the philosophers of pre-*Qin* China, many have been rather thoroughly studied and individuals such as Confucius, Mencius, Laozi, Zhuangzi, and Mozi have been given rather consistent explanations. But Ming Jia thinkers have not been studied as thoroughly and deeply. As the result, there exist various conflicting explanations of their ideas. This barrier still stands in our exchange of thoughts with the rest of the world.

Thirdly, to my knowledge, there have been two English versions of *Gongsun Longzi*, one being authored by Wang Hongyin, entitled *Gongsun Longzi in Vernacular Reading* (Shaanxi: San Qin Press, 1997), and the other by Liu Yujun, entitled *A Preliminary Interpretation of Pre-*Qin *Ming Jia* (Taipei: Zheng Yi Press, 2002). The latter has not completed the translation of all the five essays of Gongsun Long's, with his "On Essence and Change" not translated. I do think that both the two translators are excellent in their translation. However, as I see it, their versions have not been able to throw light on the essential spirit of Gongsun Long's philosophy of language, namely that of a purely theoretical inquiry, by means of speculation on concepts, into the nature of knowledge that man acquires and expresses in language. For this reason, their versions do have certain problems. Take the most famous proposition of Gongsun Long's, that of "White-horse is not horse", for example. Liu considers the essay to be a discourse of dialectical revelation of the unification of contradictions between the individual and the general, while Wang believes that Gongsun Long was trying to "seek the difference from the sameness", aiming at establishing the relationships between the actuality and the concept, and the intension and the extension, on the basis of a combination of formal logical reasoning with dialectical reasoning. I do not at all agree with the two authors' evaluation of Gongsun Long's ideas in terms of dialecticism. In my opinion, Gongsun Long was in fact riveted on the speculations on how the correctness of the meaning of a name could be determined, by differentiating strictly the two levels of analysis: that of empirical facts and that of language concepts. One finds no indication of dialecticism in Gongsun Long's writings. This is probably why in both Liu's and Wang's versions, we find points of difficulty where we cannot follow the logical reasoning of the original author. This could leave the readers at least an impression that Gongsun Long's ideas do appear to be logical, but with serious loopholes, because the readers soon encounter quite a few incoherent and even self-contradictory statements between his essays or even between sections within the same essay. And this needs to be clarified and corrected. Meanwhile, I believe that if the analytical techniques of modern western philosophy of language (such as the distinction of "use" and "mention") are applied, we may present more coherently, hence more convincingly, the ideas of philosophy of language Gongsun Long has expressed in his discourses. About this point, more will be said in my later discussion.

Finally, Gongsun Long and the other Ming Jia thinkers were said to be exclusively focused on the issue of names, i.e., they were focused on nothing else than the reflections on language problems. For this reason, they have also contributed some unique ideas to language studies in ancient China. This is of great theoretical significance for the question of the formation of a linguistic school of thought of China's at present. As is known to all, we Chinese linguists do not yet have our own independent school of linguistics theory that is internationally influential. The so-called rationalism and empiricism in Chinese linguistics that we take sides with in our study today are all introduced in from western linguistic sciences. This is especially the case in China's foreign language research circle. In the circle of the Chinese language research, there is a more active atmosphere of academy in this respect, as the scholars begin to have their own theoretical orientations, basing their viewpoints on the basic characteristics of the Chinese language. However, an internationally influential school of linguistic thought is yet to be expected. Part of the reasons for this status quo is that we have so far failed to delve into our own traditional treasures of language study, particularly of philosophy of language, from which we might have benefited tremendously. In this respect, the study on *Gongsun Longzi* may give us illuminations.

Therefore, I intend to, in this book, offer a new translation of the five essays in *Gongsun Longzi* and the 31 "sophistic paradoxes" of Hui Shi's and other Ming Jia debaters'. My comprehension and translation are based on the standpoint that the pre-*Qin* Ming Jia thinkers, represented by Gongsun Long, were a group of rationalist philosophers of language.

Mine is, of course, a conditional explanation, but as far as I know, this is the only explanation that covers in a self-consistent manner all and every "paradoxical" proposition of Ming Jia's. I do not claim that this is the ultimate explanation, but believe that it is much more reasonable and coherent than any interpretations available, since none of them, as they stand at present, can make a coherent sense of every single proposition. So far, I believe that my framework for the reinterpretation and retranslation of *Gongsun Longzi* is a more reasonable one. However, in the spirit of scientific research, I am willing to accept any better and more convincing explanations of Gongsun Long and Ming Jia in the days to come.

In the same spirit, I do not pretend that this book is a faithful reduplication of the Ming Jia thought, because historical events can never be truthfully reproduced. On the other hand, I do not see eye to eye with E. Nida's "functional equivalence" theory of translation (Nida, 1993), as there ought to be ways in which we can be helped to tell the correct from the incorrect. Although a thousand translators may end up with a thousand Gongsun Longs (to borrow the phrasing from hermeneutics), what they produce have to be Gongsun Long and no one else, after all. Since it is highly improbable, or even impossible, for us to obtain any objective standards to tell whether a translation of *Gongsun Longzi* is absolutely right or wrong, I am ready to accept the coherence theory of truth, in the hope of adopting the internal coherence of the ideas as the principle for evaluating the reliability of my translation and those of others.

By "coherence", I mean that in the course of translating, a translator should try hard to understand the original so as to establish the consistency in comprehension between a particular sentence with other sentences as well as with the entire text (an essay or a book). Dr. Du Shihong (2012) has pointed out that coherence is not a technical aspect of a text, but emerges in discourse interaction on the basis of rationality, knowledge, intention and so on. In this principle, I should not be constrained, in translating *Gongsun Longzi*, to the surface structure of the original, including its diction and syntax, but try to make sure that there is a logically sound reason why I understand a sentence in the way I do, against the framework of thought for comprehension. As to whether my comprehension framework itself is reasonable or not, I shall discuss in greater detail in Part II (Notes on the Translation of *Gongsun Longzi*) and Part III (Framework for Reinterpreting *Gongsun Longzi*).

This brings me to the choice of literal translation or indirect translation. If we were bound up by the original, we might land ourselves in explanatory traps. This is because the classical style of the Chinese language is highly condensed and concise, omitting in some cases the process of reasoning or any semantic components that can be omitted,[1] leaving the readers to infer on what connections between statements and even between sentential elements should be. This makes theoretical works such as *Gongsun Longzi* extremely difficult to read; and for this reason, it is quite necessary to express in clear terms what has originally been cached, left out or assumed. Therefore, I decide to use frequently the method of indirect translation while trying to stick to the original diction.

With my study on pre-*Qin* Ming Jia going on in recent years, I have had some new understandings of Ming Jia, which I want to share with anyone who is interested in the topic. With my study deepening, I have come to suspect the present frameworks in which we examine *Gongsun Longzi*, because no one of the interpretations generated from these frameworks is able to give a coherent explanation of Ming Jia ideas. This is what pushes me to tackle the problem of reinterpretation and retranslation in a different angle. I welcome it if my translation leads to disagreement, for that might further lead to the reflection on traditional Chinese philosophy and linguistics and to the facilitation of mutual understanding and cultural exchange between China and the rest of the world.

The arrangement of Parts in this book is as follows.

After this introduction (in Chinese and English), Part One presents my translation of *Gongsun Longzi*, altogether five essays plus one anecdote of Gongsun Long, from Classical Chinese into modern vernacular Chinese and then into English. The original is adopted from *Interpreting* Gongsun Longzi by Wang Guan.

Part Two consists of my notes on the translation, which gives explanations to why I understand and translate, in the way I have done, the essays and particularly some difficult points in them. The notes are also in both Chinese and English.

Part Three offers my theoretical framework as to how *Gongsun Longzi* should be more coherently comprehended. I shall begin from both traditional and modern misunderstandings of Ming Jia, and explain why I regard Ming Jia thinkers as rationalist philosophers of language, after I present a brief discussion on the grammatical features of the Chinese language and its implications for philosophical

---

1   This is the case partly because of the difficulty caused by the writing instruments (inscription on bamboo sticks) and, some say, partly because of the feature of the Chinese writing system itself.

mode of thought. I shall also provide an explanation of the framework with which I reinvestigate *Gongsun Longzi* and other Ming Jia propositions.

The Appendix presents my translation of the 31 "sophistic paradoxes" mentioned above, with the translator's notes explaining my ideas about them. The reason why this is needed is that a reinterpretation of these decontextualized fragments of Ming Jia's "sophistic paradoxes" certainly reinforces our understanding of what is expressed in *Gongsun Longzi*. A retranslation of these propositions gives us a complete picture of what Ming Jia stands for.

Postscript

Some of the materials and points of view in this book have been published in academic journals in China, including *Philosophical Research*, *Journal of Sichuan University* (Philosophy and Social Science Edition), *Foreign Language Research*, *Journal of Sichuan International Studies University*, and *The Forum on the Philosophy of Language*, *ProtoSociology* as well as my book, entitled *Raising Questions in and of Language: A Study on Rationalistic Philosophy of Language of Pre-Qin School of Names*, published by Sichuan University Press in 2007. The reason why I need to include them in this book is that they help constitute important theoretical basis of my translation, which makes readers understand better my translated versions and give them an idea as to how I have come to the point of view I hold.

I remain quite open to any criticisms and suggestions on my translation and my theoretical viewpoints. In addition, I have quoted from many other scholars' works and have acknowledged their contributions by marking all the sources. All the potential errors in this book are mine.

Part I English Versions of *Gongsun Longzi*

Essay I: On Name and Actuality

Heaven and Earth, with what exist and grow therein, are material objects. Objects are rightly said to be the "objects" essentially for what the objects are without any shade of undue overgeneralization, which constitutes what an "actuality" really is. Such an "actuality" represents fully and exactly an object as it should be without any looseness or ill-fitting; and this is the standard for the reference to be "in appropriate place", the very requirement that ensures the correct use of a name in talking about the objects. Any deviation from such an "in-place" requirement is bound to result in improprieties in the use of a name. The use of a name is correct, only if it satisfies completely this "in-place" requirement.

This requirement is necessary, for it is the criterion by which we rectify the deviant uses of name, or question whether the prevalent practices of rectification of name are reasonable or not.

In light of this view, the rectification of name should be built on the ascertainment of the true nature of the "actuality" that a name refers to. Only when the "actuality" is correctly determined, can the correctness of a name be established. So I propose that to rectify names in the right way we should abide by the principle of the *thisness* in *this* and the *thatness* in *that* exclusively. Specifically, "that" is not a true name of *that*, if one says "that" but does not refer exclusively to the *thatness*; nor is "this" a true name, if one says "this" but does not refer exclusively to the *thisness*. [If this principle is not followed,] One would be in fact applying the name that should refer to one object to another incorrect object, and this is what gives rise to confusions in speech exchanges.

Therefore, when "that" is used, the reference of "that" can only be the *thatness* that *that* should have and only *that* can have. This is the only case in which the name of "that" can be applied to talking about *that*. The same is true of "this"; the reference

151

of "this" can only be the *thisness* that *this* should have and only *this* can have. This is the only case in which the name "this" can be used to talk about *this*. In this way, the meaning of a name corresponds to the essence of the object it names. It is exactly such correspondence that ensures the correctness of the name one uses.

According to this principle, "that" should, and can only, refer to the *thatness* of *that*, and "this" should, and can only, refer to the *thisness* of *this*. Such is the right way to use names. If "that" is applied to *this* so that it refers in effect both to *thatness* and *non-thatness* (*thisness*), or if "this" is applied to *that* so that it refers in effect both to *thisness* and *non-thisness* (*thatness*), these are the wrong ways to use names.

The relationship between name and actuality [that we have been debating on] is, at the end of the day, a question of knowing how to use a name to correctly refer. If it is known that "this" does not correspond to *this*, which means that the *thisness* does not exist in *this* to which the name of "this" is applied, then clearly one should refrain from applying the name "this" to *this*. If it is known that "that" does not correspond to *that*, which means that the *thatness* does not exist in *that* to which the name "that" is applied, then clearly one should refrain from applying the name to *that*.

How insightful were the ancient saints! They inspected meticulously the relationship between the meaning of name and the nature of actuality, in order to use names with great caution in speech. That's where their wisdom was!

Essay II: On "White-horse Is Not Horse"

Heckler: Is it right to say "A white horse is not a horse"?

Gongsun Long: Yes, it is.

H: Why so?

G: "Horse" is a name that names a specific form, while "white" is one that names a specific color. Clearly, the name that names a color cannot be the one that names a form. That's the basis on which I state that "'White-horse' is not 'Horse'".

H: If someone has a white horse, then he cannot be said to have no horse. Since he cannot be said to have no horse, doesn't this entail that he has a horse? For what reason, then, do you insist that to have a white horse is just to have a white horse but is not to have a horse?

G: When you use the name of "horse", both yellow horse and black horse fall under the concept the name refers to. But when you use the name of "white-horse", then yellow horse and black horse do not fall under the concept. Further, let's assume "white-horse" as an equivalent name to "horse", then the two names should be exactly the same in meaning. Since they are necessarily identical in what they mean, the names of "white" and "horse" should not have any differences in meaning. Such differences simply cannot be allowed, because what are exactly the same cannot be different at the same time! However, as we've just seen, in the cases of yellow horse and black horse, there occurs the problem of satisfying or not satisfying the semantic requirement. Why is it so? Well, such a problem is caused by the confusion in determining the essential meaning of the names used. Therefore, even if "yellow horse" and "black horse" are regarded as one conceptual entity, which we can use to instantiate the meaning of having "horse", we nevertheless cannot use it to instantiate the meaning of having "white-horse". Thus, "white-horse" is not the same as "horse". Isn't this evident enough?

H: By doing so, you are talking about the issue of "A white-horse is not a horse" on the postulation that horses are colorless. But in the actual world, there exists no colorless horse. Does it follow then that there exists no horse in the world?

G: As an empirical fact, horses do have colors, and this is why we can have white horses. But when we speak of "horse" *per se*, it does not have any color as its essential property. The concept of "horse" is only the "horseness-in-itself"; how on earth can one smuggle "white-horse" into the concept? The key point is that whiteness is not a definitional quality of horseness. "White-horse" is a compound name, made up of "horse" and "white". Can it be said, just for this reason, that both the "horse" and the "white" in this compound refer to "horseness" and that exclusively? This is why I say "white-horse" is not "horse".

H: To be sure, a horse is still a horse, even if it is not white; and white color is still white, even if it does not mean the white color of a horse. However, by combining "white" and "horse", the compound name of "white-horse" is formed and that's all there is to it. You are mistaken in claiming that what has already been combined cannot be combined, because their essential properties differ. And so, to me, it is incorrect to say "A white horse is not a horse".

G: Alright, by saying "To have 'white-horse' is to have 'horse'", we mean "to have 'white-horse' is to have 'yellow-horse'"; can this be right?

H: No, certainly not.

G: So it follows that "to have 'horse'" and "to have 'yellow-horse'" are undoubtedly two different statements. In this case, "yellow-horse" is distinguishable from "horse". The two names of "yellow-horse" and "horse" are distinguishable because each of them has its own respective reference. Since you do admit that "yellow-horse" is not "horse", why must you be so bigoted as to insist that "white-horse" is "horse"? Your claims are the most self-contradictory and confusing under the sun, as absurd as saying "what flies lives in water" or "the coffin and its boards are located in different places"!

Certainly, "having white-horse" is not equivalent to "having horse". The key point is, we should isolate the essence of "whiteness" for separate inspection. It is this isolation that makes "to have white-horse" different conceptually from "to have horse". In the phrase "to have horse", the name "horse" can only refer to the horseness-in-itself and nothing else at the same time. In the same line of thought, we simply cannot take what "white-horse" refers to for what "horse" refers to, because in that case the name "white" would have to refer also to the essence of "horse" and that exclusively, too. Should we do it in this way, we would be saying in effect "to have horse-horse", which turns out ridiculous.

G: What is white does not need to reside in a specific object in order to be white. We should forget concrete white objects and isolate the whiteness-in-itself for comprehension, and this is the right way to grasp the concept the name refers to. In ordinary speech, "white" in the compound name of "white-horse" is taken for the name of a specific color fixed in a concrete object, and for this reason the "white" is in fact not a true name as it does not represent the essence of whiteness in itself. To be correct, we should realize that the definition of "horse" does not at all involve any color element and this is why yellow horses and black horses can instantiate "horse". However, the definition of "white-horse" does include in it the essence of whiteness, and as such, it cannot be instantiated by yellow horses or black horses. White horses are the only objects that fall under the concept of "white-horse". It is necessarily true, then, that what has a certain essence cannot at the same time be what does not have the same essence; hence my assertion "'White-horse' is not 'horse'".

Essay III: On the Being of Hardness and Whiteness

Heckler: Is it correct to say that the hard, the white and the stone are three things?

Gongsun Long: No, it is not.

H: Then is it right to say that they are two things?

G: Yes.

H: Why is it so?

G: One perceives the white without perceiving the hard at the same time, which makes us talk of two experiences perceived. The same is true when one feels the hard without seeing the white at the same time.

H: Having seen the white, one cannot say that there is no whiteness; and having felt the hard, one cannot say that there is no hardness, either. But the same reasoning should be applied to the perception of the stone. Doesn't this prove that the hard, the white and the stone are three things?

G: With the eyes, one sees not the hard but the white. Hardness is not experienced by the eyes. With the hand, one feels not the white but the hard. Whiteness is not experienced by the hand.

H: Without its white color, a stone could in no way be seen; without the hardness in stones, one could not say that a stone is hard. So the hard, the white and the stone are inseparable. Is it then right to say that these three things exist as an integrated whole?

G: I think it is necessary to make clear the idea of "being in and of itself". Such a being is not the same as the factual phenomenon of not being perceived.

H: A stone should be white and hard at the same time, to be a stone in the full sense of the word. How then can we understand your idea of "being in and of itself"?

G: We know a stone is white by seeing, but we know a stone is hard by touching; this clearly indicates that what manifests itself is really separated from what does not manifest itself. The non-manifested exists in its own right and does not depend on what is manifested for its being; it just is itself. Such a state of independent existence is what I mean by "being in and of itself".

H: Even according to your view on what is manifested and what is not manifested, the whiteness and the hardness are nothing but two properties of a third entity, that is, of the stone. This is just the same as the length and the width being the inseparable properties of the area. Doesn't this show that the white and the hard are inseparable from the stone?

G: A concrete object can of course be white, but it is not true to say that the white is white because it is fixed in this white object. A specific object can be hard, but it is not true to say that the hardness is hard because it is fixed in that hard object, either. These properties in themselves are not fixed in the stones, and everything else can be in possession of either of them. Why must you insist that hardness and whiteness exist only in the stones?

H: Just observe any stones. They have to be hard and white, or else they cannot be named by "stone". If there were no stone, the talk about "white stone" would be senseless. Both hardness and whiteness reside in stones, because they are the inherent properties that stones have. This is true over time!

G: Of course, when it comes to a specific stone, these are the properties it has. However, even when hardness and whiteness exist in the stone, they are two independent properties, and this explains why one is perceived while at the same time the other is not perceived by the same organ. To put it in another way, one manifests itself, while the other does not, to the same sensory modality. Necessarily then, what is perceived cannot be what is not perceived at the same time. Nor can what manifests itself be what does not manifest itself at the same time. Thus each of them has its independent being. How can you say that they are not separable?

H: Indeed, that eyes don't see the hard does not mean that hardness is not there; and that hands don't feel the white does not mean that whiteness is not there, either. But this merely shows that different sensory organs have their own special perceptive roles or functions that cannot replace each other. Nevertheless, the hardness and the whiteness are still there in the stone. Why do you say that they exist outside the stone?

G: Hardness is necessarily hard in and of itself. It is hard not because it exists in stones, nor in any specific objects. Hardness is just that which makes objects hard. Your claim is tantamount to saying that all the hard objects are hard because it is the stone that makes them hard, but you simply could never find such hardness anywhere! Hardness is just the hardness in and of itself. By the same reasoning, if whiteness is not inherently white in and of itself, how can it enable a stone or any other objects to be white? Therefore, what is white must necessarily be white; that is, the whiteness has its being in and of itself that is not fixed in any specific objects. The same is true of other colors, such as yellow or black.

If the hardness and the whiteness do not just exist in stones, how can the ideas of "hard stone" or "white stone" have come into being in the first place? To me, ideas such as "white" and "hard" come into being exactly because whiteness and hardness exist independently and for this reason they can be isolated for respective scrutiny. Such is the approach of analysis which fits in with the different essences of things. The rational knowledge obtained from this approach embodies the essence of things and is therefore far more truthful than the preliminary knowledge one gets directly from one's bodily contacts with or one's sensory perceptions of specific things.

Let's take the case of "whiteness" for further illumination. One sees white color only with the eyes, which is possible only when there is light. But the light itself does not make the white. The truth is, neither the light nor the eyes can grasp whiteness. It is the mind that grasps the whiteness. Of course, the mind does not see the white color directly; rather, it seizes the whiteness by means of separating it out [from experiences] for the extraction of the whiteness in white colors. In the same way, the hardness is sensed by the hand, and the hand does so by the action of punching. It appears as if it were the hand that grasped the hardness by punching, but in fact this is not the case. It is the mind that does, though it does not in any way experience the hard directly. [In both the cases] what the mind does is to break down what has been experienced to extract the essence, in order to apprehend what has been experienced. Such an approach of analysis for the mastery of the essence of things should be the solely correct way to the true knowledge of everything in the universe. Our knowledge can be true, only when it is obtained in this way.

Essay IV: On Essence and Change

Heckler: Does two contain ones?

Gongsun Long: No, "two" does not contain "ones".

H: Put it in another way: "Two implies a thing on the right", is this correct?

G: No, "two" does not imply anything on the right.

H: Is it right to say "Two implies a thing on the left"?

G: No, "two" does not imply anything on the left.

H: Can the left be nameed by "two"?

G: No, it cannot.

H: Can the right be nameed by "two"?

G: No, it cannot.

H: Put the left and the right together; do they make two?

G: Yes, they do.

H: Is it correct to say that changing is not unchanging?

G: Yes, it is.

H: If the right is combined with another thing, can we say a change has occurred?

G: Yes, we can.

H: What amount has it changed into?

G: The "right".

H: The right has already changed. How can you continue to call it a right? And if no change has happened to it, why do you speak of a change?

G: "Two" in itself does not contain a left or a right; on what ground can you talk about its left and its right in the first place? If we say that "sheep" and "ox", put together, can hardly mean "horse", then surely, "ox" and "sheep", put together, may mean "chicken" to a much less extent.

H: What are you driving at?

G: Sheep differ from oxen because the former have upper teeth, while the latter do not. Nevertheless, it is improper to assert that if a thing is called "ox", it should not have any property that what is called "sheep" has, or that if it is called "sheep", it should not have any property that what is called "ox" has. It is true that these two do not have all the defining properties in common, but we may have a reason to group

158

them in one category: sheep do have the essence of "having horns", and so do oxen. I must hasten to say, it is not right to claim that speaking of "ox" is equivalent to speaking of "sheep", nor vice versa. Though the essence of "having horns" exists in them both, they are of different species after all. However, the point I am making is that "sheep-ox", as one categorical entity, shares the essence of "having horns", while that of "horse" does not. Conversely, the category of "horse" has the essence of "having a long tail", while that of "sheep-ox" does not. For this reason, I say "'sheep' and 'ox', put together, can hardly mean 'horse'".

By "hardly mean 'horse'", I am talking about the essence of "horse" as being absent from the definition of "sheep-ox". In terms of the form of this "non-horse" category, "sheep" is not a two, nor is "ox", but "sheep-ox" is a two. The "two" here refers to the essence that "sheep-ox", as an integrated category, has in common, but it does not include the essence of "horse". This is certainly right. By using this example, I intend to illustrate the essential differences between concepts. The issue of "left" and "right", which we were discussing a moment ago, should be apprehended in this way.

Further, oxen and sheep have furs, but chickens have feathers. "Chicken leg", which we speak of, is one; and actual chicken legs, which we count, are two. Thus, two and one make three. In the same way, when we say "sheep-ox leg", that is one; and when we count the legs of sheep-ox, that would be four. Thus, four and one make five. "Sheep-ox" would have "five legs", while "chicken" only "three". Therefore, I say that "sheep-ox", as a category, does not contain any essential elements of "chickenness". The "non-chickenness" here means that in "sheep-ox", one is not likely to find any essential feature that chickens would have. If I am compelled to choose either "horse" or "chicken" to say whose essence "sheep-ox" might possibly tolerate, I would choose "horse", rather than "chicken". This is because "horse" might in some way have certain properties [such as having furs] in common with "sheep-ox", while "chicken" simply does not resemble it in any way, which gives us no reason to integrate "chicken" into the "sheep-ox" category. My reasoning is clear enough. I cite such examples to point out the cause of the confusion in understanding the relationship between name and actuality; that is, the meaning of name becomes incorrect when it is used to refer to improper essences.

H: Do you have more convincing illustrations?

G: Yes, of course. Such as: mixing green and white hardly makes yellow; and mixing white and green makes light green to a much lesser extent.

H: What is your point?

G: The green and the white are two primary colors, and each is not formed of the properties that the other has. Even if they are mixed up, they stand in sharp contrast as two different colors. Each has its own clearly defined scope that is not adjacent to that of the other, and even if blended, their respective essences as primary colors remain unaffected. Their different essences are their identities, enabling them to stand independently of each other. Like the "left" and the "right" we argued before, they are not just two parts of one entity.

Therefore, blending the green with the white, one cannot produce a green color, nor can one produce a white color. How then can the blend be yellow? The yellow itself is still another primary color, referred to by its own correct name, "yellow". This is just like what the king and the ministers are to a state, each meeting up to his own definition to ensure a long-lasting stable relationship.

When the green is blended with the white, the white cannot win out to make the blend purely white. Surely, the white overwhelms the green by diluting it, but in the end this is not achieved, as the white only encroaches on the green. Such encroachment can only result in different hues of light-green. But then, the light-green does not have a correct and determinable essence that the name "light green" can precisely refer to.

Thus, the green and the white are independent primary colors each, and if forced to blend, neither of them overwhelms the other, because they would vie with each other for the assertion of their respective essence. Such a grappling for self-assertion can only result in all the various hues of light-greenness, whose essential feature, however, cannot be demarcated and delineated with any certainty.

For this reason, if I am forced [to form a category of color], I would choose "yellow" rather than "light-green" [as what category "green" and "white" compose]. After all, "yellow" refers to the essence of being a primary color, which gives us a reason to include it in the category [of "primary color"], just as the case of "horse" we discussed a moment ago. However, similar to the case of "chicken" we just mentioned, the "light-green", displaying different hues, is in lack of a clearly definable essence that enables it to be included in the category!

Without a clearly determinable essence, the result would be a situation that resembles kings and ministers struggling with each other in chaos, all attempting to be the criterion. And the consequence of such struggles can be nothing else but an even more unclear essence for a correct name to refer to.

Without a correct essence, the name and the actuality are divorced from each other, just as the example of the blended motley shows. This is what I would call "double-losing grapple for self-assertion": when such grapple takes place, the true essence is lost in oblivion, and the foundation for determining the correct meaning of the name is nowhere to be found.

Essay V: On the Nature of Reference

Things are known as "things" by virtue of reference, but reference does not mean merely the denotation of specific things. Should there be no name that refers, there would be no way things existing out there could come to be known as "things". [1]

But since references do not naturally exist anywhere, does this mean that things are their own references? References do not exist out there naturally, but things do have their actual existence in Nature. It is of course erroneous to take what exist for

---

1   Professor Hsien Chung Lee does not agree with me here, claiming that the three characters of [zhī] among the total eight cannot be explained as meaning "reference" and "denotation" respectively (see Lee's "Review" for details). But I still maintain my interpretation, which in fact is not only mine. I have given a discussion in the part of my translator's notes on this essay.

Another note I have to add here involves Lee's suggestion (in his "Review") of taking the phrase (物指[wùzhǐ]) in the last paragraph of Gongsun Long's original as an independent concept, which he says is the key to the understanding of (非指[feīzhǐ]). If he is right, we must face two questions. First, since this is so important a concept, why do we find no mentioning of [wùzhǐ] in the beginning of essay when [feīzhǐ] is clearly stated? Second, throughout the essay, Gongsun Long has been talking about [zhīfeīzhǐ], which literally says "zhī is not zhī"; and this certainly shows that the truly contrasting concepts are [zhī] and [not zhī] and not anything else. We cannot find clues to the answers to these questions. What is more, if [wùzhǐ] is an independent concept, we shall have to add another concept to our distinction of "reference" and "denotation"; it would be quite unclear what should be added in and why Gongsun Long should have added it at the end of the essay, where he is not discussing the concepts but reinforcing his ideas by rhetorical questions. Therefore, I decide not to take it as an independent concept, but to stick to my reinterpretation.

what do not exist.

If there were no names that referred, then a thing could not be known as the "thing". A thing could in no way be known as the "thing" inherently, because the thing in itself is not the same as the meaning of the "thing" referred to by the name. Since they are not the same, the "thing" can only be what it is by virtue of reference.

By saying "without references, things could not be talked about as 'things'", I do not mean that a name cannot denote a specific thing. The reason why a name can denote a specific thing is that the "thing" names the thing because it refers to what the thing essentially is. Nevertheless, the meaning of "thing" is the essence of a sort of things, and as such, it is by the very nature different from the specific things that exist out there and are denoted by the name.

The point I am making by saying that references do not exist out there is that what a name refers to is not any specific thing in itself, though a thing can be denoted by a name. Specific things in themselves are not what their names refer to, but are commonly regarded as such; this is not the correct understanding of what reference truly is. In doing so, one has in fact mistaken "the actual thing that exists but is not its own reference" for "the meaning of reference that does not physically exist". This is where the problem occurs. The truth is that a reference is by its very nature the universal property [a category of] things have in common. There is no such a thing as reference that physically exists in the natural world, but one cannot say that things cannot be referred to as "things" just for this reason. The name of "thing" can be applied to a specific thing, not because the name serves as a label that picks out the specific thing. Reference is more than mere denotation of specific things; it is what things are that the name "thing" means. Thus, reference is not identical with denotation; [or to rephrase it] the relationship between what is referred to and what actually exists is not one of denotation.

If things did not exist out there, who would be discussing "things themselves that are not their references"? If there were no things, what would be the point of talking about "reference"? Should references exist without concepts of things to be what they refer to, on what basis could one say about "not merely denoting" or "there being nothing that could not be referred to"?

In all, since to refer is not the same as to denote specific things, why should one mistakenly believe that a reference is fixed to a specific thing, thus reducing it to a mere label of that thing?

Essay VI: Anecdotes of Gongsun Long

Gongsun Long was a famous Ming Jia debater during the Warring States Period (around 475-221 BC). He deplored deeply the then chaotic situation of language use, where name did not correspond to actuality. To deal with the chaos, he proposed, with his gifted intellectual ability, the theory of "whiteness in itself". He made his argument by analogy of actual things, and debated with others in defense of "whiteness being itself". One of his well-known proposition was "White-horse is not horse". According to him, by saying "White-horse is not horse", he intended to show that "white" is a name that names a color, while "horse" is one that names a form. Since a color is not a form, nor vice versa, then when a color is talked about, no form should have a part in it; and when a form is talked about, no color should be involved. Yet in actuality, [he found] these two concepts were mixed up erroneously, which was what caused confusion of ideas. That was just like looking for a white horse in the stable where there were horses of all colors except white, in which case no horse could be picked out as a white horse. No horse could be picked out, because the kind of horse that one looked for did not exist in there and to Gongsun Long, the nonexistence of any white horse there showed that a white horse was not a horse. He wished to rectify the confusion in the relationship between name and actuality on the basis of such argumentation and to indoctrinate all people in this ideology of his.

Once, Gongsun Long met Kong Chuan, a disciple of Confucianism, in the mansion of Lord Ping Yuan of the State of Zhao. Kong put forward a proposal: "I have long admired you who are a man of integrity and hope to be your student. However, I refuse to accept your theory of 'A white horse is not a horse'. If you would be willing to recant this belief of yours, I would beg you to allow me to study under you."

Gongsun replied: "What you have said is self-contradictory. I am well-known precisely for my 'White Horse' theory! Now you want me to recant it. Then I have nothing else to teach you. The reason why you take someone to be your teacher is that you do not have the ideas or special knowledge that that person has. Your asking me to give up my ideas and knowledge is just proposing that one should teach another man before asking him to be one's teacher. Isn't this self-contradictory!

"In addition, the proposition of 'White-horse is not horse' is also accepted by Confucius himself. I have been told that once the king of the State of Chu went out hunting ferocious beasts at the Yunmeng Hunting Field, where he lost his bow. His attendants volunteered to search for it, but the king said: 'You don't need to. A Chu man loses the bow and a Chu man recovers it. Why bother looking for it?' When Confucius heard the story, he commented: 'The king has expressed his benevolence and kindness, but the expression is not perfect. He could have said that a man lost the bow while a man recovered it. Why should a man be a Chu man necessarily?' Thus it can be seen that Confucius also believed that 'Chu man' and 'man' are not the same. You agree with Confucius distinction of 'Chu man' from 'man', but at the same time falsify my distinction of 'white horse' from 'horse'. This is another point of self-contradiction in your saying.

"Well, sir, you are a disciple of Confucianism, but reject what its master Confucius accepts; you intend to learn under me, but repudiate what I have to teach you. In this case, I could never expect to be a teacher in front of you, even if I were a hundred times smarter!" Kong Chuan was unable to retort him.

Gongsun Long was one of the hangers-on of the aristocrat Ping Yuan of the State of Zhao, and Kong Chuan was a descendant of Confucius family clan. When they met each other, Kong said to Gongsun: "I humbly live in the State of Lu, where I have heard about you. I admire your wisdom and appreciate your upright personality. I have long cherished the hope of being an apprentice under your guidance, and today I see you in person finally. However, if there is anything that makes me stand against you, it would be your theory of 'A white horse is not a horse'. If you are willing to recant this theory of yours, I plead that you take me as your student."

Gongsun Long replied: "What you have said is self-contradictory, sir. The most important theory I have is exactly that of 'White-horse is not horse'. If, at your request, I recanted the theory, I would have nothing to teach you. It is absurd to find someone who has nothing to teach you to be your teacher. The reason why you ask me to be your teacher is that you do not have the idea or special knowledge that I have. So, your asking me to give up my theory is nothing but proposing that one should teach another man before asking him to be one's teacher. This does not make sense.

"The paradoxical advice you were trying to give me sounds very much like what the king of the State of Qi had said to Mr. Yin Wen. Once, the king asked Yin: 'I value talents of integrity very much, but there aren't any in the State of Qi. What has gone wrong?' Yin said: 'Please tell me what sort of people can be the talents of integrity that your majesty desires.' The king could not answer it and Yin continued: 'Suppose we now have one person here, who is loyal in serving the king, dutiful to his parents, honest with his friends and benevolent to his countrymen. Can a man with these four virtues be called a talent of integrity?' The king answered: 'Excellent! He is the very man I want.' At this, Yin asked him: 'If your majesty did have such a man, would you entrust him with the position of minister?' The king replied: 'Yes, of course I would be willing to, but I don't have such a man.'"

"Since the king of Qi appreciated very much, at that time, the character of courage, Yin went on to ask him: 'If this very man is bullied or insulted in public but dares not fight back, would your majesty still let him be your minister? ' The king replied: 'Could such a man be a talent of integrity? He is insulted but has no guts to fight back; this is an utter shame! I would not use such shameful man as my minister.' To this, Yin pressed further: 'The man is just not courageous enough to fight back, but still he has the four virtues in him. Since he has not lost the four essential virtues, he should still be referred to as a talent of integrity. However, your majesty would at once appoint and not appoint him to be your minister. Doesn't this follow that the talent of integrity that you say of is at the same time not the talent of integrity?' This landed the king in awkward silence.

"Yin Wen kept on: 'At present, certain king of a state rules his country in such a way that a man is penalized for any mistake he commits, but also penalized even if he has made no mistake; meanwhile a man is rewarded for any merit he has had, but also rewarded even if he has had no merit at all. Yet the king turns up to complain that the people under him are impossible to rule. Do you think it is reasonable for the king to say so?' The king answered: 'No, it's unreasonable.' Then Yin told him: 'I have observed personally how your officials administer the State of Qi and found that what they have been doing resembles what I have just told your majesty.' At this, the king replied: 'If I indeed ran the country like what you said, sir, I could not blame the people under me, even if they were hard to rule. But as I deem it, I am not that impotent.'

"Yin went ahead with his reasoning: 'Without any evidence, do I dare to say that? Your majesty has decreed that those who kill must die and those who injure must be jailed up. As a result, people are deterred by the rigid law and dare not fight back even if they are bullied. This is the consequence of the law. Yet, your majesty considers it a shame not to fight back when insulted. To say that is a shame constitutes a negation of his behavior. The man's behavior is in fact consistent with the law, but your majesty says no to him and deprives him of his minister position for his lawful behavior. In so doing, your majesty punishes him. Thus, he is punished though he has not violated the law. In addition, your majesty believes that not fighting back is a shame and it follows that to fight should be a glory. Regarding fighting as a glory, your majesty would acknowledge the man for his behavior of fighting by appointing him to be your minister. Entrusting him to be the minister constitutes a reward. The man is rewarded even though he has had no merit at all. What is worse, what your majesty rewards is just what your officials want to crash down upon. The behavior that the king rewards is a crime stipulated by the king's own law. This throws into chaos and confusion the associations between reward, penalty, the right and the wrong. In this situation, the king simply cannot hope to put the country in order, even if he could be ten times more competent than Yellow Emperor, the ancient wise king.'

"Come back to what we were saying. I consider what advice you were offering me sounded just like what the king of the State of Qi had said, sir. You just wish to falsify my theory of 'White-horse is not horse', but you do not know on what basis you can start to criticize it. This is very similar to the fallacy of the king of Qi, who just hoped to have talents of integrity, but had no idea what such a talent was."

Part II Notes on the Translation of *Gongsun Longzi*

There are altogether six essays in *Gongsun Longzi*. One of them is a record of what Gongsun Long has said and done, written obviously by someone else. The other five essays can be regarded as authored by Gongsun Long himself, as they are consistent with the spirit of Ming Jia who were known to have been "devoted exclusively to speculations on the issues of name", i.e., they were specially engaged in metaphysical speculations on problems of language, which was quite unique in ideology, different from all the other major schools of thought during the pre-*Qin* period, especially those of Confucianism, Daoism, Mohism, etc. As Hsien Chung Lee (2011: 3) points out, "All these essays deal directly with the epistemological issue of 'how one knows', which form a complete theoretical system." As to the arrangement of the order of these six essays, opinions differ among scholars. For instance, Zhou Shan (1997: 199-200) has listed 13 different ways of arrangement by people such as Wu Feibai, Fung Yulan, and so on, and this is not the whole story yet. Certainly, every scholar has produced his own reason for his arrangement.

I think we can put the six essays in this order: 1) "On Name and Actuality", 2) "On 'White-Horse Is Not Horse'", 3) "On the Being of Hardness and Whiteness", 4) "On Essence and Change", and 5) "On the Nature of Reference". As to "Anecdotes of Gongsun Long", it is quite OK to put it at the end of the list, since it is not written by Gongsun Long himself. This is not just a show of being different, but serves to present Gongsun Long's ideas in a more reasonable pattern.

As a programmatic document, "On Name and Actuality" should be given the first place in the series, because Gongsun Long has stated in this essay the reason why he focuses on the issue of name and has proposed his principle for the discussion. The three essays that follow are Gongsun's elaboration on his basic principle and they form a gradually deepening presentation of his ideas. "On 'White-horse Is Not Horse'" has demonstrated that the meaning of name and the fact in actuality are questions different in nature, different in terms of conceptual levels. "On the Being of Hardness and Whiteness" has further proposed the independent being of conceptual entities and formulated the important proposition that concept is the result of analysis, which is quite rare and unique among traditional Chinese thoughts. And "On Essence and Change" continues to reflect on the determinacy and certainty of conceptual meaning of a name through clarifying the essence of what the name names. One cannot fail to see that in the debates presented in these three essays, a central theme becomes very protruding: that of clarifying what the meaning of a name is and what the nature of reference is, so that the true meaning of names can be correctly mastered and language correctly used. If this issue were not dealt with successfully, Gongsun Long's ideas and principles could not have been philosophically supported. For this reason, Gongsun Long has to write the fifth essay, "On the Nature of Reference", specifically to sum up his theoretical points at a more abstract level, discussing the nature of reference, in order to clarify the misunderstandings on the part of language users concerning what the meaning of name truly is and for this reason what the nature of knowledge truly is.

Thus, I think my re-ordering of these five essays gives a more reasonable presentation of the development of Gongsun Long's ideas.

1. About "On Name and Actuality"

"On Name and Actuality" should be the programmatic document of Gongsun Long's, in which he discussed what he considered to be the foundation for the correctness of name and proposed accordingly his principle for the rectification of name. This is why I have listed it before the other essays. This essay begins from the belief that things exist objectively in the world, which is the source of the meaning of name. But this is not what Gongsun Long wants to discuss. Right after this, he turns to the discussion of what ensures the correctness of the meaning of name. The point made in the essay can be summed up by the principle he proposes, namely the principle of *thisness* in *this* and *thatness* in *that* exclusively, which is the fundamental standpoint of his philosophy of language. The whole essay follows this development pattern: 1) proposing what the correct meaning of a name should be and, if one hopes to rectify names, what the foundation should be; 2) then formulating and elaborating the principle for the rectification of names; and 3) emphasizing that only the application of such a principle guarantees the correctness of speech communication.

To begin with, Gongsun Long proposes three basic concepts for the determination of the correctness of the meaning of names: specifically "物 (pronounced [wù], meaning 'thing', 'object', 'substance', etc.)", "实(pronounced [shí]; meaning 'actuality', 'substance', 'reality', etc.)" and "位(pronounced [wèi], meaning 'seat', 'position', 'status', 'in place', etc.)", which are the difficult points for translation. These terms have so far been interpreted as meaning "substantive things as entities in reality", "that these entities occupy certain amount of space" and "the position or direction of such occupation" respectively (e.g.: Fung Yulan, 1962: 339-340; Zhou Changzhong, 2005: 260-261; etc.). Besides, the term that follows these three, namely "正(pronounced [zhèng], meaning 'correctness', 'rightness', 'integrity' etc.)" has been regarded as the fourth concept. But such interpretations face one problem: if Gongsun Long were indeed talking about the way things did exist, and then about the correctness of meaning, which all agree, there should be a transition in his essay by which he must make clear how the existence of things came to be the basis on which meaning was established. No such a transition is found in the essay, however. Gongsun Long seems to have jumped from objective existence abruptly to the principle of rectification of name. And this throws the essay into a lack of coherence of idea presentation.

To make the ideas of the essay coherent, I suggest a reinterpretation of the three basic concepts of his: they are the terms for the discussion not of the objective existence of things, but of the very basis of the correctness of the meaning of name. These terms represent Gongsun Long's philosophical speculation on the correctness of the meaning of name, rather than his empirical arguments of any kind. Gongsun Long acknowledges the objective existence of things with the first sentence, but switches instantly to the question of language, proposing that when a "物([wù], 'object', 'thing')" is talked about, the meaning of "thing" is no longer the same as a real thing in existence, but the concept of the thing so named. As a concept, the "thing" does not need to occupy any space, and therefore the term "actuality ([shí])" does not mean that certain entity must occupy space, but that the essential meaning of "thing" constitutes what we talk about in language. Such a conceptual "actuality" should be the meaning of Gongsun Long's term of "实 ([shí], actuality)". His "actuality" is thus what is referred to by a name and not the same as the real thing that exists and is labeled by a name, the latter being some sort of Kantian "thing-in-itself". This interpretation of mine is shared by Dr. Hsien Chung Lee (2011: 27).

My interpretation is well-grounded. Isn't it true that the Great Debate on Names and Actuality centers on the relationship between names and things in existence? As we shall see later on, various schools of thought hold totally different and conflicting views on the relationship, but no one has ever defined what name is or what actuality is. It is these issues that Gongsun Long hopes to clarify. He attempts to show what the "actuality" being debated on essentially is, holding that the "actuality" does not mean the objects and things in the real world. Rather, such "actuality" is the conceptual mastery of the essence of things on the part of human beings, and it should be in this sense that one talks about the relationship between names and actuality for the purpose of the rectification of names. Such conceptual "actuality" should be the exact representation of the essence of things, no more no less, permitting no deviations; and this is what Gongsun Long means by "位 ([wèi], being in its right place)", which he uses to denote what he considers to be the stipulation or requirement that ensures the semantic correctness of a name. Only if this requirement is satisfied can the meaning of a name be correct, and any deviation from it would lead to an error in the use of the name. From this, I conclude that the term that follows, namely "正(pronounced [zhèng], meaning 'right', 'correct', 'direct', etc.) is not a coordinate concept as the foregoing three, but it just means what it means: the correctness. This is what the rectification of names hopes to achieve: the correctness of name meaning that is basic to speech communication. I agree with Hsien Chung Lee (2011: 28, 43) who concludes that "the so-called [wèi] means the correct relationship between what is referred to and its name".

Seen from this angle, the idea of Gongsun Long's is not the same as that of Later Mohists', who hold that the "actuality" denotes nothing but the objective world out there, similar to Aristotle's view on what constitutes the reality. This helps to explain why the Mohist theory of meaning is in effect one of correspondence, i.e. if what is said corresponds to the actual state of affairs, then the meaning of the saying is correct. But Gongsun Long's theory of meaning is not an empirical but a rationalist one, proposing that the meaning of a name is correct only if it represents necessarily and exclusively the essence of the thing to which the name is applied. This idea is closer to Plato than to Aristotle. Thus, the Ming Jia, which Gongsun Long represents, is not just a branch of Mohism, as some have claimed (e.g.: Hu Shi, 2000: 133-134), but is a school of thinkers different from Mohism in philosophical orientation.

One more word should be given to the sentence in the original, namely "疑其 所正([yí qí suǒ zhèng], meaning, 'to question the current practice of/approach to the rectification of name')". The Chinese character "疑(pronounced [yí], meaning 'to 'doubt', 'to question' and in Classical Chinese it meant also 'to determine')" has been explained and/or translated in the sense of "to determine" (e.g.: Wang Hongyin, 1997: 94; Hsien Chung Lee, 2012: 113). I do not think this is correct. We see from the context that Gongsun Long has already proposed the approach to the rectification of name on the basis of a correct mastery of the inherent essence of the thing a name names. He should follow this point by a criticism of the then various approaches to the rectification that he believes to be incorrect, and propose accordingly his own principle for and approach to the rectification. After all, the Gongsun Long's primary goal is to clarify the concepts of "name" and "actuality" themselves, in order to guarantee the correctness of the rectification of name itself. Therefore, to me, the character "疑[yí]" should not be explained as meaning "to determine"; rather, it should keep its primary meaning, i.e., "to suspect, to question". Nor do I agree with Liu Yujun (2002: 55) who has translated the sentence in question into "to cast doubt on the correct understanding". Here, Gongsun Long is questioning not the correctness of the use of any specific name, but the correctness of the theories of and the approaches to the rectification of name and raising his own rationalistic theory and approach in this respect.

Such an understanding is more coherent with the text that follows. Starting from the second paragraph, Gongsun Long proposes that his theory should be used as the criterion for the establishment of the correct meaning of names and for reflecting on the on-going practice of rectification of name itself. With this transition, Gongsun

Long continues to put forward his principle for rectification of name, the *thisness* in *this* and the *thatness* in *that* exclusively, which is an elaboration on what he means by "the [wèi]; or being in its right place".

In his elaboration on the principle of the *thisness* in *this* and the *thatness* in *that* exclusively, Gongsun Long has repeatedly used the two Chinese characters, "此 (pronounced [cǐ], meaning *this*)" and "彼(pronounced [bǐ], meaning *that*)". A point must be made here that in the Chinese language, especially at the time Gongsun Long lived in, there is no morphological difference between concrete and abstract nouns and pronouns, such as the device of "-ness" or "-lity" in English. Besides, the Chinese language is not alphabetic, which makes it impossible for its users to express their ideas concisely in the form of "Property X", or "Object y vs. Object x", or "X exists in x", etc. This is why we find expressions in Gongsun Long's original such as "知此 之在此 (literally 'knowing this is in this')" very hard to understand and if translated literally, it would be incomprehensible for modern readers. I think the repeatedly used terms in the original essay should be differentiated according to the level of their abstractness. In Chinese, "此[cǐ]" and "彼[bǐ]" can be used as denotative terms to label "this thing" or "that thing", but in this essay, Gongsun Long uses these terms frequently to represent highly abstract references, just like westerners use "a", "b", or "X", "Y", etc. as notations for generalities. In other words, Gongsun Long uses the terms not only to denote this and that, but also to refer to *thisness* and *thatness*. Seen in this way, what has been known as the difficult sentences in this essay becomes quite clear. We see unmistakably that Gongsun Long holds that when we use the name "this" to say of a this, then the meaning of "this" should be *thisness*, the essence of *this* necessarily and exclusively. To Gongsun Long, the meaning of "this" is and can only be the *thisness* of this, which guarantees the correctness in speech communication. In the essay, he has in fact put forward, through language meaning speculation, something very close to the basic law of logic proposed by Aristotle, i.e. the laws of excluded middle and of non-contradiction. Or to put it more boldly, what he has proposed in this essay is no less the Chinese language version of the Aristotelian basic rules of logic!

By the way, most scholars today interpreted the character "在 (pronounced [zài], meaning 'to be present, to be in a location, to exist', etc.)" in the sense of "a change of position in time and space" (e.g.: Hsien Chung Lee, 2011: 32). Such an interpretation is likely to fail in unveiling Gongsun Long's idea and the translation resulted from this interpretation does not seem to make the sentence coherent with the rest of the essay, leading to perplexity on the part of the readers. For instance, the English version of Wang Hongyin's (1997: 339) goes: "... when one calls 'this', but this does not correspond to it (the thing is no longer where it was) ..." Even if we brush aside the problem of unclear anaphora in this sentence, we see that Wang's translation leaves the readers an impression that Gongsun Long's theory may appear to be something like Aristotle's correspondence theory of truth. The problem is, should we take this for Gongsun Long's theoretical standpoint in this essay, we simply could not see why he should be talking about "white-horse is not horse" or "there are no ones in two" and so on later on in his other essays; nor could we appreciate the very important idea he has proposed in his "On the Nature of Reference". For this reason I believe the character "在[zài]" should be interpreted as meaning "to exist", in order to bring out Gongsun Long's rationalist belief of the meaning of language words: *the thisness exists in this*.

Out of the above-mentioned views, I decide to adopt "thisness" and "thatness" in my translation of the key terms of "此[cǐ]" and "彼[bǐ]" in the present essay. In so doing, I am inspired by the English version of Aristotle's *Categories* and *Metaphysics*, in which the Greek term "tode ti" is translated into either "a this" or "thisness"[1]. However, I must hasten to declare that philosophers disagree as to whether Aristotle's form of "tode ti" is particular or universal, but this does not constitute a problem in my translation, since in English, a suffix "-ness" transforms an adjective into a noun to mean the essential quality of being what the adjective describes, such as "red → redness, hard → hardness", etc. Such a quality should be regarded as essential, since "redness" underlies all things that are red. Philosopher Alston (1988: 2) has used examples such as "sharpness" and "treeness" to show that Plato's Ideas are but forms resulted from language meaning analysis: e.g., generalization of "treeness" from the trees that is taken to be the only reality. Obviously, such a "treeness" is something universal, consisting of the essential qualities that trees should have and only trees

---

1   See Nicholas Bunnin and Jiyuan Yu (eds.), *Dictionary of Western Philosophy*. Jiang Yi, et al., trans., Beijing: People's Press, 2001: 5.

can have. This is why I use "thisness" and "thatness" in my translation in which these two terms refer precisely to the essences of this and that respectively. Such a way to translate Gongsun Long's original text not only represents the truly metaphysical speculative nature of his thought, but also keeps its stylistic flavor, to some extent.

I am aware that my translation might appear to be a bit troublesome for ordinary readers to read, but Gongsun Long's original text itself is full of such "irregularities" of word uses. Because the pre-*Qin* Chinese language did lack abstract expressions and Gongsun Long had to rely on the same demonstrative pronouns to encode his ideas concerning the essence, the best way to re-encode his ideas in English is to embrace the unusual expressions of "thisness" and "thatness".

Guided by such basic understanding of Gongsun Long, I have translated this essay in the way I have done, believing that this is the correct way to bring out the true theme of the essay as a master piece of rationalist writing in philosophy of language. By the way, the term "philosophy of language" employed here and later on in this book does not refer to the 20th century western philosophical inquiry in the sense of analytic philosophy, but to any endeavor to reflect on metaphysical questions of what humans know and how their knowledge can be correct, through speculating on issues of language and its meaning. In ancient China, there was indeed no ontology, nor epistemology, in the sense of western metaphysical speculation, but this does not mean that the Chinese philosophers could never come to the reflection on the fundamental questions of truth and knowledge and one way that looks suitable within the Chinese language framework is to start from the reflection on the meaning of name. I believe that Gongsun Long was such a philosopher of language.

Before I end this section, I'd like to mention that at the end of the essay, Gongsun Long does have used sentences like "How wise were the previous kings". However, this is not a declaration of Gongsun Long's political viewpoint. He uses such expressions just to reiterate the vital importance of using name correctly. Just like Wu Feibai (1983: 516) says, with the two odes to the previous kings, Gongsun Long simply "intends to illustrate the profound significance of 'exclusive speculation on what is said'"! Well, at that time, it could be a normal practice among the intellectuals to hoist one's own importance by resorting to the power of kings. This is quite understandable to us.

2. About "On 'White-horse Is Not Horse'"

"On 'White-horse Is Not Horse'" is written in the style of a debate between Gongsun Long and his heckler, through which he has elaborated on his principle for the rectification of names, that of the *thisness* in *this* and the *thatness* in *that* exclusively. As one sees in his "On Name and Actuality", this principle stipulates that the "this" should and can only refer to the thisness of this, i.e., if a name is to be applied correctly to a thing, what the name refers to should be the essence that exists in the thing talked about, and this thing cannot have this essence while having another essence at the same time.

About the translation of the key expression, I have to make a statement, because there is a great trouble with the translation of the sentence "白马非马 ([báimǎfēimǎ]; literally: 'white horse not horse')" into English. This sentence is used by Gongsun Long and his heckler, but they are using it in totally different senses. Gongsun Long's utterance should be understood in the English sentence structure of "'White-horse' is not 'Horse'", focusing on the conceptual difference between "white-horse-ness" and "horseness", but his heckler's utterance should be an empirical statement: "A white horse is not a horse". The difficulty is that these two utterances are not distinguishable in the Chinese sentence form of "白马非马", because in Chinese there is no definite or indefinite articles. Nor are there any linguistic devices to mark out whether a noun is used in abstract or concrete senses. In this dialog, while Gongsun Long uses the sentence for a conceptual speculation of the abstracted meaning, his heckler uses the same sentence in the empirical sense. This is why I have to translate "白马非马" in different ways, though the original is exactly the same. The readers are reminded that in the discourse that follows, Gongsun Long is focused on the meaning of name.

With simple name (monosyllabic character of Chinese), there does not seem to be any problem. The name "马([mǎ], 'horse')" is to be applied correctly to an object that has the essence of horse, and the name "白([bái], 'white')" to anything that has the essence of whiteness. However, compound names, such as "白马([báimǎ], 'white-horse')", constitute a challenge for Gongsun Long, because what "white-horse" names does seem to have both the essence of horse and the essence of whiteness. How then can Gongsun Long adhere to his principle of the *thisness* in *this* and the *thatness* in *that* exclusively, since "white-horse" as one name refers to two essences simultaneously? Gongsun Long has to give an explanation, in order to defend his principle, which must guarantee that the compound names like "white-horse" refer exclusively to one essence, instead of being a mere combination of two essences. This, I think, should be the key to the understanding of this essay.

It should be noted that Gongsun Long does not deny that in the objective world white horses are horses, just like horses of any other colors. But what he wants to demonstrate is that "horse" and "white", as what the names refer to, are conceptual entities. He starts from the proposition that "horse" is a name that names a certain form (horse-form), while "white" is one that names a color, neither of which can be used to name the other party. To him, the reason is that these two kinds of names refer to entities of totally different nature; the concept of "horse" does not contain any definition of color, and the same is true with "white", which exists independent of all horses (independent of all things, actually).

As one sees in the whole dialog, Gongsun Long repeatedly answers the heckler's questions not in terms of empirical fact, but in terms of language concepts. The central theme of this essay is quite clear: first, Gongsun Long's arguments for the independence of the three concepts— "white", "horse" and "white-horse", hence "white-horse" being not "horse"; and second, his further clarification of the empirical and language levels for the purpose of rationalization of his own propositions, by taking advantage of loopholes in his heckler's logic.

In the first part, we find that the heckler is arguing for his point on the empirical basis, stating that all horses in the world are colored, white horses are just white-colored, and therefore white horses are horses. To this, Gongsun Long agrees, which shows that he does acknowledge that there are white horses in reality, but soon he points out that at the level of language concept, "horse" is colorless and that "white" and "horse" are the concepts different by nature. This point has not yet been underlined by traditional interpretations of this essay of his.

For instance, the sentence in his essay (in Classical Chinese language) "求马，黄、黑马皆可致；求白马，黄、黑马不可致" has been interpreted as meaning "If we seek a horse, either a yellow or a black horse will do. If we seek a white horse, then neither a yellow nor a black horse will do" (Wang, 1997: 328). If Gongsun Long were making his point in such an empirical perspective, his argument would have been powerless indeed, because his rival could have immediately retorted him: "Since asking for horse, one obtains either a yellow or a black horse, logically one can also obtain a white horse. Doesn't this prove exactly that white horses are horses?" Yet, Gongsun Long's heckler should have neglected such an obvious logic loophole! This means only one thing: our traditional interpretation is not to the point. I think people have failed to understand this statement contextually in relation to what follows, namely "使马无色，如有马已耳，安取白马？", which itself is also misinterpreted. The trouble lies with the Chinese character "使[shǐ]" in the sentence, which can be a preposition, meaning "if", but can also be a verb, meaning "to endow, to enable". Traditionally, the interpreters have adopted the former lexical meaning of the word, thus rendering the sentence an empirical statement of "if horses are colorless, how can there be white horses?" (cf. Wang, 1997: 329; Liu, 2002: 7) As the result, Gongsun Long's metaphysical speculation on language concepts and meaning of names is turned into an empirical statement. I think this serious misunderstanding not only has distorted Gongsun Long's idea, but is also divorced from what he is proposing in the statements that follow in the same essay. As I see it, we should adopt the second lexical meaning of the character "使[shǐ]", i.e. we should regard it as meaning "to enable". In fact, Gongsun Long means to say: "Let's grant that 'horse' refers to a conceptual entity, then such a 'horse' simply does not need any color as its essential property, and since 'horse' refers to the 'horseness' exclusively, how on earth can one find 'white-horse' in this concept?" Such an understanding makes the interpretation of the sentence much more coherent with the whole essay.

This point being made, Gongsun Long goes on to argue that "white-horse" as a compound name does not simply mean "white" plus "horse", but "white-horseness" independently, a concept coordinate semantically with those referred to by "white" and "horse". He is not talking about the *genus et differences* as has been traditionally understood, but is putting the three concepts, "horse-ness-in-itself", "whiteness-in-itself" and "white-horseness-in-itself" on the same part, thus granting a compound name the same semantic status as a simple name as language units, which function in the same way to refer to one concept exclusively each. He hopes to argue for the ontological "thisness" and "thatness" of the three concepts, for the purpose of defending his principle for the rectification of names, which he has proposed in "On Name and Actuality". We can today criticize him for the flaws of logic in the way he argues for the point, but one thing is undoubtedly true that this is a question raised in and of language itself, an endeavor to reflect on the relationship between names and actuality at the level of language concept, which has further significance for reflection on what the nature of knowledge humans obtain via language is. Thus understood, his idea is undoubtedly a philosophy of language.

In passing, I think Gongsun Long has, based on the peculiar structure of the Classical Chinese language, put forward an idea very close to that of "construction" in modern cognitive linguistics. If indeed constructions exist at all language levels, "white-horse" as a compound is surely a construction, with its grammatical status independent of the other constructions, such as "white" and "horse". It is not the components in a compound name that determine its meaning; on the contrary, it is the compound as a construction that decides the role and function of the words that enter the compound. This point is head-starting for us even today.

In the latter part of this essay, Gongsun Long seizes a logic loophole in the argument of his heckler to elaborate his own point. He has first laid a trap by asking his rival, "Is it permitted to use 'to have a white horse means to have a horse' to mean 'to have a white horse means to have a yellow horse'?" Surely, his rival is taken in, because he has to admit that the sentence cannot be used to mean what Gongsun Long has said, either empirically or logically. At this reply, Gongsun Long seizes the point to prove further that "horse" in itself is colorless as a concept and that "white" just refers to the essence of "whiteness"; yet, he points out, people do not differentiate in their everyday language use the inherently essential definitions of these concepts, which lead to logical errors, if pressed for clarification. If "whiteness" exists in "white-horse" concept as a definition of "horseness", then to say "white-horse" is simply equivalent to saying "horse-horse", which is meaningless. But if "whiteness" is not a definition of "horseness", then it should logically be independent of "horseness". The trick Gongsun Long has played to resolve this potential loophole is to conclude that "white-horse" means nothing but "white-horseness" in itself, which has the same independent conceptual status as "horseness".

I should add a note here that if we do not use quotation marks to re-mark the key terms in the dialog, the original text does appear to have certain errors in logical reasoning. For example, Hsien Chung Lee (2011: 77) points out that Gongsun Long commits obviously a logical error when he concludes that "white-horse is yellow-horse" from his premises of "white-horse is horse" and "yellow-horse is horse". Of course, this is logically wrong, if read at the literal level without quotation marks added. However, like I said in the previous paragraph and shown through my translation, we should understand Gongsun Long's propositions in quotation marks, which would clearly show that he is not doing the logical inference of "white-horse is yellow-horse". Rather, he is trying to speculate on the possible logical looseness in people's use of language expressions and on the essential meanings of the concepts of "'white' as whiteness in itself" and "'horse' as horseness in itself".

With this, Gongsun Long has successfully shown that his principle for the rectification of name is right, by demonstrating that it is necessarily true that a thing with a certain essence cannot be a thing that does not have this essence exclusively. This appears to be very close to Parmenides' assertion that "that which is is, and cannot not-be". Gongsun Long's "White-horse Is Not Horse" argument can be said to be a Chinese version of the Parmenidean proposition.

3. About "On the Being of Hardness and Whiteness"

If in "On 'White-horse Is Not horse'", Gongsun Long has proposed the idea of a separated conceptual analysis of "whiteness in itself" and "horseness in itself", then his "On the Being of Hardness and Whiteness" is an in-depth discussion of this idea of his, in which he intends to formulate his analysis approach and its rationale.

In terms of language, this essay is quite easy to understand and so my translation does not differ from the other versions in any radical way. However, I believe that the translations we have today fall short of a complete illumination of Gongsun Long's thought tendency. The key words in this essay are "藏([cáng], literally 'hiding, cached')", "自藏([zìcáng], literally 'self-hiding')" and "离([lí], literally 'separation')". So far, the translators have rendered these terms respectively as "hiding something up", "hiding itself up" and "separation". These understandings are not far wrong, but the problem is that these key words are explained on empirical basis, which is not compatible with Gongsun Long's thought tendency.

A case in point is the sentence "离也者，藏也" that follows up in the later context which has up till now been translated into "Separation, as I understand it, is concealment" (Wang, 1997: 331) typically. But this translation does have certain distance from what Gongsun Long intends to say, because the word "cáng" does not mean merely "hide-up". I think it means an independent existence, which is mastered by the mind via an analytical "separation". This might very well be what Gongsun Long intends to say. We can pursue further: what on earth is separated? Does "separation" denote an actual state of separating an object from its property in the empirical sense of the word? The answer is quite obvious: empirically speaking, an object and its property are inseparable; we simply cannot separate a red flower into a flower and redness by any action; nor can we separate the hardness from the stone by any means. Thus, what Gongsun Long says can be separated can only be concepts, the results of cognition of objects and their properties! Clearly, Gongsun Long is talking about the issue epistemological by nature: that of breaking things down for separate inspections. And this is undoubtedly an approach of analysis! The fact that what is separated can be hidden from perception means that they have their own existence which does not depend on any specific objects. This is why I have translated the sentence in question into "Such a state of independent existence is what I mean by 'being in and of itself'".

To fully appreciate Gongsun Long's ideas, we should give them a re-explanation in terms of rationalistic philosophy. It has been generally acknowledged that in traditional Chinese philosophy there was no metaphysical ontology or epistemology in the sense of western philosophy and that in Classical Chinese language, there were no words equivalent to "being" and "analysis" in the western languages. But this constitutes no obstacle for the Chinese thinkers in ancient times to come to the speculation on such questions. What Gongsun Long has done is exactly the speculation on issues of this nature, only that he had to rely on what linguistic means Classical Chinese language offered him.

In this essay, his argument develops in this way. Hardness and whiteness are the properties of stones, yet they are perceived respectively by different organs (eyes seeing and hand touching). This shows that the hardness and the whiteness are independent of each other. When one perception works, it receives only one of the two properties and cannot receive both at the same time, which proves that these two properties have their own unique essences. Meanwhile, hardness does not depend on the stone to be hard, because there are other things that are hard, and the same is true with whiteness. This proves that hardness and whiteness are something different from stones, or that hardness and whiteness are independent of stones. If stones can be said to exist independently, then there is no reason why we have to say hardness and whiteness do not exist independently.

Understood in this way, Gongsun Long appears indeed to be an objective idealist like Plato. But I think we should keep in mind that Gongsun Long has never proposed that the only reality is "Idea (or Form)". Meanwhile, Gongsun Long is not proposing that "objective things should be explained by the result of subjective cognition, or objective things should correspond to the subjective ideas", as Hsien Chung Lee (2011: 67) has claimed. As we see from his other essays, especially his "On Name and Actuality", Gongsun Long does not at all deny the objective existence of things out there and we do not have sufficient evidence to shovel him into the camp of Platonic objective idealism. What he has been reflecting on is unmistakably: what is the nature of knowledge human beings have obtained by means of language?

In accordance with this point of view, I think traditional explanation of the character "藏[cáng]" is basically acceptable, i.e. it means "hide-up", but as the phrase "自藏[zìcáng]" indicates, the hide-up should be understood as referring to a more abstract state of existence, the ontological reason that makes hiding-up possible. In the essay, Gongsun Long's statement ("有自藏也，非藏而藏也", literally "there is a self-hiding, and self-hiding does not mean hiding something up") clearly shows this point of view. Let's now see in what context he says this. We see that Gongsun Long's heckler claims, from the empirical viewpoint, that if there were no whiteness, we could not see stones and if there were no hardness, we could not say "stones are hard", because all stones are white and hard; then it should be true to say that the hard, the white and the stone are just an integrated whole, inseparable from each other. To the heckler's proposition, Gongsun Long replies that it is here that the question of "self-hiding" should be raised; the self-hiding of something does not mean simply that it is hidden from perception. The reason why it can be hidden from perception is that it has the property of "self-hiding". Even if hidden, the property is still there, in and of itself. "Being hidden from perception" can be an empirical phrase, meaning that humans perceive one property with one kind of perceiving organ, while at the same time the other properties are not perceived by the same organ. But the question is: that something is hidden postulates that it must be there and that such existence does not depend on human experiences, nor does it depend on any specific things. It simply is, which is the necessary prerequisite for why it appears to be what it is. In other words, independent existence is the reason for the possibility of being hidden from perception.

Then the question is how such a self-hiding, or the being in and of itself, can be known to humans. To this, Gongsun Long continues in the essay to put forward his methodological concept of "离([lí], literally 'separation')". I think this character does not merely mean "separation, to separate", as it has traditionally been claimed to mean. Rather, this character refers to the conceptualization of properties by abstracting them out of specific things, by the application of reason, in order to grasp with certainty the essence. This is certainly an approach of analysis. In the latter part of the essay, Gongsun Long repeatedly asserts that "separation" does not mean merely that "whiteness cannot be felt by hand", or "hardness cannot be seen by eyes", but emphasizes that it is the "mind (神[shén], literally 'spirit, mind')" that masters these properties, i.e. it is the mind that apperceives and apprehends the essence of these properties. Thus, his "离[lí]" is not an empirical concept of separating something, as most scholars assume it to be, but a rational concept of analysis as a function of the mind. Gongsun Long has stated unmistakably in the essay that the sensory organs themselves do not produce the perception of any properties and that the true perception can only consist in the conceptualization, or the knowledge of the properties that the mind has processed and crystallized, which is no longer dependent on or fixed to the experience of any specific things. Gongsun Long has declared clearly that such method of analysis of his is the only correct way towards true knowledge. His belief that the mind alone gives us true knowledge draws him very close to Plato, who also believes that the mind alone can understand the true existence of Ideas.

Technically if we just translate the character of "离[lí]" into "separation", then the translation would appear difficult to understand. Take Wang Hongyin's version (1997: 331-333) for an example. It goes: "Separation is concealment... only mind can see... Even mind is incapable of feeling the hardness without separating it from whiteness." I don't think this translation is conducive to a correct and logical comprehension of Gongsun Long's ideas on the part of the readers. The statements appear to be quite contradictory. Or, if we take the character to mean "the rupture and isolation of things in relationship", then we are bound to raise questions like "If all things were isolated from each other, with no relationship among them, then the subject of cognition could only cognize himself in and of himself, and then how is it possible to achieve a cognition in terms of subject-object antithesis?" (Hsien Chung Lee, 2011: 78).

In light of this consideration, I propose to translate the word "离[lí]" into "analysis". One may object that in ancient China, there was no idea of analysis and therefore such a translation is not compatible with the actual word meaning and usage at the time. This criticism makes sense, but we do see that Gongsun Long is actually trying hard to express the idea of "separate/isolate it for special inspection/scrutiny"; i.e. he hopes to conduct the study on the meanings themselves by abstracting them from actual objects and things, in order to ascertain and clarify their essences. This is undoubtedly a method of analysis. So, if we use "analysis" to translate the character "离[lí]", we can better clarify and present the main ideas of the essay and better understand why Gongsun Long is repeatedly talking about "the white" and "the hard" as not residing in stones. It is true that during the time he lived, no one among the general public and the intellectuals alike could use "离[lí]" to mean "analysis", as there was no such a concept in the first place. But this does not entail that Gongsun Long could never expect to use a character available in the language repertoire to refer to an idea close enough to analysis. I can find no convincing reason why Gongsun Long should not have been the pioneer of the approach of analysis in Chinese intellectual history. He has been misunderstood since his time, but from his essays, we see a very clear tendency of thought in language analysis, embodied in his analytical speculations on the meaning of name. It is possible for him to have developed the approach of analysis, however immature it might have been.

I would like to call the reader's attention to this point: Gongsun Long has in this essay not only raised the issue of conceptual entity of the meaning of name, which is truly philosophical in nature, but also put forward the important proposition that the conceptual entity of language meaning is the end-product of rational analysis by the human mind. This point has not been given its due in previous studies on *Gongsun Longzi*. And this point is of critical importance: who can say, then, that the morphological features of the Chinese language are not suitable for the rise of metaphysical speculations, such as that of Plato's Ideas or Aristotle's logic? About this point, I shall have more to say later on.

I think I can conclude with confidence that this essay of Gongsun Long's is not paradoxical at all, but a true essay of philosophy of language with an obvious tint of rationalism.

4. About "On Essence and Change"

Like "On 'White-horse Is Not Horse'", "On Essence and Change" also presents the main ideas through dialogs. In this essay, Gongsun Long works in further defense of his principle for rectification of name, that of the *thisness* in *this* and the *thatness* in *that* exclusively. Starting for the argument that "two" is a concept in and of itself, which does not refer to two "ones", he attempts to show that a name should only refer to the exclusive essence of a conceptual entity, through a debate with his heckler over several language concepts.

There are several difficult points for the translation of this essay, which are meanwhile the key to the correct understanding of what the author intends to argue.

The first difficult point lies in the section on "二无一([èr wú yī], literally 'Two have-no one')". In this section, the author's use of "left" and "right" may be confusing to the readers. I agree with Wang Guan's interpretation that "left" and "right" are just another way to say "two 'ones'". To help the readers understand the point better, I have translated these two concepts into "one on the left" and "one on the right". In everyday language use, a thing on the right and a thing on the left, put together, would make two. This is common sense, but Gongsun Long intends to argue that when we use the word "two", it should and can only refer to the concept of two-ness itself, and should not refer to two "ones", since "one" should refer to the essence of oneness exclusively. If we use "two" to mean two "ones", that would be a violation of his principle for the rectification of name, the *thisness* in *this* and the *thatness* in *that* exclusively, because in that case "*two*" would have to refer to two-ness and to one-ness at the same time. Readers are referred to my notes on the translation of his "On Name and Actuality", in which Gongsun Long has stipulated that the use of the name "this" is correct, if and only if the *this* talked about does have the essence of *thisness*, with no *thatness* of any kind in it at the same time. This is exactly what Gongsun Long wants to elaborate in this essay.

Another difficulty in this section has to do with the text that we have now. Specifically, the problem lies with the passage beginning from the heckler's question of "If the right is combined with another thing, can we say a change has occurred" till Gongsun Long's proposition of "'Sheep' and 'ox', put together, hardly mean 'horseness'; 'ox' and 'sheep', put together, may mean 'chickenness' to a much less degree". Because certain words are missing in the original classic essay, the existent translation versions appear to be perplexing even with the turn-taking order between Gongsun Long and his heckler, still less than the interpretation of the words and sentences. For instance, the phrase of "变只[biàn zhī]", which has been translated into at least two English phrases: "How much has it been changed into" or "What has been changed". Most versions adopt the latter, which result in a confusing transition of ideas in the essay.

To me, Wang Guan's interpretation and parsing of the dialog turns are more reasonable. And according to Wang, I have translated the phrase into "What amount has it changed into". My understanding goes like this: in the debate the heckler obviously wants to set Gongsun Long up with this question, because it has to be empirically true that a thing on the right, if added with another thing, would make two. In this way, the heckler would be successful in demonstrating that there exist ones in two. However, Gongsun Long has not been taken in, but replied that the result of the addition is still the "right". Then the heckler presses further: if "right" has changed, how can it still be called "right", or if it has not changed, how can it be said to be changed? This appears more coherent with the context. To this question, Gongsun Long points out, "two" as an independent concept on its own simply does not have a "left" nor a "right"; i.e. there is no question of "left" and "right" in the first place; therefore the heckler's question is just a pseudo-question. Then Gongsun Long goes on to elaborate on this issue with his "ox-sheep" proposition.

My translation does not conform to any versions that we have so far, but it does appear to give a greater coherence to the ideas presented by Gongsun Long in this essay.

The second point of difficulty lies exactly with Gongsun Long's proposition of "'Sheep' and 'ox', put together, hardly mean 'horseness'; 'ox' and 'sheep', put together, may mean 'chickenness' to a much less degree". To me, this proposition is not one about categories, as is ordinarily understood, but one on the essential meaning of concepts. Gongsun Long develops his argument again with an eye to the defense of his principle for the rectification of name. To him, sheep and oxen are surely two different species and therefore "sheep" cannot be used to name oxen; nor vice versa. However, in contrast to horses, oxen and sheep do share some property in common ("with horns", for instance) and neither has the property that a horse has ("with no long tails", for instance). Therefore, sheep and oxen form a sharper contrast with horses than with each other, and for this reason the former two can, standing in opposition against the latter, be grouped into one conceptual entity named by "sheep-ox". Such a "sheep-ox" concept is itself a unique one-ness, characterized by non-horseness. But now, suppose we are faced with another choice and compelled to choose either horse or chicken to form a new conceptual entity with the "sheep-ox". Gongsun Long says clearly that he would prefer horse to chicken. The reason is simple enough: compared with horses, chickens have far fewer similarities with sheep and oxen than horses do and therefore the likelihood of forming an entity of sheep-ox-chicken is even smaller than that of forming an entity of sheep-ox-horse. This is certainly right. Even according to modern biological categorization, horses, oxen and sheep are all viviparous, though they are of different species, while chickens differ even more radically from all the other three, because chickens are oviparous.

I must hasten to point out that Gongsun Long is not talking about biological categorization, but is arguing for his philosophical view that what a name refers to should and can only be the "oneness" of the thing it names. The exaggeration of the essential difference between "chicken" and "sheep-ox" aims at demonstrating that the name "chicken" refers to the essential oneness of chickens and "sheep-ox" of sheep-ox and that these two "ones" cannot be put together to form a conceptual entity of "two" in any sense. Let's infer further just on Gongsun Long's reasoning. Suppose we take "animate" as the criterion for categorization and conceptualization, then it would be highly likely that Gongsun Long would agree with us in saying "Stones, put together with chicken-sheep-ox do not mean animal" (my fabrication). For what Gongsun Long is concerned with is nothing else but the cognitive necessity of the semantic "oneness" that a name should and can only refer to. From the positive and the negative sides, Gongsun Long is able to show that the twoness referred to by a name cannot result from simple addition of two ones and that twoness is the semantic concept with a common essential property. If human beings hope to exchange ideas with each other correctly and to understand the nature of the things in the world, they must be able to master the fundamental oneness which language words refer to, through rational analysis. Or else, the name might be divorced from its true conceptual meaning, and consequently a chaos in the use of name might result, making it impossible for human being to master and express true knowledge about the world. Thus, Gongsun Long's proposition is not a biological one, but one of philosophy of language, as he is reflecting on the question of what is the true knowledge that human beings can acquire about the world, through his speculating on the nature of the meaning of language name.

The last part of the essay further verifies that my explanation of Gongsun Long's idea is correct or at least coherent. In this section, the interpretative difficulty lies with Gongsun Long's employment of some statements of traditional mystery of the "Five-element Operations of the Yin and the Yang" as well as some statements that seem to be involving political-ethical relationship between the king and the ministers. It is here that we see various interpretations, such as that Gongsun Long is influenced by Daoism in his ideology or that Gongsun Long is discussing traditional issues of social order and political ethics (cf. Wang Hongyin, 1997: 47; Hisen Chung Lee, 2011: 43 for detailed discussions). These interpretations appear to be incorrect, or at the very least quite irrelevant with the ideas in the foregoing passages of this essay as well as in the other essays of Gongsun Long's. Certainly, Gongsun Long lived over 2,500 years ago and it was just natural that he might use certain terms and sayings prevalent at the time. But in this essay, he is not using the theory of the *Yin* and the *Yang* and of Five Elements ("metal, wood, water, fire, earth" for the explanation of what the world consists of and how the world functions) to support his rationalistic idea of philosophy of language. Isn't it strange that Gongsun Long has been rationalistically attempting to clarify the issues of meaning and reference of language words in his other essays as well as the other parts in the present essay, but suddenly here he should have switched to such mysterious and illusive concepts that may contribute nothing but further confuse the ideas of the readers? He does not at all need the theory of Operation of Five Elements to support his standpoint! It is not only unnecessary, but also incompatible with his ideas expressed throughout his essays. I do not think these sentences show that Gongsun Long is making use of the Daoist ideas or that he is discussing politics or ethics. Instead, he is just making use of these expressions for the purpose of reinforcing his own idea. What then is he talking about here?

To me, what is presented in this section is just the same as what has been discussed before in this essay, namely, his argument for the exclusive nature of semantic meaning of name, except that he is using colors as another illustration. Let's look at his reasoning. Empirically speaking, if one pours the white paint into the green paint, then one obtains as the result a paint of lighter green. However, this empirical phenomenon is not what Gongsun Long focuses on. Instead, he hopes to clarify in terms of semantic logic that the names "green" and "white" refer respectively to two colors of totally different essence, which defines the two primary colors that stand in sharp contrast from each other. Even if the two colors are mixed up, the name "green" still refers to greenness as a primary color, while "white" whiteness as a primary color. The essences that these names refer to are definite and non-changeable. However, the so-called "lighter green" is neither "green" nor "white", but refers to some sort of motley whose nature cannot be precisely determined. Indeed this is true both *de re* and *de dicto*. According to Gongsun Long's argument, "green" should and can only refer to greenness and cannot refer to any color that is not green; so does "white". Empirically, one can understand and measure with certainty the color of green or of white. As to "lighter green", it is very difficult to define how light or how green the motley color of lighter green should be. For this reason, "lighter green" is not a concept with any ascertainable definition and therefore this name does not have anything true to which it refers necessarily and exclusively. After all, no one can answer this question with any certainty: How light can a light green be a true light green?

This explains why Gongsun Long continues in the essay to point out clearly again that if he were given a compulsory choice between either "lighter green" or "yellow", which he must put together with "green" and "white" to form an entity of a pure oneness, he would unhesitatingly choose "yellow", because "yellow" at least refers to a primary color that can be clearly defined. He would not choose "lighter green", because such a motley color is beyond any clear definition. This way of argument for the point is exactly the same as the "sheep-ox" and "chicken" argument afore discussed. Or, to be more to the point, Gongsun Long attempts to use these examples to finalize his proposition that "two" as a concept should and can only refer to two-ness, and cannot be used to refer to two "one-nesses" at the same time.

In retrospect, we may blame Gongsun Long for being too far-fetched in his arguments. But as I see it, his arguments are justifiable, given the purpose of what he wants to prove. He has successfully defended his principle for the rectification of name, that of the *thisness* in *this* and the *thatness* in *that* exclusively. Based on this understanding, my translation of "On Essence and Change" differs significantly from the other versions available. Yet, I believe mine is a more coherent and clearer re-presentation of what Gongsun Long may be saying.

5. About "On the Nature of Reference"

"On the Nature of Reference" is well-known as the most difficult of all pre-*Qin* writings. It totals 268 Chinese characters in length, of which 48 are "指([zhǐ], literally 'to refer, reference, to denote, denotation, to point to, finger', etc.)", the frequency of it being 17.91% in the essay. This is not only the character of the highest frequency, but also the most difficult to explain, since it is a polysemy. However, it is the key to the understanding of the entire essay. Different interpretations of the "指[zhǐ]"'s have led to completely different and in many cases conflicting and/or confusing interpretations of what Gongsun Long says. Interestingly, diversified as the interpretations are, most seem to be inclined towards the orientation of "words", "denotation" or "reference". So, it appears quite safe to say that this essay is one centering on the problem of understanding what reference is.

I agree basically with the interpretation by Lin Mingjun and Zeng Xiangyun, (2000: 180-181) who claim that Gongsun Long has used the character "指([zhǐ])" in three different senses: 1) "to pick something out by point to it"; 2) "to refer to something by naming it"; and 3) "reference" itself. They believe that Gongsun Long is mostly discussing the issue of using names to refer to things. To them, the question of things and objects has been resolved in his "On Name and Actuality", and Gongsun Long does not need to reiterate it here again. I am inclined to say this is reasonable.

However, more profound thought of this essay can be decoded and appreciated in the light of my discussion on the "paradoxical proposition" of the Ming Jia debaters' (cf. Appendix 2.13), which goes, "A reference does not reach any individual things, which are endless and inexhaustible in the universe". I think this shows that to the Ming Jia thinkers, all things out there do have their objective existence, but when people say of "things", the "things" are what language words refer to and no longer the physical things *per se*. In other words, the things that physically exist are one thing, but "things" described in language are another, the latter being the conceptual knowledge of what the things essentially are. Words refer to the conceptual meanings of things, and to refer is not the same as to denote. This means that the meaning a name refers to does not exist physically in the specific things. Meanings are conceptual and therefore what meaning essentially is should be subject to inspection.

Let's look at the first sentence of the essay. In this sentence consisting of eight Chinese characters, there are three "指[zhǐ]"'s, making the sentence a hard nut to crack. In accordance with what I have said in the previous passage, the character "物 [wù]" means the name of things; the "指[zhǐ]"'s are all nouns, meaning "referring", "reference", and "denotation" respectively. In this way, we can make the proposition expressed by this sentence very clear: things are known as "things" because they are referred to by names, but such reference is not the same as denotation. This is highly consistent with the Ming Jia debaters' proposition of "A reference does not reach any specific things, which are endless and inexhaustible in the universe". With this basic point of view, Gongsun Long proceeds on in this essay to the speculation on the nature of reference as the conceptual meaning of things. And this is a very important part of his theory of the rectification of name. "In general, [the first sentence of this essay] proposes that every object is to be known by being represented through the function of reference. But what is represented by means of reference is no longer the same as the original thing itself." (Hsien Chung Lee, 2011: 18) I agree with this conclusion of Dr. Lee's. However, I wonder why Dr. Lee does not agree with my explaining the character of "指[zhǐ]" as "reference" and "denotation" respectively (see Lee's "Review"). This is because the original text of Gongsun Long's could only be given a coherent explanation by making this distinction. With such a distinction, we can see very clearly that this essay of Gongsun Long's has a central theme: that of making out the difference between the actual thing, the name and the reference. And the reason why this essay is necessary is that at the time of the Great Debate, the participating sides were landed in confusion because they failed to perceive the difference.

Some believe that this essay is also written in the style of a debate. Well, that might be, but not necessarily, because the fact is that the original does not have the dialog structures clearly presented, such as in Gongsun Long's essays of "On 'White-horse Is Not Horse'" or "On Essence and Change". I think the questions in the essay are simply rhetorical. Just like when we write an essay today, we might forestall some questions from our potential rivals and then give answers to them ourselves.

After the keynote statement of "Things known as 'things' have come into being by virtue of the function of reference, but 'reference' does not mean merely the denotation of specific things" at the beginning of the essay, Gongsun Long continues to say that things could in no way be called "things", if there were no language. Nevertheless, since things are just what they are without any name in the natural world, the question is: can the reference of name be equivalent to the ostensive denotation of things? Gongsun Long's answer is negative, holding that things in themselves just exist out there without any inherent name. To him, name use is the way in which human beings discuss things and for this reason, what names refer to are not the concrete things themselves, but the concepts of things. Concepts of things are of course not the same as things in themselves.

What is it that human beings know about things then? To think about this question, Gongsun Long here coined the term of "non-reference", which denotes the things that are themselves nameless. Since actual things do not have any name, one cannot expect to apply an individual name to each of them one by one. But this is not to say that the non-reference is out of bounds of reference; as individuals the things are non-reference, but as categories they can be referred to. The reason why "thing" as a name can be applied to any non-reference is that reference is the conceptual meaning of the thing as it essentially is. Gongsun Long's point is that the name is the result of human cognition of things out there and therefore the meaning of name is the abstraction of the essence of things as things, rather than the things themselves.

Right after this point, Gongsun Long puts forward in his essay an important statement concerning a rigorous distinction between denotation at the empirical level and reference at the language concept level. He argues that an individual thing certainly can be denoted by a name, but this is just to call the thing by the name rather than to indicate its meaning, and therefore, this is denotation and not reference. In ordinary language communications, people often confuse *denotation* with *reference*, mistaking the concept of "things" for concrete things themselves, which results in the chaotic understanding of the relationship between name and actuality. To say that things are "non-reference" means only that they are not their own references naturally, but does not entail that they cannot be referred to. In so saying, Gongsun Long is proposing that the essential meaning of "things" can only be represented by language words and understood by human. Or else, humans can in no way know about the world. Names with what they refer to can certainly be used to denote or label things, but such denoting is far from the essence of things they refer to. These are issues of a totally different nature.

Further, Gongsun Long has clearly stated in the essay that specific things themselves are not what their names refer to, but are commonly regarded as such; this is not the correct understanding of what reference really is and that it is wrong to take "actual things that exist but are not themselves references" for "the references that are the essential meanings but do not have physical existence". This is a logically sound statement and it does not have anything to do with Laozi's Daoist sort of concepts like "Nothingness". There is nothing mysterious or intangible in his statement, as some scholars have claimed. At this point, I do not agree with Hsien Chung Lee (2011: 20), who says that by such statements, Gongsun Long has this point in mind: "what is referred and what is said belong to the same level of existence, namely that of Nothingness". I simply cannot see how this conclusion could have been reached.

In my translation of this essay, I have adopted some of the reasonable ideas from the existent translations, but abandoned their use of terms— "signifier" and "that which is signified" (such as Wang Hongyin, 1997: 337) for the key character of "指 ([zhǐ], basically a noun denoting 'finger', but with extended meanings such as 'to point to', 'to point at', 'to refer', 'to signify' and their corresponding noun forms)" and "非指([feī zhǐ], literally 'non-chǐ', 'not chǐ')". To me, such a translation is bound to come across great difficulty when it comes to sentences like "非有非指者" (according to Wang, it would have to be translated into an incomprehensible sentence: "there is no that which is signified"). Meanwhile, Hsien Chung Lee (cf. the "Review" he has written for me) regards "非指[feī zhǐ], as a key concept like "物指[wù zhǐ], literally 'object-zhǐ']". In his view, "物指[wù zhǐ]" consists of a two-way relation in cognition between the subject and the object via a "denoting function", while "非指[feī zhǐ]" should be the subject's mastery of the property of the object. As I understand it, Lee has in fact distinguished the direct denotation from the indirect conceptual reference. I agree with this distinction. Without such a distinction, this essay of Gongsun Long's would be very difficult to decode. But I do not join him in saying that "非指[feī zhǐ]" is a special concept, for the reason that syntactically this character string should be read in a separated way as meaning "not" [zhǐ] (not a reference, not a denotation, etc.) instead of reading it as a compound expressing a single concept. This is because if we regard it as a compound noun, we would run into a syntactic difficulty. Take the second part of the first sentence for example: it could not form a complete sentence, but only a juxdaposition of two nouns, which is not grammatical in pre-*Qin* Chinese and offers readers no way to infer the relationship between the two nouns. But if we read the string separately, the sentence would be expressing the idea of "this [zhǐ] is not the same as that [zhǐ]", which is not only grammatical structurally but also highly consistent semantically with Gongsun Long's principle for the rectification of name: the *thisness* in *this* and the *thatness* in *that* exclusively. In addition, if "非指[feī zhǐ]" were indeed a special concept important in the essay, we should have every reason to expect Gongsun Long to give more elaborated discussions to it as he did other concepts. However, we find no such elaboration in his essay.

For this reason, I have adopted "reference" and "denotation" for my translation of the different "指[zhǐ]"s in this essay. The use of these two words makes the whole version very coherent in ideas. For example, the first sentence is "Things are known

193

as 'things' by virtue of the function of reference, but reference does not mean merely the denotation of specific things". To me, this translation brings the main idea of the essay out: that Gongsun Long is not talking about the relationship between the words and the things they name, but about the nature of reference itself. The point he makes throughout the essay is that words are of course capable of denoting specific objects, but to denote is not to refer. Gongsun Long wants to clarify the confusion of the two concepts by the debating parties in the Great Debate on Name and Actuality, so as to master rationally the nature of reference as the meaning of words.

Thus, the very important thought put forward by Gongsun Long through this essay is: the rectification of name should not be an endeavor to establish merely the correspondence of name to actuality; rather, one should examine whether or not the meaning of name meets the requirements necessary for the representation of the essence. This thought reinforces our apprehension and appreciation of the preposterous propositions, such as "white-horse is not horse", "there is no 'one' in 'two'", "separated being of the white and the hard", etc., which he has repeatedly argued for. I am firmly convinced that these are not sophistic paradoxes at all, but are truly metaphysical speculations on the nature of meaning itself that words refer to. His real purpose is to question the appropriateness of the then current practice of rectification of name by clarifying what "name" and "actuality" are, since these are the central ideas being debated on. This is what he says he intends to do in his "On Name and Actuality".

Hsien Chung Lee (2011: 46-47) points out that the change of "actuality" starts from the affirmation of the existence of things and ends at the "name" which pins down the conceptual intension, which in turn relies on the stipulation of "actuality-name relationship, the 位[wei]". I agree partly with this judgment, but I do not think Gongsun Long is talking about "change" or "not change", though he has used these terms in the essay. Rather, Gongsun Long is concerned with the more fundamental issue of what the nature of conceptual meaning is. He is interested in the question of what does not change among things that do change and what is it that is pinned down by name. In this respect, I think what he is doing is very similar to ancient Greek philosophers who attempt to seek the "One" from the "Many". To Gongsun Long, such a "One" is the essential meaning a name refers to. He is quite aware that in everyday language uses, people are not clear about the difference between using a name to label a thing and using a name to refer to a concept. This explains why he must write this essay: in order to correctly rectify the use of name, the concepts of *reference* and *denotation* should be clarified in the first place.

Such a rigorous distinction of denotation and reference is exactly the central issue Gongsun Long tackles in the essay, in order to maintain his principle for the rectification of name. In this sense, this essay should be regarded as a sublimation of the ideas he discussed in his previous essays, which is why I list this essay as the last of his series of five.

To propose a truly correct approach to the rectification of name in the spirit of rationalism and hence to guarantee the truthfulness of human knowledge about the world, Gongsun Long should see where the problems for the then current rectification practices lied and this should be the motivation behind his writing of this essay. However, partly for the complexity and abstractedness of this issue, and partly for the non-inflectional and loose syntactic features of the pre-*Qin* Chinese language, plus the absence of ontology and epistemology in the pre-*Qin* period, this essay constitutes a great difficulty for later interpreters and translators, resulting in a variety of totally different versions which even conflict with each other. My translation might likewise be just one more opinion, but I do think that it renders the ideas expressed in this essay more logically sound and more coherent with what Gongsun Long has expressed in the rest of his essays. In this sense, this translation can be said to be faithful to the original.

Gongsun Long, a Chinese philosopher of pre-*Qin* period over 2,500 years ago, should have come to such a rationalist speculation on issues of reference and meaning; this is no less a wonder in the intellectual history of China.

6. About "Anecdotes of Gongsun Long"

Just by the title, we see that "Anecdotes of Gongsun Long" was not written by Gongsun Long himself, but is a record of some of his deeds. This essay is not difficult to understand, nor is there anything that needs special treatment. One thing I should call attention to emphatically, however, is that some statements in it do not conform to Gongsun Long's ideology, exactly because it was written by someone else who had not been able to see correctly what Gongsun Long was proposing.

For instance, the first paragraph of this essay says that Gongsun Long insisted on his own theory of "White horse is not horse" in his debates with others, wishing to popularize such a theory in order "to indoctrinate all people in this ideology of his". This is indeed what Gongsun Long hoped to accomplish and I, as the translator, have taken this as the starting point to scrutinize the other essays in *Gongsun Longzi*. However, the unknown author of this essay said that Gongsun Long was good at applying metaphors with concrete things to illustrate his ideas, which I think is not to the point. Such a judgment shows that the author was explaining Gongsun Long's theory not in the perspective of philosophy of language, but in terms of everyday experiences. The key point of the decoding of the word "object", for instance, which as I said before means not only specific objects existing in the world, but also the conceptual meaning of "object" as it is. The author seemed to have failed to perceive and appreciate Gongsun Long's metaphysical speculations on the essence of the meaning of names in an abstract philosophical manner.

Because of this failure, he who authored "Anecdotes of Gongsun Long" explained Gongsun Long's argumentation for "White-horse is not horse" in this way: "Just like one looking for a white horse in the stable where there are horses of all colors except white; in this case no horse could be picked out. No horse could be picked out, because the kind of horse that one looks for does not exist there." This is seriously mistaken. Since it is a mistake in the original, I am not responsible to correct it. But a word of caution must be given here to remind the readers that the mode of thought at the experience level is not of the same abstract nature as that of philosophy. And this discrepancy partially explains why Gongsun Long has been misunderstood in history.

This viewpoint of mine is reinforced by what the last paragraph of the essay said, where we see clearly that what truly caused Gongsun Long to repudiate Kong Chuan was that the former complained the latter as having failed to master the nature of his theory. Gongsun Long said to Kong Chuan: "You just wish to falsify my theory of 'white-horse being not horse', but you do not know on what basis you can start to criticize it." Before so saying, Gongsun Long had already illustrated, with his logically sound reasoning, that the King of Qi State used certain word without knowing what it actually meant, because he simply did not have a mastery of the essential definition of what the word referred to. Likewise in the last paragraph of the essay, Gongsun Long pointed out clearly that Kong's criticism of his "white-horse" theory was wild of the mark because Kong had failed to understand what the theory was really driving at. In other words, Gongsun's theory and Kong's criticism were not on the same plane. Metaphysical speculation is different from everyday experiences after all.

If what are cited as anecdotes in this essay are true recordings of Gongsun Long's sayings, then this last statement does give a support to the way I understand and interpret Gongsun Long in my attempt at the translation. That is, what Gongsun Long intends to discuss are not the problems in actual practice, but the questions of theoretical speculation on reference and nature of meaning, which are issues of philosophy of language in the true sense of the phrase. Gongsun Long is entitled to be a philosopher of language of the rationalistic line of thought.

Postscript

It is practically very hard to achieve at once faithfulness to the original while keeping the stylistic flavor in the translation of *Gongsun Longzi*, not only from Chinese into English, but also from its classic style into modern vernacular style of the Chinese language. Short ones as they are, the essays of Gongsun Long's have been regarded as the most difficult to read of all pre-*Qin* writings. This is especially the case with one of the essays, entitled "On the Nature of Reference", known as the "hardest nut to crack". Even just the attempt to be faithful is a challenge, because Gongsun Long and the Ming Jia school of thought he represents have traditionally been labeled as "paradoxical sophism", rejected by all the other schools of thought as well as by laypeople. As the result, we do not have ample data available for a completely true-to-the-fact reproduction of their ideas.

What I can do, then, is to attempt at a coherence of translation, on the basis of my own studies on pre-*Qin* Ming Jia in recent years, which enables me to find certain inherent connections of expressions in his essays that may comprise a convincingly adequate explanation of the essence of his thought. Before I set out translating, I had read two already published English versions, one by Wang Hongyin and the other by Liu Yujun, and many modern Chinese versions of interpretation, few of which have, in my view, achieved such coherence. This is caused partly by the difficulty of the language, with many key points still in want of reinterpretation, partly by certain misunderstanding of the way Gongsun Long expressed his philosophy. Retranslation is in need, therefore, for a better comprehension of traditional Chinese philosophy that was sprouting on the soil of the Chinese language.

I must declare that many of the ideas from the previous translators have been examined before the reinterpretation of *Gongsun Long*zi, but this translation does attempt to produce an independent version of my own. Readers will find that I am examining the great ancient Chinese thinker in a completely new light, though some reasonable points made by previous translators are incorporated. For the academic data used and cited, please refer to the bibliography of this book. Errors in the translation are all mine.

Part III Framework for Reinterpreting *Gongsun Longzi*[1]

1. Misinterpretations of *Gongsun Longzi*

The reinterpretation of *Gongsun Longzi* is necessary, because this pamphlet is a rare embodiment of the thoughts of pre-*Qin* Ming Jia, an important programmatic document which has unfortunately been interpreted in very different and frequently conflicting ways throughout history. Such great conflicts suggest that these interpretations are problematic.

The life story of Gongsun Long can only be gathered from fragmented records in some classical documents. He was known to live in the State of Zhao during the Warring States Period (475-221 BC), serving as a hanger-on under the patronage of Zhao Sheng, Lord Ping Yuan. As one of the major representatives of the pre-*Qin* Ming Jia, Gongsun Long was very active and highly influential in the Great Debate on Name and Actuality, a large-scale ideological debate that lasted over 100 years. His theory of "White-horse is not horse" has been so well-known in China that it would be what first comes into mind at the mention of his name. Legendary story goes that Gongsun Long once led a white horse to a check-point, but the guards refused to let him pass with his horse according to the decree from their superiors. Facing this, Gongsun Long argued on the spot that he was leading a white-horse which is not a horse. His arguments rendered the guards speechless and had to allow him to pass with his horse.[2] From such historical records, we come to know that Gongsun Long often engaged himself in arguments with others and that in his whole life he adhered

---

1 Some materials in this part have been published in some other journals in China (such as *Philosophical Research, Journal of Sichuan University, Foreign Languages Research*, etc.) in the process of my research in recent years. The content presented here has been significantly modified, supplemented, or rewritten.

2 For greater details of Gongsun Long's life story, please refer to Wang Guan's *Interpretation of Gongsun Longzi*, Beijing: China Book Bureau, 1992: 2-8.

to the claims such as "white-horse is not horse", "hard and white stone is in fact two entities", etc. However, the propositions put forward by Gongsun Long and the other Ming Jia debaters appeared to be totally contradictory to common-sense knowledge and their argumentation is highly demanding and mind-bending, which partly explains why their ideas and approaches were not apprehended by the people at the time, but were condemned as "sophistic paradoxes", repudiated and rejected and finally became oblivious in history. It was said that later academic and political elites should have had the urge of burning Gongsun Long's book simply because they could not understand what it said! (Du, 1963: 6)

For this reason, a greater part of Ming Jia's works have been lost. What have been left of the ideas of famous masters such as Hui Shi's are just a few fragmented sentences. Fortunately, these five essays by Gongsun Long have survived, so that we can have a glimpse of the glory of Ming Jia's thoughts. Gongsun Long was said to be a quite productive writer whose works ran up to tens of thousands of words. But what we have today includes a mere collection of five relatively complete essays of his: "On Name and Actuality", "On 'White-horse Is Not Horse'", "On the Being of Hardness and Whiteness", "On Essence and Change", and "On the Nature of Reference". The other essay, "Anecdotes of Gongsun Long", is a record of some of Gongsun Long's sayings and deeds, in which some ideas are consistent with those expressed in the five essays, but the illustrations and interpretations do not agree with them. In addition, "Anecdotes of Gongsun Long" has some parts of redundant repetition. Obviously, the essay was not written by Gongsun Long. In spite of this, I have included in my translation the essay of "Anecdotes of Gongsun Long", for the reference of the readers.

What, then, are the so-called "sophistic" paradoxes of Ming Jia's? How do people criticize and repudiate them? Are the criticisms reasonable? Let's first look at their propositions and then examine some major criticisms against them. Gongsun Long's famous paradoxes include "White-horse is not horse", "Two consists of no ones", "hardness and whiteness are separate entities". Of these propositions, later interpreters agree that the last one expresses Gongsun Long's viewpoint that regards the abstracted "hardness" and "whiteness" as something real. For this reason, Gongsun Long has been judged to be an "idealist" philosopher. The problem is this:

no matter how idealistic a philosopher is, he/she is not likely to say that a white horse is not a horse, nor that two is not composed of two ones, as Gongsun Long did. Then why should Gongsun Long have proposed such statements? What relationship do these apparent paradoxes have with his idealistic proposition of "Hardness and whiteness are separate entities"? Few have pursued questions like these. Instead, they seem to be satisfied with labeling Gongsun Long as "sophist" and then dismiss him. After all, who else would turn up with sophistic paradoxes other than the idealists? Probably it is exactly with this misunderstanding that we have missed the chance of knowing the essence of the ideas of pre-*Qin* Ming Jia, of which Gongsun Long was the major representative. One of the essays of Gongsun Long's, "On the Nature of Reference", has traditionally been regarded as the most difficult to read of all the pre-*Qin* essays, the "hardest bone to bite into" (Zhou, 1997: 234). As the result, those who see Gongsun Long as an idealist use it as further evidence of his idealism, while those who reject Gongsun Long as a sophist also take it to be a piece of writing purported at perplexing the mind of the readers, because it is exorbitantly mind-bending.

In comparison with Gongsun Long's "sophistic paradoxes" presented in his essays, the fragmented sentences, recorded in *Zhuangzi*, that were said to be given by Hui Shi and other Ming Jia debaters may appear to be just as deviant from common sense or even more grotesque:

A) Hui Shi's Ten Propositions:

A1. *The largest-in-itself entails no more space outside it, and this can be said to be the Largest One, while the smallest-in-itself entails no more space inside it, and this can be said to be the Smallest One*;

A2. *The area, with no thickness, is in no way amassed, but can be as large as one-thousand li* (A *li* equals half a kilometer in Chinese measurement system);

A3. *The sky is as low as the earth; a mountain is as flat as a lake*;

A4. *The moment the Sun reaches its apex in sky is the moment it sets down in the west; and the moment things are born is the moment they die*;

A5. *The major commonality differs from the minor commonality, the latter means merely the apparent similarities or differences among concrete things; that all categories of things are the same or different in essence should be what we mean by the major commonality*;

A6. *The south extends in such a way that it is at once limited and limitless;*

A7. *One departs for the Yue State today, but arrives yesterday;*

A8. *There exist unlocking solutions to any seamlessly interlocked rings;*

A9. *I know that the center of the universe is located at the same time north to Yan, a state in the north, and south to Yue, a state in the south;*

A10. *I have an extensive love for everything and heaven and earth are one.*

B) The Twenty-one Paradoxical Propositions of Ming Jia Debaters:

B1. *There is hair in eggs;*

B2. *The State of Ying has the universe in it;*

B3. *Dogs can be regarded as goats;*

B4. *There are eggs in horses;*

B5. *Frogs have tails;*

B6. *Mountain comes out of the mouth;*

B7. *Tortoises are longer than snakes;*

B8. *White dogs are black;*

B9. *A chicken has three feet;*

B10. *Fire is not hot;*

B11. *Wheels do not roll on the ground;*

B12. *Eyes do not see things;*

B13. *References do not reach, for what can be reached are endless;*

B14. *One cannot draw a square with a ruler; nor can one draw a circle with a pair of compasses;*

B15. *A mortise cannot wrap up the tenon;*

B16. *The shadow of a flying bird never moves;*

B17. *There are moments when a fast-flying arrow is both static and moving;*

B18. *A puppy is not a dog;*

B19. *A yellow horse and a colored ox, put together, make a three;*

B20. *An orphan pony has never had a mother;*

B21. *Take a one-foot long rod and divide it into two halves. Repeatedly dividing a half into two every day, one can never expect to finish the division.*[1]

---

1   The translations here are literal ones faithfully following the structural patterns of the original. I shall modify and re-translate them later on in this book.

Without any contextual clues, we probably could understand only some of these propositions, such as B21, which is highly consistent with the limit theory in modern mathematics and the hypothesis of matters being limitlessly divisible in physics. We might also appreciate A1, looking up to it as Hui Shi's philosophical speculation on what the essences of being the largest and of being the smallest can be (that which has no more external space and that which has no more internal space). Apart from the few understandable ones, the rest of the propositions do appear to be strange enough, which don't make any sense in terms of everyday experiences. How, for instance, can a white dog be at the same time black? Is it true that chickens have three feet? Is it possible that the sky is as low as the earth under our feet or that a mountain is as flat as a lake surface? Isn't it a pure nonsense to say that the universe is located in the north and in the south at the same time?

Probably because of such features, Ming Jia propositions have become the target of attacks from all the other schools of thought ever since the beginning. Of the criticisms, only some are intellectual and reasonable, while many are groundless and wild of the mark. I particularly deplore the fact that the criticizers, whether reasonable ones or not, have mostly failed to make clear what Ming Jia were talking about and why they should be talking in the way they did. Next, let me sum up some representative criticisms to see how and in what dimensions Ming Jia have been attacked.

1.1 Attacks on Ming Jia during the Pre-*Qin* Period

First, let's see how Ming Jia thinkers were attacked by their contemporaries, primarily by the three major schools of thought, namely Later Mohists, the Confucianists and the Daoists.

1.1.1 Later Mohists

Later Mohists stated in their Mohist Scriptures a series of propositions that contradicted sharply those of Gongsun Long's, such as: "A white horse is a horse. To ride a white horse is to ride a horse; and to ride a horse of any color is no doubt to ride a horse" (Chapter 45); "Fire is necessarily hot, because the heat in the fire makes people feel hot" (Chapter 41); "What can be seen and what cannot be seen are not separated, just like two ones make two; likewise, width and length co-exist in the same plane and hardness and whiteness co-exist in the same stone... Feeling the hardness, one sees the whiteness at the same time, for they are mutually inclusive in the same stone" (Chapter 43) and so on. For the Later Mohists, language should be a description of what is there and what happens in the world: "The sounds uttered from the mouth become words... Speech is everyone's capacity of uttering words out of mouth to denote things, just like painting a tiger... What we use to say are names and what we say of are things existing out there; a name and an actual thing couple so that the name acquires its meaning" (Chapter 42). Since this is the case, whether the meaning of a word is correct or not should be tested by its correspondence with the actuality: "One refers to things by means of name, expresses ideas by proposition and gives explanation by reasoning... The effect should be the standard for telling the right from the wrong. Any argument should be put to test by this standard. If the effect is in keeping with actual state of affairs, the argument is right, or else, the argument is wrong. This is the rule we should follow."

My comment:

The viewpoint of Later Mohists was obviously empiricist in spirit, different from that of Ming Jia. While Ming Jia talked about "Fire is not hot", Later Mohists argued that fire is hot; against Gongsun Long's proposition of "White-horse is not horse", Later Mohists reasoned in a tit-for-tat manner that white horses are horses, because to ride a white horse is to ride a horse. Such opposition is quite natural but not to the point, because we see very clearly from Gongsun Long's essays that he was speculating on the meaning of language at the conceptual level, while Later Mohists were criticizing him at the experiential level. Later Mohists pointed out definitely that language words are the means to describe the reality and therefore whether the meaning of language is right or wrong should be tested by the effect of experience and practice. A statement is right if it corresponds with the actual state of affairs, or it would be wrong if there is no such correspondence. With this standpoint, it is no wonder that Later Mohists should object to Gongsun Long's "White-horse is not horse" proposition. Are we not riding a horse if we are riding a white horse? That would sound absurd! However, Later Mohists were not looking at the issue in the same line with Ming Jia's rationalism; their criticisms are indeed quite reasonable from the empirical point of view, but do not constitute a true negation of the propositions of the latter. Later Mohists might have understood what Ming Jia people were talking about, to the philosophical standpoint of which they simply did not agree. Nevertheless, both sides were philosophers in ancient China, because they both were predisposed to the pursuit of the foundation for the certainty of knowledge. Had their ideas not died out but instead they had continued their debates, the traditional Chinese ideology would have presented a totally different picture.

1.1.2 Confucianists

Different from Later Mohists, Confucianists' criticism against Ming Jia bordered on slandering. According to *Xunzi*, the writings of Xunzi, the major representative of Confucianism at the time, Ming Jia debaters "do not model their doctrines on the Early Kings. Nor do they observe the rituals and moral principles. Instead, they are engaged in proposing grotesque theories on the basis of bizarre playing of words, in irresponsible highlighting of details and in useless debating, which can in no sense be of any value for the society, contributing nothing to the political and moral orders. However, their reasoning does appear to be well-grounded and thus their sayings appear to be sensible, which is why they can cheat the public at large" (Chapter 6). The Ming Jia theories were "unscrupulous and wicked that should be rejected in any well-ordered epoch and are blindly followed only in an age of disturbance. As to their theories of 'the interchangeability of the being and the not-being', or 'the separation of the hardness and the whiteness and of the sameness and difference' and so on and so forth, these are all what the wisest ears are unable to hear, what the most insightful eyes are unable to see and what the smartest debaters are unable to discuss. Even if one has the wisdom of a sage, one is unable to retort them easily. A gentleman is no less a gentleman even if he does not know these theories; and an inferior man is no more an inferior man even if he knows these theories. Craftsmen not knowing these would not be impaired in his skill development, while scholars not knowing these would not be hindered from achievements in his studies. But if the rulers and officials know these theories, the consequence would be a chaos of laws; if ordinary people know these, they would be landed in confusion as to what their duties should be; and if the foolish and uncultivated individuals know these, they are bound to gather up their followers to advocate such doctrines and arguments with further nonsensical examples, until they grow old and their children grow up, never realizing that they have been doing what is evil indeed. Therefore, these theories are nothing but the uttermost stupidities, meaner than even chickens and bitches!" (Chapter 8) Therefore, Xunzi demanded, "For all those unorthodox doctrines and theories that deviate from the correct Way and all those who propose such theories without authorization, a wise king should exercise his power over them, educating them with the correct Way, restraining them with decrees, retorting them by intellectual essays and penalize them by criminal laws." (Chapter 22)

My comment:

Such invectives disclose how enraged Xunzi was by Ming Jia's propositions. Xunzi himself did have proposed his own viewpoint on language, such as his correct theory that "Names are not fixed to objects, but are used to name objects by agreement. It is by convention that a name comes to be fixed with an object" (Chapter 22). And he was more empirically-minded in terms of the rectification of name compared with the a priori theory of "modeling on the Early Wise Kings" of Confucius, the founder of Confucianism. He did raise his own theory of "the mind grasping the defining characteristics", that is, the meaning of language has its source in sensory perceptions which are to be processed by thinking, the function of the mind. But in his criticism of Ming Jia, it is beyond question that Xunzi failed to understand what they were saying and for this reason he could only resort to condemning them for using wicked arguments to perplex people's normal thoughts and to subvert the political orders and moral rituals. He was virtually acting like a shrew shouting abuses in the street. And he would not stop at this, but went on to demand a wipe-out of all Ming Jia ideas by any means available, administrative, intellectual and legal. What a tyrant he was! Even if he insisted on his empirical stance, he should have criticized Ming Jia in a philosophical manner such as Later Mohists did. On the contrary, he attacked Ming Jia from the angle of politics and morality, which was wild of the mark. This explains only one thing: Xunzi's tendency of empiricism was not yet self-conscious and not philosophically well-grounded, but he was just following the practice-oriented convention of Confucian thoughts. Xunzi's thought was not yet metaphysical and for this reason he could not apprehend the philosophical quality of Ming Jia propositions. Out of his ignorance, his attack on Ming Jia's philosophy of language in the angle of political practice missed its target. However, his attacks did bring a disastrous blow on the rational speculative mode of thinking of Ming Jia, at least partly because Confucianism, of which he was a major representative, came to be the ideological pillar for the feudalist dynasties in China later on.

1.1.3 Daoists

Daoists also attacked Ming Jia. In *Zhuangzi*, the collected writings of Zhuangzi, one of the major Daoist representatives, one reads the following remarks. "Huan Tuan, Gongsun Long and their disciples are debaters with serious limitations, because what they do hoodwinks the people and subverts their normal minds. It is true that they are able to render people speechless but in the end they cannot convince them." (Chapter 32) "[They] argue that the same and the different are just one and the same, that the hardness and the whiteness are independent entities. [They] verify what is false to be what is true and justify what is unreasonable. By so doing, [they] land all other scholars in a confusion of thought and all other debaters in puzzlement. And [they] should have boasted this to be perfect reasoning!" (Chapter 17) "Once the ordinary people know these [Ming Jia's] evil and false arguments, especially their sophistic paradoxes of 'separating the hardness and the whiteness' and of 'the same being no different from the different' etc., they would certainly be confused in their minds. Therefore, the chaos and disturbances of the society would result whenever people long for such knowledge." (Chapter 10)"Hui Shi does know a lot in many fields and has written books that run up to five-cart load in amount, but what he has written are simply wrong and what he has said are not correct at all." "Hui Shi debates with others without any prudence and answers the questions others pose without even thinking over them. He attempts to give an explanation to everything in the world, but his endless talking is full of absurdities and he should have felt that he should talk more! What he does is actually to provide people with falsity and to win his fame by defeating others in debate. This is why he is not accepted by the people. He is not profound enough in learning but too ambitious to impose his views on the world, which has pushed him on to the wrong track. Evaluated against the Dao, the Way of the universe, Hui Shi's ability is as trivial as the sound of a mosquito or a gadfly. How little he contributes to our understanding of things under heaven! ... What a pity! Hui Shi is a talented man, but he has set foot on a wrong path leading to no knowledge of anything and he never realizes that he is indeed mistaken. This is just like a man who makes a sound to achieve a silence, or one who tries to cast away his own shadow. What a tragedy!" (Chapter 32)

My comment:

Zhuangzi was said to have kept on good terms with Hui Shi and so he was polite enough to take a pity on Hui Shi by saying that Hui had wasted the talent. But to Gongsun Long and other Ming Jia debaters, Zhuangzi was not as mild in criticism, but accused them of being crafty and vicious since they dumbfounded the others in debates and confused their minds. The question is, however, that Zhuangzi had not been able to apprehend the essential quality of Ming Jia's ideas. Since Zhuangzi himself admitted that the Ming Jia debaters were able to win out in debates by rendering others speechless until they could even perplex the others' minds, why didn't he probe into the reason why they could have done that? In fact, I think this is not because Zhuangzi did not want to, but because he lacked the ability to do it. Zhuangzi noted down in his writings the fragments of Hui Shi, Gongsun Long and other Ming Jia debaters, which he garbled from their argumentation, and preened himself by belittling their ideas with his own relativistic and agnostic "wisdom". He could not have dreamed that what he did has left us pieces of evidence that not only bear out the nature of Ming Jia's rationalist philosophical tendency, but also disclosed the absence of logical reasoning in his own thought. Zhuangzi was indeed a great literary figure, but was nearly a moron in analytical speculation of logic. This explains the fact that Zhuangzi and Xunzi were totally different and even antagonistic in ideological predisposition, but both of them attacked Ming Jia vehemently in the same way and both missed the point. Being impervious to reason in criticizing Ming Jia without grasping what the latter were talking about, this is true of the attacks on the part of both Zhuangzi and Xunzi.

1.1.4 Summing up of this section

The ideas of Ming Jia, characterized by rational metaphysical speculation, were not compatible with and therefore not tolerated by the pre-*Qin* social and intellectual mainstreams, because the general cultural atmosphere in ancient China was dominated by secular scholarships aimed at practical issues concerning political and ethical orders. All the other schools of thoughts criticized and repudiated Ming Jia, even though they stood different from and even antagonistic to one another in terms of theoretical ground. Except Later Mohists who were able to engage themselves, on the basis of their empiricist philosophy, in meaningful and ideologically valuable debates with Ming Jia thinkers, the rest of the schools were good at sarcasms and invectives but came up with virtually nothing of philosophical significance. It seems true to say that the discourse and debate between Ming Jia and Later Mohism did not share a certain mutual comprehensibility with the rest of the schools of thinkers.

After the pre-*Qin* period, the thought of Confucianism came to be the single ideology of the country and the burgeoning tradition of rationalist speculation was virtually ruptured. The ideas of Ming Jia was yet to be re-discovered and given attention to until the end of the *Qing* Dynasty (around 19th to early 20th century) more than two thousand years later, with the learning and thoughts introduced into China from the west. Unfortunately, what were left of the Ming Jia works included only a few fragmented sentences that stood in no relation with each other, except the five relatively complete essays written by Gongsun Long. Because of this, modern researchers have up till now provided various interpretations of what Gongsun Long was saying, some of which are even conflicting with each other.

1.2 Various Interpretations of Gongsun Long and Ming Jia

How do modern interpreters understand Gongsun Long and his Ming Jia thinkers? Let's now take a look at some most representative theoretical samples.

1.2.1 The "sophistry" theory

Even in modern time, some still regard Gongsun Long as a sophist and criticize him in terms of political ideology. For instance, Guo Moruo (1945: 280-283) blamed Gongsun Long for "mostly playing sophistic games of concepts". He believed that these sophistic propositions were not at all politically valueless; rather, they were what Gongsun Long employed to gloss over the "reactionary speeches" of the then moribund ruling class. Therefore such sophistry was not progressive in any sense, but was "a negation of the revolutionary ideas of the earlier pre-*Qin* scholars". Yet Guo did not give any convincing proof that Gongsun Long was indeed serving the ruling class. Ironically, during the so-called Cultural Revolution in China (mid-20th century), an article entitled "'White-horse Is Not Horse' Is a Challenge against Confucian 'Rectification of Name'", drafted by the Great Criticism Group of Foreign Languages Department (1974), claimed the contrary: "It was highly likely that Gongsun Long did have the common sense that 'running-dogs are dogs'. But why should he have insisted on 'A white horse is not a horse', which is quite contradictory to the common sense? The reason is simple indeed: it was needed for the class struggle at the end of the Warring States Period; there was the need to counter-attack Confucius' 'rectification of name'." Well, Gongsun Long was now lauded to be a revolutionary hero! Ideological interpretation does not make sense.

Some others did not interpret Gongsun Long ideologically, but they also dismissed his sayings as nothing but sophistry. Zhang Taiyan (1906: 386, 395) said, "Hui Shi, Gongsun Long and the people of their kind were well-known to be debaters on name; yet they were fond of splitting or isolating concepts for trivial analysis, which made their arguments sophistic"; "Their sophistic paradoxes, such as 'a chicken has three feet', 'a puppy is not a dog' and the like are too pedantic and nonsensical to worth our discussion today." Yang Zhao (2003: 77) shared the idea: "Though Hui Shi and Gongsun Long were different in their viewpoints, both of them produced theories that contradicted the facts and ran counter to reality, because they failed to start from the sense experiences. Such theories were doomed to be sophistic." Han Donghui (2001) claimed that the school of formal name "argued for the sake of arguing, were self-contradictory and turned out to be sophists", though their sophistic propositions "were of considerable philosophical significance". Even the scholars who hold positive opinions on Ming Jia ideas may still believe that at least some of the Ming Jia propositions are but sophism, such as "An orphan pony has never had a mother" (Zhang, 1996: 211-212), or that they are just "fallacies and meaningless play of words" (Liu, 2003: 300).

My comment:

It's of course very comfortable a job to simply dismiss the Ming Jia propositions as sophistic paradoxes and then forget them, but this attitude is too reckless, like those in history who were anxious to burn Gongsun Long's book just because they could not understand it. What if they are in fact not sophistic? If this is the case, doesn't it mean that we would sit on the chance to recognize a traditional treasure of Chinese culture? Even if they are truly sophistic, what we should do is to explain why Ming Jia should have given those paradoxes. Since we admit that their sophistic propositions obviously contradict common sense on the one hand, but do have philosophical implications on the other, then we should ask what such implications they are offering us are. At the very least, we need to explain why some of Ming Jia propositions are philosophical while at the same time the others are sophistry or meaningless play of words. If Ming Jia thinkers are indeed philosophers, then our mislabeling them as sophists would mean that the perspective in which we inspect their thoughts and the framework in which we explain their propositions are in fact incorrect or at least inappropriate. As to the theory of class and class struggle, I think it has absolutely nothing to do with Ming Jia's thoughts. It is very difficult to explain in the first place why Gongsun Long should have chosen to meet the need of class struggle by way of sophism. Or, if Xunzi emphasized social and political orders and demanded that the debate on name and actuality contribute to the governing of the state, but Ming Jia stood in direct opposition against Xunzi, can we then come to the conclusion that the Ming Jia thinkers were antagonistic to the ruling class at the time? I am afraid we cannot. To criticize Ming Jia in the framework of political ideology is just the same thing as Xunzi's cursing, which is not of value in inspiring our thought.

1.2.2 The labels of materialism vs. idealism

Fung Yulan, one of the great modern Chinese philosophers, has given a very high comment on pre-*Qin* Ming Jia. He said: "Few schools [of classical Chinese philosophy] have exercised any efforts self-consciously to delve into the processes and methods of thinking *per se*, aside from the so-called Ming Jia, or School of Names, which had only a fleeting existence. This is why logic, an important issue of epistemology has not been developed. ... Rare in the history of Chinese philosophy can one find schools of thoughts with any pure theoretical interest, and so if this school [Ming Jia] were left out in our discussion, the history of Chinese philosophy would appear to be all the more lopsided." (Fung, 2000, Vol.1: 8, 147) But Fung (1962: 325) labeled Gongsun Long's philosophy as "objective idealism", for the reason that Gongsun Long, in his detailed analysis of the subject and the predicate of sentences, isolated properties from objects to give each the status of abstract and absolute existence. Similarly, Hou Wailu, et al. (1957: 419) said, "There were struggles between materialism and idealism in the history of logic of ancient China, which were reflected in the division of two lines of thinking in the debate on names. One was a progressive development, beginning from Mozi and complete with the author of *Mohist Scripture, Xunzi* and *Han Fei*. The other was one of degeneration, starting from Zengzi, culminating at Zisi and Mencius, declining from Zhuangzi and Hui Shi and finally dying out with Gongsun Long and Zou Yan. The former was progressive because the thinkers purified the methods in the debate on name and actuality into a more precise study of formal logic; while the latter was degeneration because the thinkers shrugged off the positive aspects of the debate and fell into the trap of sophism." These authors regarded Hui Shi's "sophism" as "relativist idealism" and Gongsun Long's as "absolute idealism".

However, other scholars have objected the above labeling. Qu Zhiqing (1981: 50-51) pointed out that Gongsun Long's theory concerning names and things in existence is a naïve materialism; his separation of the hardness and the whiteness was not the same with the view that regarded the spiritual as the ubiquitously real and this differed him from idealists. Liu Yujun (1995) agreed that Hui Shi and Gongsun Long "were the scholars who adhered to the same philosophical theory and standpoint, whose thought was one of materialistic naturalism with dialectical way of thinking based on antithesis and unity and with an epistemology of dialectical materialism". Zeng Xiangyun argued in an even higher profile: "Ironically, Gongsun Long who has been accused of being a thorough-going idealist should have made statements that cannot be more materialistic: 'Heaven and Earth and what exist therein are all things' ... 'The name, that's what is used to describe the actuality.' Here, I would like to quote Lenin's phrasing when he was commenting on Hegel's 'Logic', to be the most appropriate comment on Gongsun Long's philosophy: 'This is materialism, pure and simple!' And in *Gongsun Longzi*, 'the so-called idealist works, there is much more materialism than idealism'. A paradox? But it is a fact!"

Another philosopher, Du Guoxiang, did not agree that Gongsun Long was a materialist philosopher, nor did he consider him an idealist in the sense of Hegelian "das Absolut", because Gongsun Long's theory "started from the analysis of sense experience and proceeded from the empirical 'object' and 'object denotation' to the non-experiential abstract 'reference'. [And this shows that Gongsun Long] attempted to find something essential that lies behind the phenomena of the things in reality. This should be noted". But still, Du labeled Gongsun Long as a "multifarious objective idealist philosopher" (Du, 1955: 23, 61).

My comment:

These different views show that one is highly likely to find good evidence in Gongsun Long's essays to classify him into the materialist or the idealist camps. Indeed, similar to what Plato did, Gongsun Long separated the properties from the objects, and abstracted them, believing that they were real and existed independently. This is no doubt idealism. However, Gongsun Long admitted unmistakably that the world was made up of things. This poses a problem. If one admits that the world is material, one cannot at the same time admits that the world is non-material, nor vice versa. How come Gongsun Long should have admitted that the world is at once material and not material? Doesn't this suggest that the framework of ontological philosophy of materialism-idealism is in fact not an appropriate one for interpreting the ideas of Gongsun Long and Ming Jia? At least, this framework cannot help us explain completely all the propositions put forward by Gongsun Long and other Ming Jia thinkers. Take the "separating the hardness and the whiteness" for example. This proposition approximates indeed Plato's objective idealism, but Gongsun Long has proposed this on the premise that the world consists of concretely existing objects. How should we explain this?

Of course, I admit that the materialism-idealism framework does have one merit: that it shows on the whole that Gongsun Long was not a sophist. This gives us a good reason to go ahead making clear what he was actually saying, without grouping Gongsun Long into either the rank of materialists or that of idealists.

1.2.3 The "logic" theory

In 1917, Hu Shi (1983: 111) wrote in *The Development of Logical Method in*

Ancient China that the School of Names [Ming Jia] "inherited the Mohist tradition of ethic and logic study and contributed to the intellectual history of China the most systematic and mature doctrines concerning logical method." Wing-Tsit Chan (1973: 232) also wrote, "Practically all major ancient Chinese philosophical schools were greatly concerned with the relationship between name and actuality, whether for its social and moral significance (as in Confucianism), for its metaphysical import (as in Taoism), or for political control (as in Legalism). None of them was interested in the logical aspect of the problem.... The only school that was primarily devoted to logical consideration was the Logicians.... They were the only group devoted to such problems as existence, relativity, space, time, quality, reality, and causes. Although the Chinese name for them is Ming-Chia (School of Names), or Ming-pien (Scholars of Names and Debaters), they were not confined to the correspondence of name and actuality. Their metaphysical and epistemological concepts are primitive, but they represent the only tendency in ancient China toward intellectualism for its own sake. ... In this they were singular in Chinese history." Zhou Yunzhi (1994: 106-107) emphatically pointed out that "in the pre-*Qin* history of logic ideas, Gongsun Long was the first to get himself engaged in the study on and generalization of the issues of name and actuality at the abstract level of logic theory. ... In our study of *Gongsun Longzi*, we would commit a grave mistake, if we do not expound his theory of rectification of name in terms of logic, rejecting his important logic doctrine for the rectification but criticizing him with his philosophical statements tinted with idealism".

However, modern Chinese logician, Sun Zhongyuan (1987: 172) has conducted an elaborated logic analysis of Gongsun Long's essays, only to conclude that Gongsun Long was indeed a "rather good amateur logician", but also a truly "famous sophist". Pang Pu (1979: 73, 75) also said, "Formally speaking, Gongsun Long did observe the logical law of 'A is A'. The problem is, he violated fundamentally the dialectic logic, the dialectics of thinking." As the result, he could only turn out to be a sophist. Gong Jiahuai (1989) further claimed that Gongsun Long's "White-horse is not horse" proposition has violated a series of logic laws, those of identity, of non-contradiction, of sufficient reason and so on; he resorted to the disguised replacement of concepts, to the change of conceptual relations, or simply to nonsensical arguments. Gong concluded that Gongsun Long's "On 'White-horse Is Not Horse'" is an outstanding sophistic essay, which is "developed by false propositions and erroneous reasoning but structurally strict and concise with the arguments tightly interlocked".

My comment:

Gongsun Long's essays do appear to be problematic, if we examine them in the light of formal logic. But the question is, was Gongsun Long expounding logical laws with his proposition of "white-horse is not horse"? How can we explain the fact that his essays, having violated a series of logical laws, should have been "structurally so strict and concise with his arguments tightly interlocked"? At least, we should give his essays a re-examination to see how this is possible. Let's change our perspective. Suppose Gongsun Long was not working on formal logical reasoning, but talking about something else. If this is true, the framework of logic is not suitable for interpreting him. To me, the framework of dialecticism is especially irrelevant to the reading of his essays, because there is nothing therein that faintly touches dialecticism. In view of the fact that his essays have been misread and misunderstood for over two thousand years, it might well be a total mistake for us to impose formal logic analysis on his essays before we truly understand what he was trying to convey. By the way, I have to point out that the word "dialectics" used by the criticizers does not mean the same as the Socrates kind of striving for truth through dialog; rather, they use the word in the sense of "antithesis and unity of the specific and the general", "the negation of negation" and so on. That is a big issue, which I cannot give a discussion in this book. The reason why I make this point here is that many of our present interpreters of *Gongsun Longzi* do use the word in this sense, but we cannot find any clue in Gongsun Long's essays to show that he did have this thought tendency. To understand *Gongsun Longzi* in this way is most likely to leave us farther away from what is right about him.

1.2.4 The "theoretical scientist" theory

There are scholars who come to regard Gongsun Long and the other Ming Jia thinkers as theoretical scientists in ancient China. For instance, Dong Yingzhe (1995) proposed that the Ming Jia propositions recorded in Zhuangzi are not sophistic at all, but rich in scientific thoughts, except two of them, namely "Chickens have three feet" and "An orphan pony has never had a mother". The same author (Dong, 2001) later wrote to elaborate on what he believed to be Ming Jia's scientific achievements in the fields of mathematics, physics, astronomy, geography, dynamics, acoustics, biology and medicine and so on. Li Dan (1998: 228-229) firmly concluded that "Hui Shi was a theoretical mathematician and physicist and not an applied mathematician or experimental physicist", because "Hui Shi's Ten Propositions are all the products of the application of logical reasoning (including formal logic and dialectical logic; primarily the latter), which differ from the *Mohist Scripture* that gives places to logical reasoning, experimentation as well as the experiences of earlier generations". By literature research, we can easily find a lot more articles that specially deal with this or that specific propositions of Ming Jia's, such as those that discuss respectively "The shadow of flying birds has itself never moved" or "Split a rod by half a day, repeat the process every day, and the process will not be over even after ten thousand years", etc. These articles are quite successful in demonstrating that such propositions of Ming Jia's are indeed highly consistent with the theories or findings of modern sciences, such as the limit theory in mathematics, to name just one.

My comment:

I agree that Later Mohists were scientists. Reading their classic *Mohist Scripture*, one cannot help marveling that there should have been such excellent scientific thoughts, definitions and conclusions in ancient China, which have covered a wide range of fields such as physics (including acoustics, optics, and dynamics), mathematics and logic. However, this is not the case with Ming Jia, in whose writings and sayings we cannot find convincing evidence to say that they were scientists like Later Mohists. They did not seem to be interested in practical experiences or empirical studies; instead they appeared to be exclusively devoted to speculating on issues of name, debating with others over the questions of the meaning of language words. In addition, it is extremely hard to understand quite a few of their propositions in the light of scientific theory, such as "White dogs are black", "Fire is not hot", "White-horse is not horse", "I know that the center of the universe is located at the same time north to Yan, a state in the north, and south to Yue, a state in the south" and so on and so forth. Therefore, all our modern interpreters who believe Ming Jia were "theoretical scientists" have to leave these propositions unexplained by concluding that except these sophistic paradoxes, the rest are scientific propositions. This makes us perplexed, however, as to why that group of scientists should have put forward at the same time sophistic paradoxes. What is more, Gongsun Long has even written essays to argue purposefully and elaborately for such sophistic paradoxes as "White-horse is not horse" and "Two is not composed of two ones". Could he have written them just for fun? If Ming Jia were truly scientists and mathematicians, then why should Gongsun Long, their major representative whose works should be a comprehensive expression of their ideas, have chosen to argue that two ones do not make two? Puzzling problems like this suggest that we may not be right to treat Gongsun Long and his comrades as theoretical scientists.

1.3 Misunderstandings Outside China

Foreign scholars have also made studies on the Chinese language and the ideas of Gongsun Long, but their views are to me problematic. For instance, Chad Hansen concluded that in the Classical Chinese language, the nouns lacked the inflections to mark singular and plural forms and so they resemble the "material nouns" that are uncountable in the western languages in a way. This feature prevented the ancient Chinese thought from conceptual abstraction that serves as the medium for cognition, such as in western philosophical ideas. In naming with Chinese nouns, names have a one-to-one relation with stuffs and for this reason the ontological abstraction in Chinese is only concrete and partial; that is, "For every abstract set of objects one can construct a concrete mereological object by regarding all of the members of the set as discontinuous stuff. Identifying different members of the set is the same as identifying spatio-temporally different parts of the same stuff. In learning names we learn to discriminate or divide reality into these mereological stuffs which names name" (Hansen, 1983: 31-32). To put it in another way, the nouns in Chinese do not name any abstracted concepts, properties, essences or ideas, as the nouns in the western languages can do, but are confined to recognizing the boundary of things. And to Hansen, it is this feature that has shaped the Chinese thought into a "behavioral nominalism". As the result, no conceptual abstraction could be formed in ancient Chinese thoughts and the question of the "Form" could not be raised at all.

As to Gongsun Long, Hansen (1983: 151-170) argued that he was conducting self-conscious speculation on language problems, but his paradox of "White-horse is not horse" was but a strict explanation of the nature of the name: a name must always *pick out* the same object. It is true that Gongsun Long did admit that "A white horse is a horse", but he argued that in the compound name of "white-horse", the component character of "horse" is not the same thing as what the character of "horse" refers to, because these two "horse" characters do not denote the same stuff. With this analysis, Hansen concluded that by proposing the white-horse paradox, Gongsun Long insisted on the one-name-one-thing principle for the rectification of name, convinced that the name in a compound noun did not have the identity with itself when it was used alone. To Hansen, Gongsun Long thus inherited the Later Mohist's error, namely, regarding all terms as names that named stuffs instead of notions. And Gongsun Long's separation of the whiteness from the white horses was actually proposing that there was no semantic relation between "white-horse" as a compound and "white" and "horse" used respectively. Hansen pointed out that this was the source for Gongsun Long's error, because if this were the case, these "names" would be unable to name anything. This is why Gongsun Long's arguments were full of loopholes and absurdities.

Another researcher, A. C. Graham (1990: 200-209) appeared to hold opinions on Gongsun Long similar to those of Hansen's, though he argued from different angle. On the one hand, Graham thought that Gongsun Long expressed with his "White-horse is not horse" proposition the idea that the whole entity made up of the white (as a color) and the horse (as a shape) is not a part of the horse (as a shape). Gongsun Long was said to have applied the name "horse" not to the whole of the white-horse, but to a part of it, i.e. to the shape of horse while keeping the white outside the shape. Thus, the white-horse was certainly not a horse, because a whole could not be a part of itself. Graham considered Gongsun Long's proposition quite logical but Gongsun Long's rivals in debate misunderstood his part-whole argument as a genus-species relation, resulting in confusions. But how is it possible for the white (color) to stay outside the horse (the shape) when "horse" is used to name that shape? Graham (1990: 208) attributed it to the way the ancient Chinese philosophers thought about things: "Things are conceived, not as being their shapes, but as 'having shape and color'."

For the lack of noun forms to refer to abstracted universalities (such as "whiteness", "hardness", etc.) in the Classical Chinese language, the characters of "坚" (hard) or "白" (white) could also be used as verbs to describe the properties of things (such as "stone"), not in the sense of "being" but of "having" that hardness or that color. In this aspect, Graham's argument would virtually agree with that of Hansen's.

Meanwhile, the Classical Chinese language was characterized by non-differentiation of the parts of speech and free transformation of the syntactic structure. Such grammatical features forced Chinese philosophers to look at things from within and not from without, different from their western counterparts. Consequently, the former could not attempt at the objectification of knowledge as the latter had done; nor could the former categorize objects in terms of genus and species as was the case with the latter. Graham pointed out that Gongsun Long took advantage of the features of the Classical Chinese and led the debate to the path favorable for his own viewpoint, treating a subordinate concept word as a coordinate concept word. In this way, he succeeded in trapping his debate rivals in a language maze, where the Classical Chinese provided no way to help them realize that "white" and "horse" were not at all coordinate concept words and that the former was in fact subordinate to the latter in a compound. Thus his rivals could never affirm that "A white horse is a horse that has a white color and not a white plus a horse". Graham considered Gongsun Long's paradox was in fact groundless and quite easy to retort; the reason why it was not retorted lied in the features of the Classical Chinese language which did not differentiate super-ordinate or subordinate words, leading to an entanglement of the genus-species relations with the part-whole relations.

My comment:

Hansen is right in concluding that Gongsun Long was a thinker who focused on the semantic problems of "name" with an obvious tendency towards "separation". Hansen's "mass-noun" hypothesis is of some help to explaining the differences between Gongsun Long and Later Mohists, but his neglect of the coherence of ideas in Gongsun Long's writings as a whole has diminished the value of Gongsun Long's thought. If we press further for an explanation of what it is that Gongsun Long has separated out, we have good reasons to believe that it is nothing but the universality, or the Form, since such a Form is said to have its own existence independent of specific objects. It is true that in the Classical Chinese, there was no term for "universality" or "Form" in the Platonic sense, but what could the character strings of "白者" ("that which is white") in "白者自白" ("that which is white is necessarily white in itself") and of "马" ("horse") in "马无色" ("Horse is colorless") have been understood to refer to, other than the universalities or the Forms? And this further indicates that conceptual abstraction is quite possible against the background of the Classical Chinese language and that Hansen's "behavioral nominalism" theory does not hold water.

Graham's theory starts from the grammatical features of the Classical Chinese and his "part-whole" interpretation of Gongsun Long's ideas are worthy of our attention. As I shall discuss later on, it is exactly because the language posed some challenges to the pre-*Qin* thinkers that gave rise to Gongsun Long and Ming Jia, who specialized in making out the nature of language meaning. If Gongsun Long were indeed just making use of the loose structures of the language to produce sophistry, then it would not be of any value of study. This is probably why in Graham's discussion, we have found such inconsistency as believing that Gongsun Long's propositions are "quite logical" on the one hand, and "paradoxes that could have been easily retorted" on the other. Apart from this, I think Graham is a bit too subjective in his analytical technique, as he frequently adds or removes words or changes the word orders in the original, which makes his conclusion less than reliable. This might have been caused by his insufficient comprehension of the original texts written in the Classical Chinese language. For instance, in his interpretation of Gongsun Long's "On the Nature of Reference" ("Meanings and Things" in his version), Graham translated the key character of "指" (pronounced [zhǐ], "finger", "to point out", "to point to", "to refer", "to denote" and so on) into "pointing things out", just like Hansen who termed it "pick out". Both of them have failed to note its polysemous property. Accordingly, Graham has translated the first sentence in the essay into "When no thing is not the pointed-out (what the name points out), to point out is not to point it out" (Graham, 2000: 213) and another phrase in the same essay into "It is not that to point out is not to point it out, it is pointing out combined with things which is not pointing it out" (1990: 215). His translations of this kind can only make western readers so perplexed that they have to believe Gongsun Long was at best muddle-headed.

It might well be that these scholars have a questionable mastery of the Chinese language and the traditional Chinese intellectual culture. To borrow a phrase from Du Shihong (2012: 201), there are not sufficient "coherence factor interfaces" between the Chinese and the foreigners not only at the cultural level but also at the linguistic level. Yet I do not deny that their framework of language does have embodied their philosophical wisdom, which is of reference value to us.

I do not mean to complain about our foreign scholars when I write the comment here. Instead, I intend to rectify the reputation for Ming Jia by demonstrating that they are truly rationalist philosophers. In a broader sense, I intend to rectify the name for traditional Chinese philosophy, because philosophy is universal and not language-specific and a philosophy even in the strict sense of western philosophy is possible on the soil of the Chinese language.

1.4 Interpreting in Terms of Philosophy of Language

If the interpretations we have seen above are all more or less problematic, what we now discuss, the interpretation in terms of philosophy of language, provides us with a key to the understanding of the essential characteristics of the ideas of Gongsun Long and Ming Jia.

It is after the 1990s that more scholars in China explained Gongsun Long's ideas under the influence of western philosophy of language and comparative studies on Chinese and western philosophies. These studies are more head-starting.

In 1991, Zhou Changzhong published his "New Explanation of *Gongsun Longzi: A Comparative Study with Western Philosophy*" and proposed that Gongsun Long's philosophy is speculative, a philosophy of cognition and a philosophy of language analysis (Zhou, 1991: 10-14). As he sees it, "The main content of *Gongsun Longzi* consists of an analytical philosophy of language and of logic. It can be said to be unique among all pre-Qin philosophical ideas, devoted to breaking through common sense by analysis of language... and having succeeded in constructing a theory considerably rich in philosophy concerning language itself." In 2005, Zhou published another book, entitled *Pre-Qin Studies on Name and Debate and Their Scientific Thoughts*, in which he further compares Gongsun Long's ideas with the ideas in western philosophy, especially western philosophy of language, to spotlight the analyticity and rationalist tendency of Gongsun Long. In general, Zhou concludes that Gongsun Long is a realist in ontology as he affirms the reality both of actual objects and of universal forms. Epistemologically, Gongsun Long claims that cognition consists of knowing the universal form and his ideas are therefore quite logical and his arguments touch upon formal logic issues such as the law of identity and the law of non-contradiction. In terms of philosophy of language, Gongsun Long has made the distinction between sense and reference and between object word and concept word in Fregean sense; he has also discussed a series of issues concerning language, such as the objectivity of reference, decision, discrimination and change.

Cui Qingtian (1997: 26-32) does not agree to regarding the study on name and debate as the study on logic, but he has made an important point: what makes Gongsun Long's discussions on name and actuality unique among all the other scholars is that he has strictly distinguished language from thinking; "in discussing language and the object of language he used 'name' and 'actuality', but in discussing thinking and existence he used 'reference' and 'object'" (1997: 145). Cui further points out, "Gongsun Long's theory on names is one of philosophy of language. His discussions about 'white-horse is not horse' and 'separation of the hardness and the whiteness' and so on intend to clarify one thing: what the meaning of language is. To Gongsun Long, the meaning of a name constitutes the actuality, but since the name and the thing existing out there must be mediated by reference, the direct meaning of a name is the reference, according to his theory. It can be seen that Gongsun Long's theory on names is rather similar to ideas in western philosophy of language." (1997: 69) However, Cui believes that Gongsun Long's idea is consistent with that of John Locke who said: "The use of words, is to be sensible marks of ideas; and the ideas they stand for are their proper and immediate signification. Words, in their primary or immediate signification, stand for nothing but the ideas in the mind of him that uses them." (Locke, 2001: 510)

More importantly, Cui (1997: 169-170) proposes that in the west, philosophy of language comes into being after a long course of ontology and the turn of epistemology, and for this reason it appears to be unthinkable that Gongsun Long should have specialized in language meaning in China at the 3rd century BC. But the rise of Gongsun Long was indeed a necessary development of the then ideological trend of debating on names. However, Gongsun Long had only a fleeting appearance and withered out soon because his philosophy lacked the philosophical soil like the history of western epistemology.

Lin Mingjun and Zeng Xiangyun (2000: 19) also agree that the pre-*Qin* Chinese study on names should be defined as theoretical study centering on "names". Such study does not take for its object the "names" as individual and specific names, but it is aimed at the general theory on them. The two authors do not think it proper to compare the pre-*Qin* name study with the dialecties of ancient Greece, because the "names" studied in China is not the same as the "concepts" in traditional western logic, nor is the debate in China equivalent to Greek dialectics. Lin & Zeng (2000: 39) suggest a reconsideration of pre-*Qin* debate on names in the light of the essence of "names", which they think should be 1) the primary function of naming things, 2) an association with the human activity of cognition and cultural exchanges, and 3) the function of reference that represents what is referred to and that accomplishes ideas communication. In this angle, they see Gongsun Long to be an outstanding scholar of semiotics with great theoretical contribution in ancient China.

My comment:

Researches on Gongsun Long and other pre-*Qin* Ming Jia have thus entered the field of philosophy of language. To me, three points are of particularly illuminative value: 1) Gongsun Long's philosophy is a philosophy of language; 2) the philosophy of language in ancient China is in the form of metaphysical speculation on the Chinese language, centering on "*name*"; and 3) Gongsun Long's philosophy is a natural development of the pre-*Qin* ideological debate, which has already given birth to the elements of ontology and epistemology in ancient China.

I hesitate to think that such development is accidental. On the contrary, I tend to hypothesize that if western philosophy of language is the result of the development from the western tradition of ontology to the epistemological turn and then to the linguistic turn, the development in China might have followed a reversed course: the rise of Chinese ontology and epistemology from the reflection on the Chinese language. It is not a patented right of western philosophy to attempt to understand human cognition, existence and truth of the world via an analytical speculation on the meaning of language. The ancient Chinese philosophers might well have been engaged in speculations of the same nature. Furthermore, Wittgenstein says, "Problems of philosophy occur when language goes on holiday." (*PI.* § 38) Philosophy has of course its own objects for study: concept, essence, existence, knowledge and the like, but without language these issues would not exist at all. I think Wittgenstein is right; western philosophy has its origin in the questions into the meaning of words and sentences, an inquiry into what is the essential meaning expressed by concepts and propositions in separation from the users of language and the contexts in which it is used, and into how one can guarantee the correctness of the meaning. It is this impulse for "being" and "truth" that set western philosophers on to the path of rationalist philosophy. The same should also be true of the origination of Chinese philosophy.

Nevertheless, I do find some problems with our present interpreters who regard Gongsun Long as a philosopher of language.

Firstly, as the researchers argue, Gongsun Long's statements resemble quite a few great western philosophers of different standpoints, including Plato's idealism and Locke's empiricism. Then a question is natural: how can we give a coherent explanation of these different and even conflicting ideas in Gongsun Long's expressions?

Secondly, it is questionable whether or not Gongsun Long did propose the distinction between "sense" and "reference" in Fregean sense. With Frege, the reference is the object and the sense is what channels us to think about the object. However, in Gongsun Long's writings, we can hardly find similar ideas. The same is true of the other distinctions. Another point is that, as we have seen before, it is quite controversial whether Gongsun Long's is a theory of logic or not; but if we deny that his writings have elements of logic, it would make our reinterpretation impossible. Can we, then, re-examine his writings by distinguishing two levels of logic, one being purely semantic or linguistic and the other experiential or empirical? Also, if Aristotle came to establish his logic theory from his speculation on language, especially on syntactic structures, could Gongsun Long have been conducting logic analysis of word meaning in accordance with the characteristics of the Chinese language, i.e., the names? So far, I have not found discussions in this respect.

Thirdly, if we agree that Gongsun Long is a rationalist philosopher of language, we must consider the retranslation of *Gongsun Longzi*, especially into foreign languages. This should also include a retranslation and reinterpretation of Hui Shi's "Ten Paradoxes" and the "Twenty-one Propositions of Ming Jia Debaters", which have been listed at the beginning of this part. This is not only to present a more coherent text for reference by scholars in the world, but also to invite academic discussions so that we may come closer to what Ming Jia's philosophy really is. This is necessary, because in addition to what I have categorically outlined in this section, there are some other misinterpretations, such as from undifferentiating holism or agnosticism, etc. (cf. Lee, 2012: Ch.3)

In a word, what I intend to do with this book is to give a more coherent reinterpretation of *Gongsun Longzi* and the other Ming Jia propositions. Concerning the present framework of philosophy of language, I think the present theorists have not yet given a due attention to the features of the Chinese language in their analysis. Instead, they have adopted directly the existing concepts and theories in their studies on Ming Jia, resulting in their proposing the explanations that appear to be unconvincing or unsupported by textual evidence. To me, the framework of philosophy of language is a desirable one, but we need to take the linguistic features of the Chinese language into consideration when we do our study in this respect. If Ming Jia thinkers were indeed speculating on problems of language, especially on the meaning of language, then their ideas should necessarily be based on the conditions provided them by the Chinese language and therefore tinted with characteristics of the language. This is a key point in our understanding the thoughts of Ming Jia.

2. The Issue of Different Types of Languages and Different Philosophies

A thought can be said to be of philosophy of language, if it is characterized by speculating on language and meaning problems in order to reflect on what it is that humans know about the world and how human knowledge can be true. This is a question worthy of speculation because the world is boundless and ever changing; yet we have only a limited means of language for our purpose of cognition. Since humans can only know and express the world by means of language, there appears to be a huge asymmetry: we know the limitless and changing world only with a limited means and the rules that do not change. It is necessary for us to inspect and evaluate the linguistic homestead of our being, because we "have to live in language" (Qian, 2005).

Besides, some of the things humans describe in language can be empirically tested while some others cannot. For example, the sentence "If it rains the ground is wet" describes the fact that if it rains the ground is wet. Whether a statement like this is true or not can be judged by seeing if it corresponds to the fact. But for sentences like "If one is merciful one is not cruel", we have more trouble testing them, simply because we can observe the factual phenomena like the rain, the wet ground, etc., but we cannot directly observe a phenomenon like mercy. For such objects we talk about, we shall have to inquire into what they definitely mean.

This also indicates that the objects we talk about are not of the same conceptual level. I have elaborated on this point in my book, entitled "Raising Questions in and of Language" (cf. Liu, 2007), in which I propose a theory of "three modes of language cognition operation" as a framework for the reinterpretation of Ming Jia.

Let me give a brief introduction to the main idea of my theory here. Human thinking is essentially a language cognition operation and language users operate with the same language in three different modes of ordinary life, science and philosophy, the difference being that they use language to operate on objects of different nature. It is true that philosophical discourse is not the same as that in ordinary life and philosophical grammar differs from ordinary language grammar, but the language of philosophy is not transcendental, meaning that the language philosophers use to talk about thought itself and language itself is the same natural language as is used to talk about things and events in everyday life. Even the language of formal logic is derived from the natural language. In everyday life situations, people use language to talk about actual objects and events; in science, the cognitive operation is indirect and language is used to structure scientists' activities in order to perform a linguistically mediated cognition of the abstracted objects (concepts and propositions concerning the properties or laws of objective phenomena); and in philosophy, the thinkers use language to operate cognitively on language itself. The objects and the test approaches in the operation at the everyday life level are direct and empirical and therefore are experientially quite certain and definite. Those at the science operation level, however, do not have such certainty because its concepts and propositions are not actual objects existing out there but are constructed and cannot be directly verified or falsified. Finally, at the philosophical level of language cognition operation, the concepts and propositions are completely linguistic constructs and the knowledge about these constructs cannot be empirically tested at all and has to be speculated on metaphysically.

I have further expounded my point in a later paper of mine, entitled "Meta-categorization of Language and Gongsun Long's Philosophy of Language"[1]: western philosophy and Chinese philosophy might well have different starting points, but both were essentially reflections born out of meta-categorization. The so-called "*meta-categorization*" is a term I have coined on the basis of the concept of categorization, employed in modern cognitive linguistics to refer to the cognitive process of parsing and classifying things and events in the world which give orders and structures to the various experieces humans have, so that they can form concepts about the orders and structures by naming them. Hence humans know about the world. At the level of everyday speech, humans categorize their perceptions and experiences of the objects and events in the world, on the basis of which they form concepts that are direct generalization of their experiences (such as "the sun, the moon, mountain, water, cold, hot" and so on). But the categorization process does not end up here. The same mechanism of categorization will continue to parse and classify the conceptual meaning of the everyday speech words and this is what I call "re-categorization". We have, for instance, further categorized our conceptual meanings and formed superordinate concepts such as "celestial body, object, class, property, relation" and so on.

Re-categorzation is not one of perceptions and experiences and there is not much direct relationship between the re-categorized concepts with empirical facts. Because it is essentially a categorization of conceptualized meanings, re-categorized concepts are more abstract and cannot be verified to be true or false directly by perceptions and experiences. At least empirically speaking, therefore, the concepts resulted

---

1   This paper was published in *Foreign Language Research*, 2011(5), a journal of Heilongjiang University.

from re-categorization are more prone to be imprecise or even false. To guarantee the certainty, universality and necessity of the knowledge we have about the world, we have to speculate purely theoretically on how the semantic meanings of the re-categorized concepts *per se* can be correct. This is where meta-categorization comes onto the stage. The concepts of "necessity, contingency, phenomenon, essence" and so on thus come into being so that we can conduct metaphysical speculations on the abstract concepts of the re-categorization operation (What, for instance, do we mean by 'property' or 'relationship'? Is a certain property essential or phenomenal, or is a certain relationship necessary or contingent? What is the nature of an essential property or a necessary relationship? How can we be ensured that we do find a necessary relationship? etc.). So, meta-categorization is in essence a metaphysical categorization, because it is an analytical investigation into the language meaning by means of language itself, only remotely having to do with experiences. One thing I need to point out is that both categorization and re-categorization are cognitive operations (parsing, classifying and abstracting) on empirical content, experiential or semantic. This is what I call "substantive conceptualization". But meta-categorization is not just a higher lever re-categorization of re-categorization, but a critical speculation on categorization and re-categorization themselves, out of human suspicion concerning the reliability of our mastery of the world by language. This is rather an evaluative conceptualization, which attempts to find out how and under what condition we can be sure that our knowledge (what we say) about the world is true. To me, this is the essence of philosophy.

The key point of my theory is that philosophy originates in such meta-categorization on language meaning itself. All nations use language to know about the world by asking questions about it. So long as they come to question and to speculate on language meaning itself, the mode of rationalist thinking can occur in them. There are enormous typological differences among various languages (for example between English and Chinese), but what is common is that language is the way in which people cognize themselves and the world. All nations are able to develop their own rationalist philosophy and the specific languages they use, with all the different individual features, can at most shape the path leading to such a philosophy.

2.1 Western Philosophy and the Western Languages

At the time western philosophy started, its thinkers were self-conscious in their reflections on language. Plato clearly said, "Language is probably the most important of all topics" (*Cratylus*, 427e); Aristotle also claimed that his logical speculation for seeking after truth consisted in the attempt to turn up with necessary conclusions in reasoning in language: "By perfect syllogism, I mean that necessary conclusions can be achieved on the basis on nothing else except the sentences stated." (Analytica Priora, 24b)

Indeed, in proposing their theories and arguments, they are doing what I call cognitive operation of pure speculations on meaning, asking questions about "being" and "truth" in and of language. This is not only my point of view. On Plato's *Form* or *Idea*, Alston (1988: 2) has the comment that Plato calls our attention to a universal feature of language; that is, a given common noun (e.g., "tree") or an adjective (e.g., "sharp") can in the same sense be truthfully applied to a large number of individuals. And so, Plato argued that a common term can be applied in the same sense to many different individuals, only if there is an entity that the term names, such as *tree-ness* and *sharpness,* whose features every individual shares. And Zhao Dunhua sums it up and says that Plato's theory is "virtually a language analysis" (Zhao, 2001: 6).

About Aristotle's logic and language reflection, Cui (2004: 131) stated:

> *Aristotle took Greek language facts into consideration and established the subject-predicate structure of the categorical propositions (copula and content words form the predicate). On the basis of the subject-predicate structure, he further put forward the classification of propositions, the extension of nouns, the square of propositions, the conversion of propositions, and the aspects of syllogism, such as its structure, figure and mood and the divisions. Therefore, there would have been no syllogism or Aristotle's logic without the Greek language and its subject-predicate structure of propositions. Aristotle's logic and his syllogism correspond with the structure of the western languages.*

Since philosophy originates in reflection on language, it is a natural development that western philosophy has followed the course from ontology to epistemology and to language analysis. In the whole 20th century, western philosophers tackled with metaphysical questions in the frame of language analysis in the hope of recasting the age-old philosophical questions in terms of language, which was known to be the linguistic turn, the second after the epistemological turn in the 17th century (cf. M. Baghramian, 1999: xxx). Of course, whatever turns it has taken, the fundamental pursuit of western philosophy has not changed: the issues of "being" and "truth". What is it that we know and how can we be sure that what we know is true? These are always the central concerns of western philosophy.

In the rise of western philosophy, the characteristics of the western languages are of important significance, and the three syntactic features are of primary importance: 1) the copula "to be"; 2) the formal distinction of nouns, especially of the concrete and abstract nouns; and 3) the clear roles of the subject and predicate of the affirmative sentences. These important syntactic features have provided western philosophers with favorable pathway towards meta-categorization on language expressions, enabling them to embark on metaphysical mode of thought.

First, the kernel category of western philosophy is the "being as being", but "being" itself is the gerund form of the copula "to be". According to Kahn's research, "to be" has in itself the three functions of being the copula, and expressing verdictives and existential meanings. These functions give "to be" the conditions of coming to be a metaphysically kernel concept (cf. Kahn, 1986). Linguistically, the copula, "to be" connects the subject and the predicate to form a sentence; and cognitively, it joins up the object talked about and the predication of the object to form a proposition. In the sentence form of "*x* is *y*", both x and y are variables and only "is" is constant. Under what conditions can the "is" connect two variable items to form a correct proposition? Questions of this nature protrude the importance of "to be". Accidentally, "to be" in the western languages also expresses the notion of existence, such as "God is". If a thing is, it exists; and if a thing is not, it does not exist. These two functions of "to be" match western philosophers' inquiry into what the nature of existence is, because "the philosophical significance of 'being' is 'entity', and each and every sense of the 'entity' can be obtained through the analysis of the logical function of the copula 'to be'"

(Zhao, 2001: 68).

Secondly, the morphological changes of the nouns are closely related to what the nouns refer to. Take English articles for example. A singular countable noun used to refer an unspecified individual has to be preceded by articles "a, an"; a plural noun that makes general references cannot be preceded by indefinite article but must be added an "-s" or its variant after the stem; while a noun that makes a definite reference, whether singular or plural, must be preceded by the definite article "the". An abstract noun can be derived from a common noun or an adjective with certain suffixes, such as "bird + -ness = birdness" or "active + -ity = activity", etc. Common nouns can be used to denote actual objects and to refer to the concept of the objects, while the abstract nouns are only used to refer to what are abstracted.

These are but common sense about the western languages, but this common sense is important for understanding why western philosophers have naturally entered into metaphysical speculation on concepts and propositions. For these nouns help form highly abstracted concepts, such as "one" and "many", "specific" and "general", "phenomenon" and "essence" and so on and so forth, semantic dichotomies that western philosophy have speculated on ever since the beginning. To seek the *One* from the *many*, to *generalize* from the *specific*, or to discover the *essence* behind *phenomena*, etc.; the rational metaphysical speculations thus are quite naturally and harmoniously compatible with the characteristics of language. This is the conceptual formation mechanism that Hansen (1983: 34-36) refers to, namely, the language mechanism that enables the *thing-in-common* to appear as *essence, idea* or *property* semantically, metaphysically, and epistemologically. In a word, the morphological features of the western languages are conducive to the language users' awareness of the possibility of the general or the universal.

Finally, still another important link is the syntactic structure that clearly grants the roles of the subject and the predicate. This is because speculations on questions of words of what semantic nature can take the place of the subject and what structure constitutes a correct predication of the subject, etc., are likely to lead to the abstract thought over the nature of entity and the logic of proposition.

About this, Zhang Dongsun (1985: 338-339) has this to say:

Philosophical discussion of ontology comes from the issue of entity in Aristotle's study on names. ... Without the thematic entity, a sentence cannot be formed. For instance, saying "This flower is red", we assert at the same time "This is a flower". In the latter, "this" cannot be left out, because in "This is a flower", "flower" is in the predicate and not the subject, although in "The flower is red", it is the subject and not in the predicate. But however we try, we cannot boil the analysis down to a bare "this". That is to say, all predicates must be about an entity. And so, Aristotle believes that the predicate is predicated of the subject which cannot itself be predicated of any other things. Or else, his three principles (of identity, of non-contradiction and of the excluded middle) could not be established. ... In general, he has made a clear distinction between the subject and the predicate. ... If there is only a subject without a predicate, it cannot be a statement, but if there is only the predicate without a subject, it is unclear what is being talked about. So a sentence must have the subject and the predicate. Aristotle's claim is based on westerners' grammar (specifically Greek grammar). Such a grammar represents the mentality of the westerners. Aristotle has abstracted their habit of thinking into a systematic theory, which is the Aristotle's logic that has dominated westerners for over two thousand years.

To Zhang Dongsun (1985: 338-339), the Chinese language lacks the structural features necessary for the occurrence of a metaphysical speculation in the sense of western philosophy. Specifically, the influences are in these aspects: 1) the lack of structural forms of the Chinese sentences makes the distinction of the subject and the predicate unclear; 2) for lack of such a distinction, the Chinese do not have the idea of "subject", the entity talked about; 3) there is no form that marks tenses, moods or cases; and 4) for these three reasons, there is no concept of logical proposition in China.

Since the metaphysical orientation of western philosophy is naturally and closely compatible with the formal features of the western languages and the Chinese language lacks such formal features, can we then come to the conclusion that rational speculations in the sense of western metaphysics simply cannot happen on the Chinese language soil, such as Zhang has claimed?

2.2 Path Towards Philosophical Speculation and the Chinese Language

About the differences between the Chinese and European languages, Chinese linguist Wang Li (1984: 53) has this comment when he talks about the frequent absence of the subject in Chinese sentences: "In terms of the structure of sentences, the western languages are rule-of-law languages, while the Chinese language, a rule-of-man language.... With the former, there is a rigid requirement that the sentence forms be consistent, while with the latter, [the forms] can be there if useful and can be absent if not so useful; so long as the listener understands what the speaker says, it's then OK."

By "rule of law", he means that European languages attach a great importance to the structural forms of syntax, with all those conjugations and declensions, such as the morphological changes of nouns according to gender, number and case and the changes of verb forms in terms of tenses and aspects. The occupation of syntactic positions in a sentence by certain parts of speech and the relationships between different words in a sentence are all strictly and clearly defined. On the contrary, the Chinese language is characterized by "rule of man", because this language does not emphasize the structural form, with practically no morphological changes. The parts of speech in Chinese cannot be distinguished by the form and words of different grammatical categories are free to assume many roles in a sentence. As Qian G. L. (2002: 8) says, to understand a sentence in Chinese requires "intellectual intervention" by pragmatic reasoning. That is, on hearing or reading a sentence in Chinese, the listener or reader needs to infer the grammatical relationships between the terms according to the linguistic context and even the situational context.

Such great language difference does seem to mean a lot for the philosophical speculation. The three essential grammatical properties of European languages closely relevant to the occurrence of western philosophy, namely, the verb "to be", the morphological change of nouns and the formal subject-predicate structure, are all absent from the Classical Chinese language.

First, there was no copula "to be" in the Classical Chinese language and the relation of the subject with its predicate, which in European languages has to be linked by copula, is established by postpositions, in the pattern of "Name[subject marker] Name[predicate marker]". The earliest use of "是([shì], near equivalent of 'to be' in English)" as a copula in Chinese was somewhere around 200-500 AD (Wang, 2000: 401), about 5 or 6 hundred years after the pre-*Qin* period, the time when traditional Chinese philosophy had already come into being. What is more important, the copula "shì" in Chinese is not as semantically rich as "to be" in the European languages. The Chinese copula only serves the function of linking the subject with the predicate, unlike its counterpart in European languages that has the copula use, veridical use, and existential use all in one. Since the Chinese language lacks such a copula, "ontology" in the western philosophical sense of the word is impossible in Chinese philosophy. This is confirmable from the heated discussion in China over the translation of the term "ontology" into Chinese and so far, there is no universally accepted translation of the term, though all philosophers in China today know what it means.

Second, the noun in Chinese, like its other parts of speech, does not have morphological changes. There is no conjugation of gender, number and case, or other inflexions. One cannot tell by its form, whether a noun in Chinese is abstract or concrete, countable or uncountable, singular or plural. For instance, Laozi has proposed a highly abstract concept of Dao (道). This character happens to express 1) "way" or "path", very specific, common-sense objects that exist, 2) "to speak, to say, to report", a term used in everyday speech to denote both the act and the content of language communication, and also 3) abstract concepts of "cause, reason, law (in the sense of 'rule and regularity')" and so on. There is no formal difference between the three different Daos. This lack of formal inflexion in Chinese is said to have prevented the Chinese philosophers from speculating on the issues of the "One" and the "many" and from generating abstract terms of universality. In the Chinese language the noun does not distinguish individuals but generally denotes mass stuffs as Hansen (1983: 32-42) sees it, which channeled ancient Chinese philosophy to the orientation of "behavioral nominalism".

Third, because of its structural flexibility, the Chinese language does not have a strict stipulation as to what parts of speech can take the position of subject in a sentence. Nouns, verbs, adjectives can all be put to the place of subject of a sentence, whether they are the real subject of a proposition or not. Let's look at a few simple examples.

(1) 走为上策[zǒu wěi shàng cè]

literally: [walk / flee as up plan/strategy]

translation: [*To flee is the best choice.*]

(2) 我吃饭[wǒ chī fàn]

literally: [I eat meal]

translation: [*I have [am having] my meal.*]

(3) 饭吃过了[fàn chī guò le]

literally: [meal eat pass already (past marker)]

translation: [*I have eaten my meal. / The meal has been eaten.*]

(4) 王冕死了父亲[wángmiǎn sǐ le fùqīn]

literally: [Wang Mian die (past marker) father]

translation: [*Wang Mian's father died.*]

In (1), the word that takes the position of the subject is a verb. In classical as well as modern Chinese, a noun can certainly be the subject, but so can verbs, or adjectives, without any morphological change. Thus, whether the subject is a noun or a verb or one of any other parts of speech is not formally distinguishable. Not only is it unclear what words are qualified to be put to the subject position, but as shown by (1), the predicate does not seem to have a qualified verb phrase, with only "as" serving the role of a verb. In (2) and (3), the noun "meal" should be in the accusative case, i.e., it serves to be the object in both sentences, propositionally the object of a behavior operation, but in (3), it is put to the syntactic position of the subject, with no formal inflexion of any kind. Therefore, at least in form, the word "meal" does not have any formal difference whether it is in the position of the object or in the position of the subject. The syntactic voices cannot be distinguished formally, but understood intuitively. In addition, the Chinese sentences can even be quite grammatical without a subject, or the noun at the position of the subject is not the subject but the one that appears at the object position is the subject, as (4) instantiates. The problem with (4) is that the sentence pattern is of the same form as sentences such as "John kisses Mary" and "Tom loves his father", yet in (4) "Wang Mian" is not the agent of the action of "die", nor is "father" the recipient of the action. In other words, "Wang Mian" is not the true subject of the sentence, though it takes the position of the subject. The true relationship between the two nouns is to be set up by assuming the accusative case. In these cases, the subject is assumed pragmatically and such a feature is often perplexing for foreign learners of the Chinese language, though Chinese themselves have no problem understanding the relationship.

As we have seen before, Zhang Dongsun (1995: 334-349) has pointed out that unlike the Greek language that channeled Aristotle to the speculation on the ontological status of the subject in a statement, there is no such a linguistic facility conducive for the Chinese philosophers to similar issues, which is why metaphysical speculation in the sense of western philosophy cannot come into being in China.

However, contrary to this linguistic interpretation of the roots of philosophical thinking, I argue that the essence of ontology lies in metaphysical speculation on the nature of existence itself. As I have discussed afore, philosophy is given rise to by a speculation on the ultimate meaning of existence, and this speculation is not language-specific. Although there is an enormous typological difference between the Chinese and European languages, there is a common property that the language systems share: they are all the way we categorize and cognize the world. When the Chinese philosophers come to the speculations on the meaning of words we use, it is possible for the occurrence of rational speculation on what there is and what is true. But the Chinese philosophy has to follow the path set up by the characteristics of their own language towards such a mode of metaphysical thinking. This path is what I call the "character-meaning-centered" meta-categorization.

This is so because the character[1] is the basic unit in which the Chinese people say about the world, and a character is an integration of sound, form and meaning, which cannot be separated (Pan, 2002: 106-113). Because of the lack of inflexions, all grammatical elements relevant to a concept are integrated in the meaning of the character, enabling a Chinese character to be a holistic entity of linguistic information. This explains why the parts of speech of Chinese words are so unclear and so freely interchangeable in their usage and why there can be multiple meanings, sometimes at different abstract levels or of different categories, with many characters. This makes it

---

1   Linguists and grammarians in China today do not even have an agreement on whether there is a grammatical category of "word" or not as it is in European languages. This is part of the reason why there is not yet a universally accepted grammar of the Chinese language.

inevitable that the Chinese approach to meta-categorization be centered on characters as "names".

In Chinese, a character is regarded as a name. If it is difficult to distinguish formally nouns, verbs, adjectives and so on, it is possible to distinguish semantically the names for things, for actions, for properties and so on. A better way to examine the Chinese language is to regard the *name* as a fundamental grammar concept. If Chinese philosophers come to the speculation on the meaning of "name", it is highly likely that they would engage themselves in metaphysical issues. I say this for two reasons. 1) Since we use names to refer to and describe what is there in the actual world, then how is a name connected with an object or a thing that it names, and how can we be sure that we are using names to truly understand the world? These questions face Chinese philosophers. 2) With no formal inflexions, the Chinese names for substances, objects and those for properties, relations and abstractions are all the same in form and in usage. If we grant the names for real objects ontological status, can we do the same for those that don't have such status, for example the names for properties? A speculation on issues such as this may as well lead to an ontological speculation with Chinese language characteristics.

In this respect, the peculiar features of the Chinese language do not at all constitute a barrier to the birth of metaphysical ontological thought in China. The Classical Chinese language did lack syntactic devices and means to symbolize or formalize logic, but one cannot say just for this reason that there could be no mode of thought in classical Chinese philosophy over the exact meaning of language. The grammatical forms of the western languages were absent in the Classical Chinese language, but the latter was characterized by characters which had multiple semantic senses in each of them. This feature is of unique value in giving rise to metaphysical speculative thought in China, because it invites the Chinese thinkers to ponder over the ontological basis of name meaning, or how can one reliably establish the correctness of the meaning of the "names", nominal, verbal or adjectival.

Another question might be that the ancient Chinese thinkers asked different types of questions. While the ancient Greek philosophy was truth-oriented, seeking after knowledge about the world, the Chinese was social-morality-oriented, interested only in political practice. This question is reasonable, and it is backed by historical facts. But there is one point that both of them share: whatever they think and talk about, philosophers, and people in general alike, have to make sure that they are using words and sentences to express correctly what they really intend to express. Of vital importance then is to make clear what one means by certain language expressions. This is true of everyday speech where one has to follow the linguistic convention concerning language use and meaning in his/her language community; or else the communication would fail. And this is essential for philosophers, because what they ponder over and talk about, such as existence, nature, etc., does not necessarily exist out there, but is the abstraction of meaning made possible by language. Likewise, They need to clarify what they mean by what they say.

As I discussed in the previous section, philosophy does have its own objects for study, such as "existence, Idea, concept, proposition" and so on and so forth, but these objects simply cannot come into being without language and without a separated speculation on what the meaning of language is. It can be argued that the Chinese thinkers could also have given rise to their own metaphysical philosophy, if they separated language from its users and the contexts of use to speculate on what the meaning should be. Though the Chinese thinkers lacked the linguistic condition to enter philosophical speculation via syntax, the Chinese language does provide another unique path for meta-categorization: to reflect on how humans think by speculating on the meaning of "names", a peculiar feature of the Chinese language. The first large-scale ideological debate in Chinese intellectual history was exactly one on the relationship between name and actuality. This is no coincidence.

Later on, we shall see that various schools of thought debated with each other over the relationship between name and actuality, but used the same terms that referred to different concepts. This made it hard for any significant results to come out of the debate. To conduct significant debate, therefore, one must first of all make clear what name itself and what actuality itself should essentially be. This is what motivated Ming Jia to come on to the debate arena as thinkers who "specialized exclusively in names *per se*".

That traditional Chinese philosophy did not begin with the question of truth does not entail that the philosophers could not come to speculations on issues of truth. As soon as the ancient Chinese philosophers began to ascertain the essential meaning of the names they used to talk about their social, political or ethical concerns, i.e. when they came to the pure language reflection on the meaning of language itself, they would start their metaphysical speculation, asking articulately questions about what is true.

2.3 Illumination of Use and Mention Distinction in Philosophy of Language

2.3.1 A language without punctuation and the Use-Mention distinction

I have already said previously that the distinction of *use* and *mention* might be a head-starter for us in our attempt to reinterpret Ming Jia's texts and propositions. What makes me associate my interpretation of *Gongsun Longzi* with the use-mention distinction is the fact that the writing system of the pre-*Qin* Chinese language did not have punctuations, which might have been a barrier for Ming Jia to perform their analytical speculations on language: they could not distinguish using a name to say of an object from using a name to talk about the name itself. To overcome such a linguistic inconvenience, Ming Jia thinkers were compelled to make use of what-ever means available in the language to define their scope of discussions within the speculation on the meaning of names and to assert their ideas thus obtained. If this is the case, then 1) the present repudiation of Ming Jia's propositions as "sophism" is an error committed when the interpreters fail to see that these are not empirical propositions but metaphysical ones about language meaning; 2) Ming Jia's strange propositions may well be their peculiar ways to argue over the meaning of name under the conditions that they could not make the *use-mention* distinction as we can today; and 3) some of their propositions, generally regarded as "inexplicable" or "insoluble" may well be their explanations of the scope of discussion and debate or the linguistic means they adopted to mark the scope of their discussion. In view of this possibility, I intend to examine their propositions in the light of the *use-mention* distinction. However, I shall not restrain myself to the existing distinction in modern western philosophy of language, but add in my new explanation into the use of this technique for analysis.

Certainly, we *use* a word to refer to something but *mention* a word to discuss the word itself. When we mention a word, that word does not refer. This has already become a common sense in the study of western philosophy of language (Quine has given quite detailed illustrations in his *Word and Object*). In the western languages, one can quite easily detect whether a word is used or mentioned, because they have the technical devices of quotation marks. If a word in a sentence is within quotation marks, it is being mentioned; or else it is used. The proposition containing a question-marked word is one for the scrutiny of the word in question, such as Quine's examples of (a) *Boston is populous* and (b) *"Boston" has six letters*. In (a), the word "Boston" has at least one object of reference. But in (b), "Boston" does not refer to anything at all; it cannot even be translated into, say, Chinese which is not alphabetic, without changing its truth value.

Frequently in our language communications, however, we mention a word not just to examine its phonetic or syntactic properties, but to reflect on the concept referred to by the word. For example, when we say "Gene is the code of biological property", we use the word "gene" to refer to DNA format. But when we say in Chinese "'基因'是一个近乎完美的借词"("'基因[*Gene* in Chinese]' is a nearly perfect loanword"), we are mentioning the word "gene", discussing the word itself. This is worth noticing: suppose someone asks us why we say "'Gene' is a perfect loanword", we shall have to illustrate how the Chinese character string of "基因" ([jī-yīn]) approximates "gene" in sound and how the meaning of "基因" (in Chinese: "basic factor, ultimate cause, fundamental element", etc.) is close to the biological concept that the word "gene" represents. We are not just analyzing the word itself in terms of its phonetic or morphemic features; instead, we are attempting to explain the meaning of the word itself, without actually referring to any gene at the same time.

More importantly, the distinction of *use* and *mention* may as well be employed as a useful means to distinguish two levels of logic speculation: the empirical and the linguistic. This idea dawns on me, when I begin to consider how I can make sense of quite a few of the seemingly "nonsense" propositions of Ming Jia's: whether a word is quotation-marked or not may in fact mark out two levels of reflections, that on empirical experiences and that on conceptual meaning of names *per se*! If we apply this distinction to our interpretation of Ming Jia's texts and propositions, we may come to very significant insights.

As I said a moment ago, the distinction of *use* and *mention* was quite difficult with the Classical Chinese at the pre-*Qin* period, because in its writing system there was no punctuation of any kind. This might have constituted a barrier for Gongsun Long and other Ming Jia thinkers: they could not adopt the ready-made devices of quotation marks to caution or to remind their audience as well as their debating rivals that their arguments were not concerned with empirical facts but with the conceptual meaning of name *per se*. Indeed, if a Ming Jia debater should hope to make clear that "Mountains do exist, but the meaning of mountain does not exist physically out there; the 'mountain' that we are now talking about is not the same as any mountains existing in the world, but is the meaning of the word 'mountain' as a concept in our mind", what linguistic devices could they fall back on, in order to ensure that their discussion or debating was rightly confined to the level of the conceptual meaning of name?

Such a question has led me to the reconsideration of what Ming Jia intended to say by propositions like "山出口; literally: '[A] mountain [is] out of [the] mouth'", which has been known to be hard to explain and dismissed by most scholars as *inexplicable* or *insoluble* (cf. below).

Expanding the scope of application of the *use-mention* distinction, we may safely say that pre-*Qin* Ming Jia might have been *using* a name to denote or refer to an object or a thing but *mentioning* a name for the purpose of speculating on the conceptual meaning of the name *per se*. This is what I add in the *use-mention* distinction in discussing Ming Jia. In this way, I think we can have a more reasonable understanding of why they were proposing those "paradoxes" in the way they did. They might well be trying to confine, in the form of sentences, their topics for debates to the area of language meaning. In other words, they needed to declare by means of sentences to the others that what they were discussing on or debating over was not an empirical phenomenon but the meaning of a name, and that their topics were aimed at making clear what the nature of language meaning was and how one could master the correct meaning of name. Understood in this way, I believe that we can see more clearly their rationalist spirit of philosophy of language.

2.3.2 Re-examining the "X out of mouth" proposition

Did the Ming Jia thinkers, then, have left any clues to us that would render my understanding reasonable? I think yes. A very important clue is the proposition of "[A] mountain [is] out of [the] mouth", one that has not been satisfactorily explained.

Some claim that this is a "scientific description" of how mountains come into being, such as the formation of volcanoes which do have "mouths" (Zhou et al., 1984: 40). But certainly not all mountains are volcanoes with mouths and Ming Jia could in no way generalize the formation of mountains as expressed in the proposition. Some others regard it as a logical contradiction caused by confusions of word concepts (Shen, 1992: 210). However, these theorists have offered neither evidence nor arguments to show what sort of confusion is involved and how they cause contradictions. There are many other explanations, which I don't think necessary to list here, but no one is popularly accepted. Probably for this reason, quite a few well-known philosophers in China have just dismissed this proposition as *inexplicable* or *insoluble* (e.g.: Hu Shi, 2000: 171; Ren Jiyu, et al, 1983:495; Chen Guying, 1983:899; etc.).

It is not inexplicable, however. As early as in the *Tang* Dynasty (618-907 AD), Buddhist Monk Cheng Xuanying proposed that this proposition simply stated that "The name of 'mountain' is uttered from the mouth". Even Shen Youding himself cited Cheng's explanation to say that this means "mountain" as a meaningful sound was uttered out of human mouths; i.e. it is a language expression. But I wonder why then Shen should have continued to complain that this is a confusion of word concepts. More recently, Ye Jingming (2003: 195) has implied in her writing that if "[A] mountain [is] out of [the] mouth" is talking about the meaningful sound of language, then this proposition should be re-written into "'Mountain' is out of the mouth", with quotation marks added according to modern academic convention; or else confusions would result because of the unclear demarcation of the conceptual level of discussion. Ye is quite right, but she has not further discussed this issue.

I agree that this proposition should be punctuated in this way. This is of key importance for our correct understanding of what it says. My reasoning is not difficult: if Ming Jia had had quotation marks at their disposal, they could have used them to show to their audience and rivals in debate that their topic was on the conceptual meaning of name instead of on empirical common-sense about objects and things. But Ming Jia had no such linguistic devices for use. What they could possibly rely on could only be the use of sentences to delimit their area of argumentation; i.e., they had to use sentences to tell their debate partners that they should focus the debate on the conceptual meaning of the names, without involving any actual objects or experiences.

It is not just a fancy that the Ming Jia debaters were doing so at the time. My suggestion can be backed up by what Xunzi said when he was attacking Ming Jia at the pre-*Qin* period. In his criticisms, Xunzi listed what he perceived as "paradoxical nonsense", such as those recorded by Zhuangzi (cf. the beginning section of this part). It is noticeable that in the first chapter of *Xunzi*, his writings, Xunzi complained that Gongsun Long, Hui Shi and other Ming Jia debaters advocated what went "in from the ear, and out of the mouth" in their discussions and debates and he criticized them for doing so. To me, this is worthy of our attention because it is not just a suggestion, but a piece of evidence noted down that Ming Jia debaters did use such sentences in their talking and debating. What is it that comes in from the ear and out of the mouth in any discussions or debates? Certainly, it is not something substantive like an object, but can only be linguistic in nature: the talking about the concept of something. Such a proposition, even taken literally, does not constitute any paradox at all, unlike other ones, such as "there is hair in eggs" or "mountains are as flat as lakes", etc., in Xunzi's and Zhuangzi's lists. To find more clues, we see that Xunzi continued to classify two categories of knowledge: one being the intellectual propositions that came in to the audience ears and were kept in the mind as a part of people's thought; the other being what he called "despicable" propositions that went into the ear and came out of the mouth, which were nothing but such silly language games that served to perplex people's mind. To Xunzi, Ming Jia's propositions were nothing but such despicable language games. What goes in from the ear and out of the mouth is linguistic: words and sentences, and to Xunzi, any propositions that do not match people's experiences, thus leaving no useful ideas in the people's mind, are just silly language games, such as what Ming Jia have put forward.

This is certainly a serious misunderstanding on the part of Xunzi, as he had never been able to perceive and appreciate the value of Ming Jia's "language games". He remained at the level of empirical facts, while Ming Jia ventured into the metaphysical speculations on the conceptual meaning of name. Nevertheless, Xunzi's accidental recording of "In from the ear, and out of the mouth" shows that Ming Jia did use such statements in their dialogs with the others and the reason why they had to do so frequently was that they were constantly reminding their rivals that in their debate, the theme was not concerned with anything existing physically, but only the meaning of the names uttered from human mouths! What is out there should not be confused with what we say about it, and our talking about things and that about the meanings are different by nature. This should be what Ming Jia had in mind when they put forward the so-called "inexplicable" proposition.

Therefore, I think Monk Cheng Xuanying's explanation is right and I also agree with Ye Jingming that the proposition should be rewritten into "'Mountain' [is] out of the mouth". What I propose further is that this was originally Ming Jia's linguistic technique to make known that they were not using the word "mountain" to refer to mountains but were mentioning the word for the purpose of speculating on the meaning of "mountain" *per se*.

Ming Jia might have also made statements like "Man is out of the mouth" or "Horse is out of the mouth" or "Whiteness is out of the mouth" and so on and so forth. It is just a matter of chance that Zhuangzi recorded "Mountain is out of the mouth". In Zhuangzi's eyes, this was certainly nonsense, because since mountains existed out there that everyone could see, how could they just come into being out of the mouth? Yet both Xunzi and Zhuangzi had failed to understand that Ming Jia were actually saying that mountains are just what exist out there, but are called "mountains" because people use the name to name them; and the meaning of the name "mountain" is not the same thing as any real mountains, but consists of the concept in the human mind. The mountains out there just exist, which one can see, but there is no question of meaning in the mountains themselves. However, when it comes to language expressions, semantic questions do arise. The meaning of "mountain" does cause the potential problems of explanation. For example, what can be said to be a "mountain"? How can one distinguish a "mountain" from a "hill"? Does "mountain" still refer to a mountain like Himalayas when we say "a mountain of a man" or "a mountain of work"? And so on. And the word might be used to refer to other irrelevent objects. In Chinese, for instance, a man can use the name of "泰山" [tàishān], literally: "Mountain Tai" to address or to refer to his father-in-law, but a woman cannot use this same name to address or to refer to her father-in-law. It is of vital importance, then, to make clear how the name acquires its meaning and what the essence of meaning is.

Thus, pre-*Qin* Ming Jia would have to convince the others that the so-called "rectification of name" should not be an effort merely to identify the correspondence of a name with an object; rather, the task should be the speculation on the nature of the meaning of name and on the laws and rules of thinking that guarantee the certainty of the meaning and the correct use of the names. This is consistent with what Gongsun Long has stated in his essay, "On Name and Actuality" (cf. my translation and translator's note).

2.3.3 Exemplary explanations

In light of such a reinterpretation of the "X out of the mouth" proposition, I believe we can achieve a more coherent and reasonable comprehension of the ideas expressed in *Gongsun Longzi* and in the propositions of other Ming Jia thinkers'.

Take Gongsun Long's most famous propositions of "White-horse is not horse" and "independent being of hardness and whiteness" for example, if we do not evaluate the truthfulness of this proposition by empirical observations but regard it as a discussion on the meaning of the names of "white-horse-ness", and "horseness" as they are uttered, we clearly see that Gongsun Long insists in his essay that "whiteness" in itself is different from the mere white color in the objects and things out there. Gongsun Long does not deny that there are white horses out there, because he has stated very clearly in his essay that horses do exist out there, which is why one can have white horses. However, he is not interested in the questions like whether white horses are a sub-set of the category of horses. Instead, he is concerned with the meaning of "horse" itself, which he says is colorless as a concept. The point he attempts to make is this: the name "horse" expresses an independent existence and so should the name of "white". "White" is a name that names a color and therefore cannot be used to name a shape. Just like the meaning of "horse" has its ontological foundation, the meaning of "white" should also have such a foundation which is whiteness-in-itself. Since whiteness-in-itself expresses an essence which is not a part of the essence of the concept of "horse", "white-horse" as a concept should certainly be different from both "white" and "horse". Such ideas are undoubtedly metaphysical in essence.

In so doing, Gongsun Long has come close to Plato's theory of Form, because he regards whiteness as having its own being. This is not just my guessing work, but is supported by Gongsun Long's discussion on the separation of "hardness" and "whiteness" in his "On the Being of Hardness and Whiteness". In the essay, he has stated very clearly that such concepts have their independent existence and that such separation is possible because of the function of the mind. He wants to show that the only true knowledge is to be obtained by the mind that organizes the sense data to extract the essence. Were Gongsun Long born in ancient Greece, he would have been an enthusiastic adherent to Plato's theory.

Applying the same analysis to some other propositions of Ming Jia's, we find that they might well be exploring the issues of how meaning can be correctly determined and further what is the nature of knowledge human beings have acquired via language. Take Hui Shi's proposition of "天与地卑、山与泽平" ("The sky is as low as the earth; mountains are as flat as lakes") for example. Empirically, this is certainly nonsense. But when we add quotation-marks to the proposition, it becomes: The "sky" is as "low" as the "earth"; "mountains" are as "flat" as "lakes".

Notice that in this proposition, there are four key nouns: "sky, earth, mountain," and "lakes" and two adjectives: "low" and "flat". In Classical Chinese, all these nouns and adjectives appear in the form of name (one Chinese character), with no morphemic inflections or any formal devices to mark their parts of speech. A question naturally arises is: we can find ontological basis on which the meaning of the nouns is established, but how can we determine the ontological basis of the adjectives? One can point to the sky and say "That's the sky" and point at the earth beneath the feet and say "This is the earth"; the same is true with "mountain" and "lake". But can anyone point at something and say in the same fashion "That is the low" or "This is the flat"? Hui Shi might well be pondering such ontological issues concerning the meaning of the names. He might be asking questions such as whether there existed anything like "lowness-in-itself" or "flatness-in-itself", in the same spirit as Gongsun Long arguing for the independent existence of "hardness" and "whiteness". If this is indeed the case, we can confidently conclude that these examples show that Gongsun Long and Hui Shi were in fact engaged in metaphysical speculation on the basis of the meaning of the Chinese adjectives. Their propositions are unmistakably rationalistic in spirit, bringing them very close to the threshold to ontology.

I don't pretend that I have done the solely correct reinterpretation of Gongsun Long's essays and other Ming Jia thinkers' propositions, but my approach is indeed able to give a more coherent and consistent explanation to all the propositions, including the ones formerly regarded as extremely difficult to understand or as simply inexplicable.

3. Ming Jia Coming onto the Arena as Rationalists

Ming Jia's self-conscious speculation on the meaning of name is an in-depth development of the pre-*Qin* debate on name and actuality. This topic necessarily involves the major schools of thoughts at the time: Confucianism, Daoism and Mohism. In addition, there were many others such as Legalism, the School of Yin and Yang and so on; but these schools did not put forward really unique ideas about language and reality (Legalism, for instance, simply followed Confucianism, especially the name theory of Xunzi), and this is why I do not include them in my discussion.

About the thought tendency of Ming Jia, Hsien Chung Lee (2011, 2012) thinks that they had very good theoretical awareness, whose rational reflection was focused on the issues of "to know" and "to express". Lee (2012: 130) pointed out that pre-*Qin* Ming Jia's "way of thinking was unique at the time, finding new questions from the existing doctrines, exploring them in a completely new light and constructing their own theory on name and actuality.... It was a true breakthrough and progress at the time". I think this evaluation is quite right; Ming Jia's ideas were indeed original, and what is more, this originality was characterized by rationalistic speculation.

3.1 Confucius' Theory of Rectification of Names

Confucius initiated the pre-*Qin* debate on name and actuality, the first philosophical debate that lasted over 100 years in Chinese history. When asked what he would do if he was offered the position of prime minister in the Lu State, Confucius replied that he would first of all rectify the names, because, he said, "If names are not rectified, speech communication is hampered; if speech communication is hampered, nothing can be done successfully; if nothing can be done successfully, the social rituals and customs cannot be put in order; if the social rituals and customs cannot be put in order, the laws and penalties are powerless; and if the laws and penalties are powerless, people simply would not know how to behave" (Confucius: Ch.13). The motivation of Confucius to demand a rectification of name was that he attributed the then social turmoil and the breakdown of the social orders and moral codes established by the good old tradition to problems in speech communication, i.e. the names were used wrongly, divorced from the right objects or things they should be applied to. Confucius was convinced the rectification of name was of fundamental significance for the rule of a state. Certainly, if the names are divorced from the actual states of affairs, it would lead to disorder in the language exchanges which in turn leads to incomprehensibility of ideas; how can there be social orders or ethical criteria? It was this idea of Confucius that aroused the great debate.

However, Confucius' rectification of name was not oriented to truth-seeking through the speculation on the meaning of language. First of all, the primary target for the rectification was one of stipulating more strictly the orders of social ranks. To him, "One who is named 'a king' should behave in accordance with the nature of a king and be treated as such; one who is named 'a minister' should behave in accordance with the nature of a minister and be treated as such; the same is true for one who is named 'a father' or a 'son'" (Confucius: Ch.12). Clearly, Confucius' rectification was concerned with social orders and moral issues instead of language analysis. He did urge people to enrich their vocabulary and to use the right names to denote the right objects (such as his advice that one should know more about the names of fauna and flora and his criticisms on the wrong use of names, such as the wrong use of "觚" [gū]; "a wine-cup of a certain shape used in China earlier than the pre-*Qin* period" to denote a wine-cup which no longer had the shape as in the former wise king's time and therefore should no longer be called "gū"), but his central concern was "to restrain oneself to restore the rituals", and his mission was to restore the social political orders and moral behavioral codes of the past glorious time. We cannot see anything that shows he has the impulse to seek the truth through language analysis.

Secondly, Confucius' rectification of name required that empirical actuality meet up to the ideal semantic criterion of name of the previous wise king's time, because the criterion defined the essence of what there is in the world. Confucius was convinced that his contemporaries were still using the names given by the previous wise kings, but the actuality no longer complied with the correct names instituted by the wise king, which resulted in the chaos of meanings that hindered language exchanges. The situation was so serious that people did not even know how to behave and what to model on, bringing the society into disorder and the rituals into collapse. So to restore the social orders, one should start from the rectification of name in strict accordance to what the previous wise kings had decreed, which could not allow any revision. If this can be counted as an idea of philosophy of language, it is certainly *a priori*, something like the idea of *language legislator* Plato proposed through the mouth of Socrates: some ancient saints were insightful enough to see the essences of things and thus able to give things their right names so that the later generation could use language correctly to talk about the world.

Of course, their ideas are just a bit similar. Plato was oriented to truth seeking via rational speculation and his theory of meaning is philosophically "essence theory" (in linguistics it was termed "naming theory"). Confucius was, however, primarily a devoted practitioner who spared no effort to restore what he believed to be the ideal social orders and his theory of the name-actuality relationship was oriented to the establishment of the basis for ethical, political and social orders. Confucius did not even clearly define his key terms of ideology, such as "仁[rén]", meaning "mercy" "kind-hearted" etc. in Chinese but in translating Confucian ideas this word is usually dubbed as "benevolence"; instead he just provided statements that described certain traits of behavior or were simply metaphorical: "One is very close to benevolence if he is self-composed, resolute, simple and taciturn" (Ch.13), "The wise is like water while the benevolent a mountain; for the wise moves while the benevolent stays firm; the wise is happy while the benevolent long-lasting" (Ch. 6); or "Is benevolence far away from us? I want benevolence and it would be with me" (Ch. 7). But what is the "benevolence"? Confucius never gave any logical or empirical explanation. Even if we were ready to accept such statements as some sort of "definite descriptions" of what benevolence could be, we would not know how we could be "like a mountain", what counted as "self-composed, resolute, simple and taciturn" and what indeed "close to benevolence" might mean because "is close to" could not be equivalent to "is". Such statements of Confucius are vague and doubtable even as instructions about how to behave. In Confucius' ideas, there is no attempt to seek after anything true, which keeps him far away from ancient Greek philosophers in the quality of spiritual pursuit. However, we see that the "actuality" in Confucius' terms consists of *a priori* standards set up by the former wise kings.

3.2 Xunzi's Theory of Rectification of Names

Another major representative of Confucianism was Xunzi, who proposed the theory of "conventionality" concerning language: "Names cannot be said to be appropriate in and of themselves; they are used to name things by agreement and their appropriateness is established by convention. Names are not inherently fixed to anything existing in reality; they come to be bound with the things they name through agreement; it is the convention that establishes the name-actuality relationship." (Ch. 22) He also pointed out that what man experienced about objects and things through his senses were likely to be imprecise and therefore these same data should be further "mind-tested", in order to grasp correctly the similarities or the differences between objects and things. Xunzi went beyond Confucius to find a more reasonable theoretical basis for the rectification of name.

Although Xunzi, like Confucius, complained that the name-actuality relationship had been ruptured which caused confusions in judging what was good and what was bad, and therefore demanded the rectification of name, his proposal was "to institute names to denote things" (Ch. 22): to make different names denote different things. In addition to asking for making the actuality comply with the criteria of the names, Xunzi said at the same time that names must be decreed to describe actuality. This makes him different from Confucius. This can be further witnessed by his discussions on "general name" and "specific name":

> *Although things in the world are enormous in number and in variety, we sometimes do not describe them individually but call them in general "things". "Thing" thus is the most general name. By analogy, we know that within a general name there are further generalizations that in turn can be further generalized until we come to the end where there is no more generalization*

possible. Sometimes we want to name specific things; this is why we have names of birds and animals. "Bird" and "animal" are themselves the greatest specific names, which we can further classify into more specific ones until we come to the end where we can no longer classify... Things that look the same but are in different places, and things that look different but are in the same place must all be specifically identified and distinguished. Things that look the same but are in different places can be said to be of the same kind, but they are still two individual things. Where things change in appearance without a change of the property, we call it a transformation. Transformation does not make a thing different from what it is; it is still the same thing. This is what we do to inspect the things and determine their numbers and it is of key importance in our institution of names. (Ch. 22)

It is clear that Xunzi was not only aware of the conceptual hierarchy of names, but also proposed the practice of instituting names according to what things are in actuality and what features they have; sometimes a name can be used to denote different objects, while sometimes different names can be applied to the same object. Therefore one must examine specific objects and things in order to make sure whether the names for them are correct or not. These are his important ideas, showing that in Xunzi's rectification of name, the objects and things occupied a more important status than in Confucius' theory. Most likely, to me, Xunzi has been influenced by the empirical philosophy of Later Mohism.

However, in terms of the purpose of the rectification of name, Xunzi did not differ from Confucius. In Chapter 22 of his writings, Xunzi said: "The former wise kings instituted names so that the established names distinguished things in the world and the universal Way was comprehended and followed by the people whom the kings could lead in uniformity.... So the sage should institute names for correct denotation, to separate the noble from the humble in social order, which is its higher level function, and to discriminate what are the same and what are different in actuality, which is its lower level function." He intended to advise the king that names should be instituted to verify the social ranks of individuals, because if this would help identify the hierarchical positions of the people in the society, each of whom would have clear and definite moral-behavioral codes. If this was done, the king could then rule the country by subjecting the people to his will. It can be seen here that like Confucius, Xunzi had in mind the central concern of social and moral orders when he demanded the rectification of name. Theirs are basically a kind of moral-behavioral pragmatism, though they two do differ in terms of the approach to the rectification.

It is a pity that Xunzi did not go further to develop his idea of "mind-test", which might have brought him to an inquiry into the universality and necessity of knowledge. I think the reason why he should have stopped short of such an inquiry is that he was oriented in the same direction as Confucius in putting forward his ideas about language: his rectification of name is also aimed at determination of social ranks and roles in order to guarantee the rule of the king. This explains why he pointed out emphatically that the king should exclusively own the right to institute names, even though he did have certain empiricist viewpoints concerning the mechanism of and principle for the rectification of name. Such a contradictory mixture of ideas in Xunzi shows that his more or less correct or reasonable views concerning language were in fact not at all based on any ontological doctrines, which stopped him from deepening his thoughts.

3.3 Laozi's Theory of the Nameless

To Confucianists' rectification of name, Daoists proposed their theory of "the Nameless". The first sentence in Laozi's *Dao De Jing* goes, "The Dao can be said, but what is said of cannot be the ultimate Dao; names can name things, but they are not the true eternal names."

Contrary to Confucius who requested that objects and things conform to the *a priori* standard of the meaning of name, Laozi thought that the things could be labeled with their names, but the meaning of the names rested with the Dao, the principle from which everything was generated and in accordance to which everything changed. His ideas can be understood in this way: it is true that humans know and talk about specific things with names, but the ultimate meaning of names lies with the principle of the Dao; rectification of name is thus in vain, because one cannot rectify the ultimate meaning which rests with the eternal Dao that cannot be said. What the mortals can talk about is only what they experience of the meaning through their following the principle of the Dao.

Laozi's Dao is a highly abstract metaphysical concept which, as I understand it, is beyond any definition, because the Dao can in no way be talked about in the sentence pattern of "The Dao is a ...". Once we do so, we would be mistaken in naming the Dao just like we name specific things, thus reducing the Dao to an ordinary thing. And when the Dao were a thing, it could no longer be the principle from which other things are generated and to which they develop and change in accordance, but should itself also be generated by the Dao and develop and change according to the Dao, like anything else. In this case, we would face a logical contradiction: the Dao that is the principle for all things cannot be the principle for anything. To avoid this contradiction, Laozi has to say "The Dao can be said, but what is said of cannot be the ultimate Dao". So in his view, language is powerless as a tool for analytical inquiry into the Dao, which cannot be said in the first place. This is the passive point of the Daoists' philosophy of language.

Therefore, Laozi believed that rectification of name is impossible. I do not mean that Laozi deliberately proposed this theory to refuse and reject Confucius' theory of the rectification. After all, Laozi and Confucius talked about "name" in different ways, the former metaphysically and the latter practically. But objectively speaking, Laozi's theory does constitute a negation of Confucius' ideas, because to Laozi the meaning of name does not lie in the things themselves, but in the Dao. Names can of course be used to denote specific things, such as calling a cup "cup" or a dog "dog" and so on, but the reason why a dog is a dog and is named by "dog", or a cup is a cup and is called "cup" is that the things have their essences principled by the Dao. The Dao is the principle for the meaning of everything, but it itself is nameless. Therefore, Laozi claimed, "names can name things, but they are not the true eternal names". What really is, is the Nameless, the Dao. Since the Dao is nameless, how can one even start rectifying the name? Thus, Laozi's theory of the Nameless has essentially constituted a deconstruction of Confucian rectification of name.

By the way, the Dao is the metaphysical principle of the world, from which everything is generated and according to which everything develops. For this reason, it is the ultimate truth of the world. In this sense, the Dao is quite similar to Heraclitus' "Logos"; both are the metaphysical principle of everything in the world and both involve the issue of language. They are the great ideas contributed to Chinese and western philosophies by Laozi and Heraclitus respectively. But the fundamental difference between the "Dao" and "Logos" is that the latter can be said and has pushed western ideas to the path of analytical inquiry into issues of existence and knowledge through speculations on language, while the former cannot be said and leads to a cut-off of language and meaning, preventing the thinkers to set foot on analytical reflection on questions of what is and how one know it. For Heraclitus, the ultimately true knowledge can be mastered by application of reason through language, while for Laozi, the Dao can only be insightfully sensed but cannot be expressed in language. Most likely, this explains the well-known Needham's puzzlement: Why is it that none of the modern sciences was born in China, since there were brilliant scientific and technological achievements in ancient China? Science requires analysis; its definitions, questions, hypotheses, conclusions and so on must be expressed in clear language, while the "Dao" values experiential insight and holism that cannot be stated definitely, unfavorable for the occurrence of analytical mode of thinking.

3.4 Zhuangzi's Theory of Speech Unable to Exhaust Meaning

Zhuangzi was a representative of the Daoist tradition initiated by Laozi, who valued meaning more than he did language. In his writings of *Zhuangzi*, he said: "Language is used to convey meaning and once the meaning is known the speech is discarded." (Ch. 26) So with Zhuangzi, language and meaning can be separated; one uses speech to carry certain meaning but the speech itself is not important. To him, one has of course to obtain meaning by means of language, but the essential meaning is not in language: "What is expressed by speaking is something gross and what is mentally apprehended is the essence." (Ch. 17) To rephrase in our terms, what is expressed by language is only phenomenal, and the essence of things can only be mastered by the mind.

I do not think Zhuangzi regarded language as a "dross", as Han Donghui (2001) claimed. In fact, Zhuangzi did have his insightful idea about language, regarding it as a symbol of actuality: "Name is the substitute of actuality" (Ch.1), meaning that a name is used to describe an object that exists, since the object is real and a name is not the real but only substitutes the real in speech. He pointed out that there is no necessary connection between a name and an object: "A path comes into being because people walk on it; a thing comes to have its name because people call it so." (Ch. 2) "If you had called me 'buffalo' in the past, then I would be a buffalo now; or if you had called me "horse", I would now be a horse." (Ch. 13) These statements show not only that Zhuangzi held the idea of language conventionalism, but also that he objected to Confucian idealization of the function of name. An object does not have an inherent name, but is given its name by people using a language. Language is the instrument with which human beings name the world. Such understandings of Zhuangzi's are close to Mohism.

However, Zhuangzi held standpoints of relativism and agnosticism, as the result of which he could not be expected to go any deeper to propose a systematic theory on language. In "Bian the Wheel-maker Cutting a Wheel" (Ch. 13), Zhuangzi told the story of Bian the Wheel-maker saying to King Huan that the book the king was reading was nothing but a dross, because the author had died long before and the true meaning of what the author had intended to convey had already been lost. Bian used his unique skill as an example to show that he had a sense of propriety about the acts in making a wheel, its speed, degree and force which he could apply with facility, but he could never put the sense into words. He could not impart in words his skill of wheel making to his own son and that was why he was still working though he was already advanced in age. How then was it possible that what the ancient author had sensed or experienced be passed on to later generations by words in the book? It seems to Zhuangzi that language can only describe something phenomenal but that which makes the phenomenon be itself (the Dao) cannot be expressed in language. To put it simply: the essential meaning cannot be known through language exchanges, but can only be sensed holistically through insightful experiences outside language.

Zhuangzi stood in opposition to any debating. To him, "From the very beginning, the Dao makes no distinctions and thus words do not have any definite and unchanging meaning; it is in debating over what something is that distinctions are made by words" (Ch. 2). He believed that the true meaning could only be sensed holistically because the Dao was an integrated whole that was beyond any effort of clarification by analysis or debate. He continued to say, "Let me mention the distinctions: those of left and right, of ordering and categorizing, of discrimination and argument, and of disagreement and contention. These are the eight practices of making distinctions. However, he who is a sage would distance himself from discussing anything beyond the six harmonies of Heaven and Earth, East, West, North and South; and even about anything within the six harmonies he would only discuss without delimitative argumentation." (Ch. 2) The contentions and debates as to who is right and who is wrong or what the correct distinctions of things should be, these are only practical and trivial and are not the metaphysical discourse of the Dao which is the ultimate basis of all things and their significance. "The universal Dao is beyond any descriptions; the true argument is beyond any words." (Ch. 2) To Zhuangzi, the profoundest truth could not be discussed in words and the most convincing viewpoint does not need argumentation.

It can be seen from his sayings that Zhuangzi had a clearer perception of the limitation human language has in terms of conveying meaning on the one hand, and on the other hand, his position was one of relativism and agnosticism: the "Dao" is not in language, nor is it anything and therefore cannot be clearly analyzed and known; it can only be sensed in certain mysteriously holistic way by individuals through their respective experiences.

3.5 Later Mohists' Empirical Standpoint for Rectification of Names

Contradictory to both Confucianism and Daoism were the empiricist ideas of Later Mohism.

Later Mohists were positive about the practical function of name. They stated in their canon *Mohist Scripture*: "A name is what is used to refer and that which is referred to is an object in existence." (Ch. 42) "When an actual object corresponds to a name, the object is called by that name; without any objects, names simply could not come into being." (Ch. 43) Note here that they think the reference of language names consists of the actual objects, and that for them actual objects are of primary importance and names are only secondary and subordinate to the objects. Thus, Later Mohism stood in direct opposition to Confucianism who advertised that the actuality should comply with the *a priari* criteria of name. They also contradicted Daoism sharply, because they proposed that rectification of name was possible because the meaning of a name was given by the object or thing it referred to, instead of lying in the mysterious and fathomless Dao. To Later Mohists, the correctness of language meaning should be tested by objective practices, which we have seen before: "The effect should be the standard for telling the right from the wrong. Any argument should be put to test by this standard. If the effect is in keeping with actual state of affairs, the argument is right, or else, the argument is wrong. This is the rule we should follow." (Ch. 45) Quite positivistic were their ideas concerning the relationship between name and actuality and between speech and meaning. For the purpose of this book, the interesting point is the debate between Later Mohists and Ming Jia thinkers. Tan Jiefu (1983: 63-75) has made a classification of the pre-*Qin* thoughts on name, grouping Gongsun Long and other Ming Jia into what he calls "School of Name-forms" and Later Mohists into "School of Names". Tan intends to show that they two are totally different and even conflicting in ideas and propositions. Indeed, As we have seen before Ming Jia and Later Mohists were antagonistic to each other in what they say. Against Gongsun Long's "White-horse is not horse", Mohists showed that "White horses are horses" and so on. But to me, one point is of vital importance: while Later Mohists were concerned with the truth of correspondence at the level of experience, Ming Jia talked about truth at the level of language concept. Take their debate over "fire" for example. When Ming Jia said "'Fire' is not hot", they were discussing "fire" not as an actual phenomenon but as the concept referred to by the word, inquiring into the nature of the "fire" which, as a concept in the mind, can not have the property of being hot. However, when Later Mohists retorted that "Fire is hot, just like what we feel when we see the sun", they were obviously talking about *fire* not as a concept expressed by the word but as a natural phenomenon. Shen Youding (1992: 203-205) finds the fact very strange that Later Mohists refuted some of Ming Jia's proposition such as "Fire is not hot", "Eyes don't see" on the one hand, but unhesitatingly accept their other propositions, such as "The shadow of flying birds has itself never moved" on the other; the Mohists also stated that "Shadows are static" and further argued for it: "When the light arrives, the shadow disappears. If the shadow remains still, it only means the object stays still and the light is also still." (Ch. 43)

　　To me, this is nothing strange, because we can see that Later Mohists were dealing with Ming Jia's propositions on the own empirical standpoint, accepting those that they saw as consistent with empirical facts and rejecting those they deemed inconsistent with empirical facts. Later Mohism and Ming Jia were certainly antagonistic in ideology, but both were attempting to retort one another intellectually on the basis of their respective tendency of thought, instead of attacking each other without an understanding of each other's point of view. Both sides turned up with their persuasive arguments in their own right. This was quite rare in pre-*Qin* times, or rather has been rare in the entire intellectual tradition of China.

3.6 Occurrence of Ming Jia Ideas as a Necessary Development

The above discussions have showed that in pre-*Qin* period, all the schools involved in the Great Debate on Name and Actuality put forward their theories concerning language and its meaning. Since they all insisted on different views, the debate among them proved very heated. But a fundamental question was how a name came to express an actual thing? About what "name" was, the scholars of different schools did not seem to disagree much, but they differed widely from each other in opinions on what "actuality" was, using the concept in different senses. If "actuality" simply consisted of specific objects that physically existed out there, then it would be quite right to just label them with names, but why then some would propose that the meaning of name rested with the "Dao" that could not be said? While some requested that things in reality conform to the requirement of the meaning of name, the only true criteria established *a priori*, or else one could not use names to say anything correctly, others argued that things were things in themselves but described by man with names, and therefore the meaning of name was just the object described. In this situation, questions would rise: what is the "actuality" which we are talking about and debating over? What is the nature of the "actuality" expressed by language? How can the actuality be correctly apprehended and expressed? Someone had to be aware of questions like these and came out to clarify the issue, promoting people to think about what it was that man knew by virtue of language and what constituted a true understanding of the world. This is exactly what Ming Jia wanted to do and actually did.

Seeing from this point, I do not agree completely with Hsien Chung Lee (2012: 130) who says, "Ming Jia inherited the tradition of rectification of name, converted to the idea of the Nameless and conflicted with the thought of pinning down the name by actuality." Certainly, Ming Jia attempted to rectify the meaning of name, but in their thought we find nothing even remotely close to the Nameless theory of Daoism; and while it is true that Ming Jia differed sharply from Later Mohism, we do find that they two shared a common pursuit of what is true. What is more, the Daoist Nameless theory is not compatible at all with the thought of empirical pinning-down of name by actuality. Such Contradictory ideas cannot coexist in the same doctrine. In light of this, my theory is this: the historical and ideological motivation for the rise of Ming Jia was their impulse to clarify the nature of "name" and the nature of "actuality", two key concepts of the Great Debate on Name and Actuality of the pre-*Qin* period, initiated by Confucius' proposal of rectification of name that had led to enormous contentions and arguments concerning language, meaning and epistemology.

"It is possible for one to think in a clear and definite way, only when one realizes that language consists of signs and that words are characterized by ambiguities in its function of reference, and accordingly makes analysis of what it is that a word refers to." (Jin, 2006: 76) Ming Jia came to the reflection on the meaning of language, because the seemingly insoluble contentions among various schools of thought around the issues of rectification of name would necessarily lead to the effort to clarify the nature of "name" and "actuality", the very key concepts themselves. Confucianism required shaping the empirical actuality by the stipulated standard of the meaning of names, hoping to restore the ideal name-actuality match established in the good old days. Daoism nullified, with their theory of the nameless Dao, the possibility of the rectification, leading to epistemological relativistic and agnostic tendency of thought. Later Mohism were convinced that names could be rectified, but the standard for determining the meaning of language should be empirical. Now that the various schools of thinkers were not using the terms "name" and "actuality" in the same sense, their debates and contentions could go nowhere, never able to straight anything out. Lacking a basic agreement on the essential definitions of the two key concepts, their debates appeared to be pointless, or worse still, they might cause further confusions of thoughts. It was in this situation that Ming Jia came on to the arena, who specialized themselves in reflecting on the problem of name and asking questions about the nature of meaning, which led them on to the path towards rationalist philosophy of language characterized by analytical speculation. This was quite unique and rare in Chinese history, however fleeting their appearance was.

Let me digress a little to see, why Ming Jia just had such a fleeting appearance in history. Most likely, Ming Jia were thrown in oblivion, partly because their mode of thought, as a highly abstract reflection on language meaning, appeared to be divorced from common sense and therefore not understood and accepted by the public, and partly because they were wrongly attacked by the mainstream schools of thought, such as Confucianism and Daoism. As we have seen before, Xunzi resorted to invectives and slanders against Ming Jia. Xunzi's indignation had its source in his inability to understand what Ming Jia were saying and he demanded a complete ban on their ideas by whatever means available. He was intellectually nothing but despotic. But he was successful in giving Ming Jia a bad reputation and making their ideas less than intelligible for the later generations. Du Guoxiang (1955: 7-8) is definitely sure that the book *Gongsun Longzi* that we have today cannot be a spurious edition, simply because its content is beyond ordinary understanding. Du has quoted this comment given by a later scholar who happened to have come cross *Gongsun Longzi*: "I tried to read it, but cannot make sense of the sayings such as 'White-horse is not horse'; nor can I understand the discourses on hardness and whiteness and on sameness and difference. ... If I want to know the correct use of names, I must put this book into fire immediately." About such comment, Du sighs: "One should have been only too anxious to burn Gongsun Long's book, just because he failed to understand it. What stupidity is that!" (1955: 7-8) To me, that's how stupid Xunzi was. He failed to understand Ming Jia propositions and then demanded to forbid them by means of criminal punishment.

Surely, Han Fei, a pupil of Xunzi, followed his mentor's thought. Han Fei formulated legal articles to ban Ming Jia ideas. As Cui Qingtian (1997: 73) says, "To Han Fei, the law is at once the rule to govern a country and the supreme stipulation of all thoughts and actions; therefore the abstract discussions of topics such as 'hardness and whiteness' would cause ungrounded suspicions among the people, which in turn might shake the foundation of the political rule of the feudalist dictatorship." It might well be that if the analytical mode of thinking did take root in the mind of the people, they would be able to raise serious doubts about the dictatorship, as the nature of such thought would always lead to questions. Han Fei, who took sides with the rulers, seemed to have a good awareness about it instinctively. Unfortunately, the result was that Ming Jia's ideas were doomed to be eliminated.

4. Ming Jia Thinkers as Rationalist Philosophers of Language

To refer to Ming Jia thinkers as "rationalist philosophers of language", I need to clarify in what sense I use the phrase. Strictly speaking, *rationalism* denotes the philosophical tradition developed by Descartes and others around 17th and 18th centuries, which claims that true knowledge comes from the exercise of human faculty of reason, since certainty cannot be established on sense data, which can be highly unreliable. But I am not using the word in this strict sense, since this line of thought is absent from the entire traditional Chinese philosophy. I use "rationalism" here to talk about Ming Jia because I think they have an ideological inclination to pursue the certainty of language meaning by appealing to reason rather than relying on practical experiences, or on mysterious meditations. It is true that the Chinese philosophy was not knowledge-oriented from its start and the issue of truth through analysis was never on the philosophical agenda, but as we have seen, Chinese philosophers like Ming Jia inevitably stepped on to the path of rationalist thought characterized by analytic speculation. It was in the Great Debate on Name and Actuality that Ming Jia came into being, first as an effort to clarify the key concepts in the debate and then in the process they formed their own rationalist philosophy concerning language meaning.

Similarly in a strict sense, "philosophy of language" refers to the trend of western philosophy in the 20th century, which attempts "to understand the nature of language and its relationship with speakers, their thoughts, and the world. ...[It involves] not only a quantitative increase in interest in matters linguistic, but also the recasting of age-old philosophical questions in linguistic terms." (Baghramian, 1999: Introduction) Of course I am not using the phrase in this sense to talk about Gongsun Long and Ming Jia. But broadly speaking, I believe that a thinker can be counted as a philosopher of language, so long as he/she speculates on language and language meaning which further involves issues of ontology and of epistemology, his questions

261

being fundamental ones such as what the basis of language meaning is, what meaning essentially is, how we can guarantee the correctness of language meaning or what is the nature of the knowledge human beings have by means of language, etc. It is in this broad sense that I ascribe the property of philosopher of language to Gongsun Long and pre-*Qin* Ming Jia.

In addition to my discussions above, I think I have the following evidence to support my claim that Ming Jia thinkers are rationalist philosophers of language.

4.1 Evidence I

The first evidence comes from one of our modern labels of Ming Jia as "a branch of Mohism". Since Ming Jia and Later Mohism were both concerned with questions of name and actuality and had very similar or even the same propositions, some scholars such as Tan Jiefu believe that Ming Jia thinkers were basically Mohists, who just deviated from some of the orthodox Mohist doctrines.

However, I do not think Ming Jia was just a branch of Mohism, because they two hold completely different philosophical viewpoints. They do have some statements that express the same ideas (e.g., both agree that shadows do not move), but those are small in number while most of what they say differ greatly (e.g., Ming Jia argue that substance is limitlessly divisible, but Later Mohists reply that everything has an end point, and when you come to the end point you cannot go on dividing). They two are discussing at different levels: one at the level of language concept, and the other that of empirical actuality. Just as Zhang Dainian (2005: 159) has pointed out, Ming Jia and Mohists "based their respective theories on different grounds, the former talking about reference and the latter objects". Zhang's comment is truly to the point. Ming Jia's "talking about reference" does not involve discussions on anything actually existing out there but is focused on the reference itself, which is very obvious in Gongsun Long's essays styled in dialogs, specifically "On 'White-horse Is Not Horse'", "On the Being of Hardness and Whiteness" and "On Essence and Change". And his "On the Nature of Reference" is a special essay on what reference is, what the relationship between reference and object is, how one should distinguish reference from denotation, etc.

I think in the dialogs of *Gongsun Longzi*, the heckler was none other than a Later

Mohist. I say this for two reasons.

First, Confucianists and Daoists were concerned with political, moral or social cultural problems instead of with knowledge and the epistemological conditions for the certainty of knowledge. Confucius, Laozi, Xunzi and Zhuangzi did express their views on issues of language, but they did not seem to have any theoretical interest in how knowledge could be true, of which we find no statements in their sayings. What is more, Laozi and Zhuangzi were also relativistic in their ideas. None of the concerns and intellectual predispositions of these thinkers finds any expression in Gongsun Long's essays presenting dialogs. The key question running through the dialogs that Gongsun Long and his heckler are concerned is: when a name is used, what the nature of its conceptual meaning is and how it can be determined to be of true knowledge.

Second, Gongsun Long and his heckler stand in opposition to each other in their debate, whose positions on the nature of word meaning are respectively characterized by rationalism and empiricism. One can see in the dialogs that the heckler is always retorting Gongsun Long's propositions on the basis of empirical facts, trying to establish the correctness of the meaning of names on the correspondence with actual states of affairs, while Gongsun Long's replies are rationalistic in nature, hoping to convince the heckler that the correctness of the meaning of names should be established on the basis of the intellectual reasoning about the essence of actual things. The heckler has demonstrated the same line of thought as the empiricist philosophy of Later Mohism expressed in *Mohist Scripture*. Gongsun Long does admit the reasonableness of the heckler's viewpoint, but further shows that such viewpoint does not constitute a proof of the correctness of name and this is why he spares no effort in persuading the heckler that one should not equate empirical experiences to rational knowledge in thinking about the correctness of name meaning. The essays in *Gongsun Longzi* might well be actual recordings of the debates between Ming Jia and Mohists. I think I can boldly say that at the pre-*Qin* period, Ming Jia debaters had the only true rival of thought in Mohists, because only they two had serious theoretical interest in pure questions of ontology and epistemology, i.e. in what it is and how it can be true. Zhuangzi's egocentric recordings of the fragments of Hui Shi and other Ming Jia debaters' sayings and his satirical and critical comments show that Zhuangzi himself failed to see what Ming Jia and Mohists were talking about and could only garble their utterances here and there.

Actually, one of the essays, "Anecdotes of Gongsun Long", in *Gongsun Longzi* has already disclosed the rationalist tendency of Gongsun Long's thought. As I have said previously in my translator's notes, Gongsun Long reasoned with Kong Chuan who pleaded to be Gongsun Long's pupil but on condition that he recant his "*White-horse is not horse*" doctrine. Facing this challenge, Gongsun Long pointed out the logical error in Kong's statements and said outright that they two were not thinking at the same level. Gongsun Long's logical reasoning often rendered Kong speechless. To me, a rationalist who thinks in a logical way would also demonstrate the characteristic of logical thinking in dealing with everyday situations.

4.2 Evidence II

Similar anecdotal records can be found also about Hui Shi, the other major representative of Ming Jia. Let's look at a record of the dialogs in *Zhuangzi* (Ch.17) between Zhuangzi himself and Hui Shi:

> *Zhuangzi and Hui Shi were one day promenading on the bank of River Hao.*
>
> *Zhuangzi said: "Look at the leisure way the fish swim! They are so happy."*
>
> *To this, Hui Shi replied: "You are not the fish. How do you know that the fish are happy?"*
>
> *Zhuangzi: "You are not me. How do you know that I don't know the fish are happy?"*
>
> *Hui Shi: "I am not you and therefore do not know what you know. It follows that you do not know the fish are happy since you are not the fish. It's just a simple reasoning!"*
>
> *Zhuangzi: "Let's come back to the original question. When you said 'How do you know that the fish are happy', you had already known that I knew the fish were happy and you should have been asking me! I knew that on the bank of River Hao!"*

Obviously, Hui Shi is not interested in whether the fish are happy or not. What he presses for an answer of is: what logically sound basis does Zhuangzi have on which he judges the fish to be happy. Hui Shi is not an empirical scientist, who would choose to infer the state of emotion of fish by the observation of their behaviors or other external features. He is not interested in knowledge *per se*, but inquires into the conditions that guarantee the certainty of knowledge. In this example, Hui Shi requires the rational proof of the affirmative statement made by Zhuangzi.

Zhuangzi is the one who uses quibbling in this debate. Unable to cope with the logical power of Hui Shi's questions, he resorts to fraudulence of changing the topic from "How" to "Where" he gets to know the fish are happy, to dodge the spearhead of Hui Shi's rational thought. Zhuangzi is said by many to be smart in so doing as he has "outwitted" Hui Shi; but in fact this only shows the ignorance of Zhuangzi in questing for true knowledge. Zhuangzi has demonstrated no wisdom of logical analysis. Some people may say that the way Zhuangzi acquires knowledge is empathy, an analogy of experiences. That may well be the case; one is surely able to infer that the fish are happy by their pattern of behavior. But obviously such inference is too subjective to be reliable and the knowledge obtained in this way does not have a high degree of certainty and necessity. What Hui Shi presses for in the dialog is none other than the necessary condition for the certainty of knowledge.

Similar dialogs between Hui Shi and Zhuangzi can be found elsewhere in *Zhuangzi*. The following dialog, for instance, is recorded in Chapter 5.

> *Hui Shi asked Zhuangzi: "It is true that human beings are born emotionless?"*
>
> *Zhuangzi replied: "Yes."*
>
> *Hui Shi: "How can they be called 'humans' without any emotions?"*
>
> *Zhuangzi: "The Dao has given them their appearances and Heaven has given them their forms. Why shouldn't they be called 'humans'?"*
>
> *Hui Shi: "Since they are called 'humans', how is it possible that they live without emotions?"*
>
> *Zhuangzi: "This is not what I mean by saying they are emotionless. What I mean is that to be emotionless, they should not harm themselves by what they like or what they dislike, but should just adapt to the Dao, without any desire for*

gains."

Hui Shi: "But if they do not desire for gains, how can they survive in the first place?"

Zhuangzi: "The Dao has given them their appearances and Heaven has given them their forms. They should not harm themselves by what they like or what they dislike. Now you exert your efforts and exhaust your spirit, murmuring by leaning at a tree or dozing off by the table. Heaven has given you the form you have, and you should have chosen to waste it on the vain discussions of 'hardness and whiteness'!"

This dialog also shows Hui Shi's pursuit of the definiteness of meaning: "emotion" as a design feature of what is called "human being"; a human being must have emotions to be a human being. Or else, the name of "human being" should not be applied. To this, Zhuangzi repeatedly says that Heaven has given human beings their forms and therefore they can be called "human beings". This is an obvious error, for the outward form does not necessarily indicate the innate essence: a stone sculpture of a human figure, for instance, does not make the stone a human being. Even if we interpret Zhuangzi's "form" as meaning "physique", it would be incomplete as a definition of what a human being is, for what defines human existence is nothing else but the rational capacity. According to modern understanding of psychology, emotions are the psychological processes resulted from the interaction between environmental stimuli and cognitive interpretation of how the subject himself/herself stands in relation to the stimuli. Some emotions (joy, anger, sadness and so on) are common among all animals including humans, while some others (morality, volition, love, patriotism and so on) are human species-specific. So, emotion is one of the designing features of human being as human being. In this respect, Hui Shi is right and Zhuangzi is wrong. What I want to emphasize is that in the entire dialog, Zhuangzi has not answered directly any of Hui Shi's questions, but mentioning such indefinable concepts of "the Dao" or "Heaven" and in the end resorting to personal abuses against his rival. Zhuangzi's sayings show that there is no analytic element in his way of thinking that leads him to the attempt to clarify any conceptual meaning and to logical thought. This in turn foils the rationalist thought tendency of Hui Shi.

From such dialogs, we see that Hui Shi, a major represtutative of Ming Jia, like Gongsun Long, is not satisfied with empirical generalizations about objects and things; nor does he accept anything of subjective guessing or mysterious speculation. No one except a true rationalist would adopt such attitude like Hui Shi's to deal with the issues of conceptual certainty of language meaning and to pose questions in an analytical way. Many people today consider that Zhuangzi has won out with his "philosophical wisdom" in the dialogs, but I hold totally different opinions. I think the loser is Zhuangzi; his thought is not philosophical at all in the strict metaphysical sense of the word. Pressed hard by Hui Shi's rational logic, Zhuangzi does not know which way to turn to, except to sophistry. Nevertheless, we should thank Zhuangzi for his egocentrism, for this has pushed him on to note down these dialogs as well as Ming Jia's propositional fragments so that we have now a chance to glimpse at the brilliance of Ming Jia's rationalistic thought.

4.3 Evidence III

The more direct evidence, of course, is found in the five essays left over to us in *Gongsun Longzi*, of which "On Name and Actuality" and "On the Nature of Reference" are the programmatic documents of Ming Jia theory, declaring the standpoint, principle and approach of their philosophy of language.

In "On Name and Actuality", Gongsun Long began with the statement of "Heaven and Earth, with what exist and grow therein, are just material objects". This shows that Gongsun Long does not deny the objective existence of actual objects in the world. He puts this statement in the beginning to say that what exist out there are the objects for human cognition. This statement is in consistency with Hui Shi's attempt "to give an explanation to everything in the world".

To Gongsun Long, objects and things are indeed what exist physically and they are the source and foundation of human knowledge. Without actual objects and things, there would have been no talking about objects and things in the first place. However, the existence of objects is one thing, but it is quite another to know what they truly are. Such knowledge would be impossible without language. After all, it is by virtue of language that humans own the world (Li, 2006). Therefore, on the basis of admitting objective existence, Gongsun Long engages himself in examining what humans come to know and master the world through strict speculation on language problems. He wants to investigate the question of what sort of actuality it is that man masters. For this purpose, Gongsun Long has proposed his principle of philosophy of language: the *thisness* in *this* and the *thatness* in *that* exclusively:

> ... *to rectify names correctly we should abide by the principle of "the thisness in this and the thatness in that exclusively". Specifically, "that" is not a true name of that, if one says 'that' but does not refer exclusively to the thatness; nor is "this" a true name, if one says "this" but does not refer exclusively to the thisness. ...when "that" is used, the meaning of "that" can only be the "thatness" that that should have and only that can have. This is the only case in which the name of "that" can be applied to talking about that. The same is true of "this"; the meaning of "this" can only be the "thisness" that this should have and only this can have. This is the only case in which the name "this" can be used to talk about this.*

Gongsun Long points out that the meaning of a word necessarily has its strict definition and to use words to talk about things and to exchange ideas correctly, it is a must that the nature of word meaning be put to strict scrutiny in order to clarify exactly what "this" refers to and what "that" refers to. To him, when we use the word "that", what we use the word to say of must have the essence of thatness which all the objects "that" names must have and only the objects "that" names can have; the same is true when we use the word "this" to say of an object "this" names. Only this stipulation guarantees the correct use of words, which in turn guarantees the truthfulness and certainty of the knowledge we obtain. This is in fact no less than the classical Chinese version of Aristotle's basic principles of logic, those of non-contradiction and of excluded middle, because what Gongsun Long expresses is exactly that an object cannot be this object and that object at the same time; in other words, an object either is or is not itself and in no case can an object be and not be itself at the same time.

As I have said before, in the Classical Chinese language, there is no copula "to be" and there is no way Gongsun Long could have posed questions concerning the syntactic forms around "to be". But his speculations around "this" and "that" are the same in essence as what the ancient Greek philosophers have done. He is asking questions of "this" and "that" as a philosophical exploration with the Chinese language characteristics into "what is" and "how it can be true". His expressions appear to be tongue-twisting and difficult to decode because the writing system of the Chinese language is not alphabetic but hieroglyphic. While the western languages provide their users with alphabetical symbols to stand for concepts, the Chinese language does not have such devices ready for Chinese philosophers like Gongsun Long, who are therefore compelled to express their meanings by means of the linguistic means available in Chinese. If we substitute the "this" and "that" in Gongsun Long's writings with the oft-used letters of "P" and "Q" etc., then we can find Gongsun Long putting forward propositions of "P must be P and cannot at the same time be not P", and "there is no case where one can say of a thing as both P and Q ($\neg$P) at the same time". Isn't this very close to Aristotle's theorems of "P $\vee \neg$P" and "$\neg$(P $\wedge \neg$P)"?

Also as we have discussed before, in "On the Nature of Reference", Gongsun Long endeavors to discuss a central question of philosophy: to explain what it is that human uses language to know about the world, through his speculations on what reference essentially is. By the function of language, what humans know about the world are not bound to specific objects and things, but generalized knowledge through the process of conceptualization, which means that we parse the world with words, grouping things into categories to master the essential characteristics of the categories. This is how our concepts are formed. Modern linguistics has developed on this understanding (cf. de Saussure, 1949: 157). Gongsun Long has already had some burgeoning ideas of this kind. In his view, words can be used to name specific objects, but as reference, the meaning of word does not necessarily have anything direct to do with specific objects. Objects existing out there do not have any inherent names and the names that we have are the result of representing the concepts of objects which are no longer the objects themselves, but the essential meaning cognized by us through parsing and categorizing the world. So, Gongsun Long points out confidently that it is the conceptual meaning that a name refers to and for this reason the *reference* is not the same as the *denotation* of objects.

This is also the meaning of the Ming Jia debaters' proposition: "A reference does not reach any specific things, which are endless and inexhaustible in the universe", because it refers to the meaning abstracted by the mind from the objects and things. Language makes our thought possible and enables human beings to transcend their immediate experiences to achieve a rational knowledge about the world. This is a view generally accepted today. If this is true, speculations on language appear to be quite necessary. Language expresses our thought and thus to explore how we can correctly speak is exactly to explore how we can think correctly.

In spite of all the problems of expression and rigidity of reasoning, the five essays in *Gongsun Longzi* have presented to the readers his system of thoughts.

First, in "On Name and Actuality", Gongsun Long has proposed that things exist objectively and that names are not just the labels of things but the symbols that refer to the essential meanings, that things differ from one another not in appearance but in the thing-ness which one thing must possess that no other thing can possess, and that therefore the principle for the rectification of name should be that of the *thisness* in *this* and the *thatness* in *that* exclusively. In this process, Gongsun Long has virtually proposed the Chinese language version of Aristotle's basic logic theorems of non-contradiction and of excluded middle.

Second, in "On 'White-horse Is Not Horse'", "On the Being of Hardness and Whiteness" and "On Essence and Change", Gongsun Long undertakes to analyze the concepts of "white-horse" and "horse", "two" and "one" and "hardness" and "whiteness" in an effort to illustrate and elaborate on his principle for the rectification of name put forward in "On Name and Actuality". Of the three essays, "On the Being of Hardness and Whiteness" is the most important one, in which he systematically discussed his ideas of "being in and of itself" based on which he comes to regard "hardness" and "whiteness" as having their own beings independent of any other things. Such conceptual beings are very close to Plato's Ideas. Gongsun Long clearly claims that such conceptual beings are to be mastered by the mind by means of analysis. Like Plato, Gongsun Long is convinced that the only true knowledge is the rational knowledge that the mind grasps through analysis. It seems to me that Gongsun Long has proposed two sorts of realities: both material and conceptual. This makes him different from Plato. But whatever is the case, his thought is a philosophy characterized by rationalism.

Third, in "On the Nature of Reference", Gongsun Long goes on to propose the distinction between *denotation* and *reference*, say that these are concepts of different levels, the former being empirical and the latter language-conceptual. He points out unmistakably that only the referential function of language gives what human beings truly know about the world. Amazingly, the special discussion on "to refer" and "to denote" occurs in the west after their linguistic turn in 20th century.

4.4 Summing up

Pre-*Qin* Ming Jia, represented by Gongsun Long, are a group of thinkers engaged in understanding the content of concept and the way human beings know the world through metaphysical speculations on language and meaning. They are indeed rationalist philosophers of language unique and rarely seen in Classical Chinese intellectual history.

In my paper, "Meta-categorization of Language and Gongsun Long's Philosophy of Language"[1], I wrote: "Gongsun Long was quite conscious in his meta-categorization of the conceptual meaning of language expressions. His speculations displayed a definite awareness of ontology and epistemology. Had the Chinese philosophical tradition developed along his line of thought, there could well have been debates over questions such as whether the 'thisness' or 'thatness' was real entities or not, similar to the debate between realism and nominalism in western tradition. Those who held that 'thisness' and 'thatness' had a real existence (like Gongsun Long himself) might have become Platonic idealists, while those who believed that meaning was nothing but the property of name whose truth or falsity should be put to test in practice (like Later Mohists) might have become nominalists. Should this have been the case, the ancient Chinese thought might well have developed its own metaphysics and logic even in the strict sense of western philosophy; the difference might have been that Chinese philosophy would have turned from philosophy of language to ontology and epistemology."

---

1 Liu Limin, "Meta-categorization of Language and Gongsun Long's Philosophy of Language", *Foreign Language Research*, 2011(1): 16.

5. Concluding Remarks

If what I have discussed in this book is right, we have confidence to say that metaphysical speculation on ontology and epistemology as a mode of abstract philosophical thinking, is not language-specific, unlike what is said by people like Derrida to be the patent right of European languages. European languages, with their emphasis on structural forms, are indeed conducive to such a philosophical rationalism, but it is equally possible for this rationalism to bud and grow on the soil of the Classical Chinese language.

The ideas of Ming Jia might have started the traditional Chinese philosophy on to the path of metaphysical speculation oriented toward truth-seeking. An analytical speculation on the concepts of the Dao and the Ren in Chinese philosophy, pressing for what the Dao is and how can man know the truth of the Dao, might have given rise to a philosophical "what-ology"with the Chinese language characteristics, an ontology without "to be" and "being". Unfortunately, the development of the rationalistic spirit in traditional Chinese philosophy was brutally curbed, with the burgeoning rationalist philosophy of Ming Jia stifled in its cradle when the intellectual prejudice and political dictatorship had done their work later on. This is not a metaphor but what happened in Chinese history. After the persecution of scholars including Ming Jia thinkers, banning their ideas and burning their books (during the *Qin* Dynasty, around 200 BC), no one has ever since attempted to raise questions in and of language in China's intellectual circle, resulting in a severe lack of logical analysis and speculative rationalism in traditional Chinese philosophy.

The classical language has no obstacle for the Chinese to speculate on what exists and what is true or false, in a manner no less speculative and rational than what western philosophers have done, only that the starting points might differ. The view that the Chinese language with its non-structural and non-formal property is unsuitable for metaphysical thoughts and therefore cannot produce a philosophy essentially the same as western philosophy is, at least to me, ungrounded and wrong. The love of wisdom is universal and not at all language-specific.

Finally, I'd like to make a declaration. I have retranslated *Gongsun Longzi* in a new framework of understanding. Is my reinterpretation and retranslation successful?

I leave this question to the readers and to history. But as the translator, I am quite confident that my translation is more reasonable and more coherent than the other versions available at present in explaining all and every proposition of Ming Jia thinkers'. This shows at least that the framework of my book approximates more closely the thought tendency of Ming Jia thinkers, compared with the other existing frameworks for interpretation.

Before finishing the revision of my book draft, I have given it to some of my friends for their reviews. One of them, Professor Du Shihong of Southwest University in China has raised this question: an age-old conundrum should have thus been resolved? He says he can accept my reinterpretation as coherent only on the basis of certain assumptions or presuppositions. And he is right. Whose interpretation of *Gongsun Longzi* and Ming Jia philosophy that we have so far is not based on any assumptions or presuppositions? If more persuasive frameworks are proposed for reinterpreting *Gongsun Longzi*, thus giving a more coherent and reasonable explanation to Ming Jia philosophy, then I would be very happy to accept their views without hesitation.

Appendix
English Version of Ming Jia's Paradoxes with Translator's Interpretations

1. Hui Shi's "10 Paradoxical Propositions"

1.1 〔English version〕

The largest-in-itself entails no more space outside it, and this can be said to be "the Oneness of the Largest", while the smallest-in-itself entails no more space inside it, and this can be said to be "the Oneness of the Smallest".

〔Interpretation〕

This proposition is Hui Shi's speculation on the definition of the essence of the "largest" and that of the "smallest". Such a speculation can only be metaphysical as the content of the proposition can in no way be verified empirically. Hui Shi could rely only on logic reasoning to achieve such a definition.

1.2 〔English version〕

The area, having no thickness, is in no way amassed, but can be one-thousand-*li* large.[1]

〔Interpretation〕

This proposition has been accepted unanimously as Hui Shi's speculative reflection on the definition of "area". What one should note is that Hui Shi is not, with this proposition, pondering on the empirical issue of how to measure an area, but is inquiring into questions concerning what the very nature of area is.

---

1   By Chinese measurement system, 1 *li* equals to 0.5 kilometers.

1.3 〔English version〕

The "sky" is as "low" as the "earth"; a "mountain" is as "flat" as a "lake".

〔Interpretation〕

Without quotation marks, this proposition does appear to be meaningless nonsense, because experiences show us that the sky cannot be as low as the earth, nor can a mountain be as flat as the lake. However, with quotation marks, we see a different picture: what Hui Shi is reflecting on is the question of the ontological foundation for the meaning of names. Names like "sky, ground, mountain, lake" do have things that really exist from which their meanings are derived. However, for names like "low, flat", on what do they fall back for their meanings? That the Chinese language does not have morphemic forms to distinguish different parts of speech is what pushes Hui Shi to the ontological speculation on the secure basis for the determination of the meaning of a name, especially the adjectives as names. This proposition is not a demonstration of "relativism", nor is it any ethical or moral judgment, as is presently assumed by most scholars.

There are some who suggest that this proposition of Hui Shi's says that "It is the height of the sky that foils the lowness of the earth; and it is the undulation of the mountain that foils the flatness of the lake". They are explaining the word "与([yǔ]; literally 'and, to give, to render, to endow', etc.)" in the sense of "to endow", believing that Hui Shi is stating that we cannot know what is "low" without the idea that the sky is high, nor what is "flat" without the idea that the mountains are not flat. Because of the fact that this is only a fragment that is left of Hui Shi's argumentation, such an explanation might make sense decontextually. The problem is that this explanation is not compatible with the ideological tendency demonstrated in the rest of Hui Shi's propositions and in those of the other Ming Jia debaters'. The argument in the form of "X is relative to Y" (such as "lowness is relative to highness" or "bigness is relative to smallness") is the way Laozi and Zhuangzi made their points. As is known today, Zhuangzi and Hui Shi stood in opposition to each other in terms of philosophical standpoints. The fact that Zhuangzi recorded this sentence of Hui Shi's as an example of what he believed to be nonsensical paradoxes shows that he did not agree with what this proposition was expressing. Therefore to me, it is not proper to explain Hui Shi's idea in the viewpoint of Zhuangzi's. If Zhuangzi was a relativist basically, then Hui Shi would resent relativism and seek instead after the certainty and correctness of meaning and knowledge. This is why I believe this proposition has expressed Hui Shi's inquiry into the ontological basis of the meaning of names, especially that of adjectives.

By the way, I would like to make an additional comment on the translation of the adjective name, "卑[bēi]", which some said should be translated into "humble" or "inferior", on the ground that in ancient Chinese ideology, "sky" (heaven) was regarded as symbolic of the "yang" (positive, plus...), representing the roles of "male, father" and so on, while "earth" was symbolic of the "yin" (negative, minus...), representing the roles of "female, mother" and so forth. With the former dominating the latter, the latter had only a subordinate and therefore humble or inferior position. At a philosophy conference in 2008, Professor Liu Runqing from Beijing Foreign Languages University raised this question to me. His theory might be sensible. However, in the light of several clues, I conclude that it is highly unlikely that Hui Shi would be here talking about ethical and moral issue with the first part of this proposition while discussing empirical actuality with the latter part of it. The clues include: 1) that the other propositions of Hui Shi's are all cognitively oriented, 2) that he himself declared clearly that he was enthusiastic of all things in the world, and 3) that Zhuangzi commented on Hui Shi's intellectual tendency as "always focused exclusively on all things out there". These compel me to the belief that what Hui Shi is speculating on by this proposition is epistemological rather than moral or social-ethical in nature. Therefore, I insist on translating the character into "low". Of course, even if one could use "humble" for the translation, it does not constitute a challenge to my framework of interpretation, because we could still say that Hui Shi, with this proposition, was inquiring into the essence of "humbleness" itself as well as the ontological status of the semantic meaning of the word.

1.4〔**English version**〕

The "moment" the Sun reaches its apex in sky is the "moment" it sets down in the west; and the "moment" things are born is the "moment" they die.

〔**Interpretation**〕

Without quotation marks added, this does appear to be a relativistic proposition, claiming that it is hard to know an empirical phenomenon as it can be at once what-it-is and not what-it-is. This has been a traditional explanation of the proposition throughout history. But the problem with this explanation is that if it were correct, then the idea it expresses would be inconsistent with many of the other propositions of Hui Shi's. It is highly unlikely for a thinker to hold at the same time a standpoint of logical rationalism and one of relativism. It is probably true to say instead that Hui Shi, with this proposition, was speculating on the nature of the concept "moment". If time itself is regarded as a river, then this river consists of numerous moments without which there would be no time. So if time does exist, then moments must logically exist. Yet just as the literal meaning of the proposition shows, the "moment" is very difficult to be ascertained experientially, because once the word "this moment" is uttered, it is already a past. The moment we are in seems never to be the "moment" we talk about. Then what is "moment"? How does it exist? In what way can humans master the essence of moment as moment in itself? Hui Shi is thus inquiring into the essence of time metaphysically. Such an explanation conforms more properly to the other propositions of his in spirit (cf. also the interpretation of 1.3).

1.5 〔**English version**〕

The "major commonality (universality)" differs from the "minor commonality (similarity)", the latter means merely the apparent similarities or differences among concrete things; that all categories of things are the same or different in essence should be what we mean by the "major commonality (universality)".

〔**Interpretation**〕

This proposition has traditionally been explained as the evidence of Hui Shi's idea of "merging the similarity and the difference", a relativist ideology that attempts to erase the similarity or difference between things, believing that everything is just the same as everything else. However, this might be a serious misinterpretation.

From the sentence expression itself, a point can be quite clear: Hui Shi thought that the "major commonality" and the "minor commonality" are concepts of different metaphysical levels. The former refers to the fundamental sameness or difference between different categories of things, which is determined by the essence that things have. This is obviously a Platonic type of ideal universality. And the "minor commonality", as is used in everyday speech, refers only to the apparent similarity or difference between specific things. Hui Shi does not think such a minor commonality, as concepts expressed in everyday speech, represents necessarily the essence of things and therefore demands a truthful determination of the commonality of things by virtue of rational reasoning on the essence of things. My explanation differs from the other available ones at present, but I believe it tallies with the rationalistic ideology of Hui Shi's.

1.6 〔English version〕

The south extends in such a way that it is at once limited and limitless.

〔Interpretation〕

The explanations available at present consider this proposition as a reflection on the issue of "limit". This does make sense, but it may not be correct to explain it as a relativistic proposition of "boundless finite", as this phrase is itself paradoxical, or rather, contradictory. Or as some others explained, this proposition says that the "limits" are contained in the "limitless", but that would be a dialectical interpretation, which is not necessarily true with Hui Shi's ideology. Indeed, Hui Shi may well be reflecting on the question of "limit", but his approach to this issue is the metaphysical speculation on the nature of space itself. In the same line of thought as in Proposition 1.4 discussed previously, Hui Shi may well be questioning in the following way. Humans seem unable to master by means of experience individual moments in time, but can do so by means of language with which they parse the time into its moments. To Hui Shi, the essence of space is a question of the same nature. The limitless space cannot be experienced but inferred on the limited spaces. Humans can experience this space or that space, but such experiences are not the nature of space itself. Since the essence of space cannot be experientially verified, what is necessary then is to conduct rational analysis of what space is, in order to say about space in a correct way. Such an explanation suits better the standpoint of Hui Shi's.

1.7 〔**English version**〕

One departs for the Yue State "today", but arrives "yesterday".

〔**Interpretation**〕

Traditional explanations of this proposition are probably totally mistaken, as they all explained it as a demonstration of Hui Shi's cognitive skepticism in line with Zhuangzi's thought. The reason why I say they are wrong is this: Zhuangzi has repeatedly asserted that his philosophy contrasts sharply with that of Hui Shi's; and indeed, the recounts in Zhuangzi's book clearly show that his cognitive skepticism and relativism have always been in conflicts with Hui Shi's logical rationalism. Therefore, it is logically erroneous to explain Hui Shi in Zhuangzi's terms. Nevertheless, this proposition is difficult to explain. Here, I attempt at a new explanation in accordance to the ideological orientation of Hui Shi's.

It is highly probable that Hui Shi was tackling the question of the identity of being, by way of reflecting on the temporality expressed by "today" and "yesterday". Such a problem arose because of the lack of the copula "to be" in the pre-*Qin* Chinese language. Suppose there were such a copula that had the predicative, veridical and existential uses in one as is true in the western languages, Hui Shi might well have been pondering the issue of "being". Yet because there was no copula "to be" in the pre-*Qin* Chinese language, and its verbs were all void of morphemic conjugations to express the tense and aspect etc., Hui Shi had no other linguistic means to rely on for speculating on being as being and not being as becoming, but to speculate on the temporal meanings as conveyed by names of "today" and "yesterday".

This is why I propose that quotation marks be added to the two names of "today" and "yesterday". Let's hypothesize that Hui Shi was speculating on the identity of an event as the event in itself. Certainly, the occurrence of an event follows a time sequence. That someone "departs for the Yue State" is an event, but once the event occurs then the language words used to describe "this event" can never refer to the "this event" any more, as it has already been an event in the past, even though it is only a past "that event" a short moment ago. Logically then, "that event" cannot be "this event". It is language that enables us to distinguish the diachronic being and the synchronic being of the event. Then the key question is: is the state of the event in the past identical with the state of the event at present? If something changes from one state to another, can it retain its identity of being itself? Can we say that an object is still that object even though it has changed? So, the phrases "depart today" and "arrive yesterday", put in one statement to say about one event, are probably purported at protruding the important question of the identity of being by means of elaborating the temporality of the past and the present to draw the readers' attention, given the grammatical features of the language. Whether such an explanation is true to the original or not is an open question, but it does appear to meet up to the criterion of the exclusive essence of the *thisness* in *this* and the *thatness* in *that*, the principle proposed by Gongsun Long for rectification of names and for this reason it is consistent with the general tendency of pre-*Qin* Ming Jia's ideology.

1.8 〔English version〕

There exist "unlocking solutions" to any seamlessly interlocked rings.

〔Interpretation〕

Empirically, a seamlessly interlocked ring cannot be unlocked. But at the level of conceptual meaning of names, a question always entails its answer. Since the ring has been locked up, then logically there is a way to unlock it, at least in terms of conceptual possibility. Even "non-unlocking" itself is an answer to the question. Such an explanation may appear to be a bit far-fetched, but it is consistent with Hui Shi's speculative perspective of language meaning reflection.

Viewed from this angle, this proposition may have deeper implications: the existence of actual objects is one thing, but to think about the objects and talk about them is another. There is no one-to-one correspondence between things in the empirical world and names in the conceptual world of language meaning. What is impossible in the actual experiences may well be possible in the conceptual world created by language.

1.9 〔English version〕

I *know* that the center of the universe is located at the same time north to *Yan*, a state in the north, and south to *Yue*, a state in the south.

〔**Interpretation**〕

Literally, this proposition is erroneous, of course. To make sense of the proposition, almost everyone has accepted such an interpretation so far: Hui Shi was saying that the Earth is round. However, this interpretation may be mistaken, because history shows that the idea of the Earth being round was not with the pre-*Qin* people. Rather, the astronomers at that time were convinced that the Earth was flat and static. To me, the key to the comprehension of this proposition is the phrase "I know", which renders this proposition different in form from all the rest and is a valuable hint at the true nature of Ming Jia's philosophical position.

It is highly likely that Hui Shi was speculating on questions of such kind: How can we evaluate the truth value when a statement is preceded by "I know"? Or, as some of us understand it today, is "I know" just an assertive behavior, which does not involve truth value? For a statement P, we can tell whether it is true or false empirically or logically (such as "Metals expand when heated", "If A>B and B>C, then A>C", etc). But when we say "I know P", can its truthfulness be evaluated? If P is true, there is no problem and the whole sentence is true. But if P is false, the question is more complex. "Knowing P" means "having the knowledge of P"; but since the P is false, it cannot be knowledge and therefore "I know P" is false. The trouble is that it is the speaker who says "I know P"; and so even if P is false, the speaker does have stated that he knows P. This is why some simply dismiss "I know P" as an assertive behavior that is itself neither true nor false. Again however, here is a problem. If the speaker says "I believe P" instead of "I know P", does that make a difference? Certainly it does. "I know P" states a fact that is acknowledgeable to be true or false, and with "I know" added to P, the truth value could remain the same as P, while "I believe P" is true whether P is true or false, because it is always "I" who believes. There is no denial of this fact itself. Such an understanding conforms to Hui Shi's rationalist characteristic of analytical speculation.

In all, this issue invites a lot of questions concerning the truth of knowledge. Over 2,500 years ago, Hui Shi might well have been thinking about this issue. The oblivion of his rationalist thought is undoubtedly a tremendous loss to China's intellectual tradition.

1.10 〔 English version 〕

Everything is there for us to know; and there is a unified order that governs all things in the universe.

〔 Interpretation 〕

Many people look upon this proposition as the gist of the other propositions of Hui Shi's, believing that he is outlining his idea that nothing is absolute and human cognition of the world is relative. But as I have pointed out before, it is just wrong to explain Hui Shi in Zhuangzi's ideology, for it cannot explain why Zhuangzi, as a relativistic philosopher, should have recorded Hui Shi's propositions as something to which he stands in opposition.

From what we have examined before, we find no evidence to convince us that Hui Shi's propositions have anything to do with things that really exist, nor do we find any discussion on human experiences. Hui Shi did not show any interest in ethical, moral or political issues, but was fond of speculating on "things" with an intensive orientation to the pursuit of truthfulness of knowledge. However, his thought was not like the later Mohists who were empiricists in essence, but oriented towards the inquiry into the logical foundation for the certainty of knowledge, a strong predisposition for rational analysis of how conceptual meaning of names could be true. What interested Hui Shi is this: seeking after the truth of everything. He worked in a way very close to his counterparts in ancient Greece, seeking after the One from the many or the essence from the phenomena. I think such an understanding is consistent with the philosophical nature of Hui Shi's thought.

Just before I finished writing this book, I had the fortune of reading a new book by Professor Hsien Chung Lee (2012), entitled "Research on Ming Jia Philosophy", in which Proposition 1.10 is translated into modern Chinese this way: "Love this world before you set out to know it." Professor Lee regards Hui Shi as a philosopher engaged in epistemological issues, which I agree. Indeed, I could have translated this saying of Hui Shi's as suggested by Lee. However, Lee considers that Hui Shi's "love" here means "bringing close the distance from one mind to another, breaking down the barriers lying between humans and reality ... Only with such empathy can one understand things in reality ... [And only in this way] can one tolerate different theories on the reality and be perceptive of their limitations and of what they talk about in various relativistic viewpoints". I do not agree with this theorization of Lee's. To me, Hui Shi as one of the major representative of Ming Jia should be such a person as to be highly insightful in examining the issues of the nature of the meaning of name by means of language logic analysis, which turns out to be his life-long struggling. In addition, we have seen in the previous part, that Hui Shi's thought is obviously characterized by logical analysis and speculation, which is quite clearly demonstrated through his arguments with Zhuangzi, a relativist in epistemology. In light of this, I think it would appear to be perplexing to explain Proposition 1.10 in terms of ideas that lead very easily to relativism. Relativism is everything but consistent with Ming Jia's analytical thought tendency.

2. "21 Paradoxes" of the Ming Jia Debaters

2.1 〔 English version 〕

There "is" hair in eggs.

〔 Interpretation 〕

In accordance to Ming Jia's rationalist philosophy of language, this proposition may well be their speculation on the meaning of "there is". In what follows, there are three more propositions (2.2, 2.4, 2.5) that have the same syntactic structure as this one, i.e. that of "x has y". If the "有([yǒu], to have, there is)" in these propositions is understood as meaning "to be in possession of", then these are nonsensical indeed. Instead, Ming Jia debaters should be reflecting, by using "有"([yǒu]) in the sense of "there is", meaning "existence".

In Chinese, "x has y" means "y exists in x" (it may also mean "x possesses y", but this is not philosophically significant). If in x there is y, the fact of the existence of y in x can be perceived, comprehended and then expressed by "there is". However, with "x has-no y", what sort of fact does it express? An important point here is that in Chinese, the word "无" ([wú]) is an antonym of "有" ([yǒu]), meaning "have-no". But, different from its counterpart in the western languages, "无" ([wú]) is a single word instead of a verbal phrase consists of "have" and "not". If "有" ([yǒu]) is the name of the fact of existence, then "无" ([wú]) is the name of the fact of non-existence. Here lies the trouble for Ming Jia: Is non-existence of y a fact? We can perceive and understand [yǒu] empirically, but can we do the same with "无" ([wú])? How can we be ensured that "无" ([wú]) expresses a truth? I think such speculations come close to those of western philosophical ideas concerning "be" and "not-be", which are certainly non-experiential and purely rationalist conception of the essence of existence.

2.2 〔English version〕

The State of Ying "has" the universe in it.

〔Interpretation〕

To understand this proposition, see also the interpretation of Proposition 2.1. Certainly the universe is not just in the State of Ying, but when we say this sentence, how can we guarantee that we have stated a truth, since it is not?

2.3 〔English version〕

"Dog" can be used to say of "goat".

〔Interpretation〕

Traditional explanation of this proposition is correct, because it certainly is not a statement of dogs can be goats in the sense of empirical facts. It is quite obvious that this is a discussion on the names *per se*. What Ming Jia debaters point out with this proposition is that the name of a thing is not inherent but conventional. There is no necessary and testable relationship between the name and what it names. This explanation is consistent with what Gongsun Long has expressed in his essays "On

Name and Actuality" and "On the Nature of Reference". Meanwhile, I also refer the readers to the translator's notes on his essay "On Essence and Change".

2.4 〔 English version 〕

There "are" eggs in horses.

〔 Interpretation 〕

To understand this proposition, see also the interpretation of Proposition 2.1. It is an empirical fact that horses do not lay eggs. But it is a problem how such "non-existence" should have been verified.

2.5 〔 English version 〕

There "exists" a tail in a frog.

〔 Interpretation 〕

To understand this proposition, see also the interpretation of Proposition 2.1.

2.6 〔 English version 〕

"Mountain" is a name uttered from the mouth.

〔 Interpretation 〕

Quite some scholars consider this proposition not explainable, while some others believe it to be saying "mountains have mouths" in the sense that mountains are formed by volcanoes. This explanation is wrong, because it tries to understand a proposition of philosophy of language in terms of actual states of affairs. To me, Cheng Xuanying of *Tang* Dynasty (618-907 AD) was right when he said that this proposition states that "mountain is a name out of man's mouth". I think the word "mountain" in the proposition should be quotation-marked, because the Ming Jia debaters intended to caution the others that "mountain" in the sentence does not denote any specific mountain in existence, but is a phonetic sound that represents the idea of mountain. There was no punctuation in pre-*Qin* Chinese and for this reason, the debaters had no other way to nail down the concepts of "use" and "mention", as is done in western philosophy of language, but to rely on such forms of expression to remind the others that the ideas they debated on were not empirical but conceptual. In this way, they drew a boundary to their debates, limiting them to the scope of philosophical speculation on conceptual meaning of names *per se*. If this understanding is correct, then this proposition is direct evidence to show that the Ming Jia debaters are indeed philosophers of language.

2.7〔English version〕

Compared with a snake, a tortoise is "longer".

〔Interpretation〕

In terms of experiential knowledge of length, a snake is certainly longer than a tortoise, which is probably what urged Zhuangzi to record this proposition as a ridiculous paradox. Later interpretation of Zhuangzi's recording goes that the snake is greater in length than a tortoise but a tortoise is greater in life expectancy than a snake. However, this is a statement of fact and not at all paradoxical. To me, the key to the explanation of this proposition is the adjective of "长 ([cháng], 'long')". The "long" applied to the length of a snake expresses a spatial concept, while applied to the life expectancy of a tortoise it expresses a temporal concept. It is here that the Ming Jia debaters have raised the question: the two measurements are of totally different nature yet expressed by the same name of "long", then what is long as long in itself? Even in modern time, we have no precise answer to this question, not to mention the ancient people. The description of the spatial and the temporal properties should be done by one single word, then how can we be sure of the essential meaning or universality of what the word refers to? How is it possible for man to use the same word to master concepts of different nature? These are truly questions of philosophy, both ontological and epistemological. Such an interpretation is consistent with the quality of rationalist speculation of Ming Jia's.

2.8〔English version〕

A "white" dog is "black".

〔**Interpretation**〕

A white dog cannot be a black dog, or else that would be a violation of the basic law of logic. Therefore, this proposition should not be taken for an empirical description of a certain fact, but a speculation on the conceptual meaning of names. I hold that the statement is coherent with the "White-horse is not horse" proposition put forward by Gongsun Long. The point Ming Jia thinkers were making might well be this: the name that names a color cannot name a shape, but must and should only name a color. Then the question occurs: "white" is a name that names a color, and so is "black"; since a color is a color, is it right to say "white" is "black"? The more profound implication of this question is: does color itself have a color? This is certainly not an empirical question but a metaphysical one. From the thought tendency demonstrated in the other propositions of Ming Jia's, I believe that they are indeed reflecting on and inquiring into questions of this nature. Zhuangzi's recording of this proposition is nothing but a garbling of their statements, because he simply failed to apprehend and appreciate the essence of Ming Jia's argumentation.

2.9 〔**English version**〕

A chicken should have three "feet".

〔**Interpretation**〕

Traditionally, there has been a unanimous agreement that this proposition should be explained in accordance with what Gongsun Long has proposed in his essay, "On Essence and Change", that there exists a "chicken foot" as a concept, which one says, and a chicken does have two feet, which one can count. Together, they make three.

One point must be made here. With propositions in this form, the Ming Jia debaters demonstrated their wisdom of driving home to the people that the meaning of a name is not the actual thing denoted. In the conceptual world constructed by language, different "things" are concepts rather than actual things out there. It is such conceptual meaning that constitutes of what we know. Specific chicken feet, as actual things, are not the same with every chicken (i.e. different in color, size, shape, etc.), they disappear sooner or later (chickens die) and they can even be deformed or fragmented. But, when a thing is called "chicken foot", it must have the essence that all chicken feet have and only chicken feet can have, whatever state it might be in. Without such essence, the thing cannot be named "chicken foot". This essence, that all chicken feet have and only chicken feet can have, is eternal, perfect and constant, thus constituting the essential meaning of the name of "chicken foot". And it is the meaning of this nature that constitutes the true knowledge man has about chicken feet. This is unmistakably a rationalistic position concerning epistemology.

In what follows, some propositions are to be understood in the same line of thought (specifically, 2.10, 2.11, 2.12, 2.14, 2.15 and 2.19). Or else, they would remain nonsensical paradoxes only, if they are explained in terms of empirical facts.

2.10〔English version〕

"Fire" is not hot at all.

〔Interpretation〕

To understand this proposition, see also the interpretation of Proposition 2.9. Empirically, it is undoubtedly true that fire is hot, but as conceptual meaning, "fire" is certainly not hot at all.

2.11〔English version〕

A "wheel" does not roll on the ground.

〔Interpretation〕

To understand this proposition, see also the interpretation of Proposition 2.9. Empirically, a wheel rolls on the ground, but as a concept, "wheel" does not.

2.12〔English version〕

"Eyes" do not see things.

〔Interpretation〕

To understand this proposition, see also the interpretation of Proposition 2.9. In his essay "On the Being of Hardness and Whiteness", Gongsun Long has illustrated that man can see things and their colors because there are lights and eyes, but lights and eyes themselves do not perceive. It is the mind that apprehends the things and the colors. His illustration is the same as the propositions of Ming Jia debaters in their metaphysical ideology. This proposition just emphasizes that as the conceptual meaning of the name, "eye" is not used to see things.

2.13 〔English version〕

A reference does not reach any individual things, which are endless and inexhaustible in the universe.

〔Interpretation〕

Some (e.g. Fung Yulan) regard the word "指" ([zhǐ]) in the first part of the statement as meaning the Plutonian "Form", which can be known but not seen. Others say that the word "指" ([zhǐ]) means pointing things out by the finger. The former, to me, is reasonable, while the latter wild of the mark.

It is most likely a programmatic proposition of the Ming Jia debaters', a clue to the realm of their thoughts. The proposition is completely consistent with what Gongsun Long has proposed in his essay "On the Nature of Reference", in which he says clearly: "Things are known as 'things' by virtue of the function of reference, but 'reference' does not mean merely the denotation of specific things." As the debaters see it, mankind can only know the world by virtue of language names, but the meaning of a name is the concept and not any concrete thing. In other words, the reference of a name is not directly linked with any object or thing that exists physically, as the objects and things are so astronomical in number that it is impossible to name them one by one in order to know them. The meaning of a name is the result of human cognition that generalizes the common features of specific things by putting them into categories. This is undoubtedly a highly commendable thought of Ming Jia's, which shows that they have already proposed that in addition to an objective world of things, there is a world of meanings constructed rationally on the basis of language. The conceptual entities in the world of meanings are the true knowledge that humans have, and it is this knowledge of the universal that enables mankind to have a rational comprehension of the objective world of things that are endless and change in various ways. It is in the light of this understanding that I agree with Fung Yulan who has suggested the word "至 ([zhì], 'reach')" in the second half of this proposition should be "物 ([wù], things, substance)" instead, which brings out the meaning better.

2.14 〔English version〕

With a ruler one cannot draw the squareness itself; nor can one draw the roundness itself with a pair of compasses.

〔Interpretation〕

To understand this proposition, see also the interpretation of Proposition 2.9. With a ruler or a pair of compasses, one can surely draw a square or a circle. These are empirical facts. But a circle is a circle because it has the essence of roundness, the same is true with a square. Such essence is the conceptual meaning represented by language and not the square or round objects any more. Therefore, one cannot draw the concept of squareness, nor can one draw the concept of roundness. The reason why Ming Jia debaters had to put forward their ideas in such a "paradoxical" way was that in the pre-*Qin* Chinese language there was simply an absence of necessary means of word-formation, such as those in English (*round* vs. *roundness*, etc.).

2.15 〔English version〕

A "mortise" cannot wrap up the "tenon".

〔Interpretation〕

To understand this proposition, see also the interpretation of Proposition 2.9. It is an empirical fact that a mortise is used to wrap up the tenon. But as a language concept, the meaning of "tenon" is not wrapped up by any mortise.

2.16 〔English version〕

The shadow of flying birds is itself never moving.

〔Interpretation〕

This proposition has traditionally been explained as meaning a flying bird moves but its shadow does not. This is acceptable. The later Mohists have also proposed the same statement: "Shadows don't move, but are static from one spot to the next." Even in modern scientific understanding, this is a correct theorization. However, in the light of the nature of Ming Jia's speculative metaphysical thought, I believe that this proposition has a deeper implication: the debaters might well have been reflecting on the nature of "movement" itself. The movement of a bird that is flying is the displacement of the object the (bird) itself, but this is not the case with the shadow of the flying bird, which is only the projection of the bird's movement. Thus, what appears to be movement may not be movement in the true sense of the word. It is very probable that the Ming Jia debaters, with this proposition, were speculating on the essence of movement itself, instead of just making an empirical observation.

2.17 〔English version〕

There are moments when a fast-flying arrow is both static and moving.

〔Interpretation〕

There does not seem to be any disagreement over this proposition that it means a flying arrow is at once moving and static. But most scholars tend to understand this proposition in terms of dialecticism, which is not coherent with the rationalism of Ming Jia thought. In fact, this proposition is very similar to Zeno's paradox of "Flying arrow does not move" in ancient Greece. If the value of Zeno's paradox lies in that it highlights the importance of rational logical analysis of sense experiences, this proposition of Ming Jia debater's should be appreciated in the same way. In the viewpoint of the debaters, "flying" is of course a process, which can be analyzed into as many brief moments as possible. Then, at any one of these moments, is the arrow moving or static? To say it either way, there is a problem that prohibits a precise definition of "flying". If it is moving, then logically the arrow can only be in one place at a moment and cannot be in one place and in another at the same moment; but if it is static, how can a series of static moments compose a movement? Clearly, the meaning of "static" conflicts with that of "moving". What is the essence of "movement" then? This is the question that the debaters are inquiring into by this proposition.

2.18 〔English version〕

A puppy is not a dog.

〔Interpretation〕

This proposition contains a philosophically significant point: a dog, when it is young, is called "puppy", but when grown up, is called "dog". However, the identity of existence does not tolerate the process of "becoming". Whatever is, either is or is not. Existence should transcend experiences. Such a reflection resembles very closely Parmenides' speculation on "being" and "becoming". Similar interpretation should be given to Proposition 2.20.

2.19 〔English version〕

A "yellow" horse and a "colored" ox, put together, make a three.

〔Interpretation〕

To understand this proposition, see also the interpretation of Propositions 2.8 and 2.9. "Yellow" is a name that names color, and so is "colored". "Horse" and "ox" name two respective animals. Therefore, these are the names of three concepts.

2.20 〔English version〕

An orphan pony has never had a mother.

〔Interpretation〕

See also the interpretation of Proposition 2.18. Because of the lack of tense inflections with Chinese verbs, the Ming Jia debaters added an adverb "never" to the verb "has", in order to highlight the issue of time, which point has not been given due attention to by traditional explanation of this proposition. It is highly likely that the debaters were speculating on the identity of being, via a semantic analysis of "orphan pony". An orphan pony certainly had a mother, but "had" is not the same as "has" whether empirically or formally. To say "an orphan pony has a mother" is a semantic contradiction, but to say "an orphan pony has no mother" is no longer philosophically interesting. Either way, Ming Jia debaters could not bring home to the audience what they intend to express, limited by the non-conjugation feature of the Chinese verbs. As with this proposition, the "has never had" highlights the question of being and becoming. Is the pony that "had a mother" the same as the pony who "has no mother" the same pony? Which one should be true of the orphan pony itself, the one in the past or the one at present that is represented by the phrase "orphan pony"? Again, we see that is a profound philosophical question concerning the essence of "being" and "becoming". This proposition is of the same nature as that of Hui Shi's commented before (cf. the interpretation of Proposition 1.7).

2.21 〔English version〕

Split a rod by half a day, repeat the process every day, and the process will not be over even after ten thousand years.

〔Interpretation〕

About this proposition, there is almost no disagreement among the interpreters, who accept that it expresses an idea of limit that conforms to modern mathematics theory. I also see eye to eye with the accepted explanation, but hope to point out one thing: that the pre-*Qin* Ming Jia debaters arrived at this theory not from generalization on the basis of practical experiences, but from their pure speculation on concepts. What they were speculating on is the question of whether substance is infinitely divisible. And this is consistent with their general thought tendency. It is worth mentioning that the later Mohists at the pre-*Qin* period also came to discuss the question of divisibility, but they concluded, on their empiricist ground, that substance is not infinitely divisible because the division cannot go on any more when it comes to the end point or the "extremity" as they termed it. Indeed, this is an empiricist view, but the empiricism of the later Mohists serves to foil the rationalist spirit of the Ming Jia debaters.

Postscript

Besides the above 31 propositions recorded in Zhuangzi's works, there are still some other propositions of pre-*Qin* Ming Jia debaters' scattered in other writings, such as in Xunzi's essay. Yet none of those propositions is beyond the argument scope of Hui Shi's ten propositions and the 21 propositions of the debaters and therefore they are not included in this translation, in order to ward off repetitions.

The above propositions are listed in the order as Zhuangzi has recorded them. But obviously, they can be re-grouped into different categories according to their contents. Here I would like to provide my idea of the re-listing which I have done in another book, entitled *Asking Questions in and of Language: A Study on Rationalistic Philosophy of Language of Pre-Qin School of Names* (Sichuan University Press, 2007), for the readers' reference. See the above interpretations for the reason of the re-grouping.

      A) Hui Shi's Ten Propositions

          Group I: 1.1, 1.2, 1.5, 1.10

          Group II:1.3

          Group III: 1.4, 1.6, 1.7, 1.8

          Group IV: 1.9

      B) The Debaters' 21 Propositions

          Group I: 2.6

          Group II: 2.13

          Group III: 2.16, 2.17, 2.21

          Group IV: 2.7, 2.8

          Group V: 2.3, 2.18

          Group VI: 2.1, 2.2, 2.4, 2.5, 2.20

          Group VII: 2.9, 2.10, 2.11, 2.12, 2.14, 2.15, 2.19

Before this book, I have published two research papers on the ten propositions of Hui Shi's and the twenty-one paradoxes of Ming Jia debaters' respectively in *Philosophy and Social Sciences Edition of Journal of Sichuan University* (2007) and *Philosophical Research* (2009). The translated versions presented here in this part have been enriched by adopting some of my latest results of research on the same topic.

主要参考文献

阿尔斯顿.语言哲学［M］.牟博，等，译.北京：生活·读书·新知三联书店，1988.

陈鼓应.庄子今注今译［M］.北京：中华书局，1983.

陈嘉映.语言哲学［M］.北京：社会科学文献出版社，2003.

崔清田.名学与辩学［M］.太原：山西教育出版社，1997.

崔清田.墨家逻辑与亚里士多德逻辑比较研究［M］.北京：人民出版社，2004.

德里达.书写与差异［M］.张宁，译.北京：生活·读书·新知三联书店，2001.

董英哲，等.辩者论题的科学思想与反向思维［J］.西北大学学报：自然科学版，
  1995（3）：265-270.

董英哲，等.先秦名家科学思想概论［J］.科学技术与辩证法，2001（6）：67-71.

杜国庠.先秦诸子的若干研究［M］.北京：生活·读书·新知三联书店，1955.

杜世洪.脉络连贯——话语理解的语言哲学研究［M］.北京：人民出版社，2012.

冯友兰.中国哲学简史［M］.北京：北京大学出版社，1996.

冯友兰.中国哲学史［M］.1931年初版.上海：华东师范大学出版社，2000.

郭沫若.名辩思潮的批判［A］.//《郭沫若全集》（历史篇 第2卷）［C］.郭沫若著
  作编辑出版委员会1982年编辑出版.北京：人民出版社，1945.

龚家淮.试析公孙龙的《白马论》［J］.内蒙古师大学报：汉文哲学社会科学版，
  1989（第4期增刊）：89-95.

韩东晖.先秦时期的语言哲学问题［J］.中国社会科学，2001（5）：59-68.

侯外庐，等.中国思想通史［M］.北京：人民出版社，1957.

胡适.中国哲学史大纲［M］.上海：上海古籍出版社，2000.

胡适.先秦名学史［M］.《先秦名学史》翻译组，译.上海：学林出版社，1983.

霍凯特.现代语言学教程［M］.索振羽，等，译.北京：北京大学出版社，2002.

金克木.书读完了［C］.黄德海，编选.上海：汉语大词典出版社，2006.

李耽.先秦形名之家考察［M］.长沙：湖南大学出版社，1998.

李洪儒.系词——人在语句中的存在家园［J］.外语学刊，2006（2）：29-33.

李贤中.公孙龙子有关认识问题之研究［M］.新北：花布兰出版社，2011.

李贤中.名家哲学研究［M］.新北：花布兰出版社，2012.

林铭钧，等.名辩学新探［M］.广州：中山大学出版社，2000.

刘利民.在语言中盘旋——先秦名家"诡辩"命题的纯语言思辨理性研究［M］.成
都：四川大学出版社，1997.

刘文典.庄子补正.昆明：云南人民出版社，1980.

刘玉俊.浅论先秦名家［M］.台北：正谊出版社，2002.

墨翟.墨子全译.孙以楷，甄长松，译注.成都：巴蜀书社，2000.

庞朴.公孙龙子研究［M］.北京：中华书局，1979.

钱冠连.语言：人类最后的家园［M］.北京：商务印书馆，2005.

屈志清.公孙龙子新注［M］.武汉：湖北人民出版社，1981.

任继愈.中国哲学发展史（先秦）［M］.北京：人民出版社，1983.

沈有鼎.中国古代辩者的悖论［C］// 沈有鼎文集.北京：人民出版社，1992.

四川大学古籍整理所，中华诸子宝藏编纂委员会.老子道德经.诸子集成（新编一）.
成都：四川人民出版社，1998.

四川大学古籍整理所，中华诸子宝藏编纂委员会.论语.成都：四川人民出版社，
1998.

孙中原.中国逻辑史（先秦）［M］.北京：中国人民大学出版社，1987.

索绪尔.普通语言学教程［M］.北京：商务印书馆，1949.

谭戒甫.公孙龙子形名发微［M］.北京：中华书局，1983.

王琯.公孙龙子悬解.北京：中华书局，1992.

王宏印.白话解读公孙龙子［M］.西安：三秦出版社，1997.

王力.王力文集［M］.1卷.济南：山东教育出版社，1984.

王力.王力语言学论文集［M］.北京：商务印书馆，2000.

王先谦.荀子集解［M］.沈啸寰，王星贤，点校.北京：中华书局，1988.

汪奠基.中国逻辑思想史料分析［M］.北京：中华书局，1961.

伍非百.中国古名家言［M］.北京：中国社会科学出版社，1983.

杨武金.墨经逻辑研究［M］.北京：中国社会科学出版社，2004.

杨钊.先秦诸子与古史散论［M］.北京：北京师范大学出版社，2003.

叶锦明.逻辑分析与名辩哲学［M］.台北：学生书局，2003.

曾祥云. 对公孙龙哲学评价的质疑［J］. 学术界，2004（4）：130-136.

张岱年. 中国哲学大纲［M］. 北京：生活·读书·新知三联书店，2005.

张东荪. 理性与良知［C］. 张汝伦，编. 上海：上海远东出版社，1995.

张新. 中国名家［M］. 北京：宗教文化出版社，1996.

章太炎. 论诸子学［A］// 章太炎选集［C］. 朱维铮，姜义华，编注. 上海：上海人民出版社，1906.

赵敦华. 西方哲学简史［M］. 北京：北京大学出版社，2001.

周昌忠. 公孙龙子新论——和西方哲学的比较研究［M］. 上海：上海社会科学院出版社，1991.

周昌忠. 先秦名辩学及其科学思想［M］. 北京：科学出版社，2005.

周山. 绝学复苏——近现代的先秦名家研究［M］. 沈阳：辽宁教育出版社，1997.

周云之. 公孙龙子正名学说研究——校诠、今译、剖析、总论［M］. 北京：社会科学文献出版社，1994.

Baghramian, M. *Modern Philosophy of Language*［C］. Washington D. C.: Counterpoint, 1999.

Carnap, R. Empiricism, Semantics, and Ontology［A］(1947) // Maria Baghramian, Ed. *Western Philosophy of Language*［C］. Washington D. C.: Counterpoint, 1999.

Chan, Wing-Tsit. *A Source Book in Chinese Philosophy*［M］. New Jersey: Princeton University Press, 1973.

Graham, A. C. *Studies in Chinese Philosophy and Philosophical Literature*［M］. New York: State University of New York Press, 1990.

Hansen, Chad. *Language and Logic in Ancient China*［M］. Ann Arbor: The University of Michigan Press, 1983.

Kahn, C. H. Retrospect on the Verb "to be" and the Concept of Being［A］// *The Logic of Being: Historical Studies*［C］. Simo Knuuttila, ed. Dordrecht: D. Reidel Publishing Company, 1986.

Liu, C. "*Ming-Jia* (the Logicians) and Zeno: A Comparative Study"［A］// Bo Mou, ed. *Comparative Approaches to Chinese Philosophy*［C］. Burlington, VT：Ashgate Publishing Company, 2003.

Locke, John. Of Words［Z］. Originally published in 1690, as a part of "An Essay Concerning Human Understanding", in *The Philosophy of Language*［C］. 4th edition.

A. P. Martinich, ed. Oxford: Oxford University Press, 2001.

Mou, B. A Double Reference Account: Gongsun Long's "White-Horse-Not-Horse" Thesis [J] . *Journal of Chinese Philosophy*, 2007 (Vol. 34, No.4): 493-513.

Nida, E. *Language, Culture and Translating* [M] . Shanghai: Foreign Language Education Press, 1993.

Nye, A. *Philosophy of Language: The Big Questions* [C] . Boston, Mass: Blackwell Publishers, 1998.

Quine, W. V. O. *Word and Object* [C] . Boston, Mass.: The Technology Press of MIT, 1960.

Russell, B. *The Principles of Mathematics* [M] . New York: W. W. Norton & Company, 1938.

Wittgenstein, L. *Tractatus Logico-philosophicus/Philosophical Investigations* [M] . Beijing: China Social Sciences Press, 1999.